The Ways of the World

The Ways of the World

DAVID HARVEY

OXFORD
UNIVERSITY PRESS

OXFORD
UNIVERSITY PRESS

Oxford University Press is a department of the University of Oxford.
It furthers the University's objective of excellence in research, scholarship,
and education by publishing worldwide. Oxford is a registered trade mark of
Oxford University Press in the UK and in certain other countries

Published in the United States of America by Oxford University Press
198 Madison Avenue, New York, NY 10016, United States of America

First published in Great Britain in 2016 by PROFILE BOOKS LTD

Copyright © David Harvey 2016

ISBN 978-0-19-046944-3

Printed by Sheridan Books, USA

Contents

Picture Credits

Figure 4.2 (top) © Photothèque des Musées de la Ville de Paris/Briant; (bottom) © Photothèque des Musées de la Ville de Paris/Joffre

Figure 4.3 (left) © Photothèque des Musées de la Ville de Paris/Habouzit; (right) © Photothèque des Musées de la Ville de Paris/Pierrain

Figure 4.5 © Photothèque des Musées de la Ville de Paris/Lifeman

Figure 4.6 © Photothèque des Musées de la Ville de Paris/Joffre

Figure 4.7 © Photothèque des Musées de la Ville de Paris/Joffre

Figure 4.8 © Photothèque des Musées de la Ville de Paris/Joffre

Figure 4.9 © Photothèque des Musées de la Ville de Paris/Degraces

Figure 4.10 © Photothèque des Musées de la Ville de Paris/Joffre

Figure 4.11 © Photothèque des Musées de la Ville de Paris/Degraces

Foreword

I've been lucky enough to be involved in publishing many of David Harvey's books, from his first in 1969 to this one forty-seven years later. The former was *Explanation in Geography*, in which he recast the ways geographers collected, classified and interpreted data and how they generalised and based theories on it. He did so in the light of a range of other disciplines, especially philosophy, statistics and mathematics. He sought to bring what he called 'decent intellectual standards for rational argument' to geographical methodology and theorising. The book was a tour de force and swiftly acclaimed throughout the world. Harvey finished it while a lecturer in the Department of Geography at Bristol University. By the time it was published he had become an associate professor in the Department of Geography and Environmental Engineering at the Johns Hopkins University in Baltimore. Here his experience of the city in the aftermath of the 1968 riots dramatically changed the focus of his research and marked the start of his long association with the works of Karl Marx. The transition became evident two years later in 'Revolutionary and Counter-Revolutionary Theory in Geography and the Problem of Ghetto Formation', published here as Chapter 1. Its subject is in marked contrast to the book that preceded it, but Harvey's concern for the meticulous collection and analysis of data and rigorous interpretation of its significance for theory and practice is just as evident in both. It has remained characteristic of his work ever since.

In his commmentary on Chapter 1 Harvey notes that his findings on the causes of housing problems in Baltimore won the admiration of city officials, landlords and financiers. In this case he admits he had failed to mention the Marxist basis of his analysis. His explorations of the protean nature of capital have continued to win plaudits from the capitalists he criticises, even when explicitly framed in Marxist terms: *The Enigma of Capital*, for example, published in 2010, was favourably reviewed in the *Financial Times* and the IMF's *Finance and Development*. You can see why when you read the sparklingly clear account of how capital evolves in Chapter 11. Like his illustrious predecessor, Harvey is a brillantly perceptive analyst of capital's history and adaptability, even as he diagnoses the causes of its crises and the inevitability of its demise.

My own favourites among the book's many high points include the account of what lies behind the building of Sacré-Coeur in Paris in Chapter 4, the exposition of time–space compression in his examination of postmodernism in Chapter 5, and the account in Chapter 8 of the strike by car workers in Oxford that moves from an analysis of the tensions between local action and global causes to a close consideration of the novels of Raymond Williams, as well as the theme recurring throughout the book of how problems of over-accumulation spill over, all too visibly, into unbridled urbanisation and the social ills that go with it.

This cornucopia of David Harvey's writing from every period, thus far, of his long and productive career will appeal to everyone already familiar with his work as much as it will to those coming to it for the first time.

John Davey
Oxford, August 2015

Introduction

Some astonishing news reports are coming out of China. The United States Geological Survey, which keeps tabs on these things, reports that China consumed 6,651 million tonnes of cement in the years 2011–13 compared with the 4,405 million tonnes the United States used over the period 1900–1999. In the United States we have poured a lot of concrete, but the Chinese must be pouring it everywhere at unconscionable rates. How and why could this be? And with what environmental, economic and social consequences?

These are the kinds of questions that this book is designed to shed light on. So let us look at the context of this bare fact and then consider how we can create a general framework for understanding what is happening.

The Chinese economy faced a serious crisis in 2008. Its export industries fell on hard times. Millions of workers (30 million by some estimates) were laid off because consumer demand in the United States (the chief market for Chinese goods) had fallen off a cliff: millions of households in the US either lost or were threatened with losing their homes to foreclosure and they were certainly not rushing out to the shopping malls to buy consumer goods. The property boom and bubble in the United States from 2001 to 2007 was a response to the crash of the earlier 'dot-com' stock market bubble in 2001. Alan Greenspan, Chair of the US Federal Reserve, then engineered low interest rates so capital being rapidly withdrawn from the stock market moved into the property market as its preferred destination until the property bubble burst in 2007. Thus do the crisis tendencies of capital get moved around. The crisis of 2008, manufactured mainly in the housing markets of the American South-West (California, Arizona and Nevada) and South (Florida and Georgia) produced millions of unemployed workers in the industrial regions of China by early 2009.

The Chinese Communist Party knew it had to put all those unemployed workers back to work or face the threat of massive social unrest. By the end of 2009 a detailed joint study of the International Monetary Fund and the International Labour Organisation estimated that the net job loss in China as a result of the crisis was around 3 million (compared to 7 million in the United States). The Chinese Communist Party somehow managed to create around 27 million jobs in a year. This is a phenomenal, if not unprecedented, performance.

So what did the Chinese do and how did they do it? They engineered a massive wave of investment in physical infrastructures. These were designed in part to spatially integrate the Chinese economy by setting up communication links between the vibrant industrial zones of the East Coast with the largely underdeveloped interior, as well as improving connectivity between southern and northern industrial and consumer markets which had hitherto been rather isolated from each other. This was coupled with a vast programme of forced urbanisation, building whole new cities as well as expanding and reconstructing the developed ones.

This response to conditions of economic crisis was not new. Napoleon III brought Haussmann to Paris in 1852 to restore employment by rebuilding the city after the economic crash and revolutionary movement of 1848. The United States did the same after 1945 when it deployed much of its increased productivity and surplus cash to build the suburbs and metropolitan regions (in the style of Robert Moses) of all the major cities while also integrating the South and West into the national economy through the construction of the interstate highway system. The aim in both cases was to create relatively full employment for surpluses of capital and labour and thereby assure social stability. The Chinese after 2008 did the same but, as the data on cement consumption indicate, they did so through a shift in scale. Such a shift had also been seen before: Robert Moses worked at a far larger metropolitan region scale than Baron Haussmann, who focused on the city alone. After 2008 at least a quarter of China's GDP was derived from housing construction alone and when to this is added all the physical infrastructures (such as high-speed rail lines, highways, dam and water projects, new airports and container terminals, etc.), roughly half of China's GDP and almost all of its growth (which bordered on 10 per cent until recently) were attributable to investment in the built environment. This was how China got out of the recession. Hence the pouring of all that concrete.

The knock-on effects of these Chinese initiatives were dramatic. China consumed some 60 per cent of the world's copper and more than half of world's output of iron ore and cement after 2008. Accelerating demand for raw materials meant that all those countries supplying minerals, oil, agricultural products (timber, soya beans, hides, cotton, etc.) quickly shook off the effects of the crash of 2007–08 and experienced rapid growth (Australia,

Chile, Brazil, Argentina, Ecuador…). Germany, which supplied the Chinese with high-quality machine tools, also thrived (as opposed to France, which did not). Crisis resolutions move around as fast as crisis tendencies. Hence the volatility in the geography of uneven developments. But there is no question that China took a leading role in saving global capitalism from disaster after 2008 with its massive urbanisation and investments in the built environment.

How did the Chinese do it? The basic answer is simple. They debt-financed. The Central Committee of the Communist Party told the banks to lend no matter what the risk. Municipalities as well as regional and village administrations were told to maximise their developmental initiatives, while the terms of borrowing for investors and consumers were relaxed to buy apartments for either living or investing in. As a result, the growth of the Chinese debt has been spectacular. It has nearly doubled since 2008. China's debt to GDP ratio is now one of the highest in the world. But unlike Greece, the debt is owed in renminbis and not dollars or euros. The Chinese central bank has plenty of foreign reserves to cover the debt if need be and could print its own money at will. The Chinese took Ronald Reagan's (surprising) view that deficits and debt do not matter. But by 2014 most municipalities were bankrupt, a shadow banking system had also grown up to disguise the gross overextension of bank lending to non-earning projects and the property market had become a veritable casino of speculative volatility. Threats of devaluation of property values and of overaccumulated capital in the built environment began to materialise by 2012 and crested in 2015. China experienced, in short, a predictable problem of overinvestment in the built environment (as had happened to Haussmann in Paris in 1867 and to Robert Moses between the end of the 1960s and the New York fiscal crisis of 1975). The massive wave of fixed capital investment should have increased productivity and efficiency within the space of the Chinese economy as a whole (as happened in the case of the interstate highway system in the United States during the 1960s). Investing half of GDP growth in fixed capital that produces declining growth rates is not a good proposition. The positive knock-on effects of China's growth were reversed. As China's growth slowed, commodity prices fell, sending the economies of Brazil, Chile, Ecuador, Australia etc. into a tail spin.

So how do the Chinese propose to deal with their current problems of disposing of their surplus capital in the face of overaccumulation in the built environment and rapidly escalating indebtedness? The answers are just as startling as the data on cement use. To start with, the Chinese are planning to build a single city to house 130 million people (the combined population of Britain and France). Centred on Beijing and pinned together by high-speed transport and communications networks (that will 'annihilate space through time' as Marx once put it) in a territory no bigger than Kentucky, this debt-financed project is designed to absorb surpluses of capital and of labour well into the future. How much cement will be poured is anybody's guess, but it will surely be huge.

China is not the only place contemplating projects of this sort. Smaller versions can be found everywhere. The recent dramatic urbanisation of the Gulf States is one obvious example. Turkey plans to convert Istanbul into a city of some 45 million (it is currently around 18) and has begun a huge programme of urbanisation on the northern end of the Bosphorus. A new airport and bridge over the Bosphorus are already under construction. Unlike China, however, Turkey cannot do this by going into debt in its own currency and international bond markets are turning nervous about the risks. This particular project threatens to stall. Building booms, with rising property prices and rents, are in evidence in almost every major city in the world. We certainly have one in New York City. They had a vigorous one in Spain until it all collapsed in 2008. And when the collapse comes it reveals a lot about the wastefulness and foolishness of the investment schemes that get left behind. A whole new airport costing a billion or more euros was built in Ciudad Real just south of Madrid. But no planes came and the airport venture went bankrupt. The top bid when it was put up for auction in the spring of 2015 was 10,000 euros.

But for the Chinese, doubling down on city building is not enough. They are also looking beyond their borders for ways to absorb their surplus capital and labour. There is a project to rebuild the so-called 'Silk Road' that linked China to Western Europe through Central Asia in medieval times. 'Creating a modern version of the ancient trade route has emerged as China's signature foreign policy initiative under President Xi Jinping,' write Charles Clover and Lucy Hornby in the *Financial Times* (12 October 2015). The rail network would run from the East Coast of China through Inner and Outer Mongolia and the central Asian states to Tehran and Istanbul, from where it will fan out across Europe as well as branching off to Moscow. It is already the case that commodities from China can get to Europe by this route in four days instead of the seven taken by ocean transport. Lower costs and faster times on the Silk Road in the future will convert a largely empty area in central Asia into a string of thriving metropolises. This is already happening. In exploring the rationale for the Chinese project, Clover and Hornby pointed to the pressing need to absorb the vast surpluses of capital and of materials like cement and steel in China. The Chinese, who have absorbed and then created an increasing mass of surplus capital over the last thirty years now desperately seek what I call a 'spatial fix' (see chapter 2) to their problems of surplus capital.

This is not the only global infrastructure project that interests the Chinese. The Initiative for the Integration of the Regional Infrastructure in South America (IIRSA) was launched in 2000 as an ambitious programme to create transport infrastructures for the circulation of capital and commodities over twelve South American states. Transcontinental links pass through ten growth poles. The most ambitious projects connect the West (Peru and Ecuador) to the East (Brazilian) Coast. But the Latin American countries do not have the finance. Enter China, which is particularly interested in opening up Brazil to their trade without the time-consuming detours of sea routes. In 2012 they signed an agreement with Peru to begin upon the route over the Andes towards Brazil. The Chinese are also interested in financing the new canal through Nicaragua to compete with that in Panama. In Africa the Chinese are already hard at work (using their own labour and capital) integrating the transport systems of East Africa and are interested in constructing transcontinental railways from one coast to the other.

I recount these stories to illustrate how the world's geography has been and is being constantly made, remade and sometimes even destroyed in order to absorb rapidly accumulating surpluses of capital. The simple answer to the question of why this is happening is: because the reproduction of capital accumulation requires it. This sets the stage for a critical evaluation of the potential social, political and environmental consequences of such processes and raises the issue of whether we can afford to continue on this path or whether we need to check or abolish the impulse to the endless accumulation of capital that lies at its root. This is the unifying theme that links together the seemingly disparate chapters in this book.

That creative destruction of the world's geographical environment is going on all the time is obvious – we see it around us, read of it in the press and hear about it on the news every day. Cities like Detroit flourish for a while and then collapse as other cities boom. Ice caps melt and forests shrink. But the idea that to understand all this might require something more than mere description, that we need to create new frameworks for understanding how and why 'things happen' the way they do, is more than a little revolutionary. Economists, for example, typically construct their theories as if geography is the fixed and unchanging physical terrain upon which economic forces play out. What could be more solid than mountain ranges like the Himalayas, the Andes or the Alps or more fixed than the shape of the continents and the climatic zones that girdle the earth? Recently, respected analysts like Jeffrey Sachs in *The End of Poverty: Economic Possibilities of our Time* (2005) and Jared Diamond in *Guns, Germs and Steel: The Fates of Human Societies* (1997) have written best-selling books suggesting that geography construed as the fixed and unchanging physical environment is destiny. Most of the differentials in the wealth of nations, notes Sachs, correlate with distance from the equator and access to navigable water. Others, like Daron Acemoglu and James Robinson in *Why Nations Fail: The Origins of Power, Prosperity, and Poverty* (2012), write best-selling books disputing that view. Geography, they say, has nothing to do with it. The historically and culturally constructed institutional framework is what matters. The one party says Europe grew wealthy and became the birthplace of free market capitalism because of its rainfall regime, jagged coastline and regional ecological diversity, while China was held back by a smooth coastline that inhibited easy navigation and a hydrological regime that required centralised and bureaucratic state management hostile to free markets and individual initiative. The other party says that institutional innovations stressing private property and a fragmented structure of state and regional powers emerged perhaps by accident from Europe to impose an extractive imperialism upon densely populated parts of the world (like India and China) which until recently held their economies down, contrasting radically with the openness of settler colonialism in the Americas and Oceania that stimulated free market economic growth. Compelling histories of humanity have been constructed around analogous themes: think of Arnold Toynbee's monumental *Study of History*, in which environmental challenges and human responses lie at the root of historical transformations, or the more recent surprising popularity of Jared Diamond's *Guns, Germs and Steel*, where environment dictates all.

What I suggest in the essays assembled here is at odds with both these traditions, not least because both are, quite simply, wrong. They are wrong not because they get the details wrong, which they plainly do (the smoothness of China's coastline versus the jagged coastline of Europe depends entirely on the scale of the map one consults), but because their definition of what is or is not geographical makes no sense: it depends on an artificial Cartesian separation of nature from culture, whereas it is impossible on the ground and in the streets to see where nature ends and culture begins. Imposing a dichotomy where there is none is a fatal mistake. Geography is expressive of the unity of culture and nature and not the product of some causal interaction with feedback, as it is so commonly represented. This fiction of a duality produces all manner of political and social disasters.

As the recent history of China shows, the geography of the world is not fixed but constantly changing. Shifts in the time and cost of transportation, for example, are perpetually redefining the relative spaces of the global economy. The draining of wealth from East to West from the eighteenth century onwards could not have occurred without the new technologies of transportation and military dominance that changed the space-time coordinates of the global economy (particularly with the coming of the railways and the steamship). It is relative and not absolute space that matters. Hannibal had a lot of trouble getting his elephants over the Alps but the building of the Simplon Tunnel dramatically changed the ease of movement of commodities and people between most of Europe and northern Italy.

In these essays I aim to find a framework to understand the processes making and remaking our geography and the consequences thereof for human life and the environment of planet earth. I say a 'framework' rather than a specific and tightly ordered theory because the geography is constantly changing, not merely because humans are active agents in creating environments conducive to the reproduction of their mode of production (such as capitalism), but because simultaneous transformations are taking place in the world's ecosystems under other impulsions. Some, but by no means all, of these changes are unintended consequences of human actions: think of global climate change, sea level rises, ozone hole formation, degraded air and water qualities, oceanic debris and declining fish stocks, species extinctions, and the like. Meanwhile, new pathogens and viruses (HIV/AIDS, Ebola, West Nile virus) arise and older pathogens are either eliminated (smallpox) or, like malaria, appear recalcitrant in the face of attempts by humans to control them. The natural world we inhabit is also in constant motion as the movement of tectonic plates spews out volcanic lavas and sparks earthquakes and tsunamis, while sunspots affect the earth in disparate ways.

The reproduction of our geographical environment occurs in myriad ways and for all manner of reasons. Haussmann's boulevards in Paris were partly conceived of as military installations designed for military and social control of a traditionally restive urban population, just as the current spate of dam building in Turkey is mainly designed to destroy by flooding the agrarian base of the autonomous Kurdish movement while criss-crossing south-east Anatolia with a series of moats to inhibit the movement of the insurgent guerrillas seeking Kurdish independence. That the building of both the boulevards and the dams absorbs surplus capital and labour appears entirely incidental. Cultural perceptions and mores are constantly being built into the landscape in specific ways as the landscape itself becomes a series of mnemonics (like Sacré-Coeur in Paris or a mountain like Mont Blanc) that signal identity and social and collective meanings. The hilltop towns and villages of Tuscany contrast with the bare hilltops regarded as sacred and untouchable spaces in Korea. To try to cram diverse features of this sort into a single coherent theory is plainly impossible. But this does not mean the production of geography surpasses all human understanding. That is why I write of 'frameworks' for understanding the making of new geographies, the dynamics of urbanisation and uneven geographical developments (why some places thrive while others decline) and the economic, political social and environmental consequences for life on planet earth in general and daily life in the mosaic of neighbourhoods, towns and regions into which the world is divided.

To create such frameworks requires that we explore process-based philosophies of enquiry and embrace more dialectical methods in which the typical Cartesian dualities (such as that between nature and culture) are dissolved into a single flow of historical and geographical creative destruction. While this may at first seem hard to grasp, it is possible to locate events and processes such that we might better divine how to navigate dangerous seas and venture onto uncharted lands. There is nothing, of course, that guarantees that the framework will prevent shipwrecks or stop us falling into quicksands, getting becalmed or becoming so discouraged we just give up. Anyone looking at the contemporary tangle of relations and interactions occurring in the Middle East can surely understand my meaning.

The cognitive maps provide some pegs and handholds with which to survey how such messes can occur and perhaps hints as to how we might take an exit from the predicaments we face. This is a bold claim. But in these difficult times it takes a certain boldness and the courage of our convictions, to go anywhere. And we should do so in the certainty we will make mistakes. Learning, in this instance, means extending and deepening the cognitive maps we carry in our heads. These maps are never complete and in any case are rapidly changing, these days at faster and faster rates. The cognitive maps, compiled over some forty years of working, thinking and dialoguing with others, are incomplete. But perhaps they provide a foundation for a critical understanding of the ways of the complicated geography in which we live and have our being.

This raises questions about what the ways of our future world might look like. Do we want to live in a city of 130 million people? Is pouring concrete everywhere in order to keep capital from falling into crisis a reasonable thing to do? I don't find the vision of that new Chinese city particularly attractive for all manner of reasons – social, environmental, aesthetic, humanistic and political. Maintaining any sense of personal or collective worth, dignity and meaning in the face of such a developmental juggernaut appears a mission destined for failure, productive of the deepest alienations. I can't imagine that many of us would personally will it, promote it or plan it, though, evidently, there are some futurologists who are fanning the flames of these utopian visions and enough serious journalists who are convinced or captivated enough to want to report on the initiatives, along with financiers controlling capital surpluses ready and desperate to deploy them and make the visions real.

It is, I recently concluded in *Seventeen Contradictions and the End of Capitalism*, both logical and imperative in our times to seriously consider the changing geography of the world from a critical anti-capitalist perspective. If sustaining and reproducing capital as a dominant form of political economy requires, as seems to be the case, pouring concrete everywhere at an ever-increasing rate, then surely it is time to at least question if not reject the system that produces such excesses. Either that, or the apologists for contemporary capitalism have to show that the reproduction of capital can be achieved by other less violent and less destructive means. I await that debate with interest.

Chapter 1

Revolutionary and Counter-Revolutionary Theory in Geography and the Problem of Ghetto Formation

How and why would we bring about a revolution in geographic thought? In order to gain some insight into this question, it is worth examining how revolutions and counter-revolutions occur in all branches of science. Kuhn[1] provides an interesting analysis of this phenomenon as it occurs in the natural sciences. He suggests that most scientific activity is what he calls normal science. This amounts to the investigation of all facets of a particular paradigm (a paradigm being a set of concepts, categories, relationships and methods which are generally accepted throughout a community of scientists at a given point in time). In the practice of normal science, certain anomalies arise – observations or paradoxes which cannot be resolved within an existing paradigm. These anomalies become the focus of increasing attention until science is plunged into a period of crisis in which speculative attempts are made to solve the problems posed by the anomalies. Out of these attempts there eventually arises a new set of interlocking concepts, categories, relationships and methods which resolve the existing dilemmas while preserving and incorporating the worthwhile aspects of the old paradigm. Thus, a new paradigm is born and is followed once more by the onset of normal scientific activity.

Kuhn's schema is open to criticism on a number of grounds. I shall discuss two problems very briefly. First, there is no explanation as to how anomalies arise and how, once they have arisen, they generate crises. This criticism could be met by distinguishing between significant and insignificant anomalies. For example, it was known for many years that the orbit of Mercury did not fit Newton's calculations, yet this anomaly was insignificant because it had no relevance to the use of the Newtonian system in an everyday context. If certain anomalies had arisen in bridge construction, then they would obviously have been deemed highly significant. The Newtonian paradigm remained satisfactory and unchallenged until something of practical importance and relevance could not be accomplished by appealing to it.

Secondly, there is the question, never satisfactorily answered by Kuhn, concerning the way in which a new paradigm becomes accepted. Kuhn admits that acceptance is not a matter of logic. He suggests rather that it involves a leap of faith. What is this leap of faith based on? Underlying Kuhn's analysis is a guiding force which is never explicitly examined. In his history this guiding force is rooted in a fundamental belief in the virtues of control and manipulation of the natural environment. The leap of faith, apparently, is based on the belief that the new paradigm will extend and deepen this power. But which aspect of nature? Presumably it will be an aspect of nature which is important in terms of everyday activity and everyday life at a particular point in history.

The central criticism of Kuhn, which these two criticisms point to, is his abstraction of scientific knowledge-making from its historical materialist context. Kuhn provides an *idealist* interpretation of scientific advancement, when it is clear that scientific thought is fundamentally geared to material activities. The historical materialist basis for the advancement of scientific knowledge has been explored by Bernal.[2] Material activity involves the manipulation of nature in the interests of man, and scientific understanding cannot be interpreted independently of that general thrust. However, at this juncture, we are forced to add a further perspective because 'the interest of man' is subject to a variety of interpretations, depending on which sector of society we are thinking of. Bernal points out that the sciences in the West have until very recently been the preserve of a middle-class group, and even recently, with the rise of what is often called the 'meritocracy', the scientist is often drawn into middle-class ways of life and thought in the course of his or her career. We may thus expect the natural sciences tacitly to reflect a drive for manipulation and control over those aspects of nature which are relevant to the middle class. Far more important, however, is the harnessing of scientific activity by a process of patronage and funded research to the special interests of those who are in control of the means of production and finance. The coalition of industry and government heavily directs scientific activity. Consequently, 'manipulation and control' means manipulation and control in the interests of particular groups in society (specifically, the industrial and financial community together with the middle class) rather than in the interests of society as a whole.[3] With these perspectives we are better able to understand the general thrust of scientific advancement hidden within the recurrent scientific revolutions which Kuhn has so perceptively described.

It has frequently been questioned whether Kuhn's analysis could be extended to the social sciences. Kuhn appears to view the social sciences as 'pre-scientific' in the sense that no one social science has really established that corpus of generally accepted concepts, categories, relationships and methods which form a paradigm. This view of the social sciences as pre-scientific is, in fact, quite general among philosophers of science.[4] However, a quick survey of the history of thought in the social sciences shows that revolutions in thinking do indeed occur and that they are marked by many of the same features which Kuhn identified in the natural sciences. There is no question that Adam Smith provided a paradigmatic formulation for economic thought which was subsequently built upon by Ricardo. In modern times Keynes succeeded in doing something essentially similar to Smith and he provided a paradigmatic formulation which dominated economic thought in the West until 1970 or so. Johnson[5] explores such revolutions in thought in economics. His analysis parallels in many respects that of Kuhn, adding, however, several extra twists. At the heart of the Keynesian revolution, Johnson asserts, was a crisis generated by the failure of pre-Keynesian economics to deal with the most pressing and significant problem of the 1930s – unemployment. Thus, unemployment provided the significant anomaly. Johnson suggests that:

> By far the most helpful circumstance for the rapid propagation of a new and revolutionary theory is the existence of an established orthodoxy which is clearly inconsistent with the most salient facts of reality, and yet is sufficiently confident of its intellectual power to attempt to explain those facts, and in its efforts to do so exposes its incompetence in a ludicrous fashion.

Thus the objective social realities of the time overtook the conventional wisdom and served to expose its failings.

> In this situation of general confusion and obvious irrelevance of orthodox economics to real problems, the way was open for a new theory that offered a convincing explanation of the nature of the problem and a set of policy prescriptions based on that explanation.

So far, the similarity to Kuhn is quite remarkable. But Johnson then adds new considerations, some of which really stem from the sociology of science itself. He asserts that a newly accepted theory had to possess five main characteristics:

> First, it had to attack the central proposition of conservative orthodoxy ... with a new but academically acceptable analysis that reversed the proposition ... Second, the theory had to appear to be new, yet absorb as much as possible of the valid or at least not readily disputable components of existing orthodox theory. In this process, it helps greatly to give old concepts new and confusing names, and to emphasise as crucial analytical steps that have previously been taken as platitudinous ... Third, the new theory had to have the appropriate degree of difficulty to understand ... so that senior academic colleagues would find it neither easy nor worthwhile to study, so that they would waste their efforts on peripheral theoretical issues, and so offer themselves as easy marks for criticism and dismissal by their younger and hungrier colleagues. At the same time the new theory had to appear both difficult enough to challenge the intellectual interest of younger colleagues and students, but actually easy enough for them to master adequately with sufficient investment of intellectual endeavour ... Fourth, the new theory had to offer to the more gifted and less opportunistic scholars a new methodology more appealing than those currently available ... Finally, [it had to offer] an important empirical relationship ... to measure.

The history of geographic thought in the last ten years is exactly mirrored in this analysis. The central proposition of the old geography was the qualitative and the unique. This clearly could not resist the drive in the social sciences as a whole towards tools of social manipulation and control which require an understanding of the quantitative and the general. Nor can there be any doubt that during the transition process old concepts were given new and confusing names and that fairly platitudinous assumptions were subject to rigorous analytical investigation. Moreover, it cannot be denied that the so-called quantitative revolution in geography allowed the opportunity to pillory the elder statesmen in the discipline, particularly when they ventured into issues related to the newly emerging orthodoxy. Certainly, the quantitative movement provided a challenge of appropriate difficulty and opened up the prospect for new methodologies – many of which were to be quite rewarding in terms of the analytic insights they generated. Lastly, new

13

things to measure were in abundance; and in the distance–decay function, the threshold, the range of a good, and the measurement of spatial patterns geographers found four apparently crucial new empirical topics which they could spend an inordinate amount of time investigating. The quantitative movement can thus be interpreted partly in terms of a challenging new set of ideas to be answered, partly as a rather shabby struggle for power and status within a disciplinary framework, and partly as a response to outside pressures to discover the means for manipulation and control in what may broadly be defined as 'the planning field'. In case anyone misinterprets these remarks as pointing a finger at any one particular group, let me say that all of us were involved in this process and that there was and is no way in which we could or can escape such involvement.

Johnson also introduces the term 'counter-revolution' into his analysis. In this respect his thought is not very enlightening, since he clearly has an axe to grind in criticising the monetarists, whom he designates as counter-revolutionaries, even though a significant anomaly (the combination of inflation and unemployment) exists as a pressing challenge to the Keynesian orthodoxy. But there is something very important in this term which requires analysis. It seems intuitively plausible to think of the movement of ideas in the social sciences as a movement based on revolution and counter-revolution, in contrast to the natural sciences to which such a notion does not appear so immediately applicable.

We can analyse the phenomena of counter-revolution by using our insight into paradigm formation in the natural sciences. This is based on the extension of man's ability to manipulate and control naturally occurring phenomena. Similarly, we can anticipate that the driving force behind paradigm formation in the social sciences is the desire to manipulate and control human activity and social phenomena in the interest of man. Immediately the question arises as to who is going to control whom, in whose interest is the controlling going to be exercised, and if control is exercised in the interest of all, who is going to take it upon himself or herself to define that public interest? We are thus forced to confront directly in the social sciences what arises only indirectly in the natural sciences, namely, the social bases and implications of control and manipulation. We would be extraordinarily foolish to presuppose that these bases are equitably distributed throughout society. Our history shows that usually these bases are highly concentrated within a few key groupings in society. These groups may be benevolent or exploitive with respect to other groups. This, however, is not the issue. The point is that social science formulates concepts, categories, relationships and

14

methods which are not independent of the existing social relationships. As such, the concepts are the product of the very phenomena they are designed to describe. A revolutionary theory upon which a new paradigm is based will gain general acceptance only if the nature of the social relationships embodied in the theory is actualised in the real world. A counter-revolutionary theory is one which is deliberately proposed to deal with a revolutionary theory in such a manner that the threatened social changes which general acceptance of the revolutionary theory would generate are, either by co-optation or subversion, prevented from being realised.

This process of revolution and counter-revolution in social science is explicit in the relationship between the political economic theories of Adam Smith and Ricardo and those of Karl Marx, about which Engels, in his Preface to volume 2 of *Capital*, provides some quite extraordinary insights.[6] At issue was the charge that Marx had plagiarised the theory of surplus value. Marx, however, clearly acknowledged that both Adam Smith and Ricardo had discussed and partially understood the nature of surplus value. Engels sets out to explain what was new in Marx's utterances on surplus value and how it was that Marx's theory of surplus value 'struck home like a thunderbolt out of a clear sky'. To accomplish this he describes an incident in the history of chemistry (quite coincidentally, this turns out to be one of the inspirations for Kuhn's[7] thesis regarding the structure of revolutions in the natural sciences) concerning the relationship between Lavoisier and Priestley in the discovery of oxygen. Both conducted similar experiments and produced similar results. However, there was an essential difference between them. Priestley insisted for the rest of his life on interpreting his results in terms of the old phlogiston theory and therefore called his discovery 'dephlogisticated air'. Lavoisier, on the other hand, recognised that his discovery could not be reconciled with the existing phlogiston theory and, as a consequence, was able to reconstruct the theoretical framework of chemistry on a completely new basis. Thus Engels, and Kuhn after him, states that Lavoisier was the 'real discoverer of oxygen vis-à-vis the others who had only produced it without knowing what they had produced'. Engels continues:

> Marx is related to his predecessors in the theory of surplus value as Lavoisier is to Priestley ... The existence of the part of the value produced that we now call surplus-value was established long before Marx; what it consists of, i.e. the product of labour, for which the appropriator had paid no equivalent, was also formulated with a greater or lesser degree of clarity. But this was as far as it went ... [all economists] remained captive of the

economic categories as they had found them. Then Marx appeared. And he stood in direct opposition to all his predecessors. Where they had seen a solution, he saw only a problem. He saw that what was involved here was neither de-phlogisticated air nor fire-air, but oxygen: that it was neither a matter of recording a simple economic fact, nor of a conflict between this fact and eternal justice and true morality, but rather of a fact which was destined to revolutionise economics, and which provided the key to the understanding of the whole of capitalist production – for the person who knew how to use it, that is. With the aid of this fact Marx investigated all of the existing categories of economics, as Lavoisier had investigated the existing categories of phlogistic chemistry with the aid of oxygen.[8]

It is remarkable, of course, to find Engels expositing on this mode of thinking nearly a century before Kuhn supposedly revolutionised our thinking about scientific progress. The Marxist economic theory was clearly dangerous in that it appeared to provide the key to understanding capitalist production from the position of those *not* in control of the means of production. Consequently, the categories, concepts, relationships and methods which had the potential to form a new paradigm were an enormous threat to the power structure of the capitalist world. The subsequent emergence of the marginal theory of value (especially among the Austrian school of economists such as Bohm-Bawerk and Menger) did away with many of the basics of Smith's and Ricardo's analysis (in particular the labour theory of value) and also, incidentally, served to turn back the Marxist challenge in economics. The counter-revolutionary co-optation of Marxist theory in Russia after Lenin's death, and a similar counter-revolutionary co-optation of much of the Marxist language into Western sociology (so much so that some sociologists suggest that we are all Marxists now) without conveying the essence of Marxist thinking, have effectively prevented the true flowering of Marxist thought and, concomitantly, the emergence of that humanistic society which Marx envisaged. Both the concepts and the projected social relationships embodied in the concepts were frustrated.

Revolution and counter-revolution in thought are therefore characteristic of the social sciences in a manner apparently not characteristic of the natural sciences. Revolutions in thought cannot ultimately be divorced from revolutions in practice. This may point to the conclusion that the social sciences are indeed in a pre-scientific state. The conclusion is ill founded, however, since the natural sciences have never been wrested for any length of time out of the control of a restricted interest group. It is this fact, rather than anything inherent in the nature of natural science itself, that accounts for the lack of counter-revolutions in the natural sciences. In other words, those revolutions of thought which are accomplished in the natural sciences pose no threat to the existing order since they are constructed with the requirements of that existing order broadly in mind. This is not to say that there are not some uncomfortable social problems to resolve en route, for scientific discovery is not predictable and it can therefore be the source of social tension. What this does suggest, however, is that the natural sciences are in a pre-social state. Accordingly, questions of social action and social control, which the techniques of natural science frequently help to resolve, are not incorporated into natural science itself. In fact there is a certain fetishism about keeping social issues out of the natural sciences since incorporating them would supposedly 'bias' research conducted at the behest of the existing social order. The consequent moral dilemmas for those scientists who take their social responsibility seriously are real indeed. Contrary to popular opinion, it seems appropriate to conclude that the philosophy of social science is *potentially* much superior to that of natural science and that the eventual fusion of the two fields of study will come about not through attempts to 'scientise' social science but instead by the socialisation of natural science.[9] This may mean the replacement of manipulation and control with the realisation of human potential as the basic criterion for paradigm acceptance. In such an event all aspects of science would experience both revolutionary and counter-revolutionary phases of thought which would undoubtedly be associated with revolutionary changes in social practice.

Let us return now to the initial question. How and why would we bring about a revolution in geographic thought? The quantitative revolution has run its course, and diminishing marginal returns are apparently setting in; yet another piece of factorial ecology, yet another attempt to measure the distance–decay effect, yet another attempt to identify the range of a good, serve to tell us less and less about anything of great relevance. In addition, there are younger geographers now, just as ambitious as the quantifiers were in the early 1960s, a little hungry for recognition, and somewhat starved for interesting things to do. So there are murmurs of discontent within the social structure of the discipline as the quantifiers establish a firm grip on the production of graduate students and on the curricula of various departments. This sociological condition within the discipline is not sufficient to justify a revolution in thought (nor should it), but the condition is there. More importantly, there is a clear disparity between the sophisticated theoretical and methodological framework which we are using and our ability to say anything really meaningful about events as they unfold around us. There are too many anomalies between what we purport to explain and manipulate and what actually happens. There is an ecological problem, an urban problem, an international trade problem, and yet we seem incapable of saying anything of depth or profundity about any of them. When we do say something, it appears trite and rather ludicrous. In short, our paradigm is not coping well. It is ripe for overthrow. The objective social conditions demand that we say something sensible or coherent or else forever (through lack of credibility or, even worse, through the deterioration of the objective social conditions) remain silent. It is the emerging objective social conditions and our patent inability to cope with them which essentially explain the necessity for a revolution in geographic thought.

How should we accomplish such a revolution? There are a number of paths we could take. We could, as some suggest, abandon the positivist basis of the quantitative movement for an abstract philosophical idealism and hope either that the objective social conditions will improve of their own accord, or that concepts forged through idealist modes of thought will eventually achieve enough content to facilitate the creative change of objective social conditions. It is, however, a characteristic of idealism that it is forever doomed to search fruitlessly for real content. We could, on the other hand, reject the positivist basis of the 1960s in favour of phenomenological interpretations. This appears more attractive than the idealists' course since it at least serves to keep us in contact with the concept of 'man' as a being in constant sensuous interaction with the social and natural realities which surround us. Yet phenomenological approaches can lead us into idealism or back into naive positivist empiricism just as easily as they can into a socially aware form of materialism. The so-called behavioural revolution in geography points in both of these directions. Therefore the most fruitful strategy at this juncture is to explore that area of understanding in which certain aspects of positivism, materialism and phenomenology overlap to provide adequate interpretations of the social reality in which we find ourselves. This overlap is most clearly explored in Marxist thought. Marx, in the *Economic and Philosophic Manuscripts of 1844* and in the *German Ideology*, gave his system of thought a powerful and appealing phenomenological basis.

There are also certain things which Marxism and positivism have in common. They both have a materialist base and both resort to an analytic method. The essential difference, of course, is that positivism simply seeks to understand the world whereas Marxism seeks to change it. Put another way, positivism draws its categories and concepts from an existing reality with all of its defects while Marxist categories and concepts are formulated through the application of the dialectical method to history as it unfolds, here and now, through events and actions. The positivist method involves, for example, the application of traditional bi-valued Aristotelian logic to test hypotheses (the null hypothesis of statistical inference is a purely Aristotelian device): hypotheses are either true or false and once categorised remain ever so. The dialectic, on the other hand, proposes a process of understanding which allows the interpenetration of opposites, incorporates contradictions and paradoxes, and points to the processes of resolution. Insofar as it is relevant to talk of truth and falsity, truth lies in the dialectical process rather than in the statements derived from the process. These statements can be designated as 'true' only at a given point in time and, in any case, can be contradicted by other 'true' statements. The dialectical method allows us to invert analyses if necessary, to regard solutions as problems, to regard questions as solutions.

And so at last I come to the question of ghetto formation. The reader may at present feel that the foregoing was an elaborate introduction which has only fringe relevance to the question of understanding ghetto formation and devising solutions to the ghetto problem. In fact, it is crucial to the case, for I shall argue that we are able to say something relevant to the problem only if we self-consciously seek, in the process, to establish a revolutionary geographical theory to deal with it. I shall also argue that we can devise this understanding using many of the tools which are currently available to us. However, we must be prepared to interpret those tools in a new and rather different way. In short, we need to think in terms of oxygen instead of in terms of dephlogisticated air.

The ghetto has attracted a good deal of attention as one of the major social problems of the American city. Throughout the 1960s it became the centre of wave after wave of social unrest culminating in urban uprisings in Detroit, Los Angeles and a whole host of other cities in the wake of the assassination of Martin Luther King in April of 1968. It has anchored what has come to be known as 'the urban crisis' in the United States and posed problems for political power that cry out for public responses and interventions. In British cities, fears of 'polarisation' and 'ghettoisation' have also been rising. It is generally held that ghettos are bad things and that it would be socially desirable to eliminate them, preferably without eliminating the populations they contain. (Banfield's position with respect to the latter question appears somewhat ambiguous.) The intention here is not to attempt a detailed analysis of the literature on the ghetto nor to become embroiled in definitions of it.

Instead, examination shall be made of those geographical theories which appear to have some relevance for understanding ghetto formation and ghetto maintenance. The most obvious corpus of theory which calls for examination here is, of course, urban land-use theory.

One large segment of urban land-use theory in geography draws its inspiration from the Chicago school of sociologists. Park, Burgess and McKenzie[10] wrote voluminously on the city and elaborated an interpretation of city form in ecological terms. They noted the concentration of low-income groups and various ethnic groups within particular sections of the city. They also discovered that cities exhibited a certain regularity of spatial form. From this, Burgess elaborated what came to be known as the concentric zone theory of the city. Park and Burgess both appeared to regard the city as a sort of humanly produced, ecological complex within which the processes of social adaptation, specialisation of function and of lifestyle, competition for living space and so on acted to produce a coherent spatial structure, the whole being held together by some culturally derived form of social solidarity which Park[11] called 'the moral order'. The various groups and activities within the city system were essentially bound together by this moral order, and they merely jockeyed for position (both social and spatial) within the constraints imposed by the moral order. The main focus of interest was to find out who ended up where and what conditions were like when they got there. The main thrust of the Chicago school was necessarily descriptive. This tradition has had an extraordinarily powerful influence over geographic and sociological thinking and, although the techniques of description have changed somewhat (factorial ecology essentially replacing descriptive human ecology), the essential direction of the work has not changed greatly. The Chicago school of urban geographers is firmly derivative of the Chicago school of sociologists.[12] It is curious to note, however, that Park and Burgess did not pay a great deal of attention to the kind of social solidarity generated through the workings of the economic system nor to the social and economic relationships which derive from economic considerations. They did not ignore the issue, of course, but it was of secondary importance to them. As a result, the urban land-use theory which they developed has a critical flaw when it is used to explain the ghetto. It is interesting to observe that Engels, writing some eighty years before Park and Burgess, noted the phenomenon of concentric zoning in the city, but sought to interpret it in economic class terms. The passage is worth quoting, for it has several insights into the spatial structure of cities:

Manchester contains, at its heart, a rather extended commercial district, perhaps half a mile long and about as broad, and consisting almost wholly of offices and warehouses. Nearly the whole district is abandoned by dwellers, and is lonely and deserted at night ... This district is cut through by certain main thoroughfares upon which the vast traffic concentrates, and in which the ground level is lined with brilliant shops. In these streets the upper floors are occupied, here and there, and there is a good deal of life upon them until late at night. With the exception of this commercial district, all Manchester proper, all Salford and Hulme ... are all unmixed working people's quarters, stretching like a girdle, averaging a mile and a half in breadth, around the commercial district. Outside, beyond this girdle, lives the upper and middle bourgeoisie, the middle bourgeoisie in regularly laid out streets in the vicinity of working quarters ... the upper bourgeoisie in remoter villas with gardens ... in free, wholesome country air, in fine, comfortable homes, passed once every half or quarter hour by omnibuses going into the city. And the finest part of the arrangement is this, that the members of this money aristocracy can take the shortest road through the middle of all the labouring districts to their places of business, without ever seeing that they are in the midst of the grimy misery that lurks to the right and the left. For the thoroughfares leading from the Exchange in all directions out of the city are lined, on both sides, with an almost unbroken series of shops, and are so kept in the hands of the middle and lower bourgeoisie ... [that] they suffice to conceal from the eyes of the wealthy men and women of strong stomachs and weak nerves the misery and grime which form the complement to their wealth ... I know very well that this hypocritical plan is more or less common to all great cities; I know, too, that the retail dealers are forced by the nature of their business to take possession of the great highways; I know that there are more good buildings than bad ones upon such streets everywhere, and that the value of land is greater near them than in remote districts, but at the same time I have never seen so systematic a shutting out of the working class from the thoroughfares, so tender a concealment of everything which might affront the eye and the nerves of the bourgeoisie, as in Manchester. And yet, in other respects, Manchester is less built according to plan, after official regulations, is more an outgrowth of accident, than any other city; and when I consider in this connection the eager assurances of the middle class, that the working class is doing famously, I cannot help feeling that the liberal manufacturers, the Big Wigs of Manchester, are not so innocent after all, in the matter of this sensitive method of construction.[13]

21

The line of approach adopted by Engels in 1844 was and still is far more consistent with hard economic and social realities than was the essentially cultural-ecological approach of Park and Burgess. In fact, with certain obvious modifications, Engels's description could easily be made to fit the contemporary American city (concentric zoning with good transport facilities for the affluent who live on the outskirts, sheltering of commuters into the city from seeing the grime and misery which is the complement of their wealth, etc.). It seems a pity that contemporary geographers have looked to Park and Burgess rather than to Engels for their inspiration. The social solidarity which Engels noted was not generated by any superordinate 'moral order'. Instead, the miseries of the city were an inevitable concomitant to an evil and avaricious capitalist system. Social solidarity was enforced through the operation of the market exchange system. Engels reacted to London thus:

> These Londoners have been forced to sacrifice the best qualities of their human nature, to bring to pass all the marvels of civilisation which crowd their city, a hundred powers which slumbered within them have remained inactive, have been suppressed in order that a few might be developed more fully and multiply through union with those of others ... The brutal indifference, the unfeeling isolation of each in his private interest becomes the more repellent and offensive, the more these individuals are crowded together within a limited space ... The dissolution of mankind into monads, of which each one has a separate principle, the world of atoms, is here carried out to its utmost extreme ... Hence it comes too, that the social war, the war of each against all, is here openly declared ... people regard each other only as useful objects; each exploits the other, and the end of it all is, that the stronger treads the weaker under foot, and that the powerful few, the capitalists, seize everything for themselves, while to the weak many, the poor, scarcely a bare existence remains ... Everywhere barbarous indifference, hard egotism on one hand, and nameless misery on the other, everywhere social warfare, every man's house in a state of siege, everywhere reciprocal plundering under the protection of the law, and all so shameless, so openly avowed that one shrinks before the consequences of our social state as they manifest themselves here undisguised, and can only wonder that the whole crazy fabric still hangs together.[14]

If we cleaned up the language a bit (by eliminating the references to capitalism, for example), we would have a description worthy of the Kerner Commission Report,[15] one of the primary attempts by the Johnson administration to come to terms with the urban crisis that had been roiling the United States during the 1960s.

The common spatial structure of cities noted by Engels and by Park and Burgess can thus be analysed from economic and cultural points of view. The question which Engels posed, concerning the way in which such a system could evolve without guidance from the 'Big Wigs' and yet be to their clear advantage, has subsequently been the subject of detailed economic analysis. The possibility of using marginalist economic principles to explain this phenomenon in terms of land rent was initially indicated in the work of von Thunen in an agricultural context. This laid the basis for an economic theory of the urban land-market in the relatively recent work of Alonso and Muth.[16] The details of this theory need not detain us, but it is worth examining its contribution to an understanding of ghetto formation.

Urban land use, it is argued, is determined through a process of competitive bidding for the use of the land. The competitive bidding proceeds so that land rents are higher nearer the centre of activity (in the theory it is usually assumed that all employment is concentrated in one central location). If we now consider the residential choice open to two groups in the population (one rich and one poor) with respect to one employment centre, we can predict where each must live by examining the structure of their bid rent curves (defined as that which social groups can afford to pay for living space). For the poor group the bid rent curve is characteristically steep since the poor have very little money to spend on transportation; and therefore their ability to bid for the use of the land declines rapidly with distance from the place of employment. The rich group, on the other hand, characteristically has a shallow bid rent curve since its ability to bid is not greatly affected by the amount of money spent on transportation. When put in competition with each other, we find the poor group forced to live in the centre of the city, and the rich group living outside (just as Engels described it). This means that the poor are forced to live on high-rent land. The only way they can adjust to this, of course, is to save on the quantity of space they consume and crowd into a very small area. The logic of the model indicates that poor groups will be concentrated in high-rent areas close to the city centre in overcrowded conditions. Now, it is possible to construct a number of variants to the model, since the shape of the bid rent curve of the rich is really a function of their preference for space relative to transportation cost. Lave[17] points out that the spatial structure of the city will change if the preferences of the rich group change. If congestion costs increase in the central city, for example, and the rich decide that the time and frustration of long commutes are not worth it, then they can with ease alter their bid rent function and move back into the centre of the city. Various city structures can be predicted depending on the shape of the bid rent curves, and it is perfectly feasible to find the rich living in the centre of the city and the poor located on the outskirts. In this case, the poor are forced to adjust, for example by exchanging time for cost distance so that they expend large quantities of time walking to work in order to save on transport costs (a condition not unknown in Latin American cities). All this actually means that the rich group can always enforce its preferences over a poor group because it has more resources to apply either to transport costs or to obtaining land in whatever location it chooses. This is the natural consequence derived from applying marginalist economic principles (the bid rent curve being a typical marginalist device) to a situation in which income differences are substantial. The theory rests on the achievement of what is usually called 'Pareto optimality' in the housing market.

It is possible to use theoretical formulations of this sort to analyse disequilibrium in a city system and to devise policies which will serve to bring conditions back into equilibrium. With the rapid suburbanisation of employment in the United States since 1950, we would anticipate an outward shift of poor populations (given their bid rent functions) as they attempt to locate nearer their employment centres. This shift has *not* occurred because of the exclusive residential zoning in suburban areas. We may thus attribute the seriousness of the ghetto problem in modern society to a function of those institutions which prevent the achievement of equilibrium. Political and institutional barriers exist to achieving supposedly rational economic solutions. We may, through court suits and the like, challenge the legality and constitutionality of exclusive zoning. (Interestingly enough, this effort is supported by both civil rights groups and corporations, since the former regard suburban zoning as discriminatory whereas the latter are concerned by the lack of low-income labour in suburban locations.) We may also try to modify land-use controls so that the kind of situation reported for some twenty communities in the Princeton, New Jersey, area, in which there is industrial and commercial zoning for 1.2 million jobs and residential zoning adequate for only 144,000 workers, would be avoided.[18] We might also try to overcome the problem of insufficient transportation from inner-city areas to outer suburbs by subsidising transport systems or organising special transport facilities to get ghetto residents out to suburban employment. Of necessity, this requires the ghetto resident to substitute time for cost (if service is subsidised). Most of these programmes have been failures. We might also try to get back into equilibrium by attracting employment back into the city centre by urban renewal projects, support of Black capitalism, and the like. All of these solutions have as their basis the tacit assumption that there is disequilibrium in urban land use and that policy should be directed towards getting urban land use back into balance. These solutions are liberal in that they recognise inequity but seek to cure that inequity within an existing set of social mechanisms (in this case, mechanisms which are consistent with the von Thunen theory of urban land use).

How can we identify more revolutionary solutions? Let us go back to Muth's[19] presentation of the von Thunen theory. After an analytic presentation of the theory, Muth seeks to evaluate the empirical relevance of the theory by testing it against the existing structure of residential land use in Chicago. His tests indicate that the theory is broadly correct, with, however, certain deviations explicable by such things as racial discrimination in the housing market. We may thus infer that the theory is a true theory. This truth, arrived at by classical positivist means, can be used to help us identify the problem. What for Muth was a successful test of a social theory becomes for us an indicator of what the problem is. The theory predicts that poor groups must, of necessity, live where they can least afford to live.

Our objective is to eliminate ghettos. Therefore, the only valid policy with respect to this objective is to eliminate the conditions which give rise to the truth of the theory. In other words, we wish the von Thunen theory of the urban land market to become *not* true. The simplest approach here is to eliminate those mechanisms which serve to generate the theory. The mechanism in this case is very simple – competitive bidding for the use of the land. If we eliminate this mechanism, we will presumably eliminate the result. This is immediately suggestive of a policy for eliminating ghettos, which would presumably supplant competitive bidding with a socially controlled urban land market and socialised control of the housing sector. Under such a system, the von Thunen theory (which is a normative theory anyway) would become empirically irrelevant to our understanding of the spatial structure of residential land use. This approach has been tried in a number of countries. In Cuba, for example, all urban apartments were expropriated in 1960. Rents were paid to the government 'and were considered as amortisation towards ownership by the occupants, who must pay promptly and regularly and maintain the premises'.[20] Change of occupancy could occur only through a state institution.

> Those living in homes built in or prior to 1940 were to cease payment in 1965 if rent had been paid punctually since 1959. And after May 1961, all

new vacant units were distributed to families who had to pay rent equal to ten per cent of the family income. Moreover, in mid-1966, the right to live rent free for the rest of their lives was granted to all occupants of run-down tenements who had made at least 60 months payment. A total of 268,089 families no longer were paying rent in 1969.[21]

Obviously, a small country, such as Cuba, in a fairly primitive stage of economic development, is going to suffer chronic housing shortages, and poor housing per se cannot be eliminated through such action. However, the solutions adopted are interesting in that they will ultimately render the Alonso–Muth theory of the urban land market irrelevant to an understanding of residential spatial structure, and this, presumably, is what might happen if we succeed in eliminating the ghetto.

This approach to the ghetto land and housing market is suggestive of a different framework for analysing problems and devising solutions. Notice, for example, that all old housing became rent-free in the Cuba case. If we regard the total housing stock of an urban area as a social (as opposed to a private) good, then obviously the community has already paid for the old housing. By this calculus, all housing in an urban area built before, say, 1940 (and some of it built since) has been paid for. The debt on it has been amortised and retired. The only costs attached to it are maintenance and service charges. We have an enormous quantity of social capital locked up in the housing stock, but in a private market system for land and housing, the value of the housing is not always measured in terms of its use as shelter and residence, but in terms of the amount received in market exchange, which may be affected by external factors such as speculation. In many inner-city areas at the present time, houses patently possess little or no exchange value. This does not mean, however, that they have no use value. As a consequence, we are throwing away use value because we cannot establish exchange values. This waste would not occur under a socialised housing market system and it is one of the costs we bear for clinging tenaciously to the notion of private property. It has, of course, been an assumption of economic theory for some time that use value is embodied in exchange value. While the two are obviously related, the nature of the relationship depends upon who is doing the using. In the inner-city housing market we get quite different use values when we contrast the landlord, who uses the house as a source of income, and a tenant, who is interested in shelter.

This argument with respect to the Alonso–Muth residential land-use theory is too simplistic. Since it is frequently the case that a mechanism which is assumed for the purposes of the theory is not necessarily the same as the real mechanisms which generate results in accordance with the theory, it would be dangerous indeed to point immediately to competitive market processes as being the root cause of ghetto formation. All a successful test of the theory should do, therefore, is to alert us to the possibility that it is the competitive market mechanism which is at fault. We need to examine this mechanism in some detail.

A market functions under conditions of scarcity. Put another way, the allocation of scarce resources is the foundation for the market economy. It is thus important for us to look at the content of the two concepts 'resource' and 'scarcity'. Geographers have long recognised that a resource is a technical and social appraisal.[22] This means that materials and people become natural and human resources only when we possess the appropriate technology and social form to be able to make use of them. Uranium became a resource with technological advances in nuclear physics, and people become resources when they are forced to sell their labour on the market in order to survive (this is the real content of the term 'human resources' and 'human capital'). The concept of scarcity, likewise, does not arise naturally, but becomes relevant only in terms of social action and social objectives.[23] Scarcity is socially defined and not naturally determined. A market system becomes possible under conditions of resource scarcity, for only under these conditions can price-fixing commodity exchange markets arise. The market system is a highly decentralised control device for the coordination and integration of economic action. The extension of this coordinative ability has historically allowed an immense increase in the production of wealth. We therefore find a paradox, namely that wealth is produced under a system which relies upon scarcity for its functioning. It follows that if scarcity is eliminated, the market economy, which is the source of productive wealth under capitalism, will collapse. Yet capitalism is forever increasing its productive capacity. To resolve this dilemma many institutions and mechanisms are formed to ensure that scarcity does not disappear. In fact many institutions are geared to the maintenance of scarcity (universities being a prime example, although this is always done in the name of 'quality'). Other mechanisms ensure control over the flow of other factors of production. Meanwhile, the increasing productive power has to find an outlet and hence the process of waste (on military ventures, space programmes, and the like) and the process of need creation. What this suggests, of course, is that scarcity cannot be eliminated without also eliminating the market economy. In an advanced productive society, such as the United States, the major barrier to eliminating scarcity lies in the complicated set of interlocking institutions (financial, judicial, political, educational, and so on) which support the market process. Let us examine how this situation is revealed in the inner-city housing market.

There are some curious features about ghetto housing. One paradox is that the areas of greatest overcrowding are also the areas with the largest number of vacant houses. There are about 5,000 vacant structures in Baltimore – a good many of which are in reasonable condition – and they are all located in areas of greatest overcrowding. Other cities are experiencing something similar. The same areas are characterised by a large proportion of houses being let go in lieu of property taxes. Landlords in the inner-city housing market, contrary to popular opinion, are not making huge profits. In fact, the evidence suggests that they are making less than they would elsewhere in the housing market.[24] Some are unethical, of course, but good, rational, ethical landlord behaviour provides a relatively low rate of return. Yet the rents such landlords charge are very high relative to the quality of the accommodations, while properties, if they do change hands, do so at negligible prices. The banks, naturally, have good rational business reasons for not financing mortgages in inner-city areas. There is a greater uncertainty in the inner city and the land is, in any case, frequently regarded as 'ripe' for redevelopment. The fact that failure to finance mortgages makes it even riper is undoubtedly understood by the banking institutions, since there are good profits to be reaped by redevelopment under commercial uses. Given the drive to maximise profits, this decision cannot be regarded as unethical. In fact, it is a general characteristic of ghetto housing that if we accept the mores of normal, ethical, entrepreneurial behaviour, there is no way in which we can blame anyone for the objective social conditions which all are willing to characterise as appalling and wasteful of potential housing resources. It is a situation in which we can find all kinds of contradictory statements 'true'. Consequently, it seems impossible to find a policy within the existing economic and institutional framework which is capable of rectifying these conditions. Federal subsidies to private housing fail; rent subsidies are quickly absorbed by market adjustments; and public housing has little impact because it is too small in quantity, too localised in distribution (usually in those areas where the poor are forced to live anyway) and devised for use by the lowest classes in society only. Urban renewal merely moves the problem around and in some cases does more harm than good.

Engels, in a set of essays entitled *The Housing Question*, published in 1872, predicted that this was the impasse into which capitalist solutions to housing problems would inevitably lead. Theoretically, his prediction can be derived from criticising von Thunen's analysis in exactly the same way as Marx criticised Ricardo's formulations. Since the conceptualisation of rent in von Thunen's model (and in the Alonso–Muth model) is essentially the same as Ricardo's (it merely arises under somewhat different circumstances), we can use Marx's[25] arguments with respect to it directly. Rent, according to Marx, was but one manifestation of surplus value under capitalist institutions (such as private property), and the nature of rent could not be understood independently of this fact. To regard rent as something 'in itself', independent of other facets of the mode of production and independent of capitalist institutions, is to commit a conceptual error. It is precisely this error which is committed in the Alonso–Muth formulations. Further, this 'error' is manifest in the capitalist market process itself, for it requires that rents (or return on capital) be maximised rather than realising a maximum social surplus value. Since rent is merely one possible and partial manifestation of surplus value, the drive to maximise rent rather than the surplus value which gives rise to it is bound to create tensions in the capitalist economy. In fact it sets in motion forces which are antagonistic to the realisation of surplus value itself – hence the decline in production which results as potential workforces are separated from workplaces by land-use changes brought about both by commercial interests seeking to maximise the return on the land under their control, and by communities seeking to maximise their available tax bases. In *The Housing Question* Engels points to the whole gamut of consequences which flowed from this sort of competitive market process:

> The growth of the big modern cities gives the land in certain areas, particularly in those which are centrally situated, an artificial and colossally increasing value; the buildings erected on these areas depress this value, instead of increasing it, because they no longer correspond to the changed circumstances. They are pulled down and replaced by others. This takes place above all with worker's houses which are situated centrally and whose rents, even with the greatest overcrowding, can never, or only very slowly, increase above a certain maximum. They are pulled down and in their stead shops, warehouses and public buildings are erected.[26]

This process (which is clearly apparent in every contemporary city) results from the necessity to realise a rate of return on a parcel of land which is consistent with its location rent. It has nothing necessarily to do with facilitating production. The process is also consistent with certain other pressures.

Modern natural science has proved that so-called 'poor districts' in which the workers are crowded together are the breeding places of all those epidemics which from time to time afflict our towns ... Capitalist rule cannot allow itself the pleasure of creating epidemic diseases among the working class with impunity; the consequences fall back on it and the angel of death rages in its ranks as ruthlessly as in the ranks of the workers. As soon as this fact had been scientifically established the philanthropic bourgeoisie began to compete with one another in noble efforts on behalf of the health of their workers. Societies were founded, books were written, proposals drawn up, laws debated and passed, in order to close the sources of the ever-recurring epidemics. The housing conditions of the workers were examined and attempts were made to remedy the most crying evils ... Government Commissions were appointed to inquire into the hygienic conditions of the working classes.[27]

Today it is social pathology – drugs and crime – which is important, but the problem does not seem essentially different. The solutions devised still have the same characteristics. Engels states:

In reality the bourgeoisie has only one method of solving the housing question after its fashion – that is to say, of solving it in such a way that the solution continually reproduces the question anew. This method is called 'Haussmann' ... By 'Haussmann' I mean the practice which has now become general of making breaches in the working class quarters of our big towns, and particularly in areas which are centrally situated, quite apart from whether this is done from considerations of public health and for beautifying the town, or owing to the demand for big centrally situated business premises, or owing to traffic requirements, such as the laying down of railways, streets (which sometimes appear to have the strategic aim of making barricade fighting more difficult) ... No matter how different the reasons may be, the result is everywhere the same; the scandalous alleys disappear to the accompaniment of lavish self-praise from the bourgeoisie on account of this tremendous success, but they appear again immediately somewhere else and often in the immediate neighbourhood! ... The breeding places of disease, the infamous holes and cellars in which the capitalist mode of production confines our workers night after night, are not abolished; they are merely shifted elsewhere! The same economic necessity which produced them in the first place, produces them in the next place also. As long as the capitalist mode of production continues to

30

exist, it is folly to hope for an isolated solution of the housing question or of any other social question affecting the fate of the workers. The solution lies in the abolition of the capitalist mode of production and the appropriation of all the means of life and labour by the working class itself.[28]

The experience gained from implementing urban policies in contemporary American cities indicates some disturbing similarities to Engels's account, and it is difficult to avoid concluding that the inherent contradiction in the capitalist market mechanism contributes to it. Therefore, there is good reason to believe that our initial suspicion is correct and that the market mechanism is the culprit in a sordid drama. If we think in these terms, we can explain why almost all policies devised for the inner city have both desirable and undesirable outcomes. If we 'urban renew', we merely move the poverty around; if we don't, we merely sit by and watch decay. If we prevent block-busting, we also prevent Blacks from getting housing. The frustration consequent upon such a situation can easily lead to contradictory conclusions. The poor can be blamed for conditions (a conclusion which Banfield finds appropriate), and we can institute policies based on 'benign neglect' which will at least not provoke the kinds of questions which policy failures inevitably raise. It is therefore interesting to note that urban policy at the present time appears to involve a shift in emphasis from trying to save the inner cities (where programmes are doomed to failure) to trying to preserve the 'grey areas' where the market system is still sufficiently vigorous to make it possible to achieve some degree of success. Whether such a policy will prevent disaffection and the spread of decay may be doubted. However, unfortunately it also entails writing off the accumulated use values in the inner cities as well as the fates and lives of those 15–25 million people who are currently condemned to live out their existence in such locations. This seems a high price to pay for merely avoiding a realistic consideration of both the conclusion which Engels reached and the theoretical basis upon which that conclusion rests. The point I am working towards is that although all serious analysts concede the seriousness of the ghetto problem, few call into question the forces which rule the very heart of our economic system. Thus we discuss everything except the basic characteristics of a capitalist market economy. We devise all manner of solutions except those which might challenge the continuance of that economy. Such discussions and solutions serve only to make us look foolish, since they eventually lead us to discover what Engels was only too aware of in 1872 – that capitalist solutions provide no foundation for dealing with deteriorated social conditions. They are merely 'dephlogisticated air'. We can, if we will, discover oxygen and all that goes with it by subjecting the very basis of our society to a rigorous and critical examination. It is this task which a revolutionary approach to theory must first accomplish. What does this task entail?

Let me say first what it does not entail. It does not entail yet another empirical investigation of the social conditions in the ghettos. In fact, mapping even more evidence of man's patent inhumanity to man is counter-revolutionary in the sense that it allows the bleeding-heart liberal in us to pretend we are contributing to a solution when in fact we are not. This kind of empiricism is irrelevant. There is already enough information in congressional reports, newspapers, books, articles and so on to provide us with all the evidence we need. Our task does not lie here. Nor does it lie in what can only be termed 'moral masturbation' of the sort which accompanies the masochistic assemblage of some huge dossier on the daily injustices to the populace of the ghetto, over which we beat our breasts and commiserate with each other before retiring to our fireside comforts. This, too, is counter-revolutionary for it merely serves to expiate guilt without our ever being forced to face the fundamental issues, let alone do anything about them. Nor is it a solution to indulge in that emotional tourism which attracts us to live and work with the poor 'for a while' in the hope that we can really help them improve their lot. This, too, is counter-revolutionary – so what if we help a community win a playground in one summer of work to find that the school deteriorates in the autumn? These are the paths we should *not* take. They merely serve to divert us from the essential task at hand.

This immediate task is nothing more nor less than the self-conscious and aware construction of a new paradigm for social geographic thought through a deep and profound critique of our existing analytical constructs. This is what we are best equipped to do. We are academics, after all, working with the tools of the academic trade. As such, our task is to mobilise our powers of thought to formulate concepts and categories, theories and arguments, which we can apply to the task of bringing about a humanising social change. These concepts and categories cannot be formulated in abstraction. They must be forged realistically with respect to the events and actions as they unfold around us. Empirical evidence, the already assembled dossiers, and the experiences gained in the community can and must be used here. But all of those experiences and all of that information means little unless we synthesise it into powerful patterns of thought.

However, our thought cannot rest merely on existing reality. It has to embrace alternatives creatively. We cannot afford to plan for the future on the basis of positivist theory, for to do so would merely reinforce the status quo. Yet, as in the formation of any new paradigm, we must be prepared to incorporate and reassemble all that is useful and valuable within that corpus of theory. We can restructure the formulation of existing theory in the light of possible lines of future action. We can criticise existing theories as 'mere apologetics' for the dominant force in our society – the capitalist market system and all its concomitant institutions. In this manner we will be able to establish both the circumstances under which location theory can be used to create better futures, and the circumstances in which it reinforces modes of thought conducive to the maintenance of the status quo. The problem in many cases is not the marginalist method per se nor optimising techniques per se, but that these methods are being applied in the wrong context. Pareto optimality as it enters location theory is a counter-revolutionary concept, as is any formulation which calls for the maximisation of any one of the partial manifestations of surplus value (such as rent or return on capital investment). Yet programming solutions are clearly extremely relevant devices for understanding how resources can best be mobilised for the production of surplus value. Formulations based on the achievement of equality in distribution are also counter-revolutionary unless they are derived from an understanding of how production is organised to create surplus value. By examining questions such as these, we can at least begin to evaluate existing theory and in the process (who knows?) perhaps begin to derive the lineaments of new theory.

A revolution in scientific thought is accomplished by marshalling concepts and ideas, categories and relationships into such a superior system of thought when judged against the realities which require explanation that we succeed in making all opposition to that system of thought look ludicrous. Since we are, for the most part, our own chief opponents in this matter, many of us will find that a first initial step on this path will be to discomfort ourselves, to make ourselves look ludicrous to ourselves. This is not easy, particularly if we are possessed of intellectual pride. Further, the emergence of a true revolution in geographic thought is bound to be tempered by commitment to revolutionary practice. Certainly, the general acceptance of revolutionary theory will depend upon the strengths and accomplishments of revolutionary practice. There will be many hard personal decisions to make – decisions that require 'real' as opposed to 'mere liberal' commitment. Many of us will undoubtedly flinch before making such a commitment, for it is indeed very comfortable to be a mere liberal. However, if conditions are as serious as many of us believe, then we will increasingly come to recognise that nothing much can be lost by that kind of commitment and that almost everything stands to be gained should we make it and succeed.

So what, then, are the prospects for constructing revolutionary theory in the discipline of geography? There are a number of positive tasks to be undertaken. We have to clear away the counter-revolutionary clutter that surrounds us. We also have to recognise the status quo apologetic quality of the rest of our theory. We have to recognise that:

1. Each discipline locates problems and solutions through a study of real conditions mediated through a theoretical framework consisting of categorisations, propositions, suggested relationships and general conclusions.

2. There are three kinds of theory:

   i *Status quo theory* – a theory which is grounded in the reality it seeks to portray and which accurately represents the phenomena with which it deals at a particular moment in time. But, by having ascribed a universal truth status to the propositions it contains, it is capable of yielding prescriptive policies which can result only in the perpetuation of the *status quo.*

   ii *Counter-revolutionary theory* – a theory which may or may not *appear* grounded in the reality it seeks to portray, but which obscures, be-clouds and generally obfuscates (either by design or by accident) our ability to comprehend that reality. Such a theory is usually attractive and hence gains general currency because it is logically coherent, easily manipulable, aesthetically appealing, or just new and fashionable; but it is in some way quite divorced from the reality it purports to represent. A counter-revolutionary theory automatically frustrates either the creation or the implementation of viable policies. It is therefore a perfect device for non-decision-making, for it diverts attention from fundamental issues to superficial or non-existent issues. It can also function as spurious support and legitimisation for counter-revolutionary actions designed to frustrate needed change.

   iii *Revolutionary theory* – a theory which is firmly grounded in the reality it seeks to represent, the individual propositions of which are ascribed a contingent truth status (they are in the process of becoming true or false dependent upon the circumstances). A revolutionary theory is dialectically formulated and it can encompass conflict and contradiction within itself. A revolutionary theory offers real choices for future moments in the social process by identifying immanent choices in an existing situation. The implementation of these choices serves to validate the theory and to provide the grounds for the formulation of new theory. A revolutionary theory consequently holds out the prospect for creating truth rather than finding it.

3. Individual propositions and, indeed, whole theoretical structures are not necessarily *in themselves* in any one of the above categories. They only enter a category in the process of use in a particular social situation. Otherwise propositions and theories remain abstracted, idealised and ethereal formulations which possess form but not content (they are words and symbols merely). Counter-revolutionary formulations are frequently kept permanently in this content-less state.

4. A theoretical formulation can, as circumstances change and depending upon its application, move or be moved from one category to another. This suggests two dangers which must be avoided:

   i *Counter-revolutionary co-optation* – the perversion of a theory from a revolutionary to a counter-revolutionary state.

   ii *Counter-revolutionary stagnation* – the stagnation of a revolutionary theory through failure to reformulate it in the light of new circumstances and situations – by this means a revolutionary theory may become a *status quo* theory. But there are also two important revolutionary tasks:

   a) *Revolutionary negation* – taking counter-revolutionary theory and exposing it for what it really is.

   b) *Revolutionary reformulation* – taking *status quo* or *counter-revolutionary* formulations, setting them into motion or providing them with real content, and using them to identify real choices immanent in the present.

These tasks can be pursued and these dangers can be avoided only if the counter-revolutionary posture of the organised pursuit of knowledge (and in particular disciplinary division) is recognised and reality is confronted directly.

Commentary
This text circulated at the Boston meeting of the Association of American

Geographers in 1971. It emerged from detailed studies of the housing conditions that had contributed to the urban uprising of the Black population of Baltimore (as well as in many other cities across the United States) following the assassination of Martin Luther King in April 1968. I participated in these housing studies shortly after arriving at Johns Hopkins in Baltimore in the autumn of 1969. In the report we wrote, I experimented with the idea, taken from Marx's *Capital*, of analysing the commodity character of housing provision in terms of the contradictory relation between use and exchange value, pointing out that reliance on market mechanisms prevented the delivery of adequate housing qualities to low-income populations. I also noted how public policies generally failed to solve housing problems but just moved them around. I concealed for obvious tactical reasons the origin of these ideas in the report and was pleasantly surprised that city officials, landlords and financiers found such formulations helpful, commonsensical and intriguing. This encouraged me to continue exploring Marx's ideas, which at the time were new to me. The urban uprising of April 2015 in Baltimore, occurring as it did in the wake of a huge wave of housing foreclosures that hit single-headed households (mainly women) and the African-American population of the city particularly hard, echoed the events of 1968. It sadly offered (as did the acclaimed TV series *The Wire*, set in Baltimore over the period 2002–08) grim confirmation of the persistently appalling consequences for low-income and marginalised populations of the urban process in the United States. It's astonishing how relevant the text written by Engels in 1872 was to mine written a century later and how the subjects discussed in them find instant recognition in Istanbul, São Paulo, London and Shanghai as well as Manchester then and Baltimore today.

Chapter 2
The Geography of Capitalist Accumulation

A Reconstruction of the Marxian Theory

The need of a constantly expanding market for its products chases the bourgeoisie over the whole surface of the globe. It must nestle everywhere, settle everywhere, establish connexions everywhere ... All old established national industries have been destroyed or are daily being destroyed. They are dislodged by new industries, whose introduction becomes a life and death question for all civilised nations, by industries that no longer work up indigenous raw material but raw material drawn from the remotest zones; industries whose products are consumed, not only at home, but in every quarter of the globe. In place of the old wants, satisfied by the productions of the country, we find new wants, requiring for their satisfaction the products of distant lands and climes. In place of the old local and national seclusion and self-sufficiency, we have intercourse in every direction, universal interdependence of nations.[1]

The geographical dimension of Marx's theory of the accumulation of capital has for too long been ignored. This is, in part, Marx's own fault, since, in spite of the dramatic depiction of the global conquests of the bourgeoisie in *The Communist Manifesto*, his writings on the topic are fragmentary, casually sketched, and unsystematic. His intention was, apparently, not to leave matters in such an unordered state. He planned books on the state, the world market, and crisis formation, but these works never materialised. Careful scrutiny of his unfinished works reveals, however, a scaffold of thought on the subject that can bear the weight of substantive theorising and historical interpretation. My purpose is to give more explicit shape and substance to that scaffold and so to lay the basis for a theory of the spatial dynamics of accumulation. This will, I hope, help us elucidate and interpret the actual historical geography of capitalism.

The importance of such a step scarcely needs stressing. Phenomena as diverse as urbanisation, uneven geographical development, interregional interdependence and competition, restructurings of the regional and international division of labour, the territoriality of community and state functions, imperialism, and the geopolitical struggles that flow therefrom all stand to be elucidated and incorporated into the grand corpus of theory that Marx bequeathed us. The trick is to unravel the relation between the temporal dynamics of accumulation of capital and the production of new spatial configurations of production, exchange, and consumption.

The path to such an understanding is littered with all manner of obstacles. The theory that Marx did complete usually treats capitalism as a closed system. External space relations and internal spatial organisation apparently play no role in shaping temporal dynamics. Most Marxists have followed Marx in this. The result has been an extraordinary bias against any explicit theorisation of space and space relations within the Marxist tradition. How, then, can we rectify this omission and insert space and geography back into the argument? In what follows I shall insist that space and geography not be treated as afterthoughts, as mere appendages to already achieved theory. There is more to the problem than merely showing how capitalism shapes spatial organisation, how it produces and continuously revolutionises its geographical landscape of production, exchange, and consumption. I shall argue that space relations and geographical phenomena are fundamental material attributes that have to be present at the very beginning of the analysis and that the forms they assume are not neutral with respect to the possible paths of temporal development. They are to be construed, in short, as fundamental and 'active moments' within the contradictory dynamics of capitalism. The production of space is, to put it in more conventional Marxist language, a force of production. My grounds for this insistence are twofold.

First, I interpret Marx's method not as seeking firm and immutable conceptual building blocks from which to derive conclusions but as a process that moves dialectically. At each new phase of his enquiries, Marx extends, revises and expands interpretations of the basic categories with which the investigation commenced. His conceptual apparatus evolves with the movement of the argument. The investigation of the dynamics of crisis formation, of the circulation of fixed capital, of the operations of the credit system, for example, all lead to significant reformulations of basic concepts like 'use value' and 'value'. Withholding consideration of space and geography at the outset, as Marx tends to do, has no necessarily bad effects upon final understandings, provided we reformulate our conceptual apparatus as we proceed.

Second, there is abundant textual evidence that this is exactly what Marx thought to do. The first chapters of *Capital* incorporate several spatial concepts (community, place, world market, etc.). The language he uses frequently evokes a connection between spatial and geographical phenomena on the one hand and the basic conceptual apparatus on the other. Early in *Capital*,[2] for example, Marx notes that 'money is a *crystal*' formed 'of necessity' through 'the historical progress and *extension*' of exchange which 'develops the contrast, latent in commodities, between use value and value'. It then follows that 'the value of commodities more and more expands into an embodiment of human labour in the abstract' in 'proportion as exchange *bursts its local bonds*'.[3] This is a familiar theme in Marx. The growth of trade across the world market is fundamental to the use value/value distinction as well as to the distinction between concrete and abstract labour. To the degree that the latter distinction is 'the pivot upon which a clear comprehension of Political Economy turns', who can doubt that the study of the geographical integration of market exchange and the circulation of capital, of changing space relations, has much to say about the interpretation to be put on value itself? And this is no isolated instance either. We find Marx[4] arguing, for example, that transportation over space is 'productive of value', that the capacity to overcome spatial barriers belongs to 'the productive forces', that the detail and social division of labour depends upon the agglomeration of labourers and the concentration of productive force in space, that differentials in labour productivity have a 'basis' in natural differentiations, that the value of labour power varies according to geographical circumstances, and the like. Whenever spatial and geographical phenomena are introduced, the fundamental conceptual apparatus is usually not far behind. Spatial phenomena have therefore to be accorded a fundamental position in the overall theory.

Our task, then, is to bring spatial relations and geographical phenomena explicitly into the main corpus of Marx's theory and to trace the effects of such an insertion upon interpretations of fundamental concepts. The first step is to search among the clues liberally sprinkled in Marx's own writings to get a sense of directions to take and paths to explore. The harder we push this kind of research, the closer we shall come to creating a theory with which to understand the dynamics of capitalism's historical geography.

Transportation relations, spatial integration, and the annihilation of space by time

The circulation of capital in its standard form can be defined as a continuous process: money is used to buy commodities (labour power and means of production), which, when transformed through production, allows a fresh commodity to be thrown upon the market in exchange for the initial money outlay plus a profit. The *circulation of commodities*, however, refers simply to the patterns of market exchange of commodities. While there can be market exchange of commodities without the circulation of capital, the latter presupposes the former. For purposes of analysis, therefore, we can begin by isolating the exchange of commodities as a single transitional moment in the overall circulation of capital. By analysing the conditions of the spatial circulation of commodities, we can prepare the way for a more thorough understanding of the circulation of capital in space.

When mediated by money, says Marx, the circulation of commodities 'bursts through all the temporal, spatial and personal barriers imposed by the direct exchange of products'.[5] Selling in one place and buying in another while holding money in between becomes a normal social act. When aggregated, the innumerable acts of buying and selling define the circulation processes of both money and commodities. These processes entail costs of two sorts.[6] What Marx calls the '*faux frais*' of circulation are regarded as necessary but unproductive costs, necessary deductions from surplus value created in production. These include costs of circulation such as storage, bookkeeping, and the labour expended and profit extracted from retailing, wholesaling, banking, legal and financial services, and the like. These costs contrast with the expenditure of labour power to move commodities, money and information from one place to another which are productive of value.

An analysis of the separation between buying and selling in space leads directly, therefore, to a consideration of the role of transport and communications in the circulation of commodities and money, and, hence, of capital. Marx has a fair amount to say on this topic. The industry that 'sells change of location' as its product, he argues, is directly productive of value because 'economically considered, the spatial condition, the bringing of the product to market, belongs to the production process itself. The product is really finished only when it is on the market.'[7] This means that capital can be productively invested to enhance the circulation of commodities across space. However, the industry has its own peculiar laws of production and realisation, because transportation is itself produced and consumed simultaneously at the moment of its use, while it also typically relies heavily upon fixed capital (roadbeds, ocean terminals, rolling stock, and the like). Although there is potential here for direct surplus value production, there are good reasons for capitalists not to engage in its production except under certain favourable circumstances. The state is often, therefore, very active in this sphere of production.[8]

Any reduction in the cost of transportation is important, Marx argues, because 'the expansion of the market and the exchangeability of the product', as well as the prices of both raw materials and finished goods, are correspondingly affected.[9] The ability to draw in raw materials over long distances and to dispatch products to distant markets is obviously affected by these costs. Such cost reductions depend upon the production of 'improved, cheaper and more rapid transportation'.[10] Viewed from the standpoint of production in general, therefore, 'the reduction of the costs of real circulation (in space) belongs to the development of the forces of production by capital'.[11]

Put in the context of Marx's general proposition of the impulsion, under capitalism, to perpetually revolutionise the productive forces, this implies an inevitable trend towards perpetual improvements in transportation and communications. Marx provides some hints as to how pressure is brought to bear to achieve such improvements. 'The revolution in the modes of production of industry and agriculture made necessary a revolution … in the means of communication and transport,' so that they 'gradually adapted themselves to the mode of production of large-scale industry by means of a system of river steamers, railways, ocean steamers and telegraphs'.[12]

Elsewhere, he advances the following general proposition: 'the more production comes to rest on exchange value, hence on exchange, the more important do the physical conditions of exchange – the means of communication and transport – become for the costs of circulation. Capital by its nature drives beyond every spatial barrier. Thus the creation of the physical conditions of exchange … becomes an extraordinary necessity for it.'[13] The consequent reduction in transport costs opens up fresh pastures for the circulation of commodities and, hence, of capital. 'The direct product can be realised in distant markets in mass quantities,' and new 'spheres of realisation for labor driven by capital' can be opened up.[14]

But the movement of commodities over greater distances, albeit at lower cost, tends to increase the time taken up during circulation. The effect is to increase the turnover time of capital – defined as the production time plus the circulation time[15] – unless there are compensating improvements in the speed of circulation. Since the longer the turnover time of a given capital the smaller its annual yield of surplus value, the speed of commodity circulation

41

is just as important to the circulation of capital as the cost. Marx takes up this idea explicitly. Speeding up 'the velocity of circulation of capital' in the spheres of both production and exchange contributes to the accumulation of capital. From the standpoint of the circulation of commodities, this means that 'even spatial distance reduces itself to time: the important thing is not the market's distance in space, but the speed ... with which it can be reached'.[16] There is every incentive, therefore, to reduce the circulation time of commodities to a minimum.[17] A dual need, to reduce both the cost and the time of movement, therefore arises out of the imperatives of accumulation of capital: 'While capital must on one side strive to tear down every spatial barrier to intercourse, i.e., to exchange, and conquer the whole earth for its market, it strives on the other side to annihilate this space with time ... The more developed the capital ... the more does it strive simultaneously for an even greater extension of the market, and for greater annihilation of space by time.'[18]

The phrase 'annihilation of space by time' is of great significance within Marx's thinking. It suggests that the circulation of capital makes time the fundamental dimension of human affairs. Under capitalism, after all, it is socially necessary labour time that forms the substance of value, surplus labour time that lies at the origin of profit, and the ratio of surplus labour time to socially necessary turnover time that defines the rate of profit and, ultimately, the average rate of interest. Under capitalism, therefore, the meaning of space and the impulse to create new spatial configurations of human affairs can be understood only in relation to such temporal requirements. The phrase 'annihilation of space by time' does not mean that the spatial dimension becomes irrelevant. It poses, rather, the question of how and by what means space can be used, organised, created and dominated to fit the rather strict temporal requirements of the circulation of capital.

Consideration of that question leads Marx down a number of interesting paths. He argues, for example, that the continuity of flow across space and the regularity of delivery play significant roles in relation to turnover time – the reduction of reserve stocks and of inventories of all types reduces the quantity of capital necessarily kept idle within the overall turnover process. It follows that there is a strong need to organise the transport and communications system to guarantee regularity of delivery as well as speed and low cost.[19]

But the temporal requirements of the circulation of capital prompt further important adjustments[20] within the organisation of capitalism to deal with the spatial barriers it encounters. Long-distance trade, because it separates production and consumption by a relatively long time interval, poses serious problems for the continuity of capital flow. Herein, in Marx's opinion, lies 'one of the material bases' of the credit system. Marx elsewhere develops this argument at greater length in language that renders explicit the relations between time, space and the credit system under capitalism:

> Circulation appears as an essential process of capital. The production process cannot be begun anew before the transformation of the commodity into money. The constant continuity of this process, the unobstructed and fluid transition of value from one form into the other, or from one phase of the process into the next, appears as a fundamental condition for production based on capital to a much greater degree than for all earlier forms of production. [But] while the necessity of this continuity is given, its phases are separate in time and space ... It thus appears as a matter of chance ... whether or not its essential condition, the continuity of the different processes which constitute its process as a whole, is actually brought about. The suspension of this chance element by capital itself is credit ... Which is why credit in any developed form appears in no earlier mode of production. There were borrowing and lending in earlier situations as well, and usury is even the oldest of the antediluvian forms of capital. But borrowing and lending no more constitute credit than working constitutes industrial labour or free wage labour. And credit as an essential, developed relation of production appears historically only in circulation based on capital or free wage labour.[21]

The credit system permits money to circulate in space independently of the commodities for which that money is an equivalent. The circulation of credit on the world market then becomes one of the chief mechanisms for the annihilation of space by time and dramatically enhances the capacity to circulate commodities (and hence capital) across space. In the process a certain power devolves upon the money capitalists vis-à-vis industrialists, while the contradictions inherent in the credit system also take on specific geographical expression.[22]

The efficiency with which commodities can be circulated over space depends also upon the activities of the merchant capitalists. Marx here contrasts the historical role of the merchant – buying cheap in order to sell dear; mediating between geographically dispersed producers at low levels of development; accumulating capital through profiteering, robbery and violence; and forming the world market[23] – with the position of the merchant under a purely capitalist mode of production. In the latter instance, Marx argues, the merchant's role is to lower the cost and speed up the circulation of commodities (and hence of capital) by specialising in the marketing function.[24] Profits are to be had out of the efficient performance of such a role. But, like that of the money capitalists, the position of the merchants in the overall circulation process of capital gives them a certain power vis-à-vis the industrial capitalists and provides all too frequent opportunity for free expression of their penchant for speculation, profiteering, cheating and excessive accumulation. Nevertheless, to the degree that the heart of the modern form of capitalism is shaped by the necessity to produce on an ever-enlarged scale,[25] so the formation of the world market can no longer be attributed to the activities of the merchant but must be traced back to its origins in capitalist production.

The direct relaxation of spatial constraints through revolutions that reduce the cost and time of movement and improve its continuity and efficiency can therefore be supplemented by the increasing efficiency of organisation of the credit and marketing systems. The latter help to annihilate space with time and so increase the capacity for spatial integration between geographically dispersed producers. The industrial capitalists, however, can achieve much the same effect through their organisation of production, their location decisions and their technological choices. Let us see how Marx deals with such a possibility.

The capacity to procure surplus value is linked to the physical productivity of the labour employed. Capitalists can here exploit those variations that have their origin in nature.[26] Superior locations can similarly be exploited in trade. Under the coercive laws of competition, therefore, we might reasonably expect the location of production to be increasingly sensitive to natural variation and locational advantage. Marx rejects such an idea without, however, denying the basis of human activity in nature and location. He insists, first of all, that fertility, productivity and location are *social* determinations, subject to direct modification through human action and equally subject to re-evaluation through changing technologies of production: 'the capital-relation arises out of an economic soil that is the product of a long process of development. The existing productivity of labour, from which it proceeds as its basis, is a gift, not of nature, but of a history embracing thousands of centuries.'[27] Fertility can be built up in the soil, relative locations altered by transport improvements, and new productive forces embedded by human labour in the land itself.[28] Furthermore, the advantage of access to, say, a waterfall as a power source can be eliminated overnight by the advent of the steam engine. Marx is primarily interested in the way in which transformations of this sort liberate capitalist production from natural constraints and produce a humanly created 'second nature' as the arena for human action. And if circumstances arise (and Marx concedes this was frequently the case in the agriculture of his time) where natural fertility and location continue to give permanent advantages to privileged producers, then the benefit could be taxed away as ground rent.

The location of production cannot, therefore, be interpreted as a mere response to natural conditions but as the outcome of a social process in which modifications of nature, of locational advantage and of the labour process are linked. The persistence of spatial and resource endowment constraints has then to be interpreted as an effect internal to the logic of capitalist development rather than as something that resides in external nature. And this brings us back to the idea that one of the principles internal to the logic of capitalist organisation of production is the annihilation of space by time and the reduction of spatial barriers.

For example, when capitalists seeking relative surplus value strive to mobilise and appropriate labour's powers of cooperation, they do so by concentrating activity within a relatively smaller space.[29] The reorganisation of the detail division of labour for the same purpose demands that processes that were once successive in time 'go on side by side in space' simultaneously.[30] The application of machinery and the rise of the factory system consolidate this tendency towards the spatial concentration of labour and productive forces within a restricted space. This same principle carries over to questions of inter-industry linkages within the social division of labour. The agglomeration of production within a few large urban centres, the workshops of capitalist production, is a tendency inherent in the capitalist mode of production.[31] In all of these instances we see that the rational organisation of production in space is fundamental to the reduction of turnover time and costs within the circulation process of capital.

The tendency towards the agglomeration of population and productive forces in large urban centres is reinforced by a number of other processes of considerable significance. Technological innovations that liberate industry from close dependence upon a particular and localised raw material or energy source permit greater concentration of production in urban centres. This was precisely the importance of the steam engine, which 'permitted production to be concentrated in towns' because it was 'of universal application and relatively speaking, little affected by its choice of residence by local circumstances'.[32] Improvements in the means of transportation also tend in the direction of the already existing market, that is to say 'towards the major centres of production and population, towards export ports, etc.' ... The 'particular ease of commerce and the consequent acceleration in the turnover of capital ... gives rise to an accelerated concentration of both the centre of production and its market'.[33]

The resultant 'concentration of masses of men and capital thus accelerated at certain points' is even further emphasised because 'all branches of production which, owing to the nature of their product, are oriented principally to local outlets, such as breweries, thus develop to their greatest extent in the major centres of population'.[34] What Marx in effect depicts is powerful cumulative forces making for the production of urbanisation under capitalism. And he helps us see these forces as part and parcel of the general processes seeking the elimination of spatial barriers and the annihilation of space by time. 'With the development of the means of transport, the speed of movement in space is accelerated, and spatial distance is thus shortened in time.'[35]

But this process also requires the agglomeration of labourers, the concentration of population, within the restricted space of urban centres. 'The more rapidly capital accumulates in an industrial or commercial town, the more rapidly flows the stream of exploitable human material.'[36] This flow can arise out of 'the constant absorption of primitive and physically uncorrupted elements from the country', which presupposes the existence there of 'a constant latent surplus population' that can be dislodged by primitive accumulation – enclosures or other violent means of expropriation from the land.[37] The importation of Irish labourers into the industrial and commercial centres of England was of particular interest to Marx, for it not only provided a necessary flow of surplus labourers but did so in a way that divided the working-class movement.[38] In the absence of such migrations, the expansion of the labour force depended upon the 'rapid renewal' and 'absolute increase' of a labouring population through fundamental and distinctively urban transformations in the social conditions of reproduction of labour power – earlier marriage, employment opportunities for children that encouraged labourers to 'accumulate' children as their only source of wealth, and so on. And in the event of labour shortage, technological change tended to produce a 'floating' industrial reserve army concentrated 'in the centres of modern industry'.[39] Even under conditions of technologically induced high unemployment, the capitalists could still leave the reproduction of labour power to 'the labourer's instincts of self-preservation and of propagation'.[40] The accumulation of capital in space goes hand in hand with 'the accumulation of misery, the torment of labour, slavery, ignorance, brutalisation, and moral degradation', while children are raised in 'conditions of infamy'.[41]

Limits obviously exist to the progressive concentration of productive forces and labouring populations in a few large urban centres, even though such agglomeration may help reduce turnover times and circulation costs. Such concentrations of human misery form breeding grounds for class consciousness and organisation, while overcrowding both in the factory and in the living space can become a specific focus of social protest.[42] But capital does not wait upon the emergence of such problems to set in motion its own quest for dispersal. The tendency to create the world market is, after all, 'given in the concept of capital itself'. The creation of surplus value at 'one point requires the creation of surplus value at another point', which means 'the production of a constantly widening sphere of circulation' through complementary tendencies to create new points of production and exchange. The exploration of 'all nature in order to discover new, useful qualities of things', as well as to gain access to raw materials, entails 'universal exchange of the products of all alien climates and lands'.[43] The tendency towards agglomeration is partially offset, therefore, by an increasingly specialised 'territorial division of labour which confines special branches of production to special districts of a country', coupled with the rise of a 'new and international division of labour' responsive to the needs of modern industry.[44] And all of this is facilitated by new transport and credit systems that facilitate long-distance movement, reduce spatial barriers, and annihilate space by time.

The conception towards which Marx appears to be moving is of a geographical landscape beset by a pervasive tension between forces making for agglomeration in place and forces making for dispersal over space in the struggle to reduce turnover time and so gain surplus value. If there is any general structure to it all – and Marx is far from explicit on the point – it is that of a progressive concentration of forces of production (including labour power) at particular places together with rapid geographical expansion of market opportunities. With the accumulation of capital, Marx comments, 'flows in space' increase remarkably; while the 'market expands spatially, the periphery in relation to the center is circumscribed by a constantly expanding radius'.[45] Some sort of centre–periphery relation, perhaps an echo of that original antithesis between town and country which lies at the origin of the social division of labour,[46] appears almost certain to arise.

But such a structure is perpetually being recast in the restless quest for accumulation. The creation of absolute surplus value rests upon 'the production of a constantly widening sphere of circulation', while the production of relative surplus value entails 'quantitative expansion of existing consumption: ... creation of new needs by propagating existing ones in a wide circle' and 'production of new needs and discovery and creation of new use values' through 'the exploration of the earth in all directions'. Marx then goes on to integrate the rise of science, the definition of new social wants and needs, and the transformation of world culture into his general picture of the global transformations necessarily wrought through an expansionary capitalism powered by the impulsion of accumulation for accumulation's sake:

> Capital drives beyond national barriers and prejudices as much as beyond nature worship, as well as all traditional, confined, complacent, encrusted satisfactions of present needs, and reproductions of old ways of life. It is destructive towards all of this and constantly revolutionises it, tearing down all the barriers which hem in the development of the forces of production, the expansion of needs, the all-sided development of production, and the exploitation and exchange of natural and mental forces.[47]

To the degree that capitalist production 'moves in contradictions which are constantly overcome but just as constantly posited', so we find contradictions internal to this overall expansionary dynamic. In particular, the search for 'rational' geographical configurations of production and consumption runs up against the impulsion to revolutionise the productive forces in transport and communications. Expansion occurs in a context where transformations in the cost, speed, continuity and efficiency of movement over space alter 'the relative distances of places of production from the larger markets'. This entails 'the demise of old centres of production and the emergence of new ones'. 'There is simultaneously a further shift and displacement as a result of the change in the relative situation of production and market places which itself results from the changes in the means of communication.'[48] Marx is apparently perfectly comfortable with the idea that space is relative and dependent on investments in transport and communications. The resultant instability is exacerbated by processes of technological and organisational change that either liberate production from specific locational requirements (access to a particular raw material or energy supplies, dependence upon particular labour skills) or confirm the trend towards increasing specialisation within a territorial division of labour. And the shifting physical and social capacity of the labourers to migrate (on a temporary or permanent basis) also enters into the picture.[49]

The shifts in spatial configurations produced by such processes become problematic to the degree that capitalism requires fixed and immobile infrastructures, tied down as specific use values in particular places, to facilitate production, exchange, transportation and consumption. Capitalism, after all, 'establishes its residence on the land itself and the seemingly solid presuppositions given by nature [appear] in landed property as merely posited by industry'.[50] The value embodied in such use values embedded in the land cannot be moved without being destroyed. Capital thus must represent itself in the form of a physical landscape created in its own image, as use values created through human labour and embedded in the land to facilitate the further accumulation of capital. The produced geographical landscape constituted by fixed and immobile capital is both the crowning glory of past capitalist development and a prison that inhibits the further progress of accumulation precisely because it creates spatial barriers where there were none before. The very production of this landscape, so vital to accumulation, is in the end antithetical to the tearing down of spatial barriers and the annihilation of space by time.

This contradiction grows with increasing dependence upon fixed capital (machinery, plant, physical infrastructures of all kinds). The problem arises because with 'fixed capital the value is imprisoned within a specific use value',[51] while the degree of fixity increases with durability, other things being equal.[52] Marx describes the conditions governing the circulation of fixed capital in the following terms: 'The value of fixed capital is reproduced only insofar as it is used up in the production process. Through disuse it loses its value without its value passing on to the product. Hence the greater the scale on which fixed capital develops ... the more does the continuity of the production process or the constant flow of reproduction become an externally compelling condition for the mode of production founded on capital.'[53] The employment of fixed and immobile capital, in short, exerts a strong claim upon the future circulation of capital and the future deployment of labour power. Until the capital invested in such assets is amortised through use, capital and labour power are constrained geographically to patterns of circulation that help realise the value embodied in all improvements 'sunk in the soil ... every form in which the product of industry is welded fast to the surface of the earth'.[54]

Capitalist development has to negotiate a knife-edge path between preserving the values of past capital investments embodied in the land and destroying them in order to open up fresh geographical space for accumulation. A perpetual struggle ensues in which physical landscapes appropriate to capitalism's requirements are produced at a particular moment in time only to be disrupted and destroyed, usually in the course of a crisis, at a subsequent point in time.

This contradiction hides an irony that is nowhere more apparent than in the transport industry itself. The elimination of spatial barriers and the annihilation of space by time requires 'a growth of that portion of social wealth which, instead of serving as direct means of production, is invested in means of transportation and communication and in the fixed and circulating capital required for their operation'.[55] In other words, the production of a fixed configuration of space (e.g., the rail, road and port systems) is the only means open to capital to overcome space. At some point the impulsion to overcome space must render the initial investments obsolete and redundant, perhaps well before the value embodied in them has been realised through use.

The location theory in Marx (if we may call it that) is not much more specific than this (although there is much of peripheral interest in his analyses of rent and fixed capital formation). The virtue of his fragmentary remarks lies not in their sophistication but in the vision they project of the role of the production and restless restructuring of geographical landscapes and space relations as active moments within the dynamics of capital accumulation. Revolutions in the productive forces embedded in the land, in the capacity to overcome space and annihilate space with time, are not afterthoughts to be added on in the final chapter of some analysis. They are fundamental because it is only through them that we can give flesh and meaning to those most pivotal of all Marxian categories, concrete and abstract labour.

This last point is of sufficient importance to warrant reflection. The expenditure of human labour power 'in a special form and with a definite aim' to produce use values in a given place and time is, as Marx puts it, 'an eternal natural necessity, which mediates the metabolism between man and nature, and therefore human life itself'.[56] The different qualities of concrete labour are brought into relation with each other through exchange and, ultimately, through the circulation of capital. And that process of bringing different concrete labour activities into a general social relation gives that same labour process abstract qualities tied to value as socially necessary labour time, the labour time 'required to produce an article under the normal conditions of production, and with the average degree of skill and intensity prevalent at the time'.[57] The 'normal conditions' and 'average skill and intensity' cannot be specified, however, except with reference to a given space of exchange and capital circulation. The processes of formation of the world market, of spatial integration, of the international and territorial division of labour, of the geographical concentration of production (labour power and productive force), are therefore fundamental to understanding how a concrete labour process acquires abstract, universal qualities. For the geographer this must surely be one of Marx's most profound insights. For it not only puts the study of space relations and geographical differentiation into the heart of Marx's theorising but also points the way to a solution of the problem that has for so long bedevilled the geographical imagination: how to make universal generalisations about the evident unique particularities of space. The answer lies, of course, not in philosophical speculation but in a study of exactly how the processes of capital circulation bring the unique qualities of human action in given places and times into a framework of universal generality. And that, presumably, was exactly what Marx meant by that stunning conception that bears repeating: 'Abstract wealth, value, money, hence abstract labour, develop in the measure that concrete labour becomes a totality of different modes of labour embracing the world market.'

Foreign trade

While some of Marx's scattered comments on foreign trade (he never completed a projected work on the world market) can be interpreted as logical extensions of his views on location and space relations, the focus is more on how the history and dynamics of capital accumulation were and are expressed through pre-existing geographical structures – the nation-state in particular – rather than on the processes that give rise to spatial configurations in the first place. By accepting the fiction of capital accumulation as primarily a national affair, Marx was, of course, making concessions to a long line of thought that passed from the mercantilists via the physiocrats to Adam Smith and the Ricardian doctrine of comparative advantage. The strength of that tradition in political economy inexorably drew Marx to a critique of some of its fundamental propositions and a partial acceptance of others. And if the picture he portrays appears somewhat at odds with that which we have previously outlined, it is no less legitimate for all that. It is, as it were, the world of geographical interactions seen from a rather different window. A full understanding of Marx's views must rest on a synthesis of two rather disparate but both equally legitimate perspectives on the geography of capitalist accumulation.

Marx sees the development of foreign trade, the formation of the world market and the rise of capitalism as integrally related within a process in which consequences at one stage become preconditions for the next. The drive to overcome spatial barriers, for example, presages the absorption, dissolution or transformation of all non-capitalist modes of production ultimately under the homogenising force of the circulation of capital. Monetisation, commodity exchange and, finally, the imposition of capitalist relations of production represent various steps in such a process.

The mere penetration of the money form, he declares, has a 'dissolving' influence on the isolated community and draws 'new continents into the metabolism of circulation'.[58] Capital can then be accumulated directly from that 'metabolism of circulation' once it is established. The towns accumulate use values and hence values from the countryside, while commercial capital, as a historically prior form of organisation to producers' capital,

> exploits the difference between production prices in various countries ... [and] appropriates for itself a preponderant part of the surplus product: partly by acting as middleman between communities whose production is still basically oriented to use value ... and partly because in those earlier modes of production the principal proprietors of the surplus product whom the merchant trades with i.e. the slave-owner, the feudal lord and the state (e.g. the oriental despot) represent the consumption of wealth that the merchant sets out to trap ... Commercial capital, when it holds a dominant position, is thus in all cases a system of plunder, just as its development in the trading peoples of both ancient and modern times is directly bound up with violent plunder, piracy, the taking of slaves and subjugation of colonies ... The development of trade and commercial capital always gives production a growing orientation to exchange values, expands its scope, diversifies it and renders it cosmopolitan, developing money into world money. Trade always has, to a greater or lesser degree, a solvent effect on the pre-existing organisations of production, which in all their various forms are principally oriented to use-value. But how far it leads to the dissolution of the old mode of production depends first and foremost on the solidity and inner articulation of this mode of production itself. And what comes out of this process of dissolution, i.e., what new mode of production arises in place of the old, does not depend on trade, but rather on the character of the old mode of production itself.[59]

Merchants' capital played a crucial role in the redistribution of wealth and power from the countryside to the city or from the whole world to a few dominant capitalist nations. But all this changed when merchants' capital became subservient to industrial capital and so was forced to respect the rules of fair exchange. The merchant then became the mere agent who imposed more basic forms of capitalist domination. For example:

The cheapness of the articles produced by machinery, and the revolution in the means of transport and communication provide weapons for the conquest of foreign markets. By ruining the handicraft production of finished products in other countries, machinery forcibly converts them into fields for the production of its raw material. Hence India was compelled to produce cotton, wool, hemp, jute and indigo for Great Britain. By constantly turning workers into 'supernumeraries', large scale industry, in all countries where it has taken root, spurs on rapid increases in emigration and the colonisation of foreign lands, which are thereby converted into settlements for growing the raw materials of the mother country, just as Australia, for example, was converted into a colony for the growing of wool. A new and international division of labour springs up, one suited to the requirements of the main industrial countries, and it converts one part of the globe into a chiefly agricultural field of production for supplying the other part, which remains a pre-eminently industrial field.[60]

The exact geography of this new international division of labour depends, however, upon a whole host of 'special factors' and contradictory effects which make capitalist production's path to global domination peculiarly torturous.

In the case of colonies, for example, Marx insists on what he sees as a key distinction:

There are colonies proper, such as the United States, Australia, etc. Here the mass of the farming colonists, although they bring with them a larger or smaller amount of capital from the motherland, are not capitalists, nor do they carry on capitalist production. They are more or less peasants who work themselves and whose main object, in the first place, is to produce their own livelihood. In the second type of colonies – plantations – where commercial speculations figure from the start and production is intended for the world market, the capitalist mode of production exists, although only in a formal sense, since the slavery of Negroes precludes free wage labour, which is the basis of capitalist production. But the business in which slaves are used is conducted by capitalists.[61]

The two kinds of colony evolve very differently in relation to global processes of accumulation. Colonies of the second sort, no matter whether they are actively founded or fashioned out of a transformation of some pre-capitalist society (as in Eastern Europe), stand to be highly profitable, at least initially, because of the high rates of exploitation achievable through the reduction of necessities to a bare minimum. This tendency to transform necessities into luxuries

> determines the whole social pattern of backward nations ... which are associated with a world market based on capitalist production. No matter how large the surplus product they (the noncapitalist producers) extract from the surplus labor of their slaves in the simple form of cotton or corn, they can adhere to this simple undifferentiated labor because foreign trade enables them to convert these simple products into any kind of use value.[62]

The inability to revolutionise the productive forces under such conditions of created underdevelopment is what in the long run renders such colonies vulnerable.

In contrast, colonies made up of small independent producers, trading some surplus into the market, are typically characterised by labour shortages and high wages (particularly where abundant, cheap land is available). Colonies of this sort are not so amenable to capitalist forms of exploitation and may even actively resist the penetration of the capitalist mode of production:

> There the capitalist regime constantly comes up against the obstacle presented by the producer who, as owner of his own conditions of labour, employs that labour to enrich himself instead of the capitalist. The contradiction between these two diametrically opposed economic systems has its practical manifestation here in the struggle between them. Where the capitalist has behind him the power of the mother country, he tries to use force to clear out of the way the modes of production and appropriation which rest on the personal labour of the independent producer.[63]

Innumerable populist and radical movements spawned among settlers in frontier regions in the United States, Canada, Australia and other countries testify to the importance of such a conflict. But since such colonies are shaped by the spin-off of surplus population backed by small quantities of capital from the main centres of accumulation, and since they also often form expanding markets for capitalist production, they, too, eventually become integrated into a hegemonic capitalist mode of production. Thus the United States was being transformed in Marx's own time from an independent, largely non-capitalistic production system into a new centre for capital accumulation. 'Capitalist production advances there with gigantic strides,'

Marx noted, 'even though the lowering of wages and the dependence of the wage-labourer has by no means yet proceeded so far as to reach the normal European level.'[64]

But there are other 'special factors' to be taken into account. Marx recognises, for example, that 'the productiveness of labour is fettered by physical conditions' and that differences in nature therefore form 'a physical basis for the social division of labour'. But he is equally emphatic that such differences represent possibilities only (and not unmodifiable by human action at that) because in the final analysis the productiveness of labour 'is a gift, not of Nature, but of history embracing thousands of centuries'.[65] Furthermore, to the degree that productivity is defined under capitalism to mean the capacity of the labourer to produce surplus value for the capitalist,[66] so national and regional differences in the value of labour power become crucial:

> In comparing the wages in different nations, we must therefore take into account all the factors that determine changes in the amount of the value of labour power; the price and extent of the prime necessities of life in their natural and historical development, the cost of training the workers, the part played by the labour of women and children, the productivity of labour, and its extensive and intensive magnitude ... The average intensity of labour changes from country to country; here it is greater, there less. The national averages form a scale whose unit of measurement is the average unit of universal labour. The more intense national labour, therefore, as compared to the less intense, produces in the same time more value, which expresses itself in more money.[67]

The productivity of labour and the value of labour power, he concedes, can vary quite substantially, even within a country.[68] And capitalist production, far from eradicating such differences, can all too easily emphasise or even create them. 'In proportion as capitalist production is developed in a country, so, in the same proportion, do the national intensity and productivity of labour there rise above the international level.'[69] The penetration of money relations and simple commodity exchange appears powerless to modify such a condition of uneven geographical development. And this has important implications:

> Capital invested in foreign trade can yield a higher rate of profit, firstly because it competes with commodities produced by other countries with less developed production facilities, so that the more advanced country

sells its goods above their value even though still more cheaply than it competitors ... The privileged country receives more labour in exchange for less, even though this difference, this excess, is pocketed by a particular class.[70]

On this basis certain peculiarities can arise in the terms of trade between developed and underdeveloped societies, between centres and peripheries.[71] Furthermore, such differentials can persist. Countries may establish a monopoly over the production of particular commodities, while other factors may also prevent any direct 'levelling out of values by labour time and even the levelling out of cost prices by a general rate of profit'.[72] Even more startling is Marx's admission that:

Here the law of value undergoes essential modification. The relationship between labour days of different countries may be similar to that existing between skilled, complex labour and unskilled, simple labour within a country. In this case the richer country exploits the poorer one, even when the latter gains by the exchange.[73]

This assertion appears totally at odds with the main thrust of Marx's argument, that of inevitable global integration of capitalist production and exchange under a single law of value represented by universal money. It is, after all, only in 'the world markets that money first functions to its full extent as the commodity whose natural form is also the directly social form of realisation of human labour in the abstract'.[74]

Furthermore:

It is only foreign trade, the development of the market to a world market, which causes money to develop into world money and abstract labour into social labour. Abstract wealth, value, money, hence abstract labour, develop in the measure that concrete labour becomes a totality of different modes of labour embracing the world market. Capitalist production rests on the value or the transformation of the labour embodied in the product into social labour. But this is only possible on the basis of foreign trade and the world market. This is at once the pre-condition and the result of capitalist production.[75]

Can we discern here a faint echo of that same contradiction that Marx makes more explicit in his consideration of location: that the elimination of geographical differentiations entails the construction of fresh differentiations? It certainly seems as if specific material geographical structures mediate between the abstract aspects of labour (a social determination achieved through exchange on the world market) and labour's concrete qualities (the particularities of the labour process as undertaken by particular people in a particular place and time). The merchant capitalist, as we have seen, 'appropriates an overwhelming portion of the surplus product partly as a mediator between communities which still substantially produce for use values'.[76]

These are the kinds of 'special factors' that make of foreign trade a very complex issue. These complexities do not derive from the failure of capitalist development to overcome the social and cultural barriers to its global hegemony (although these barriers can be exceedingly resistant and in some cases determinant). They stem, rather, from the inherent contradictions within the capitalist mode of production itself. Much of the complexity we encounter in the case of foreign trade must be interpreted, therefore, as global manifestations of the internal contradictions of capitalism. And underlying all such manifestations is the very real possibility that in the end capitalism creates the greatest barriers (geographical as well as social) to its own development.

Commentary

The lack of any geographical perspectives (other than that on colonialism and imperialism) in most left theorising and in Marxian political economy in particular was a hot topic in radical geography in the early 1970s. An awkward relationship existed, which even Lenin failed to resolve, between theories focused on the exploitation of one class by another and those based on the exploitation of people in one territory by those in another. Several geographers in Marxist circles in the USA and the UK were actively involved in remedying the deficiency, as were those around Yves Lacoste and Henri Lefebvre in France. It became clear that the anarchist tradition in geography, founded in the work of Pyotr Kropotkin and Élisée Reclus, had within it a far more sensitive approach to questions of space, place and environment than mainstream Marxism. Anarchism, however, lacked the powerful political economic theory that Marx pioneered. My own contribution was to see if there was anything in Marx's texts that could usefully contribute to the discussion. Marx often referred to issues of the production of space and the spatial dimensions of social relations in the dynamics of capital but he usually did so in asides, parentheses or in out-of-the-way places. I decided to assemble these bits and pieces to see if they could be synthesised into something more systematic. I was pleased with the result and naively imagined that mainstream Marxist political economists would greatly appreciate the new insights. But they largely ignored it, in part, I suspect, because most mainstream Marxists did not then believe geographers could contribute anything relevant to Marxism, in much the same way mainstream geographers had a hard time getting their heads around the idea that Marx's thinking might be of relevance to geography. Such mutual disbelief has faded somewhat over time but has by no means disappeared. This speaks volumes about the limits imposed by dividing intellectual labour into disciplines. I incorporated many of the ideas and insights that came from creating this text into the last chapters of *The Limits to Capital*, which first appeared in 1982.

Chapter 3
The Urban Process under Capitalism

A Framework for Analysis

My objective is to understand the urban process under capitalism. I confine myself to the capitalist forms of urbanisation because I accept the idea that the 'urban' has a specific meaning under the capitalist mode of production which cannot be carried over without a radical transformation of meaning (and of reality) into other social contexts.

Within the framework of capitalism, I hang my interpretation of the urban process on the twin theories of *accumulation* and *class struggle*. The two themes are integral to each other and have to be regarded as different sides of the same coin – different windows from which to view the totality of capitalist activity. The class character of capitalist society means the domination of labour by capital. Put more concretely, a class of capitalists is in command of the work process and organises that process for the purposes of producing profit. The labourer, however, has command only over his or her labour power, which must be sold as a commodity on the market. The domination arises because the labourer must yield the capitalist a profit (surplus value) in return for a living wage. All of this is extremely simplistic, of course, and the actual class relations (and relations between factions of classes) within an actual system of production (comprising production, services, necessary costs of circulation, distribution exchange, etc.) are highly complex. The essential Marxist insight, however, is that profit arises out of the domination of labour by capital and that the capitalists as a class must, if they are to reproduce themselves, continuously expand the basis for profit. We thus arrive at a conception of a society founded on the principle of 'accumulation for accumulation's sake, production for production's sake'. Accumulation is the means whereby the capitalist class reproduces both itself and its domination over labour. Accumulation cannot, therefore, be isolated from class struggle.

The contradictions of capitalism

We can spin a whole web of argument concerning the urban process out of an analysis of the contradictions of capitalism. Let me set out the principal forms these contradictions take.

Consider, first, the contradictions that lie within the capitalist class itself. In the realm of exchange each capitalist operates in a world of individualism, freedom and equality and can and must act spontaneously and creatively. Through competition, however, the inherent laws of capitalist production are asserted as 'external coercive laws having power over every individual capitalist'. A world of individuality and freedom on the surface conceals a world of conformity and coercion underneath. But the translation from individual action to behaviour according to class norms is neither complete nor perfect – it never can be because the *process* of exchange under capitalist rules always presumes individuality, while the law of value always asserts itself in social terms. As a consequence, individual capitalists, each acting in his or her own immediate self-interest, can produce an aggregate result that is wholly antagonistic to the collective class interest. To take a rather dramatic example, competition may force each capitalist to so lengthen and intensify the work process that the capacity of the labour force to produce surplus value is seriously impaired. The collective effects of individual entrepreneurial activity can seriously endanger the social basis for future accumulation.

Consider, secondly, the implications of accumulation for the labourers. We know from the theory of surplus value that the exploitation of labour power is the source of capitalist profit. The capitalist form of accumulation therefore rests upon a certain violence that the capitalist class inflicts upon labour. Marx showed, however, that this appropriation could be worked out in such a way that it did not offend the rules of equality, individuality and freedom as they must prevail in the realms of exchange. Labourers, like capitalists, 'freely' trade the commodity they have for sale in the marketplace. But labourers are also in competition with each other for employment, while the work process is under the command of the capitalist. Under conditions of unbridled competition, the capitalists are forced willy-nilly into inflicting greater and greater violence upon those whom they employ. Individual labourers are powerless to resist because they too are locked in competition with each other. The only solution is for the labourers to constitute themselves as a class and find collective means to resist the depredations of capital. The capitalist form of accumulation consequently calls into being overt and explicit class struggle between labour and capital. This contradiction between the classes explains much of the dynamic of capitalist history and is fundamental to understanding the accumulation process.

The two forms of contradiction are integral to each other. They express an underlying unity and are to be construed as different aspects of the same reality. Yet we can usefully separate them. The internal contradiction within the capitalist class is rather different from the class confrontation between capital and labour, no matter how closely the two may be linked. In what follows I first focus on the accumulation process in the absence of any overt response on the part of the working class. I then broaden the perspective and consider how the organisation of the working class and its capacity to mount an overt class response affect the urban process under capitalism.

Other contradictions could enter in to supplement the analysis. For example, the capitalist production system often exists in an antagonistic relation to non- or pre-capitalist sectors that may exist within (the domestic economy, peasant and artisan production sectors, etc.) or without it (pre-capitalist societies, socialist countries, etc.). We should also note the contradiction with 'nature' which inevitably arises out of the relation of the dynamics of accumulation and the 'natural resource base' as capital defines it. Such matters obviously have to be taken into account in any analysis of the history of urbanisation under capitalism.

The laws of accumulation

I begin by sketching the structure of flows of capital within a system of production and realisation of value. This I do with the aid of a series of diagrams which appear highly 'functionalist' and perhaps unduly simple, but which nevertheless help us understand the basic logic of the accumulation process. We shall also see how problems arise because individual capitalists produce a result inconsistent with their class interest and consider some of the means whereby solutions to these problems might be found. In short, I attempt a summary of Marx's argument in *Capital* in the ridiculously short space of three or four pages.

The primary circuit of capital

In volume 1 of *Capital*, Marx presents an analysis of the capitalist production process. The drive to create surplus value rests either on an increase in the length of the working day (absolute surplus value) or on the gains to be made from continuous revolutions in the 'productive forces' through reorganisations of the work process which raise the productivity of labour power (relative surplus value). The capitalist captures relative surplus value from the organisation of cooperation and division of labour within the work process or by the application of fixed capital (machinery). The motor for these continuous revolutions in the work process, for the rising productivity of labour, lies in capitalist competition as each capitalist seeks an excess profit by adopting a production technique superior to competitors and the social average.

The implications of this for labour are explored in a chapter entitled 'The general law of capitalist accumulation'. Marx here examined alternations in the rate of exploitation and in the temporal rhythm of changes in the work process in relation to the supply conditions of labour power (in particular, the formation of an industrial reserve army), assuming all the while that a positive rate of accumulation must be sustained if the capitalist class is to reproduce itself. The analysis proceeds around a strictly circumscribed set of interactions, with all other problems assumed away or held constant. Figure 3.1 portrays the relations examined.

The second volume of *Capital* closes with a model of accumulation on an expanded scale. The problems of proportionality involved in the aggregate production of means of production and of consumption are examined, with all other problems held constant (including technological change, investment in fixed capital, etc.). The objective here is to show the potential for crises of disproportionality within the production process. But Marx has now broadened the structure of relationships put under the microscope (Figure 3.2). Note, however, that in both cases Marx tacitly assumes that all commodities are produced and consumed within one time period. The structure of relations examined in Figure 3.2 can be characterised as the *primary circuit of capital*.

Much of the analysis of the falling rate of profit and its countervailing tendencies in volume 3 similarly presupposes production and consumption within one time period, although there is some evidence that Marx intended to broaden the scope of this. But it is useful to consider the first part of the volume 3 analysis as a synthesis of the arguments presented in the first two volumes. It describes what happens within the primary circuit of capital as individual capitalists act in a way that goes against their collective class interest. The tendency is to produce a condition of *overaccumulation* – too much capital is produced relative to the opportunities to employ that capital. This tendency is manifest in a variety of guises. We have:

1. Overproduction of commodities – a glut on the market.
2. Falling rates of profit in pricing terms (to be distinguished from

the falling rate of profit in value terms, which is a theoretical construct).

3. Surplus capital, which can be manifest either as idle productive capacity or as money capital lacking opportunities for profitable employment.

4. Surplus labour and/or a rising rate of exploitation of labour power.

One or a combination of these manifestations may be present simultaneously. We have here a preliminary framework for the analysis of capitalist crises.

The secondary circuit of capital

I now drop the tacit assumption of production and consumption within one time period and consider the problem posed by production and use of commodities requiring different working periods, circulation periods and the like. This is an extraordinarily complex problem, which Marx addresses to some degree in volume 2 of *Capital* and the *Grundrisse*. Here I confine myself to some remarks regarding the formation of *fixed capital* and the *consumption fund*. Fixed capital, Marx argues, requires special analysis because of certain peculiarities that attach to its mode of production and realisation. These peculiarities arise because fixed capital items can be produced in the normal course of capitalist commodity production, but they are used as aids to the production process rather than as direct raw material inputs. They are also used over a relatively long time period. We can also usefully distinguish between fixed capital enclosed within the production process and fixed capital that functions as a physical framework for production. The latter I call the 'built environment for production'.

On the consumption side we have a parallel structure. The consumption fund is formed out of the commodities that function as aids rather than as direct inputs to consumption. Some items are directly enclosed within the consumption process (consumer durables such as stoves, washing machines, etc.) while others act as a physical framework for consumption (houses, pavements, etc.) – the latter I call the 'built environment for consumption'.

We should note that some items in the built environment function jointly for both production and consumption – the transport network, for example – and that items can be transferred from one category to another by changes in use. Also, fixed capital in the built environment is immobile in space in the sense that the value incorporated in it cannot be moved geographically without being destroyed. Investment in the built environment therefore

63

Figure 3.1 **The relations considered in Marx's 'general law of accumulation'**

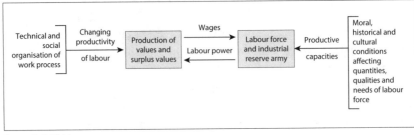

Source: *Capital*, Vol. 1

Figure 3.2 **The relations considered in Marx's model of 'reproduction on expanded scale'**

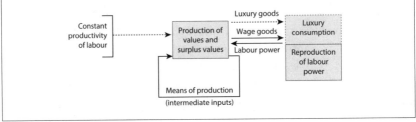

Source: *Capital*, Vol. 2

entails the creation of a whole physical landscape for the purposes of production, circulation, exchange, and consumption.

I call the capital flows into fixed asset and consumption fund formation the secondary circuit of capital. Consider, now, the manner in which such flows can occur. There must obviously be a 'surplus' of both capital and labour in relation to current production and consumption needs in order to facilitate the movement of capital into the formation of long-term assets, particularly those constituting the built environment. The tendency towards overaccumulation produces such conditions within the primary circuit on a periodic basis. One feasible if temporary solution to this overaccumulation problem would therefore be to switch capital flows into the secondary circuit.

Individual capitalists will often find it difficult to bring about such a switch in flows for a variety of reasons. The barriers to individual switching of capital are particularly acute with respect to the built environment, where investments tend to be large-scale and long-lasting, often difficult to price in the ordinary way, and in many cases open to collective use by all individual capitalists.

Indeed, individual capitalists left to themselves will tend to undersupply their own collective needs for production precisely because of such barriers. Individual capitalists tend to overaccumulate in the primary circuit and to underinvest in the secondary circuit; they have considerable difficulty organising a balanced flow of capital between the primary and secondary circuits.

A general condition for the flow of capital into the secondary circuit is, therefore, the existence of a functioning capital market and, perhaps, a state willing to finance and guarantee long-term, large-scale projects with respect to the creation of built environments. At times of overaccumulation, a switch of flows from the primary to the secondary circuit can be accomplished only if the various manifestations of overaccumulation can be transformed into money capital that can move freely and unhindered into these forms of investment. This switch of capital flows cannot be accomplished without a money supply and credit system that create 'fictitious capital' in advance of actual production and consumption. This applies as much to the consumption fund (hence the importance of consumer credit, housing mortgages, municipal debt, etc.) as it does to fixed capital. Since the production of money and of credit is a relatively autonomous process, we have to conceive of the financial and state institutions controlling the process as a kind of collective nerve centre governing and mediating the relations between the primary and secondary circuits of capital. The nature and form of these financial and state institutions and the policies they adopt can play important roles in checking or enhancing flows of capital into the secondary circuit of capital or into certain specific aspects of it, such as transportation, housing, public facilities, and so on. An alteration in these mediating structures can therefore affect both the volume and the direction of capital flows, by constricting flows down some channels and opening up new conduits elsewhere.

The tertiary circuit of capital

In order to complete the picture of the circulation of capital in general, we have to conceive of a tertiary circuit of capital which comprises, first, investment in science and technology (the purpose of which is to harness science to production and thereby to contribute to the processes that continuously revolutionise the productive forces in society) and, second, a wide range of social expenditures that relate primarily to the reproduction of labour power. The latter can usefully be divided into investments directed towards the qualitative improvement of labour power from the standpoint of capital (investments in education and health by means of which the capacity of labourers to engage in the work process will be enhanced) and investments in co-optation, integration, and repression of the labour force by ideological, military, and other means.

Individual capitalists find it hard to make such investments as individuals, no matter how desirable they may regard them. Once again, the capitalists are forced to some degree to constitute themselves as a class – usually through the agency of the state – and thereby find ways to channel investments into research and development and into the quantitative and qualitative improvement of labour power. We should recognise that capitalists often need to make such investments in order to fashion an adequate social and political basis from further accumulation. But with regard to social expenditures, the investment flows are very strongly affected by the state of class struggle. The amount of investment in repression and in ideological control is directly related to the threat of organised working-class resistance to the depredations of capital. And the need to co-opt labour arises only when the working class has accumulated sufficient power to require co-optation. Since the state can become a field of active class struggle, the mediations that are accomplished by no means fit exactly with the requirements of the capitalist class. The role of the state requires careful theoretical and historical elaboration in relation to the organisation of capital flows into the tertiary circuit.

The circulation of capital as a whole and its contradictions

Figure 3.3 portrays the overall structure of relations constituting the circulation of capital among the three circuits. The diagram looks very structuralist-functionalist because of the method of presentation. I can conceive of no other way to communicate clearly the various dimensions and paths of capital flow. We now have to consider the contradictions embodied within these flows and relations. I shall do so initially as if there were no overt class struggle between capital and labour. This enables us to see that the contradiction between individual capitalists and capital in general is itself a major source of instability within the accumulation process.

We have already seen how the contradictions internal to the capitalist class generate a tendency towards overaccumulation within the primary circuit of capital. And I have argued that this tendency can be overcome, temporarily at least, by switching capital into the secondary or tertiary circuits. Capital has, therefore, a variety of investment options open to it – fixed capital or consumption fund formation, investment in science and technology, investment in 'human capital' as labour is usually called in bourgeois literature, or outright repression. At particular historical conjunctures capitalists may not be capable of taking up all of these options with equal vigour, depending

Figure 3.3 **The structure of relations between the primary, secondary and tertiary circuits of capital**

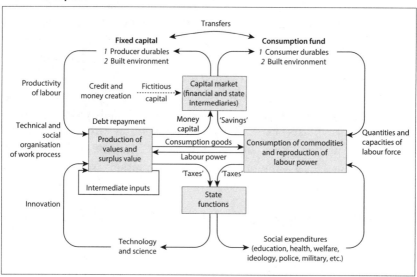

upon the degree of their own organisation, the institutions they have created, and the objective possibilities dictated by the state of production and the state of class struggle. I shall assume away such problems for the moment in order to concentrate on how the tendency to overaccumulation, which I have identified so far only with respect to the primary circuit, manifests itself within the overall structure of circulation of capital. To do this I first need to specify the concept of productivity of investments, in particular those directed into the secondary and tertiary circuits of capital.

On the productivity of investments in the secondary and tertiary circuits

I choose the concept of 'productivity' rather than 'profitability' for a variety of reasons. First of all, the rate of profit as Marx treats of it in volume 3 of *Capital* is measured in value rather than pricing terms and takes no account of the distribution of the surplus value into its component parts of interest on money capital, profit on productive capital, rent on land, profit of merchant's capital, etc. The rate of profit is regarded as a social average earned by individual capitalists in all sectors, and it is assumed that competition effectively ensures its equalisation. This is hardly a suitable conception for examining the flows between the three circuits of capital. To begin with, the formation of fixed capital in the built environment – particularly the collective means of production in the form, say, of transport networks – cannot be understood without understanding the formation of the capital market and the distribution of part of the surplus value in the form of interest. Second, many of the commodities produced in the secondary and tertiary circuits cannot be priced in the ordinary way, while collective action by way of the state cannot be examined in terms of the normal criteria of profitability. Third, the rate of profit that holds is perfectly appropriate for understanding the behaviours of individual capitalists or corporations in competition with each other, but cannot be translated into a concept suitable for examining the behaviour of capitalists as a class without some major assumptions (treating the total social profit as equal to the total surplus value produced within the capitalist system, as Marx does, for example).

The concept of productivity helps us to bypass some of the problems if we specify it carefully enough. For the fact is that capitalists as a class – often through the agency of the state – do invest in the production of conditions that they hope will be favourable to future accumulation, to their own reproduction as a class, and to their continuing domination over labour. This leads us immediately to a definition of productive investment as one that directly or indirectly expands the basis for the production of surplus value. Plainly, investments in the secondary and tertiary circuits have the potential under certain conditions to do this. The problem – which besets the capitalists as much as it confuses us – is to identify the conditions and means that will allow this potential to be realised.

Investment in new machinery is the easiest case to consider. It is directly productive if it expands the basis for producing surplus value and unproductive if those benefits fail to materialise. Similarly, investments in science and technology may or may not produce new forms of scientific knowledge which can be applied to expand accumulation. But what of investment in roads, housing, healthcare and education, police forces and the military, and so on? If workers are being recalcitrant in the workplace, then judicious investment by the capitalist class in a police force to intimidate the workers and break their collective power may indeed be productive indirectly of surplus value for the capitalists (this was the origin of the nineteenth-century Pinkertons in the USA). If, however, the police are employed to protect the bourgeoisie in the conspicuous consumption of their revenues in callous disregard of the poverty and misery that surrounds them, then the police are not acting to facilitate accumulation. The distinction may be fine but it demonstrates the dilemma. How can the capitalist class identify, with reasonable precision, the opportunities for indirect and direct productive investment in the secondary and tertiary circuits of capital?

This is what a lot of public policy debates are about. The costs of bad investments are bound to register somewhere and perhaps even underpin a certain kind of crisis formation (often centred on public expenditures and policies).

On the forms of crisis under capitalism

Crises are the real manifestations of the underlying contradictions within the capitalist process of accumulation. The argument that Marx seems to propose in *Capital* is that there is always the potential within capitalism to achieve 'balanced growth', but that this potential can never be realised because of the structure of the social relations prevailing in capitalist society. This structure leads individual capitalists to produce results in aggregate that are antagonistic to their own class interests and to inflict insupportable violence upon the working class which is bound to elicit its own response in the field of overt class struggle.

We have already seen how the capitalists tend to generate states of over-accumulation within the primary circuit of capital and have considered the various manifestations that result. As the pressure builds, either the accumulation process grinds to a halt or new investment opportunities are found as capital flows down the various channels into the secondary and tertiary circuits. This movement might start as a trickle and become a flood as the potential for expanding the production of surplus value by such means becomes apparent. But the tendency towards overaccumulation is not eliminated. It is transformed, rather, into a pervasive tendency towards over-investments in the secondary and tertiary circuits. This overinvestment is in relation solely to the needs of capital and has nothing to do with the real needs of the people, which inevitably remain unfulfilled. Manifestations of crisis thus appear in both the secondary and the tertiary circuits of capital. But there is a substantial time-lag because of the long turnover time of such investments. It may take many years before their failure or success becomes evident. But at some point manifestations of crisis thus appear in both the secondary and the tertiary circuits of capital.

As regards fixed capital and the consumption fund, the crisis takes the form of a crisis in the valuation of assets. Chronic overproduction results in the devaluation of fixed capital and consumption fund items – a process that affects the built environment as well as producer and consumer durables. We can likewise observe crisis formation at other points in the structure of capital flows – crises in social expenditures (health, education, military repression), in consumption fund formation (housing), and in technology and science. In each case the crisis occurs because the potential for productive investments within each of these spheres is exhausted. Further flows of capital do not expand the basis for the production of surplus value. We should also note that crises of any magnitude in any of these spheres is registered as a crisis within the financial and state structures, while the latter, because of their relative autonomy, can be an independent source of crises (we can thus speak of financial, credit, and monetary crises alongside fiscal crisis of state expenditures).

Crises are the 'irrational rationalisers' of the capitalist mode of production. They are indicators of imbalances and force a rationalisation (which may be painful for certain sectors of the capitalist class as well as for labour) of the process of production, exchange, distribution, and consumption. They may also force a rationalisation of institutional structures (financial and state institutions in particular). From the standpoint of the total structure of relationships I have portrayed, we can distinguish different kinds of crises:

1. *Partial crises*, which affect a particular sector, geographical region, or set of mediating institutions. These can arise for any number of reasons but are potentially capable of being resolved within that sector, region, or set of institutions. We can witness autonomously forming monetary crises, for example, which can be resolved through regulation and institutional reforms, crises in the formation of the built environment in certain places which can be resolved by bankruptcy or a revival in the local economy, etc.
2. *Switching crises*, which involve a major reorganisation and restructuring of capital flows and/or a major restructuring of mediating institutions in order to open up new channels for productive investments. There are two kinds of switching crises:
   i) *Sectoral switching crises*, which entail switching the allocation of capital from one sphere (e.g. fixed capital formation) to another (e.g. education).
   ii) *Geographical switching crises*, which involve switching capital flows from one place or region to another. This form of crisis is particularly important for investments in the built environment because these are immobile in space.
3. *Global crises*, which affect, to a greater or lesser degree, all sectors, spheres and regions within the capitalist system. We will thus see widespread devaluations of fixed capital and the consumption

fund, a fiscal crisis of state expenditures, a crisis of productivity and profits, all manifest at the same time everywhere. I note in passing that there have been only two global crises of this sort in the twentieth century – that of the 1930s and its World War II aftermath; the second after 1973 but which had been steadily building from 1968 onwards.

Crises can build from partial to global. The switching crises that relate to and underpin uneven geographical developments within capitalism are particularly interesting to study.

Commentary

This was my first attempt to construct a theoretical basis – using Marx's categories – for an interpretation of urbanisation by examining its links to capital accumulation. It brought the analysis of the geography of capitalist accumulation down to the specifics of the urban level. Although the theory may seem oversimplified and in need of elaboration and development (particularly concerning the roles of the state and credit), I think it still provides a robust way for thinking through the role of long-term fixed capital investments in the built environment in the reproduction of capital. It also invites enquiries into how the tendency towards overaccumulation gets transferred from one circuit of capital to another and with what effects. The obvious danger is a crisis of overaccumulation in the built environment. The framework explains how China compensated for a substantial decline in its export trade after 2008, following the collapse of consumer demand in the USA, by a state-led strategy of forcing surplus capital and labour into huge urbanisation and physical infrastructure projects. These allowed China to maintain relatively high rates of growth after 2009 while the rest of the world floundered. Much the same could be said of the United States after 1945 when the country resorted to its favourite way of warding off crises by 'building houses and filling them with things' (i.e. suburbanisation). In 2007/08 this solution ran out of possibilities in the USA, sparking an international financial crisis. As I write this in 2015, there is growing evidence of overinvestment in the built environment in China: it will be interesting to see what transpires as the authorities struggle to prevent overaccumulation in the secondary circuit threatening the health of not only China's economy but that of the whole world.

The analysis of the circuits of capital developed in this chapter is consistent with Marx's organic, ecosystemic and evolutionary way of thinking about the production and reproduction of capital through growth. Lefebvre mentions the idea of the secondary circuit in *The Urban Revolution*. The only other analysis of this sort, though from a very different angle, is by the Brazilian geographer Milton Santos, with whom I had some productive discussions in the 1970s.

For the sake of brevity, I have omitted the latter part of the article. This presented some historical data on class struggles and investments in the secondary circuit of capital which were broadly consistent with what was being explored theoretically.

Chapter 4
Monument and Myth

The Building of the Basilica of the Sacred Heart

Strategically placed atop a hill known as the Butte Montmartre, the Basilica of Sacré-Coeur occupies a commanding position over Paris. Its five white marble domes and the campanile that rises beside them can be seen from every quarter of the city. Occasional glimpses of it can be caught from within the dense and cavernous network of streets which makes up old Paris. It stands out, spectacular and grand, to the young mothers parading their children in the Jardins de Luxembourg, to the tourists who painfully plod to the top of Notre-Dame or who painlessly float up the escalators of the Centre Beaubourg, to the commuters crossing the Seine by metro at Grenelle or pouring into the Gare du Nord, to the Algerian immigrants who on Sunday afternoons wander to the top of the rock in the Parc des Buttes-Chaumont. It can be seen clearly by the old men playing 'boules' in the place du Colonel Fabien, on the edge of the traditional working-class quarters of Belleville and La Villette – places that have an important role to play in our story.

On cold winter days when the wind whips the fallen leaves among the ageing tombstones of the Père Lachaise cemetery, the basilica can be seen from the steps of the tomb of Adolphe Thiers, first president of the Third Republic of France. Though now almost hidden by the modern office complex of La Défense, it can be seen from more than twenty kilometres away in the Pavillon Henry IV in St Germain-en-Laye, where Adolphe Thiers died. But by a quirk of topography, it cannot be seen from the famous Mur des Fédérés in that same Père Lachaise cemetery where, on 27 May 1871, some of the last few remaining soldiers of the Commune were rounded up after a fierce fight among the tombstones and summarily shot. You cannot see Sacré-Coeur from that ivy-covered wall now shaded by an ageing chestnut. That place of pilgrimage for socialists, workers and their leaders is hidden from a place of

Figure 4.1 The Basilica of Sacré-Coeur

pilgrimage for the Catholic faithful by the brow of the hill on which stands the grim tomb of Adolphe Thiers.

Few would argue that the Basilica of Sacré-Coeur is beautiful or elegant (Figure 4.1). But most would concede that it is striking and distinctive, that its direct Byzantine style achieves a kind of haughty grandeur which demands respect from the city spread out at its feet. On sunny days it glistens from afar, and even on the gloomiest of days its domes seem to capture the smallest particles of light and radiate them outward in a white marble glow. Floodlit by night it appears suspended in space, sepulchral and ethereal. Thus does Sacré-Coeur project an image of saintly grandeur, of perpetual remembrance. But remembrance of what?

The visitor drawn to the basilica in search of an answer to that question must first ascend the steep hillside of Montmartre. Those who pause to catch their breath will see spread out before them a marvellous vista of rooftops, chimneys, domes, towers, monuments – a vista of old Paris that has not changed much since that dull and foggy October morning in 1872, when the archbishop of Paris climbed those steep slopes only to have the sun miraculously chase both fog and cloud away to reveal the splendid panorama of Paris spread out before him. The archbishop marvelled for a moment before crying out loud: 'It is here, it is here where the martyrs are, it is here that the Sacred Heart must reign so that it can beckon all to it!'[1] So who are the martyrs commemorated here in the grandeur of this basilica?

The visitor who enters into that hallowed place will most probably first be struck by the immense painting of Jesus which covers the dome of the apse. Portrayed with arms stretched wide, the figure of Christ wears an image of the Sacred Heart upon his breast. Beneath, two words stand our directly from the Latin motto – GALLIA POENITENS. And beneath that stands a large gold casket containing the image of the Sacred Heart of Jesus, burning with passion, suffused with blood and surrounded with thorns. Illuminated day and night, it is here that pilgrims come to pray.

Opposite a life-size statue of St Marguerite-Marie Alacoque, words from a letter written by that saintly person – date: 1689; place: Paray-le-Monial – tell us more about the cult of the Sacred Heart:

THE ETERNAL FATHER WISHING REPARATION FOR THE BITTERNESS AND ANGUISH THAT THE ADORABLE HEART OF HIS DIVINE SON HAD EXPERIENCED AMONGST THE HUMILIATION AND OUTRAGES OF HIS PASSION DESIRES AN EDIFICE WHERE THE IMAGE OF THIS DIVINE HEART CAN RECEIVE VENERATION AND HOMAGE.

Prayer to the Sacred Heart of Jesus which, according to the scriptures, had been exposed when a centurion thrust a lance through Jesus's side during his suffering upon the cross, was not unknown before the seventeenth century. But Marguerite-Marie, beset by visions, transformed the worship of the Sacred Heart into a distinctive cult within the Catholic Church. Although her life was full of trials and suffering, her manner severe and rigorous, the predominant image of Christ which the cult projected was warm and loving, full of repentance and suffused with a gentle kind of mysticism.[2]

Marguerite-Marie and her disciples set about propagating the cult with great zeal. She wrote to Louis XIV, for example, claiming to bring a message from Christ in which the king was asked to repent, to save France by dedicating himself to the Sacred Heart, to place its image upon his standard and to build a chapel to its glorification. It is from that letter of 1689 that the words now etched in stone within the basilica are taken.

The cult diffused slowly. It was not exactly in tune with eighteenth-century French rationalism, which strongly influenced modes of belief among Catholics and stood in direct opposition to the hard, rigorous and self-disciplined image of Jesus projected by the Jansenists. But by the end of the eighteenth century it had some important and potentially influential adherents. Louis XVI privately took devotion to the Sacred Heart for himself and his family. Imprisoned during the French Revolution, he vowed that within three months of his deliverance he would publicly dedicate himself to the Sacred Heart and thereby save France (from what, exactly, he did not say, nor did he need to). And he vowed to build a chapel to the worship of the Sacred Heart. The manner of Louis XVI's deliverance did not permit him to fulfil that vow. Marie Antoinette did no better. The queen delivered up her last prayers to the Sacred Heart before keeping her appointment with the guillotine.

These incidents are of interest because they presage an association, important for our story, between the cult of the Sacred Heart and the reactionary monarchism of the *ancien régime*. This put adherents to the cult in firm opposition to the principles of the French Revolution. Believers in the principles of liberty, equality and fraternity, who were in any case prone to awesome anticlerical sentiments and practices, were, in return, scarcely enamoured of such a cult. Revolutionary France was no safe place to attempt to propagate it. Even the bones and other relics of Marguerite-Marie, now displayed in Paray-le-Monial, had to be carefully hidden during those years.

The restoration of the monarchy in 1815 changed all that. The Bourbon monarchs sought, under the watchful eye of the European powers, to restore whatever they could of the old social order. The theme of repentance for the excesses of the revolutionary era ran strong. Louis XVIII did not fulfil his dead brother's vow to the Sacred Heart, but he did build, with his own money, a Chapel of Expiation on the spot where his brother and his family had been so unceremoniously interred – GALLIA POENITENS.

A society for the propagation of the cult of the Sacred Heart was founded, however, and proceedings for the glorification of Marguerite-Marie were transmitted to Rome in 1819. The link between conservative monarchism and the cult of the Sacred Heart was further consolidated. The cult spread among conservative Catholics but was viewed with some suspicion by the liberal progressive wing of French Catholicism. But now another enemy was ravaging the land, disturbing the social order. France was undergoing the stress and tensions of capitalist industrialisation. In fits and starts under the July Monarchy (installed in 1830 and just as summarily dispensed with in the revolution of 1848) and then in a great surge in the early years of the Second Empire of Napoleon III, France saw a radical transformation in certain sectors of its economy, in its institutional structures and in its social order.[3]

The cult of the Sacred Heart now assembled under its banner not only those devotees drawn by temperament or circumstances to the image of a gentle and forgiving Christ, not only those who dreamed of a restoration of the political order of yesteryear, but also all those who felt threatened by the materialist values of the new social order, in which money had become the Holy Grail, the papacy of finance threatened the authority of the Pope, and Mammon had supplanted God as the primary object of worship. From the standpoint of conservative Catholics, the transformation threatened much that was sacred in French life, since it brought within its train a crass and heartless materialism, an ostentatious and morally decadent bourgeois culture, and a sharpening of class tensions.

To these general conditions, French Catholics could also add some more specific complaints in the 1860s. Napoleon III had finally come down on the side of Italian unification and committed himself politically and militarily to the liberation of the central Italian states from the temporal power of the Pope. The latter did not take kindly to such politics and under military pressure retired to the Vatican, refusing to come out until such time as his temporal power was restored. From that vantage point, the Pope delivered searing condemnations of French policy and the moral decadence which, he felt, was sweeping over France. In this manner he hoped to rally French Catholics in the active pursuit of his cause. The moment was propitious.

Marguerite-Marie was beatified by Pius IX in 1864. The cult of the Sacred Heart became a rallying cry for all forms of conservative opposition. The era of grand pilgrimages to Paray-le-Monial began. The pilgrims, many carried to their destination by the new railways that the barons of high finance had helped to build, came to express repentance for both public and private transgressions. They repented for the materialism and decadent opulence of France. They repented for the restrictions placed upon the temporal power of the Pope. They repented for the passing of the traditional values embodied in an old and venerable social order. GALLIA POENITENS.

Just inside the main door of the Basilica of Sacré-Coeur in Paris, the visitor can read the following inscription:

THE YEAR OF OUR LORD 1875 THE 16TH JUNE IN THE REIGN OF HIS HOLINESS POPE PIUS IX IN ACCOMPLISHMENT OF A VOW FORMULATED DURING THE WAR OF 1870–71 BY ALEXANDER LEGENTIL AND HUBERT ROHAULT DE FLEURY RATIFIED BY HIS GRACE MSGR. GUIBERT ARCHBISHOP OF PARIS; IN EXECUTION OF THE VOTE OF THE NATIONAL ASSEMBLY OF THE 23 JULY 1873, ACCORDING TO THE DESIGN OF THE ARCHITECT ABADIE; THE FIRST STONE OF THIS BASILICA ERECTED TO THE SACRED HEART OF JESUS WAS SOLEMNLY PUT IN PLACE BY HIS EMINENCE CARDINAL GUIBERT ...

Let us flesh out that capsule history and find out what lies behind it. As Bismarck's battalions rolled to victory after victory over the French in the summer of 1870, an impending sense of doom swept over France. Many interpreted the defeats as righteous vengeance inflicted by divine will upon an errant and morally decadent France. It was in this spirit that the Empress Eugénie was urged to walk with her family and court, all dressed in mourning, from the Palace of the Tuileries to Notre-Dame, to publicly dedicate themselves to the Sacred Heart. Though the Empress received the suggestion favourably, it was, once more, too late. On 2 September, Napoleon III was defeated and captured at Sedan; on 4 September, the Republic was proclaimed on the steps of the Hôtel-de-Ville and a Government of National Defence was formed. On that day also the Empress Eugénie took flight from Paris, having prudently, and at the Emperor's urging, already packed her bags and sent her more valuable possessions on to England.

The defeat at Sedan ended the Empire but not the war. The Prussian armies rolled on, and by 20 September they had encircled Paris and put that city under a siege that was to last until 28 January of the following year. Like many other respectable bourgeois citizens, Alexander Legentil fled Paris at the approach of the Prussian armies and took refuge in the provinces. Languishing in Poitiers and agonising over the fate of Paris, he vowed in early December that 'if God saved Paris and France and delivered the sovereign pontiff, he would contribute according to his means to the construction in Paris of a sanctuary dedicated to the Sacred Heart'. He sought other adherents to this vow and soon had the ardent support of Hubert Rohault de Fleury.[4]

The terms of Legentil's vow did not, however, guarantee it a very warm reception, for, as he soon discovered, the provinces 'were then possessed of hateful sentiments towards Paris'. Such a state of affairs was not unusual, and we can usefully divert for a moment to consider its basis.

Under the *ancien régime*, the French state apparatus had acquired a strongly centralised character which was consolidated under the French Revolution and Empire. This centralisation thereafter became the basis of French political organisation and gave Paris a peculiarly important role in relation to the rest of France. The administrative, economic and cultural predominance of Paris was assured. But the events of 1789 also showed that Parisians had the power to make and break governments. They proved adept at using that power and were not loath, as a result, to regard themselves as privileged beings with a right and duty to foist all that they deemed 'progressive' upon a supposedly backward, conservative and predominantly rural France. The Parisian bourgeois despised the narrowness of provincial life and found the peasant disgusting and incomprehensible.[5]

From the other end of the telescope, Paris was generally seen as a centre of power, domination and opportunity. It was both envied and hated. To the antagonism generated by the excessive centralisation of power and authority in Paris were added all of the vaguer small-town and rural antagonisms towards any large city as a centre of privilege, material success, moral decadence, vice and social unrest. What was special in France was the way in which the tensions emanating from the 'urban–rural contradiction' were so intensely focused upon the relation between Paris and the rest of France.

Under the Second Empire these tensions sharpened considerably. Paris experienced a vast economic boom as the railways made it the hub of a process of national spatial integration. At the same time, falling transport costs and the free trade policies signalled by the Anglo-French Treaties of Commerce in 1860 brought the city into a new relationship with an emerging global economy. Its share of an expanding French export trade increased dramatically, and its population grew rapidly, largely through a massive immigration of rural labourers.[6] Concentration of wealth and power proceeded apace as Paris became the centre of financial, speculative and commercial operations. The contrasts between affluence and poverty became ever more startling and were increasingly expressed in terms of a geographical segregation between the bourgeois quarters of the west and the working-class quarters of the north, east and south. Belleville became a foreign territory into which the bourgeois citizens of the west rarely dared to venture. The population of that place, which more than doubled between 1853 and 1870, was pictured in the bourgeois press as 'the dregs of the people' caught in 'the deepest depths of poverty and hatred' where 'ferments of envy, sloth and anger bubble without cease'.[7] The signs of social breakdown were everywhere. As economic growth slowed in the 1860s and as the authority of Empire began to fail, Paris became a cauldron of social unrest, vulnerable to agitators of any stripe.

And to top it all, Haussmann, at the Emperor's urging, had set out to 'embellish Paris' with spacious boulevards, parks and gardens, monumental architecture of all sorts. The intent was to make Paris a truly imperial city, worthy not only of France but of Western civilisation. Haussmann had done this at immense cost and by the slipperiest of financial means, a feat which scarcely recommended itself to the frugal provincial mind. The image of public opulence which Haussmann projected was only matched by the conspicuous consumption of a bourgeoisie, many of whom had grown rich speculating on the benefits of his improvements.[8]

Small wonder, then, that provincial and rural Catholics were in no frame of mind to dig into their pockets to embellish Paris with yet another monument, no matter how pious its purpose. But there were even more specific objections which emerged in response to Legentil's proposal. The Parisians had with their customary presumptuousness proclaimed a republic when provincial and rural sentiment was heavily infused with monarchism. Furthermore, those who had remained behind to face the rigours of the siege were showing themselves remarkably intransigent and bellicose, declaring they would favour a fight to the bitter end, when provincial sentiment showed a strong disposition to end the conflict with Prussia. And then the rumours and hints of a new materialist politics among the working class in Paris, spiced with a variety of manifestations of revolutionary fervour, gave the impression that the city had, in the absence of its more respectable bourgeois citizenry, fallen prey to radical and even socialist philosophy. Since the only means of communication between a besieged Paris and the non-occupied territories was pigeon or balloon, abundant opportunities arose for

Figure 4.2 The fires that raged in Paris during the closing days of the Commune left behind an enormous train of destruction. Among the many photos available (mostly anonymous), we find one of the rue Royale with the fires still smouldering. Many of the major public buildings, such as the Hôtel-de-Ville, the Ministry of Finance and the Palace of the Tuileries, were reduced to ruins. The palace was eventually torn down by the republican administration that came to power in the 1880s, in part because of the cost to rebuild it, but also because it was a hated symbol of royal and Napoleonic power.

misunderstanding, which the rural foes of republicanism and the urban foes of monarchism were not beyond exploiting.

Legentil therefore found it politic to drop any specific mention of Paris in his vow. But towards the end of February the Pope endorsed it, and from then on the movement gathered some strength. And so on 19 March, a pamphlet appeared which set out the arguments for the vow at some length.[9] The spirit of the work had to be national, the authors urged, because the French people had to make national amends for what were national crimes. They confirmed their intention to build the monument in Paris. To the objection that the city should not be further embellished they replied, 'Were Paris reduced to cinders, we would still want to avow our national faults and to proclaim the justice of God on its ruins.'

The timing and phrasing of the pamphlet proved fortuitously prophetic. On 18 March, Parisians had taken their first irrevocable steps towards establishing self-government under the Commune. The real or imagined sins of the Communards were subsequently to shock and outrage bourgeois opinion. And as much of Paris was indeed reduced to cinders in the course of a civil war of incredible ferocity, the notion of building a basilica of expiation upon these ashes became more and more appealing. As Rohault de Fleury noted, with evident satisfaction, 'In the months to come, the image of Paris reduced to cinders struck home many times.'[10] Let us rehearse a little of that history.

The origins of the Paris Commune lie in a whole series of events which ran into each other in complex ways. Precisely because of its political importance within the country, Paris had long been denied any representative form of municipal government and had been directly administered by the national government. For much of the nineteenth century, a predominantly republican Paris was chafing under the rule of monarchists (either Bourbon 'legitimists' or 'Orléanists') or authoritarian Bonapartists. The demand for a democratic form of municipal government was long-standing and commanded widespread support within the city.

The Government of National Defence set up on 4 September 1870 was neither radical nor revolutionary,[11] but it was republican. It also turned out to be timid and inept. It laboured under certain difficulties, of course, but these were hardly sufficient to excuse its weak performance. It did not, for example, command the respect of the monarchists and lived in perpetual fear of the reactionaries of the right. When the Army of the East, under General Bazaine, capitulated to the Prussians at Metz on 27 October, the general left the impression that he did so because, being monarchist, he could not bring himself to fight for a republican government. Some of his officers who resisted the capitulation saw Bazaine putting his political preferences above the honour of France. This was a matter which was to dog French politics for several years. Rossel, who was later to command the armed forces of the Commune for a while, and who was summarily executed by the invading forces of Versailles for his role, was one of the officers shocked to the core by Bazaine's evident lack of patriotism.[12]

But the tensions between the different factions of the ruling class were nothing compared to the real or imagined antagonisms between a traditional and remarkably obdurate bourgeoisie and a working class that was beginning to find its feet and assert itself. Rightly or wrongly, the bourgeoisie was greatly alarmed during the 1860s by the emergence of working-class organisation and political clubs, by the activities of the Paris branch of the International Working Men's Association, by the effervescence of thought within the working class and the spread of anarchist and socialist philosophies. And the working class – although by no means as well organised or as unified as their opponents feared – was certainly displaying abundant signs of an emergent class-consciousness.

The Government of National Defence could not stem the tide of Prussian victories or break the siege of Paris without widespread working-class support. And the leaders of the left were only too willing to give it in spite of their initial opposition to the Emperor's war. Blanqui promised the government 'energetic and absolute support', and even the International's leaders, having dutifully appealed to the German workers not to participate in a fratricidal struggle, plunged into organising for the defence of Paris. Belleville, the centre of working-class agitation, rallied spectacularly to the national cause, all in the name of the Republic.[13]

The bourgeoisie sensed a trap. They saw themselves, wrote a contemporary commentator drawn from their ranks, caught between the Prussians and those whom they called 'the reds'. 'I do not know,' he went on, 'which of these two evils terrified them most; they hated the foreigner but they feared the Bellevillois much more.'[14] No matter how much they wanted to defeat the foreigner, they could not bring themselves to do so with the battalions of the working class in the vanguard. For what was not to be the last time in French history, the bourgeoisie chose to capitulate to the Germans, leaving the left as the dominant force within a patriotic front. In 1871, fear of the 'enemy within' was to prevail over national pride.

The failure of the French to break the siege of Paris was first interpreted as the product of Prussian superiority and French military ineptitude. But as sortie after sortie promised victory only to be turned into disaster, honest patriots began to wonder if the powers that be were not playing tricks which bordered on betrayal and treason. The government was increasingly viewed as a 'Government of National Defection' – a description that Marx later used to great effect in his impassioned defence of the Commune.[15] The government was equally reluctant to respond to the Parisian demand for municipal democracy. Since many of the respectable bourgeois had fled, it looked as if elections would deliver municipal power into the hands of the left. Given the suspicions of the monarchists of the right, the Government of National Defence felt it could not afford to concede what had long been demanded. And so it procrastinated endlessly.

As early as 31 October, these various threads came together to generate an insurrectionary movement in Paris. Shortly after Bazaine's ignominious surrender, word got out that the government was negotiating the terms of an armistice with the Prussians. The population of Paris took to the streets and, as the feared Bellevillois descended en masse, took several members of the government prisoner, agreeing to release them only on the verbal assurance that there would be municipal elections and no capitulation. This incident was guaranteed to raise the hackles of the right. It was the immediate cause of the 'hateful sentiments towards Paris' which Legentil encountered in December. The government lived to fight another day. But, as events turned out, they were to fight much more effectively against the Bellevillois than they ever fought against the Prussians.

So the siege of Paris dragged on. Worsening conditions in the city now added their uncertain effects to a socially unstable situation. The government proved inept and insensitive to the needs of the population and thereby added fuel to the smouldering fires of discontent.[16] The people lived off cats or dogs, while the more privileged partook of pieces of Pollux, the young elephant from the zoo (forty francs a pound for the trunk). The price of rats – the 'taste is a cross between pork and partridge' – rose from sixty centimes to four francs apiece. The government failed to take the elementary precaution of rationing bread until January, when it was much too late. Supplies dwindled, and the adulteration of bread with bone meal became a chronic problem which was made even less palatable by the fact that it was human bones from the catacombs which were being dredged up for the occasion. While the common people were thus consuming their ancestors without knowing it, the luxuries of café life were kept going, supplied by hoarding merchants at exorbitant prices. The rich that stayed behind continued to indulge their pleasures according to their custom, although they paid dearly

Figure 4.3 The cartoonist Cham joined with an ageing Daumier to try and extract some humour from the desolate months of the 1870s siege of Paris. Here we see Parisians queuing for their nightly share of rat meat; Cham also advises his viewer to take care, when eating mouse, that the cat does not give pursuit.

for it. The government did nothing to curb profiteering or the continuation of conspicuous consumption by the rich in callous disregard for the feelings of the less privileged.

By the end of December, radical opposition to the Government of National Defence was growing. It led to the publication of the celebrated Affiche Rouge of 7 January. Signed by the central committee of the twenty Parisian arrondissements, it accused the government of leading the country to the edge of an abyss by its indecision, inertia and foot-dragging; suggested that the government knew not how to administer or to fight; and insisted that the perpetuation of such a regime could end only in capitulation to the Prussians. It proclaimed a programme for a general requisition of resources, rationing and mass attack. It closed with the celebrated appeal 'Make way for the people! Make way for the Commune!'[17]

Placarded all over Paris, the appeal had its effect. The military responded decisively and organised one last mass sortie, which was spectacular for its military ineptitude and the carnage left behind. 'Everyone understood,' wrote Lissagaray, 'that they had been sent out to be sacrificed.'[18] The evidence

Figure 4.4 Thiers had been a frequent subject for Daumier ever since the 1840s. His sudden reappearance on the political stage in 1870 provided another chance for critical comment. In the figure to the left (published 24 February 1871), Thiers is seen orchestrating the newly elected National Assembly in Bordeaux (but 'one can't see the prompter'), and on the right (published 21 April, after the Commune has been declared) we see Thiers frenetically whipping his horses, harnessed to the coach of state, in the direction of Versailles. Paris, depicted in the statuesque figure of Liberty, is left with horses straining in the opposite direction, but with head turned disapprovingly towards Thiers. The break-up of the state is ominously foretold.

of treason and betrayal was by now overwhelming for those close to the action. It pushed many an honest patriot from the bourgeoisie, who put love of country above class interest, into an alliance with the dissident radicals and the working class.

Parisians accepted the inevitable armistice at the end of January with sullen passivity. It provided for national elections to a constituent assembly which would negotiate and ratify a peace agreement. It specified that the French army lay down its arms but permitted the National Guard of Paris, which could not easily be disarmed, to remain a fighting force. Supplies came into a starving city under the watchful eye of the Prussian troops. Most of the remaining bourgeoisie fled to their rural retreats, while the influx of impoverished, unpaid and demoralised soldiers into the city added to the social and political stresses there. In the February elections, the city returned its quota of radical republicans (Louis Blanc, Hugo, Gambetta and even Garibaldi). But rural and provincial France voted solidly for peace. Since the left was antagonistic to capitulation, the republicans from the Government of National Defence seriously compromised by their management of the war and the Bonapartists discredited, the peace vote went to the monarchists. Republican Paris was appalled to find itself faced with a monarchist majority in the National Assembly.

Thiers, by then seventy-three years old, was elected president in part because of his long experience in politics and in part because the monarchists did not want to be responsible for signing what was bound to be an ignoble peace agreement. He ceded Alsace and Lorraine to Germany. Worse still, in Parisians' eyes, he agreed to the symbolic occupation of Paris by the Prussian troops on 1 March, which could have easily become a bloodbath since many in Paris threatened an armed fight. Only the organisational power of the left (who understood the Prussians would destroy them and thus do Thiers's work for him) and the influence of a shadowy new group called the Central Committee of the National Guard prevented a debacle. The Prussians paraded down the Champs-Elysées, watched in stony silence by the crowds with all the major monuments shrouded in black crêpe. The humiliation was not easy to forgive and Thiers was held to blame. Thiers also agreed to a huge war indemnity. But he was enough of a patriot to resist Bismarck's suggestion that Prussian bankers float the loan required. Thiers reserved that privilege for the French and turned this year of troubles into one of the most profitable ones ever for the gentlemen of French high finance.[19] The bankers informed Thiers that if he was to raise the money, he must first deal with 'those rascals in Paris'. This he was uniquely equipped to do. As minister of the interior under Louis Philippe, he had, in 1834, been responsible for the savage repression of one of the first genuine working-class movements in French history. Ever contemptuous of 'the vile multitude', he had long had a plan for dealing with them – a plan which he had proposed to Louis Philippe in 1848 and which he was now finally in a position to put into effect.[20] The plan was simple. He would use the conservatism of the country to smash the radicalism of the city.

On the morning of 18 March, the population of Paris awoke to find that the remains of the French army had been sent to Paris to relieve that city of its cannons in what was obviously a first step towards the disarmament of a populace which had, since 4 September, joined the National Guard in massive numbers (Figure 4.5). The populace of working-class Paris set out spontaneously to reclaim the cannons as their own. Had they not, after all, made the cannons with their own hands out of metals they had collected and melted down during the siege? On the hill on Montmartre, weary French

Figure 4.5 The cannons of Montmartre, depicted in this remarkable photo, were mainly created in the Parisian workshops during the siege out of melted-down materials contributed by the populace. They were the flash point of contention that sparked the break between Paris and Versailles.

soldiers stood guard over the powerful battery of cannons assembled there, facing an increasingly restive and angry crowd. General Lecomte ordered his troops to fire. He ordered once, twice, thrice. The soldiers had not the heart to do it, raised their rifle butts in the air, and fraternised joyfully with the crowd. An infuriated mob took General Lecomte prisoner. They stumbled across General Clément-Thomas, remembered and hated for his role in the savage killings of the June Days of 1848. The two generals were taken to the garden of No. 6, rue des Rosiers, and, amid considerable confusion and angry argument, put up against a wall and shot.

This incident is of crucial importance. The conservatives now had their martyrs. Thiers could brand the insubordinate population of Paris as murderers and assassins. But the hilltop of Montmartre had been a place of martyrdom for Christian saints long before. To these could now be added the names of Lecomte and Clément-Thomas. In the months and years to come, as the struggle to build the Basilica of Sacré-Coeur unfolded, frequent appeal was to be made to the need to commemorate these 'martyrs of yesterday who died in order to defend and save Christian society'. This phrase was actually used by the Committee of the National Assembly appointed to report on the proposed law that would make the basilica a work of public utility.[21] On that sixteenth day of June in 1875 when the foundation stone was laid, Rohault de Fleury rejoiced that the basilica was to be built on a site which, 'after having been such a saintly place had become, it would seem, the place chosen by Satan and where was accomplished the first act of that horrible saturnalia which caused so much ruination and which gave the church two such glorious martyrs'. 'Yes,' he continued, 'it is here where Sacré-Coeur will be raised up that the Commune began, here where generals Clément-Thomas and Lecomte were assassinated.' He rejoiced in the 'multitude of good Christians who now stood adoring a God who knows only too well how to confound the evil-minded, cast down their designs and to place a cradle where they thought to dig a grave'. He contrasted this multitude of the faithful with a 'hillside, lined with intoxicated demons, inhabited by a population apparently hostile to all religious ideas and animated, above all, by a hatred of the Church'.[22]

GALLIA POENITENS.

Thiers's response to the events of 18 March was to order a complete withdrawal of military and government personnel from Paris. From the safe distance of Versailles, he prepared methodically for the invasion and reduction of Paris. Bismarck proved not at all reluctant to allow the reconstitution of a French army sufficient to the task of putting down the radicals in Paris and released prisoners and material for that purpose.

Left to their own devices, and somewhat surprised by the turn of events, the Parisians, under the leadership of the Central Committee of the National Guard, arranged for elections on 26 March. The Commune was declared a political fact on 28 March. It was a day of joyous celebration for the common people of Paris and a day of consternation for the bourgeoisie.

The politics of the Commune were hardly coherent. While a substantial number of workers took their place as elected representatives of the people for the first time in French history, the Commune was still dominated by radical elements from the bourgeoisie. Composed as it was of diverse political currents shading from middle-of-the-road republican through the Jacobins, the Proudhonists, the socialists of the International and the Blanquist revolutionaries, there was a good deal of factionalism and plenty of contentious argumentation as to what radical or socialist path to take. Yet their legislation was progressive. They put a moratorium on rental payments and suspended night work in the bakeries. Their reorganisation of education and the arts, the opening of the latter to mass participation along with the

Figure 4.6 Barricade of the Communards on the rue d'Allemagne, March 1871.

dissolution of a hitherto deep segregation between high art and daily life, and their exploration of new forms of democratic participation … in all these respects the innovations within the Commune were remarkable, leading an initially negative and sceptical Marx to offer his wholehearted support to the Communards.[23]

Much of this proved moot, however, since whatever pretensions to a socialist modernity and progressive politics the Communards may well have had, they were about to be overwhelmed by a tidal wave of reactionary conservativism. Thiers attacked in early April and the second siege of Paris began. Rural France was being put to work to destroy working-class Paris.

What followed was disastrous for the Commune. When the Versailles forces finally broke through the outer defence of Paris – which Thiers had had constructed in the 1840s – they swept quickly through the bourgeois sections of western Paris and cut slowly and ruthlessly down the grand boulevards that Haussmann had constructed into the working-class quarters of the city. Barricades were everywhere, but the military was prepared to deploy cannons to blast them apart and use incendiary shells to destroy buildings that housed hostile forces. So began one of the most vicious bloodlettings in an often bloody French history. The Versailles forces gave no quarter. To the

Figure 4.7 Some 300 of the last Communards captured at the end of the 'bloody week' of May 1871 were arbitrarily shot at the Mur des Fédérés in Père Lachaise cemetery, turning the wall into a place of pilgrimage for decades to come. (Gouche by Alfred Darjon)

Figure 4.8 Communards shot by the Versailles forces (photo attributed to Disdéri). Someone has placed a white wreath in the hands of the young woman at the bottom right (a symbol of Liberty, once again about to be interred?).

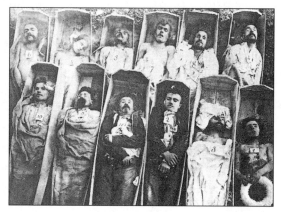

deaths in the street fighting, which were not, by most accounts, too extensive, were added an incredible number of arbitrary executions without judgement. A renowned doctor was put to death for his socialist utopian views, a republican deputy and critic of the Commune, Milière, was put to death because an army captain happened not to like his newspaper articles. He was forced to his knees on the steps of the Pantheon and told to beg forgiveness for his sins

Figure 4.9 The toppling of the Vendôme Column, here depicted by Meaulle and Viers, created a lot of interest, illustrating how buildings and monuments were deeply political symbols to Parisians.

– for the first time in his life he cried 'Vive la Commune' instead. The Luxembourg Gardens, the barracks at Lobau, the celebrated and still-venerated wall in the cemetery of Père Lachaise, echoed ceaselessly to the sound of gunfire as the executioners went to work. Between twenty and thirty thousand Communards died thus. GALLIA POENITENS – with vengeance.

Out of this sad history there is one incident which commands our attention. On the morning of 28 May, an exhausted Eugène Varlin – bookbinder, union and food cooperative organiser under the Second Empire, member of the National Guard, intelligent, respected and scrupulously honest, committed socialist and brave soldier – was recognised and arrested. He was taken to that same house on rue des Rosiers where Lecomte and Clément-Thomas died. Varlin's fate was worse. Sentenced immediately to die, he was paraded around the hillside of Montmartre, some say for ten minutes and others for hours, abused, beaten and humiliated by a fickle mob. He was finally propped up against a wall and shot. He was just thirty-two years old. They had to shoot twice to kill him. In between fusillades he cried, evidently unrepentant, 'Vive la Commune!' His biographer called it 'the Calvary of Eugène Varlin'. The left can have its martyrs too. And it is on that spot that Sacré-Coeur is built.[24]

The 'bloody week', as it was called, also involved an enormous destruction of property. Paris burned. To the buildings set afire in the course of the bombardment were added those deliberately fired for strategic reasons by the retreating Communards. From this arose the myth of the 'incendiaries' of the Commune who recklessly took revenge, it was said, by burning everything they could. The Communards, to be sure, were not enamoured of the privileges of private property and were not averse to destroying hated symbols. The Vendôme Column – which Napoleon III had doted upon – was, after all, toppled in a grand ceremony to symbolise the end of authoritarian rule. The painter Courbet was later held responsible for this act and condemned to pay for the construction of the monument out of his own pocket. The Communards also decreed, but never carried out, the destruction of the Chapel of Expiation by which Louis XVIII had sought to impress upon Parisians their guilt in executing his brother. And when Thiers had shown his true colours, the Communards took a certain delight in dismantling his Parisian residence, stone by stone, in a symbolic gesture which de Goncourt[25] felt had an 'excellent bad effect'.

But the wholesale burning of Paris was another matter entirely. To the buildings set afire in the course of the bombardment were added those deliberately fired by the retreating Communards. From this arose the myth of the 'incendiaries' of the Commune who recklessly took revenge, it was said, by burning everything they could. The false myth of the hideous woman 'petroleuse' was circulated by the Versailles press and women under suspicion were arbitrarly shot on the spot.[26] A bourgeois diarist, Audéoud,[27] complacently recorded how he denounced a well-dressed woman in the rue Blanche as a 'petroleuse' because she was carrying two bottles (filled with what we will never know). When she pushed a lunging and rather drunken soldier away, the soldier shot her in the back.

No matter what the truth of the matter, the myth of the incendiaries was strong. Within a year, the Pope himself was describing the Communards as 'devils risen up from hell bringing the fires of the inferno to the streets of Paris'. The ashes of the city became a symbol of the Commune's crimes against the Church and were to fertilise the soil from which the energy to build Sacré-Coeur was to spring. No wonder that Rohault de Fleury[28] congratulated himself upon that felicitous choice of words – 'were Paris to be reduced to cinders'. That phrase could strike home with redoubled force, he noted, 'as the incendiaries of the Commune came to terrorise the world'.

The aftermath of the Commune was anything but pleasant. Bodies littered the streets and the stench became unbearable. To take just one example, the three hundred or so bodies dumped in the lake in Haussmann's beautiful new park at Buttes-Chaumont (once a site for hanging petty criminals and later a municipal dump) had to be dragged out after they surfaced, horribly bloated, several days later; they were burned in a funeral pyre that lasted for days. Audéoud[29] delighted in the sight of all the bodies 'riddled with bullets, foul and rotting' and took 'the stink of their corpses' as an 'odor of peace and if the all-too sensitive nostril revolts, the soul rejoices'. 'We too,' he went on, 'have become cruel and pitiless, and we should find it a pleasure to bathe and wash our hands in their blood.' But the bloodletting began to turn the stomachs of the bourgeoisie until all but the most sadistic of them had to cry 'stop!' The celebrated diarist Edmond de Goncourt tried to convince himself of the justice of it all when he wrote:

> It is good that there was neither conciliation nor bargain. The solution was brutal. It was by pure force. The solution has held people back from cowardly compromises ... the bloodletting was a bleeding white; such a purge, by killing off the combative part of the population defers the next revolution by a whole generation. The old society has twenty years of quiet ahead of it, if the powers that be dare all that they may dare at this time.[30]

These sentiments were exactly those of Thiers. But when de Goncourt later passed through Belleville and saw the 'faces of ugly silence', he could not help but feel that here was a 'vanquished but unsubjugated district'. Was there no other way to purge the threat of revolution?

The experiences of 1870–71, when taken together with the confrontation between Napoleon III and the Pope and the decadent 'festive materialism' of the Second Empire, plunged Catholics into a phase of widespread soul-searching. The majority of them accepted the notion that France had sinned, and this gave rise to manifestations of expiation and a movement of piety that was both mystical and spectacular.[31] The intransigent and ultramontane Catholics unquestionably favoured a return to law and order and a political solution founded on respect for authority. And it was the monarchists, generally themselves intransigent Catholics, who held out the promise for that law and order. Liberal Catholics found all of this disturbing and distasteful, but they were in no position to mobilise their forces – even the Pope described them as the 'veritable scourge' of France. There was little to stop the consolidation of the bond between monarchism and intransigent Catholicism. And it was such a powerful alliance that was to guarantee the building of Sacré-Coeur.

The immediate problem for the progenitors of the vow was, however, to operationalise a pious wish. This required official action. Legentil and Rohault de Fleury sought the support of the newly appointed archbishop of Paris. Monseigneur Guibert, a compatriot of Thiers from Tours, had required some persuading to take the position in Paris. The three previous

Figure 4.10 This view, from the hilltop of Montmartre, of Paris burning in the final days of the Commune captures something of what Rohault de Fleury had in mind when he commented on how fortuitously appropriate it had been to make the vow to build Sacré-Coeur even if 'Paris were reduced to ashes'.

archbishops had suffered violent deaths: the first during the insurrection of 1848, the second by the hand of an assassin in 1863, and the third during the Commune. The Communards had early decided to take hostages in response to the butchery promised by Versailles. The archbishop was held as a prime hostage for whom the Communards sought the exchange of Blanqui. Thiers refused that negotiation, apparently having decided that a dead and martyred archbishop (who was a liberal Catholic in any case) was more valuable to him than a live one exchanged against a dynamic and aggressive Blanqui. During the 'bloody week', certain segments of the Communards (the Blanquists in particular) took whatever vengeance they could. On 24 May, with the Versailles forces hacking their way into Paris in the most brutal and bloody fashion, arbitrarily executing anyone they suspected of playing any kind of role in the Commune, the archbishop was shot. In that final week, seventy-four hostages were shot, of whom twenty-four were priests. That awesome anticlericalism was as alive under the Commune as it had been in 1789. But

Figure 4.11 Remorse and revulsion for what happened in the Commune were initially confined to republicans of a social democratic persuasion. Manet (top) was deeply moved by the events, and drew several representations mourning the deaths on the barricades. Daumier (bottom), in one of his last drawings, commented sadly and poignantly on 'when workers fight each other'.

with the massive purge which left more than twenty thousand Communards dead, nearly forty thousand imprisoned and countless others in flight, Thiers could write reassuringly on 14 June to Monseigneur Guibert: 'The "reds," totally vanquished, will not recommence their activities tomorrow; one does not engage twice in fifty years in such an immense fight as they have just lost.'[32] Reassured, Monseigneur Guibert came to Paris.

The new archbishop was much impressed with the movement to build a monument to the Sacred Heart. On 18 January 1872, he formally accepted responsibility for the undertaking. He wrote to Legentil and Rohault de Fleury thus:

> You have considered from their true perspective the ills of our country ... The conspiracy against God and Christ has prevailed in a multitude of hearts and in punishment for an almost universal apostasy, society has been subjected to all the horrors of war with a victorious foreigner and an even more horrible war amongst the children of the same country. Having become, by our prevarication, rebels against heaven, we have fallen during our troubles into the abyss of anarchy. The land of France presents the terrifying image of a place where no order prevails, while the future offers still more terrors to come ... This temple, erected as a public act of contrition and reparation ... will stand amongst us as a protest against other monuments and works of art erected for the glorification of vice and impiety.[33]

By July 1872, an ultraconservative Pope Pius IX, still awaiting his deliverance from captivity in the Vatican, formally endorsed the vow. An immense propaganda campaign unfolded, and the movement gathered momentum. By the end of the year, more than a million francs were promised, and all that remained was to translate the vow into its material, physical representation.

The first step was to choose a site. Legentil wanted to use the foundations of the still-to-be-completed Opera House, which he considered 'a scandalous monument of extravagance, indecency and bad taste'.[34] Rohault de Fleury's initial design of that building had, in 1860, been dropped at the insistence of Count Walewski ('who had the dubious distinction of being the illegitimate son of Napoleon I and the husband of Napoleon III's current favourite').[35] The design that replaced it (which exists today) most definitely qualified in the eyes of Legentil as a 'monument to vice and impiety', and nothing could be more appropriate than to efface the memory of Empire by constructing the basilica on that spot. It probably escaped Legentil's attention that the Communards had, in the same spirit, toppled the Vendôme Column.

By late October 1872, however, the archbishop had taken matters into his own hands and selected the heights of Montmartre because it was only from there that the symbolic domination of Paris could be assured. Since the land on that site was in part public property, the consent or active support of the government was necessary if it was to be acquired. The government was considering the construction of a military fortress on that spot. The archbishop pointed out, however, that a military fortress could well be very unpopular, while a fortification of the sort he was proposing might be less offensive and more sure. Thiers and his ministers, apparently persuaded that ideological protection might be preferable to military, encouraged the archbishop to pursue the matter formally. This the latter did in a letter of 5 March 1873.[36] He requested that the government pass a special law declaring the construction of the basilica a work of public utility. This would permit the laws of expropriation to be used to procure the site.

Such a law ran counter to a long-standing sentiment in favour of the separation of Church and State. Yet conservative Catholic sentiment for the project was very strong. Thiers procrastinated, but his indecision was shortly rendered moot. The monarchists had decided that their time had come. On 24 May, they drove Thiers from power and replaced him with the arch-conservative royalist Marshal MacMahon, who, just two years before, had led the armed forces of Versailles in the bloody repression of the Commune. France was plunged, once more, into political ferment; a monarchist restoration seemed imminent.

The MacMahon government quickly reported on the law, which then became part of its programme to establish the rule of moral order in which those of wealth and privilege – who therefore had an active stake in the preservation of society – would, under the leadership of the king and in alliance with the authority of the Church, have both the right and the duty to protect France from the social perils to which it had recently been exposed and thereby prevent the country falling into the abyss of anarchy. Large-scale demonstrations were mobilised by the Church as part of a campaign to re-establish some sense of moral order. The largest of these demonstrations rook place on 29 June 1873, at Paray-le-Monial. Thirty thousand pilgrims, including fifty members of the National Assembly, journeyed there to dedicate themselves publicly to the Sacred Heart.[37]

It was in this atmosphere that the committee formed to report on the law presented its findings on 11 July to the National Assembly, a quarter of whose members were adherents to the vow. The committee found that the proposal to build a basilica of expiation was unquestionably a work of public utility. It was right and proper to build such a monument on the heights of Montmartre for all to see, because it was there that the blood of martyrs – including those of yesterday – had flowed. It was necessary 'to efface by this work of expiation, the crimes which have crowned our sorrows', and France, 'which has suffered so much', must 'call upon the protection and grace of Him who gives according to His will, defeat or victory'.[38]

The debate which followed on 22 and 23 July in part revolved around technical-legal questions and the implications of the legislation for State–Church relations. The intransigent Catholics recklessly proposed to go much further. They wanted the assembly to commit itself formally to a national undertaking which 'was not solely a protestation against taking up of arms by the Commune, but a sign of appeasement and concord'. That amendment was rejected. But the law passed with a handsome majority of 244 votes.

A lone dissenting voice in the debate came from a radical republican deputy from Paris:

> When you think to establish on the commanding heights of Paris – the fount of free thought and revolution – a Catholic monument, what is in your thoughts? To make of it the triumph of the Church over revolution. Yes, that is what you want to extinguish – what you call the pestilence of revolution. What you want to revive is the Catholic faith, for you are at war with the spirit of modern times ... Well, I who know the sentiments of the population of Paris, I who am tainted by the revolutionary pestilence like them, I tell you that the population will be more scandalised than edified by the ostentation of your faith ... Far from edifying us, you push us towards free thought, towards revolution. When people see these mani-festations of the partisans of monarchy, of the enemies of the Revolution, they will say to themselves that Catholicism and monarchy are unified, and in rejecting one they will reject the other.[39]

Armed with a law which yielded powers of expropriation, the committee formed to push the project through to fruition acquired the site atop the Butte Montmartre. They collected the moneys promised and set about solic-iting more so that the building could be as grand as the thought that lay behind it. A competition for the design of the basilica was set and judged. The building had to be imposing, consistent with Christian tradition, yet quite distinct from the 'monuments to vice and impiety' built in the course of the Second Empire. Out of the seventy-eight designs submitted and exhibited to the public, that of the architect Abadie[40] was selected. The grandeur of its domes, the purity of the white marble and the unadorned simplicity of its detail impressed the committee – what, after all, could be more different from the flamboyance of that awful Opera House?

By the spring of 1875, all was ready for putting the first stone in place. But radical and republican Paris was not, apparently, repentant enough even yet. The archbishop complained that the building of Sacré-Coeur was being treated as a provocative act, as an attempt to inter the principles of 1789. And while, he said, he would not pray to revive those principles if they happened to become dead and buried, this view of things was giving rise to a deplorable polemic in which the archbishop found himself forced to participate. He issued a circular in which he expressed his astonishment at the hostility expressed towards the project on the part of 'the enemies of religion'. He found it intolerable that people dared to put a political interpretation upon thoughts derived only out of faith and piety. Politics, he assured his readers, 'had been far, far from our inspirations; the work had been inspired, on the contrary, by a profound conviction that politics was powerless to deal with the ills of the country. The causes of these ills are moral and religious and the remedies must be of the same order.' Besides, he went on, the work could not be construed as political because the aim of politics is to divide, 'while our work has for its goal the union of all ... Social pacification is the end point of the work we are seeking to realise.'[41]

The government, now clearly on the defensive, grew extremely nervous at the prospect of a grand opening ceremony which could be the occasion for an ugly confrontation. It advised caution. The committee had to find a way to lay the first stone without being too provocative. The Pope came to their aid and declared a day of dedication to the Sacred Heart for all Catholics everywhere. Behind that shelter, a much-scaled-down ceremony to lay the first stone passed without incident. The construction was now under way. GALLIA POENITENS was taking shape in material symbolic form.

The forty years between the laying of the foundation stone and the final consecration of the basilica in 1919 were often troubled ones. Technical difficulties arose in the course of putting such a large structure on a hilltop rendered unstable by years of mining for gypsum. The cost of the structure increased dramatically, and, as enthusiasm for the cult of the Sacred Heart diminished somewhat, financial difficulties ensued. And the political controversy continued. The committee in charge of the project had early decided upon a variety of stratagems to encourage the flow of contributions. Individuals and families could purchase a stone, and the visitor to Sacré-Coeur will see the names of many such inscribed upon the stones there. Different regions and organisations were encouraged to subscribe towards the construction of particular chapels. Members of the National Assembly, the army, the clergy and the like all pooled their efforts in this way. Each particular chapel has its own significance.

Among the chapels in the crypt, for example, the visitor will find that of Jesus-Enseignant, which recalls, as Rohault de Fleury put it, 'that one of the chief sins of France was the foolish invention of schooling without

Figure 4.12 The Statue of Liberty in its Paris workshop before being shipped to New York.

God'.[42] Those who were on the losing side of the fierce battle to preserve the power of the Church over education after 1871 put their money here. And next to that chapel, at the far end of the crypt, close to the line where the rue des Rosiers used to run, stands the Chapel to Jesus-Ouvrier. That Catholic workers sought to contribute to the building of their own chapel was a matter for great rejoicing. It showed, wrote Legentil, the desire of workers 'to protest against the fearsome impiety into which a large part of the working class is falling' as well as their determination to resist 'the impious and truly infernal association which, in nearly all of Europe, makes of it its slave and victim'.[43] The reference to the International Working Men's Association is unmistakable and understandable, since it was customary in bourgeois circles at that time to attribute the Commune, quite erroneously, to the nefarious influence of that 'infernal' association. Yet, by a strange quirk of fate, which so often gives an ironic twist to history, the chapel to Jesus-Ouvrier stands almost exactly at the spot where ran the course of the 'Calvary of Eugène Varlin'. Thus it is that the basilica, erected on high in part to commemorate the blood of two recent martyrs of the right, commemorates unwittingly in its subterranean depths a martyr of the left.

Legentil's interpretation of all this was in fact somewhat awry. In the closing stages of the Commune, a young Catholic named Albert de Munn watched in dismay as the Communards were led away to slaughter. Shocked, he fell to wondering what 'legally constituted society had done for these people' and concluded that their ills had in large measure been visited upon them through the indifference of the affluent classes. In the spring of 1872, he went into the heart of hated Belleville and set up the first of his Cercles-Ouvriers.[44] This signalled the beginnings of a new kind of Catholicism in France – one which sought through social action to attend to the material as well as the spiritual needs of the workers. It was through organisations such as this, a far cry from the intransigent ultramontane Catholicism that ruled at the centre of the movement for the Sacred Heart, that a small trickle of worker contributions began to flow towards the construction of a basilica on the hilltop of Montmartre.

The political difficulties mounted, however. France, finally armed with a republican constitution (largely because of the intransigence of the monarchists), was now in the grip of a modernisation process fostered by easier communications, mass education and industrial development. The country moved to accept the moderate form of republicanism and became bitterly disillusioned with the backward-looking monarchism that had dominated the National Assembly elected in 1871. In Paris the 'unsubjugated' Bellevillois, and their neighbours in Montmartre and La Villette, began to reassert themselves rather more rapidly than Thiers had anticipated. As the demand for amnesty for the exiled communards became stronger in these quarters, so did the hatred of the basilica rising to their midst (Figure 4.13). The agitation against the project mounted.

On 3 August 1880, the matter came before the city council in the form of a proposal – a 'colossal statue of Liberty will be placed on the summit of Montmartre, in front of the church of Sacré-Coeur, on land belonging to the city of Paris'. The French republicans at that time had adopted the United States as a model society which functioned perfectly well without monarchism and other feudal trappings. As part of a campaign to drive home the point of this example, as well as to symbolise their own deep attachment to the principles of liberty, republicanism and democracy, they were then raising funds to donate the Statue of Liberty that now stands in New York harbour. Why not, said the authors of this proposition, efface the sight of the hated Sacré-Coeur by a monument of similar order?[45]

No matter what the claims to the contrary, they said, the basilica symbolised the intolerance and fanaticism of the right – it was an insult to civilisation, antagonistic to the principles of modern times, an evocation of the past, and a stigma upon France as a whole. Parisians, seemingly bent on demonstrating their unrepentant attachment to the principles of 1789, were determined to efface what they felt was an expression of 'Catholic fanaticism' by building exactly that kind of monument which the archbishop had previously characterised as a 'glorification of vice and impiety'. By 7 October the city council had changed its tactics. Calling the basilica 'an incessant provocation to civil war', the members decided by a majority of sixty-one to three to request the government to 'rescind the law of public utility of 1873' and to use the land, which would revert to public ownership, for the construction of a work of truly national significance. Neatly sidestepping the problem of how those who had contributed to the construction of the basilica – which had hardly yet risen above its foundations – were to be indemnified, it passed along its proposal to the government. By the summer of 1882, the request was taken up in the Chamber of Deputies.

Archbishop Guibert had, once more, to take to the public defence of the work. He challenged what by now were familiar arguments against the basilica with familiar responses. He insisted that the work was not inspired by politics but by Christian and patriotic sentiments. To those who objected to the expiatory character of the work he simply replied that no one can ever afford to regard their country as infallible. As to the appropriateness of the cult of the Sacred Heart, he felt only those within the Church had the right to judge. To those who portrayed the basilica as a provocation to civil war he replied: 'Are civil wars and riots ever the product of our Christian temples? Are those who frequent our churches ever prone to excitations and revolts against the law? Do we find such people in the midst of disorders and violence which, from time to time, trouble the streets of our cities?' He went on to point out that while Napoleon I had sought to build a temple of peace at Montmartre, 'it is we who are building, at last, the true temple of peace'.[46]

He then considered the negative effects of stopping the construction. Such an action would profoundly wound Christian sentiment and prove divisive. It would surely be a bad precedent, he said (blithely ignoring the precedent set by the law of 1873 itself), if religious undertakings of this sort were to be subject to the political whims of the government of the day. And then there was the complex problem of compensation not only for the contributors but for the work already done. Finally, he appealed to the fact that the work was giving employment to six hundred families – to deprive 'that part of Paris of such a major source of employment would be inhuman indeed'.

The Parisian representatives in the Chamber of Deputies, which, by

1882, was dominated by reformist republicans such as Gambetta (from Belleville) and Clemenceau (from Montmartre), were not impressed by these arguments. The debate was heated and passionate. The government for its part declared itself unalterably opposed to the law of 1873 but was equally opposed to rescinding the law, since this would entail paying out more than twelve million francs in indemnities to the Church. In an effort to defuse the evident anger from the left, the minister went on to remark that by rescinding the law, the archbishop would be relieved of the obligation to complete what was proving to be a most arduous undertaking at the same time as it would provide the Church with millions of francs to pursue works of propaganda which might be 'infinitely more efficacious than that to which the sponsors of the present motion are objecting'.

The radical republicans were not about to regard Sacré-Coeur in the shape of a white elephant, however. Nor were they inclined to pay compensation. They were determined to do away with what they felt was an odious manifestation of pious clericalism and to put in its place a monument to liberty of thought. They put the blame for the civil war squarely on the shoulders of the monarchists and their intransigent Catholic allies.

Clemenceau rose to state the radical case. He declared the law of 1873 an insult, an act of a National Assembly which had sought to impose the cult of the Sacred Heart on France because 'we fought and still continue to fight for human rights, for having made the French Revolution'. The law was the product of clerical reaction, an attempt to stigmatise revolutionary France, 'to condemn us to ask pardon of the Church for our ceaseless struggle to prevail over it in order to establish the principles of liberty, equality and fraternity'. We must, he declared, respond to a political act by a political act. Not to do so would be to leave France under the intolerable invocation of the Sacred Heart.[47]

With impassioned oratory such as this, Clemenceau fanned the flames of anticlerical sentiment. The chamber voted to rescind the law of 1873 by a majority of 261 votes to 199. It appeared that the basilica, the walls of which were as yet hardly risen above their foundations, was to come tumbling down.

The basilica was saved by a technicality. The law was passed too late in the session to meet all the formal requirements for promulgation. The government, genuinely fearful of the costs and liabilities involved, quietly worked to prevent the reintroduction of the motion into a chamber which, in the next session, moved on to consider matters of much greater weight and moment. The Parisian republicans had gained a symbolic but pyrrhic parliamentary victory. A relieved archbishop pressed on with the work.

Figure 4.13 Sacré-Coeur as vampire, a poster for *La Lanterne*, around 1896.

Yet somehow the matter would not die. In February 1897, the motion was reintroduced.[48] Anticlerical republicanism had by then made great progress, as had the working-class movement in the form of a vigorous and growing socialist party. But the construction atop the hill had likewise progressed. The interior of the basilica had been inaugurated and opened for worship in 1891, and the great dome was well on the way to completion (the cross which surmounts it was formally blessed in 1899). Although the basilica was still viewed as a 'provocation to civil war', the prospect for dismantling such a vast work was by now quite daunting. And this time it was none other than Albert de Munn who defended the basilica in the name of a Catholicism that had, by then, seen the virtue of separating its fate from that of a fading monarchist cause. The Church was beginning to learn a lesson, and the cult of the Sacred Heart began to acquire a new meaning in response to a changing social situation. By 1899, a more reform-minded Pope dedicated the cult to the ideal of harmony among the races, social justice and conciliation.

But the socialist deputies were not impressed by what they saw as manoeuvres of co-optation. They pressed home their case to bring down the hated symbol, even though almost complete, and even though such an act would entail indemnifying eight million subscribers to the tune of thirty million francs. But the majority in the chamber blanched at such a prospect. The motion was rejected by 322 to 196.

This was to be the last time the building was threatened by official action. With the dome completed in 1899, attention switched to the building of the campanile, which was finally finished in 1912. By the spring of 1914, all was ready and the official consecration set for 17 October. But war with Germany intervened. Only at the end of that bloody conflict was the basilica finally consecrated. A victorious France – led by the fiery oratory of Clemenceau – joyfully celebrated the consecration of a monument conceived of in the course of a losing war with Germany a generation before. GALLIA POENITENS at last brought its rewards.

Muted echoes of this tortured history can still be heard. In February 1971, for example, demonstrators pursued by police took refuge in the basilica. Firmly entrenched there, they called upon their radical comrades to join them in occupying a church 'built upon the bodies of communards in order to efface the memory of that red flag that had for too long floated over Paris'. The myth of the incendiaries immediately broke loose from its ancient moorings, and an evidently panicked rector summoned the police into the basilica to prevent the conflagration. The 'reds' were chased from the church amid scenes of great brutality. Thus was the centennial of the Paris

Commune celebrated on that spot. And as a coda to that incident, a bomb exploded in the basilica in 1976, causing quite extensive damage to one of the domes. On that day, it was said, the visitor to the cemetery of Père Lachaise would have seen a single red rose on August Blanqui's grave.

Rohault de Fleury had desperately wanted to 'place a cradle where [others] had thought to dig a grave'. But the visitor who looks at the mausoleum-like structure that is Sacré-Coeur might well wonder what it is that is interred there. The spirit of 1789? The sins of France? The alliance between intransigent Catholicism and reactionary monarchism? The blood of martyrs like Lecomte and Clément-Thomas? Or that of Eugène Varlin and the twenty thousand or so Communards mercilessly slaughtered along with him?

The building hides its secrets in sepulchral silence. Only the living, cognisant of this history, who understand the principles of those who struggled for and against the embellishment of that spot, can truly disinter the mysteries that lie entombed there and thereby rescue that rich experience from the deathly silence of the tomb and transform it into the noisy beginnings of the cradle.

Commentary

Understanding urbanisation requires more than an analysis of capital flows or migratory streams. Citizenship, belonging, alienation, solidarities, class and other forms of collective politics have crucial roles in the production of spaces of intimacy and social relations as well as the spaces occupied by public functions. The urban process is equally about movements, encounters, conflicts and political confrontations. Much of what happens in a city is symbolic. At the time I wrote this piece on Sacré-Coeur I was reading a lot of Dickens (whom I had detested having to read in my youth!) and was mightily impressed with how he managed to convey so brilliantly the sense, smell and movement of city life. It seemed vital to inject something similar into my own writing on cities as a complement to capital theory. In 1976/77 I had a Guggenheim Fellowship to go to Paris, ostensibly to study Marxist theory. While there I wondered about the origins of the building on the hill and why I found it so creepy to be inside it. I decided to see if I could discover what ghosts might be buried there. The more I found out, the more fascinated I got. This led me not only to write this piece but also to set my theoretical studies in Paris alongside an account of what happened during Haussmann's remodelling of the city in the Second Empire. The first version of this chapter came out in 1979. It was a joy to write. It kept me alive and interested when life was grim and politics dead.

The work also proved a wonderful framework in which to set a dialogue between history and theory on the one hand and Marx and historical geography on the other. I arrived in Paris with one conception of how Marx's political economy should be read and left with a markedly different reading. The experience of the Commune had a big influence over Marx's thinking on how we should shape alternatives. It certainly influenced (and continues to influence) mine. Much can be learned from an immersion in the history of the Commune. Its continuing relevance is explored in Kristin Ross's recent book, *Communal Luxury: The Political Imaginary of the Paris Commune.*

Paris, Capital of Modernity, of which a revised version of this piece is a seminal part, was published in 2003. This and *The Limits to Capital* span what my work has been about.

Chapter 5
Time–Space Compression and the Postmodern Condition

How have the uses and meanings of space and time shifted with the transition from Fordism to flexible accumulation? I want to suggest that we have been experiencing, these last two decades, an intense phase of time–space compression that has had a disorienting and disruptive impact upon political-economic practices and the balance of class power, as well as upon cultural and social life. While historical analogies are always dangerous, I think it no accident that postmodern sensibility evidences strong sympathies for certain of the confused political, cultural and philosophical movements that occurred at the beginning of the twentieth century (in Vienna, for example) when the sense of time–space compression was also peculiarly strong. I also note the revival of interest in geopolitical theory since around 1970, the aesthetics of place, and a revived willingness (even in social theory) to open the problem of spatiality to a general reconsideration.[1]

The transition to flexible accumulation was in part accomplished through the rapid deployment of new organisational forms and new technologies in production. Though the latter may have originated in the pursuit of military superiority, their application had everything to do with bypassing the rigidities of Fordism and accelerating turnover time as a solution to the grumbling problems of Fordism–Keynesianism that erupted into open crisis in 1973. Speed-up was achieved in production by organisational shifts towards vertical disintegration – subcontracting, outsourcing, etc. – that reversed the Fordist tendency towards vertical integration and produced an increasing roundaboutness in production even in the face of increasing financial centralisation. Other organisational shifts – such as the 'just-in-time' delivery system that reduces stock inventories – when coupled with the new technologies of electronic control, small-batch production, etc., all reduced turnover times in many sectors of production (electronics, machine tools, automobiles, construction, clothing, etc.). For the labourers this all implied an intensification (speed-up) in labour processes and an acceleration in the de-skilling and re-skilling required to meet new labour needs.

Accelerating turnover time in production entails parallel accelerations in exchange and consumption. Improved systems of communication and information flow, coupled with rationalisations in techniques of distribution (packaging, inventory control, containerisation, market feedback, etc.), made it possible to circulate commodities through the market system with greater speed. Electronic banking and plastic money were some of the innovations that improved the speed of the inverse flow of money. Financial services and markets (aided by computerised trading) likewise speeded up, so as to make, as the saying has it, 'twenty-four hours a very long time' in global stock markets.

Of the many developments in the arena of consumption, two stand out as being of particular importance. The mobilisation of fashion in mass (as opposed to elite) markets provided a means to accelerate the pace of consumption not only in clothing, ornament and decoration but also across a wide swathe of lifestyles and recreational activities (leisure and sporting habits, pop music styles, video and children's games, and the like). A second trend was a shift away from the consumption of goods and into the consumption of services – not only personal, business, educational and health services, but also entertainments, spectacles, happenings and distractions. The 'lifetime' of such services (a visit to a museum, going to a rock concert or movie, attending lectures or health clubs), though hard to estimate, is far shorter than that of an automobile or washing machine. If there are limits to the accumulation and turnover of physical goods (even counting the famous six thousand pairs of shoes of Imelda Marcos), then it makes sense for capitalists to turn to the provision of very ephemeral services in consumption. This quest may lie at the root of the rapid capitalist penetration, noted by Mandel and Jameson,[2] of many sectors of cultural production from the mid-1960s onwards.

Of the innumerable consequences that have flowed from this general speed-up in the turnover times of capital, I shall focus on those that have particular bearing on postmodern ways of thinking, feeling and doing.

The first major consequence has been to accentuate volatility and ephemerality of fashions, products, production techniques, labour processes, ideas and ideologies, values and established practices. The sense that 'all that is solid melts into air' has rarely been more pervasive (which probably accounts for the volume of writing on that theme in recent years). The effect of this on labour markets and skills has been considerable. My interest here is to look at the more general society-wide effects.

In the realm of commodity production, the primary effect has been to emphasise the values and virtues of instantaneity (instant and fast foods, meals and other satisfactions) and of disposability (cups, plates, cutlery, packaging, napkins, clothing, etc.). The dynamics of a 'throwaway' society, as writers like Alvin Toffler[3] dubbed it, began to become evident during the 1960s. It meant more than just throwing away produced goods (creating a monumental waste-disposal problem), but also being able to throw away values, lifestyles, stable relationships and attachments to things, buildings, places, people and received ways of doing and being. These were the immediate and tangible ways in which the 'accelerative thrust in the larger society' crashed up against 'the ordinary daily experience of the individual'.[4] Through such mechanisms (which proved highly effective from the standpoint of accelerating the turnover of goods in consumption) individuals were forced to cope with disposability, novelty and the prospects for instant obsolescence.

'Compared to the life in a less rapidly changing society, more situations now flow through the channel in any given interval of time – and this implies profound changes in human psychology.' This transience, Toffler goes on to suggest, creates 'a temporariness in the structure of both public and personal value systems' which in turn provides a context for the 'crack-up of consensus' and the diversification of values within a fragmenting society. The bombardment of stimuli, simply on the commodity front, creates problems of sensory overload that make Simmel's dissection of the problems of modernist urban living at the turn of the century seem to pale into insignificance by comparison. Yet, precisely because of the relative qualities of the shift, the psychological responses exist roughly within the range of those which Simmel identified – the blocking out of sensory stimuli, denial and cultivation of the blasé attitude, myopic specialisation, reversion to images of a lost past (hence the importance of mementoes, museums, ruins) and excessive simplification (either in the presentation of self or in the interpretation of events). In this regard, it is instructive to see how Toffler,[5] at a much later moment of time–space compression, echoes the thinking of Simmel, whose ideas were shaped at a moment of similar trauma more than seventy years before.

The volatility, of course, makes it extremely difficult to engage in any long-term planning. Indeed, learning to play the volatility right is now just as important as accelerating turnover time. This means either being highly adaptable and fast-moving in response to market shifts, or masterminding the volatility. The first strategy points mainly towards short-term rather than long-term planning, and cultivating the art of taking short-term gains wherever they are to be had. This has been a notorious feature of US management in recent times. The average tenure of company executive officers has come down to five years, and companies nominally involved in production frequently seek short-term gains through mergers, acquisitions or operations in financial and currency markets. The tension of managerial performance in such an environment is considerable, producing all kinds of side-effects, such as the so-called 'yuppie flu' (a psychological stress condition that paralyses the performance of talented people and produces long-lasting flu-like symptoms) or the frenzied lifestyle of financial operators whose addiction to work, long hours and the rush of power makes them excellent candidates for the kind of schizophrenic mentality that Jameson depicts.

Mastering or intervening actively in the production of volatility, on the other hand, entails manipulation of taste and opinion, either through being a fashion leader or by so saturating the market with images as to shape the volatility to particular ends. This means, in either case, the construction of new sign systems and imagery, which is itself an important aspect of the postmodern condition – one that needs to be considered from several different angles. To begin with, advertising and media images have come to play a very much more integrative role in cultural practices and now assume a much greater importance in the growth dynamics of capitalism. Advertising, moreover, is no longer built around the idea of informing or promoting in the ordinary sense, but is increasingly geared to manipulating desires and tastes through images that may or may not have anything to do with the product to be sold. If we stripped modern advertising of direct reference to the three themes of money, sex and power there would be very little left. Furthermore, images have, in a sense, themselves become commodities. This phenomenon has led Baudrillard[6] to argue that Marx's analysis of commodity production is outdated because capitalism is now predominantly concerned with the production of signs, images and sign systems rather than with commodities themselves. The transition he points to is important, though there are in fact no serious difficulties in extending Marx's theory of commodity production to cope with it. To be sure, the systems of production and marketing of images (like markets for land, public goods or labour power) do exhibit some special features that need to be taken into account. The consumer turnover time of certain images can be very short indeed (close to that ideal of the 'twinkling of an eye' that Marx saw as optimal from the standpoint of capital circulation). Many images can also be mass-marketed instantaneously over space. Given the pressures to accelerate turnover time (and to overcome spatial barriers), the commodification of images of the most ephemeral sort would seem to be a godsend from the standpoint of capital accumulation, particularly when other paths to relieve overaccumulation seem blocked. Ephemerality and instantaneous communicability over space then become virtues to be explored and appropriated by capitalists for their own purposes.

But images have to perform other functions. Corporations, governments, political and intellectual leaders, all value a stable (though dynamic) image as part of their aura of authority and power. The mediatisation of politics has now become all-pervasive. This becomes, in effect, the fleeting, super-ficial and illusory means whereby an individualistic society of transients sets forth its nostalgia for common values. The production and marketing of such images of permanence and power require considerable sophistication, because the continuity and stability of the image have to be retained while stressing the adaptability, flexibility and dynamism of whoever or whatever is being imaged. Moreover, image becomes all-important in competition, not only through name-brand recognition but also because of various asso-ciations of 'respectability', 'quality', 'prestige', 'reliability' and 'innovation'. Competition in the image-building trade becomes a vital aspect of inter-firm competition. Success is so plainly profitable that investment in image-building (sponsoring the arts, exhibitions, television productions, new buildings, as well as direct marketing) becomes as important as investment in new plant and machinery. The image serves to establish an identity in the marketplace. This is also true in labour markets. The acquisition of an image (by the purchase of a sign system such as designer clothes and the right car) becomes a singularly important element in the presentation of self in labour markets and, by extension, becomes integral to the quest for individual identity, self-realisation and meaning. Amusing yet sad signals of this sort of quest abound. A California firm manufactures imitation car telephones, indistinguishable from the real ones, and they sell like hot cakes to a populace desperate to acquire such a symbol of importance. Personal image consultants have become big business in New York City, the *International Herald Tribune* has reported, as a million or so people a year in the city region sign up for courses with firms called Image Assemblers, Image Builders, Image Crafters and Image Creators. 'People make up their minds about you in around one tenth of a second these days,' says one image consultant. 'Fake it till you make it,' is the slogan of another.

It has always been the case, of course, that symbols of wealth, status, fame and power as well as of class have been important in bourgeois society, but probably nowhere near as widely in the past as now. The increasing material affluence generated during the post-war Fordist boom posed the problem of converting rising incomes into an effective demand that satisfied the rising aspirations of youth, women and the working class. Given the ability to produce images as commodities more or less at will, it becomes feasible for accumulation to proceed at least in part on the basis of pure image production and marketing. The ephemerality of such images can then be interpreted in part as a struggle on the part of the oppressed groups of whatever sort to establish their own identity (in terms of street culture, musical styles, fads and fashions made up for themselves) and the rush to convert those innovations to commercial advantage (Carnaby Street in the late 1960s proved an excellent pioneer). The effect is to make it seem as if we are living in a world of ephemeral created images. The psychological impacts of sensory overload, of the sort that Simmel and Toffler identify, are thereby put to work with a redoubled effect.

The materials to produce and reproduce such images, if they were not readily to hand, have themselves been the focus for innovation – the better the replication of the image, the greater the mass market for image making could become. This is in itself an important issue and it brings us more explicitly to consider the role of the 'simulacrum' in postmodernism. By 'simulacrum' is meant a state of such near-perfect replication that the difference between the original and the copy becomes almost impossible to spot. The production of images as simulacra is relatively easy, given modern techniques. Insofar as identity is increasingly dependent upon images, this means that the serial and recursive replications of identities (individual, corporate, institutional and political) become a very real possibility and problem. We can certainly see it at work in the realm of politics as the image makers and the media assume a more powerful role in the shaping of political identities. But there are many more tangible realms where the simulacrum has a heightened role. With modern building materials it is possible to replicate ancient buildings with such exactitude that authenticity or origins can be put into doubt. The manufacture of antiques and other art objects becomes entirely possible, making the high-class forgery a serious problem in the art collection business. We not only possess, therefore, the capacity to pile images from the past or from other places eclectically and simultaneously upon the television screen, but even to transform those images into material simulacra in the form of built environments, events and spectacles and the like, which become in many respects indistinguishable from the originals. What happens to cultural forms when the imitations become real, and the real takes on many of the qualities of an imitation, is a question to which we shall return.

The organisation and conditions of labour prevailing within what we might broadly refer to as the 'image production industry' are also quite special. An industry of this sort has to rely, after all, upon the innovative powers of the direct producers. The latter have an insecure existence, tempered by very high rewards for the successful and at least a semblance of command over their own labour process and creative powers. The growth of cultural output has in fact been phenomenal. Taylor[7] contrasts the art market condition in New York in 1945, when there were a handful of galleries and no more than a score of artists regularly exhibiting, and the two thousand or so artists who practised in or around Paris in the mid-nineteenth century, with the 150,000 artists in the New York region who claim professional status, exhibiting at some 680 galleries, producing more than 15 million artworks in a decade (compared to 200,000 in late-nineteenth-century Paris). And this is only the tip of an iceberg of cultural production that encompasses local entertainers and graphic designers, street and pub musicians, photographers, as well as the more established and recognised schools for teaching art, music, drama and the like. Dwarfing all of this, however, is what Daniel Bell[8] calls 'the cultural mass', defined as:

> Not the creators of culture but the transmitters: those working in higher education, publishing, magazines, broadcast media, theatre, and museums, who process and influence the reception of serious cultural products. It is in itself large enough to be a market for culture, purchase books, prints and serious music recordings. And it is also the group which, as writers, magazine editors, movie-makers, musicians, and so forth, produce the popular materials for the wider mass-culture audience.

This whole industry specialises in the acceleration of turnover time through the production and marketing of images. This is an industry where reputations are made and lost overnight, where big money talks in no uncertain terms, and where there is a ferment of intense, often individualised, creativity poured into the vast vat of serialised and recursive mass culture. It is the organiser of fads and has always been fundamental to the experience of modernity. It becomes a social means to produce that sense of collapsing time horizons which it in turn so avidly feeds upon.

The popularity of a work like Alvin Toffler's *Future Shock* lay precisely in its prescient appreciation of the speed with which the future has come to be discounted into the present. Out of that, also, comes a collapse of cultural distinctions between, say, 'science' and 'regular' fiction (in the works of, for example, Thomas Pynchon and Doris Lessing), as well as a merging of the cinema of distraction with the cinema of futuristic universes. We can link the schizophrenic dimension to postmodernity which Jameson emphasises with accelerations in turnover times in production, exchange and consumption that produce, as it were, the loss of a sense of the future except and insofar as the future can be discounted into the present. Volatility and ephemerality similarly make it hard to maintain any firm sense of continuity. Past experience gets compressed into some overwhelming present. Italo Calvino[9] reports the effect on his own craft of novel writing this way:

> Long novels written today are perhaps a contradiction: the dimension of time had been shattered, we cannot live or think except in fragments of time each of which goes off along its own trajectory and immediately disappears. We can rediscover the continuity of time only in the novels of that period when time no longer seemed stopped and did not yet seem to have exploded, a period that lasted no more than a hundred years.

Baudrillard,[10] never afraid to exaggerate, considers the United States as a society so given over to speed, motion, cinematic images and technological fixes as to have created a crisis of explanatory logic. It represents, he suggests, 'the triumph of effect over cause, of instantaneity over time as depth, the triumph of surface and of pure objectivisation over the depth of desire'. This, of course, is the kind of environment in which deconstructionism can flourish. If it is impossible to say anything of solidity and permanence in the midst of this ephemeral and fragmented world, then why not join in the language games? Everything, from novel writing and philosophising to the experience of labouring or making a home, has to face the challenge of accelerating turnover time and the rapid write-off of traditional and historically acquired values. The temporary contract in everything, as Lyotard remarks, then becomes the hallmark of postmodern living.

But, as so often happens, the plunge into the maelstrom of ephemerality has provoked an explosion of opposed sentiments and tendencies. To begin with, all sorts of technical means arise to guard against future shocks. Firms subcontract or resort to flexible hiring practices to discount the potential unemployment costs of future market shifts. Futures markets in everything, from corn and pork bellies to currencies and government debt, coupled with the 'securitisation' of all kinds of temporary and floating debts, illustrate techniques for discounting the future into the present. Insurance hedges of all kinds against future volatility become much more widely available.

Deeper questions of meaning and interpretation also arise. The greater the ephemerality, the more pressing the need to discover or manufacture some kind of eternal truth that might lie therein. The religious revival that has become much stronger since the late 1960s and the search for authenticity and authority in politics (with all of its accoutrements of nationalism and localism and of admiration for these charismatic and 'protean' individuals with their Nietzschean 'will to power') are cases in point. The revival of interest in basic institutions (such as the family and community), and the search for historical roots, are all signs of a search for more secure moorings and longer-lasting values in a shifting world. Rochberg-Halton,[11] in a sample study of North Chicago residents in 1977, finds, for example, that the objects actually valued in the home were not the 'pecuniary trophies' of a materialist culture which acted as 'reliable indices of one's socio-economic class, age, gender and so on', but the artefacts that embodied 'ties to loved ones and kin, valued experiences and activities, and memories of significant life events and people'. Photographs, particular objects (like a piano, a clock, a chair) and events (the playing of a record of a piece of music, the singing of a song) become the focus of a contemplative memory, and hence a generator of a sense of self that lies outside the sensory overloading of consumerist culture and fashion. The home becomes a private museum to guard against the ravages of time–space compression. At the very time, furthermore, that postmodernism proclaims the death of the author and the rise of anti-auratic art in the public realm, the art market becomes ever more conscious of the monopoly power of the artist's signature and of questions of authenticity and forgery (no matter that the Rauschenberg is itself a mere reproduction montage). It is, perhaps, appropriate that the postmodernist developer building, as solid as the pink granite of Philip Johnson's AT&T building, should be debt-financed, built on the basis of fictitious capital, and architecturally conceived of, at least on the outside, more in the spirit of fiction than of function.

The spatial adjustments have been no less traumatic. The satellite communications systems deployed since the early 1970s have rendered the unit cost and time of communication invariant with respect to distance. It costs the same to communicate over 500 miles as it does over 5,000 via satellite. Air freight rates on commodities have likewise come down dramatically, while containerisation has reduced the cost of bulk sea and road transport. It is now possible for a large multinational corporation like Texas Instruments to operate plants with simultaneous decision-making with respect to financial, market, input costs, quality control and labour process conditions in more than fifty different locations across the globe.[12] Mass television ownership coupled with satellite communication makes it possible to experience a rush of images from different spaces almost simultaneously, collapsing the world's spaces into a series of images on a television screen. The whole world can watch the Olympic Games, the World Cup, the fall of a dictator, a political summit, a deadly tragedy … while mass tourism, films made in spectacular locations, make a wide range of simulated or vicarious experiences of what the world contains available to many people. The image of places and spaces becomes as open to production and ephemeral use as any other.

We have, in short, witnessed another fierce round in that process of annihilation of space through time that has always lain at the centre of capitalism's dynamic. Marshall McLuhan described how he thought the 'global village' had now become a communications reality in the mid-1960s:

> After three thousand years of explosion, by means of fragmentary and mechanical technologies, the Western World is imploding. During the mechanical ages we had extended our bodies in space. Today, after more than a century of electronic technology, we have extended our central nervous system itself in a global embrace, abolishing both space and time as far as our planet is concerned.

In recent years a whole spate of writing has taken this idea on board and tried to explore, as for example Virilio[13] does in his *L'Esthétique de la Disparition*, the cultural consequences of the supposed disappearance of time and space as materialised and tangible dimensions to social life.

But the collapse of spatial barriers does not mean that the significance of space is decreasing. Not for the first time in capitalism's history, we find the evidence pointing to the converse thesis. Heightened competition under conditions of crisis has coerced capitalists into paying much closer attention to relative locational advantages, precisely because diminishing spatial barriers give capitalists the power to exploit minute spatial differentiations to good effect. Small differences in what the space contains in the way of labour supplies, resources, infrastructures and the like become of increased significance. Superior command over space becomes an even more important weapon in class struggle. It becomes one of the means to enforce speed-up and the redefinition of skills on recalcitrant workforces. Geographical mobility and decentralisation are used against a union power which traditionally concentrated in the factories of mass production. Capital flight, deindustrialisation of some regions and the industrialisation of others, the destruction of traditional working-class communities as power bases in class struggle, become leitmotifs of spatial transformation under more flexible conditions of accumulation.[14]

As spatial barriers diminish so we become much more sensitised to what the world's spaces contain. Flexible accumulation typically exploits a wide range of seemingly contingent geographical circumstances, and reconstitutes them as structured internal elements of its own encompassing logic. For example, geographical differentiations in the mode and strengths of labour control together with variations in the quality as well as the quantity of labour power assume a much greater significance in corporate locational strategies. New industrial ensembles arise, sometimes out of almost nothing (as the various silicon valleys and glens) but more often on the basis of some pre-existing mix of skills and resources. The 'Third Italy' (Emilia-Romagna) builds upon a peculiar mix of cooperative entrepreneurialism, artisan labour and local communist administrations anxious to generate employment, and inserts its clothing products with incredible success into a highly competitive world economy. Flanders attracts outside capital on the basis of a dispersed, flexible and reasonably skilled labour supply with a deep hostility to unionism and socialism. Los Angeles imports the highly successful patriarchal labour systems of South-East Asia through mass immigration, while the celebrated paternalistic labour control system of the Japanese and Taiwanese is imported into California and South Wales. The story in each case is different, making it appear as if the uniqueness of this or that geographical circumstance matters more than ever before. Yet it does so, ironically, only because of the collapse of spatial barriers.

While labour control is always central, there are many other aspects of geographical organisation that have risen to a new prominence under conditions of more flexible accumulation. The need for accurate information and speedy communication has emphasised the role of so-called 'world cities' in the financial and corporate system (centres equipped with teleports, airports, fixed communication links, as well as a wide array of financial, legal, business and infrastructural services). The diminution of spatial barriers results in the reaffirmation and realignment of hierarchy within what is now a global urban system. The local availability of material resources of special qualities, or even at marginally lower costs, starts to be ever more important, as do local variations in market taste that are today more easily exploited under conditions of small-batch production and flexible design. Local differences in entrepreneurial ability, venture capital, scientific and technical know-how, and social attitudes also enter in, while the local networks of influence and power, the accumulation strategies of local ruling elites (as opposed to nation-state policies), also become more deeply implicated in the regime of flexible accumulation.

But this then raises another dimension to the changing role of spatiality in contemporary society. If capitalists become increasingly sensitive to the spatially differentiated qualities of which the world's geography is composed, then it is possible for the peoples and powers that command those spaces to alter them in such a way as to be more rather than less attractive to highly mobile capital. Local ruling elites can, for example, implement strategies of local labour control, of skill enhancement, of infrastructural provision, of tax policy, state regulation, and so on, in order to attract development within their particular space. The qualities of place stand thereby to be emphasised in the midst of the increasing abstractions of space. The active production of places with special qualities becomes an important stake in spatial compe-tition between localities, cities, regions and nations. Corporatist forms of governance can flourish in such spaces, and themselves take on entrepre-neurial roles in the production of favourable business climates and other special qualities. And it is in this context that we can better situate the striving for cities to forge a distinctive image and to create an atmosphere of place and tradition that will act as a lure to both capital and people 'of the right sort' (i.e. wealthy and influential). Heightened inter-place competition should lead to the production of more variegated spaces within the increasing homoge-neity of international exchange. But to the degree that this competition opens up cities to systems of accumulation, it ends up producing what Boyer[15] calls a 'recursive' and 'serial' monotony, 'producing from already known patterns or moulds places almost identical in ambience from city to city: New York's South Street Seaport, Boston's Quincy Market, Baltimore's Harbor Place'.

We thus approach the central paradox: the less important the spatial barriers, the greater the sensitivity of capital to the variation of place within space, and the greater the incentive for places to be differentiated in ways attractive to capital. The result has been the production of fragmentation, insecurity and ephemeral uneven development within a highly unified global space economy of capital flows. The historic tension within capitalism between centralisation and decentralisation is now being worked out in new ways. Extraordinary decentralisation and proliferation of industrial produc-tion ends up putting Benetton or Laura Ashley products in almost every serially produced shopping mall in the advanced capitalist world. Plainly, the new round of time–space compression is fraught with as many dangers as it offers possibilities for survival of particular places or for a solution to the overaccumulation problem.

The geography of devaluation through deindustrialisation, rising local unemployment, fiscal retrenchment, write-offs of local assets, and the like, is indeed a sorry picture. But we can at least see its logic within the frame of the search for a solution to the overaccumulation problem through the push into flexible and more mobile systems of accumulation. But there are also a priori reasons to suspect (as well as some material evidence to support the idea) that regions of maximum churning and fragmentation are also regions that seem best set to survive the traumas of devaluation in the long run. There is more than a hint that a little devaluation now is better than massive devaluation later in the scramble for local survival in the world of severely constrained opportunities for positive growth. Reindustrialising and restructuring cannot be accomplished without deindustrialising and devaluing first.

None of these shifts in the experience of space and time would make the sense or have the impact they do without a radical shift in the manner in which value gets represented as money. Though long dominant, money has never been a clear or unambiguous representation of value, and on occasion it becomes so muddled as to become itself a major source of insecurity and uncertainty. Under the terms of the post-war settlement, the question of world money was put on a fairly stable basis. The US dollar became the medium of world trade, technically backed by a fixed convertibility into gold, and backed politically and economically by the overwhelming power of the US productive apparatus. The space of the US production system became, in effect, the guarantor of international value. But, as we have seen, one of the signals of the breakdown of the Fordist–Keynesian system was the breakdown of the Bretton Woods agreement, of convertibility of US dollars to gold, and the shift to a global system of floating exchange rates. The breakdown in part occurred because of the shifting dimensionalities of space and time generated out of capital accumulation. Rising indebtedness (particularly within the United States) and fiercer international competition from the reconstructed spaces of the world economy under conditions of growing accumulation had much to do with undermining the power of the US economy to operate as an exclusive guarantor of world money.

The effects have been legion. The question of how value should now get represented, what form money should take, and the meaning that can be put upon the various forms of money available to us has never been far from the surface of recent concerns. Since 1973, money has been 'dematerialised' in the sense that it no longer has a formal or tangible link to precious metals (though the latter have continued to play a role as one potential form of money among many others), or for that matter to any other tangible commodity. Nor does it rely exclusively upon productive activity within a particular space. The world has come to rely, for the first time in its history, upon immaterial forms of money – i.e. money of account assessed quantitatively in numbers of some designated currency (dollars, yen, Deutschmarks, sterling, etc.). Exchange rates between the different currencies of the world have also been extremely volatile. Fortunes could be lost or made simply by holding the right currency during the right phases. The question of which currency I hold is directly linked to which place I put my faith in. That may have something to do with the competitive economic position and power of different national systems. That power, given the flexibility of accumulation over space, is itself a rapidly shifting magnitude. The effect is to render the spaces that underpin the determination of value as unstable as value itself. This problem is compounded by the way that speculative shifts bypass actual economic power and performance, and then trigger self-fulfilling expectations. The delinking of the financial system from active production and from any material monetary base calls into question the reliability of the basic mechanism whereby value is supposed to be represented.

These difficulties have been most powerfully present in the process of devaluation of money, the measure of value, through inflation. The steady inflation rates of the Fordist–Keynesian era (usually in the 3 per cent range, and rarely above 5 per cent) gave way from 1969 onwards, and then accelerated in all the major capitalist countries during the 1970s into double-digit rates. Worse still, inflation became highly unstable, between as well as within countries, leaving everyone in doubt as to what the true value (the buying power) of a particular money might be in the near future.

Money consequently became useless as a means of storing value for any length of time (the real rate of interest, measured as the money rate of interest minus the rate of inflation, was negative for several years during the 1970s, so dispossessing savers of the value they were seeking to store). Alternative means had to be found to store value effectively, and so began the vast inflation in certain kinds of asset prices – collectibles, art objects, antiques, houses, and the like. Buying a Degas or Van Gogh in 1973 would surely outstrip almost any other kind of investment in terms of capital gain. Indeed it can be argued that the growth of the art market (with its concern for authorial signature) and the strong commercialisation of cultural production since around 1970 have had a lot to do with the search to find alternative means to store value under conditions where the usual money forms were deficient. Commodity and general price inflation, though to some degree brought under control in the advanced capitalist countries during the 1980s, has by no means diminished as a problem. It is rampant in countries like Mexico, Argentina, Brazil and Israel (all with recent rates in hundreds of per cent), and the prospect of generalised inflation looms in the advanced capitalist countries, where it is in any case arguable that the inflation of asset prices (housing, works of art, antiques, etc.) has taken over where commodity and labour market inflation left off in the early 1980s.

The breakdown of money as a secure means of representing value has itself created a crisis of representation in advanced capitalism. It has also been reinforced by, and added its very considerable weight to, the problems of time–space compression. The rapidity with which currency markets fluctuate across the world's spaces, the extraordinary power of money capital flow in what is now a global stock and financial market, and the volatility of what the purchasing power of money might represent, define, as it were, a high point of that highly problematic intersection of money, time and space as interlocking elements of social power in the political economy of postmodernity.

It is, furthermore, not hard to see how all of this might create a more general crisis of representation. The central value system, to which capitalism has always appealed to validate and gauge its actions, is dematerialised and shifting, time horizons are collapsing, and it is hard to tell exactly what space we are in when it comes to assessing causes and effects, meanings or values. The intriguing exhibition at the Pompidou Centre in 1985 on 'The Immaterial' (an exhibition for which none other than Lyotard acted as one of the consultants) was perhaps a mirror image of the dissolution of the material representations of value under conditions of more flexible accumulation, and of the confusions as to what it might mean to say, with Paul Virilio, that time and space have disappeared as meaningful dimensions to human thought and action.

There are, I would submit, more tangible and material ways than this to go about assessing the significance of space and time for the condition of postmodernity. It should be possible to consider how, for example, the changing experience of space, time and money has formed a distinctive material basis for the rise of distinctive systems of interpretation and representation, as well as opening a path through which the aestheticisation of politics might once more reassert itself. If we view culture as that complex of signs and significations (including language) that mesh into codes of transmission of social values and meanings, then we can at least begin upon the task of unravelling its complexities under present-day conditions by recognising that money and commodities are themselves the primary bearers of cultural codes. Since money and commodities are entirely bound up with the circulation of capital, it follows that cultural forms are firmly rooted in the daily circulation process of capital. It is, therefore, with the daily experience of money and the commodity that we should begin, no matter if special commodities or even whole sign systems may be extracted from the common herd and made the basis of 'high' culture or that specialised imaging which we have already had cause to comment upon.

The annihilation of space through time has radically changed the commodity mix that enters into daily reproduction. Innumerable local food systems have been reorganised through their incorporation into global commodity exchange. French cheeses, for example, virtually unavailable except in a few gourmet stores in large cities in 1970, are now widely sold across the United States. And if this is thought a somewhat elite example, the case of beer consumption suggests that the internationalisation of a product, which traditional location theory always taught should be highly market-oriented, is now complete. Baltimore was essentially a one-beer town (locally brewed) in 1970, but first the regional beers from places like Milwaukee and Denver, and then Canadian and Mexican beers followed by European, Australian, Chinese, Polish, etc., beers became cheaper. Formerly exotic foods became commonplace while popular local delicacies (in the Baltimore case, blue crabs and oysters) that were once relatively inexpensive jumped in price as they too became integrated into long-distance trading.

The marketplace has always been an 'emporium of styles' (to quote Raban's phrase) but the food market, just to take one example, now looks very different from what it was twenty years ago. Kenyan haricot beans, Californian celery and avocados, North African potatoes, Canadian apples and Chilean grapes all sit side by side in a British supermarket. This variety also makes for a proliferation of culinary styles, even among the relatively poor. Such styles have always migrated, of course, usually following the migration streams of different groups before diffusing slowly through urban cultures. The new waves of immigrants (such as the Vietnamese, Koreans, Filipinos, Central Americans, etc., that have added to the older groups of Japanese, Chinese, Chicanos and all the European ethnic groups that have also found their culinary heritage can be revived for fun and profit) make a typical United States city such as New York, Los Angeles or San Francisco (where the last census showed the majority of the population to be made up of minorities) as much an emporium of culinary styles as it is an emporium of the world's commodities. But here, too, there has been an acceleration, because culinary styles have moved faster than the immigration streams. It did not take a large French immigration to the United States to send the croissant rapidly spreading across America to challenge the traditional doughnut, nor did it take a large immigration of Americans to Europe to bring fast-food hamburgers to nearly all medium-sized European cities. Chinese takeaways, Italian pizza-parlours (run by a US chain), Middle Eastern falafel stalls, Japanese sushi bars ... the list is now endless in the Western world.

The whole world's cuisine is now assembled in one place in almost exactly the same way that the world's geographical complexity is nightly reduced to a series of images on a static television screen. This same phenomenon is exploited in entertainment palaces like Epcott and Disney World; it becomes possible, as the US commercial put it, 'to experience the Old World for a day without actually having to go there'. The general implication is that through the experience of everything from food, to culinary habits, music, television, entertainment, and cinema, it is now possible to experience the world's geography vicariously, as a simulacrum. The interweaving of simulacra in daily life brings together different worlds (of commodities) in the same space and time. But it does so in such a way as to conceal almost perfectly any trace of origin, of the labour processes that produced them, or of the social relations implicated in their production.

The simulacra can in turn become the reality. Baudrillard,[16] in *L'Amérique*, even goes so far, somewhat exaggeratedly in my view, to suggest that US reality is now constructed as a giant screen: 'the cinema is everywhere, most of all in the city, incessant and marvellous film and scenario'. Places portrayed in a certain way, particularly if they have the capacity to attract tourists, may begin to 'dress themselves up' as the fantasy images prescribe. Medieval castles offer medieval weekends (food, dress, but not of course the primitive heating arrangements). Vicarious participation in these various worlds has real effects on the ways in which these worlds get ordered. Jencks[17] proposes that the architect should be an active participant in this:

> Any middle class urbanite in any large city from Teheran to Tokyo is bound to have a well-stocked, indeed over-stocked 'image bank' that is continually restuffed by travel and magazines. His *musée imaginaire* may mirror the pot-pourri of the producers but it is nonetheless natural to his way of life. Barring some kind of totalitarian reduction in the heterogeneity of production and consumption, it seems to be desirable that architects learn to use this inevitable heterogeneity of languages. Besides, it is quite enjoyable. Why, if one can afford to live in different ages and cultures,

restrict oneself to the present, the locale? Eclecticism is the natural evolution of a culture with choice.

Much the same can be said of popular music styles. Commenting on how collage and eclecticism have recently come to dominate, Chambers[18] goes on to show how oppositional and subcultural musics like reggae, Afro-American and Afro-Hispanic have taken their place 'in the museum of fixed symbolic structures' to form a flexible collage of 'the already seen, the already worn, the already played, the already heard'. A strong sense of 'the Other' is replaced, he suggests, by a weak sense of 'the others': the loose hanging together of divergent street cultures in the fragmented spaces of the contemporary city re-emphasises the contingent and accidental aspects of this 'otherness' in daily life. This same sensibility exists in postmodern fiction. It is, says McHale,[19] concerned with 'ontologies', with a potential as well as an actual plurality of universes, forming an eclectic and 'anarchic landscape of worlds in the plural'. Dazed and distracted characters wander through these worlds without a clear sense of location, wondering, 'Which world am I in and which of my personalities do I deploy?' Our postmodern ontological landscape, suggests McHale, 'is unprecedented in human history – at least in the degree of its pluralism'. Spaces of very different worlds seem to collapse upon each other, much as the world's commodities are assembled in the supermarket and all manner of subcultures get juxtaposed in the contemporary city. Disruptive spatiality triumphs over the coherence of perspective and narrative in postmodern fiction, in exactly the same way that imported beers coexist with local brews, local employment collapses under the weight of foreign competition, and all the divergent spaces of the world are assembled nightly as a collage of images upon the television screen.

There seem to be two divergent sociological effects of all of this in daily thought and action. The first suggests taking advantage of all of the divergent possibilities, much as Jencks recommends, and cultivating a whole series of simulacra as milieux of escape, fantasy and distraction:

All around us – on advertisement hoardings, bookshelves, record covers, television screens – these miniature escape fantasies present themselves. This, it seems, is how we are destined to live, as split personalities in which the private life is disturbed by the promise of escape routes to another reality.[20]

From this standpoint I think we have to accept McHale's argument that postmodern fiction is mimetic of something, much as I have argued that the emphasis upon ephemerality, collage, fragmentation and dispersal in philosophical and social thought mimics the conditions of flexible accumulation. And it should not be surprising either to see how all of this fits in with the emergence since 1970 of a fragmented politics of divergent special and regional interest groups.

But it is exactly at this point that we encounter the opposite reaction that can best be summed up as the search for personal or collective identity, the search for secure moorings in a shifting world. Place-identity, in this collage of superimposed spatial images that implode in upon us, becomes an important issue, because everyone occupies a space of individuation (a body, a room, a home, a shaping community, a nation), and how we individuate ourselves shapes identity. Furthermore, if no one 'knows their place' in this shifting collage world, then how can a secure social order be fashioned or sustained?

There are two elements within this problem that deserve close consideration. First, the capacity of most social movements to command place better than space puts a strong emphasis upon the potential connection between place and social identity. This is manifest in political action. The defensiveness of municipal socialism, the insistence on working-class community, the localisation of the fight against capital, become central features of working-class struggle within an overall patterning of uneven geographical development. The consequent dilemmas of socialist or working-class movements in the face of a universalising capitalism are shared by other oppositional groups – racial minorities, colonised peoples, women, etc. – who are relatively empowered to organise in place but disempowered when it comes to organising over space. In clinging, often of necessity, to a place-bound identity, however, such oppositional movements become a part of the very fragmentation which a mobile capitalism and flexible accumulation can feed upon. 'Regional resistances', the struggle for local autonomy, place-bound organisation, may be excellent bases for political action, but they cannot bear the burden of radical historical change alone. 'Think globally and act locally' was the revolutionary slogan of the 1960s. It bears repeating.

The assertion of any place-bound identity has to rest at some point on the motivational power of tradition. It is difficult, however, to maintain any sense of historical continuity in the face of all the flux and ephemerality of flexible accumulation. The irony is that tradition is now often preserved by being commodified and marketed as such. The search for roots ends up at worst being produced and marketed as an image, as a simulacrum or pastiche (imitation communities constructed to evoke images of some folksy past, the fabric of traditional working-class communities being taken over by an urban gentry). The photograph, the document, the view and the reproduction become history precisely because they are so overwhelmingly present. The problem, of course, is that none of these are immune from tampering or downright faking for present purposes. At best, historical tradition is reorganised as a museum culture, not necessarily of high modernist art, but of local history, of local production, of how things once upon a time were made, sold, consumed and integrated into a long-lost and often romanticised daily life (one from which all trace of oppressive social relations may be expunged). Through the presentation of a partially illusory past it becomes possible to signify something of local identity and perhaps to do it profitably.

The second reaction to the internationalism of modernism lies in the search to construct place and its meanings qualitatively. Capitalist hegemony over space puts the aesthetics of place very much back on the agenda. But this, as we have seen, meshes only too well with the idea of spatial differentiations as lures for a peripatetic capital that values the option of mobility very highly. Isn't this place better than that place, not only for the operations of capital but also for living in, consuming well and feeling secure in a shifting world? The construction of such places, the fashioning of some localised aesthetic image, allows the construction of some limited and limiting sense of identity in the midst of a collage of imploding spatialities.

The tension in these oppositions is clear enough but it is hard to appreciate their intellectual and political ramifications. Here, for example, is Foucault[21] addressing the issue from his own perspective:

> Space is fundamental in any form of communal life; space is fundamental in any exercise of power ... I recall having been invited in 1966, by a group of architects, to do a study of space, of something that I called at the time 'heterotopias', those singular spaces to be found in some given social spaces whose functions are different or even the opposite of others. The architects worked on this, and at the end of the study someone spoke up – a Sartrean psychologist – who firebombed me saying that space is reactionary and capitalist but history and becoming are revolutionary. This absurd discourse was not at all unusual at the time. Today everyone would be convulsed with laughter at such a pronouncement, but not then.

The proposition the Sartrean critic offers is, though crude and oppositional, nowhere near as laughable as Foucault avers. On the other hand, postmodernist sentiment definitely leans towards Foucault's position. Whereas modernism looked upon the spaces of the city, for example, as 'an epiphenomenon of social functions', postmodernism tends to disengage urban space from its dependence on functions, and to see it as an autonomous formal system incorporating 'rhetorical and artistic strategies, which are independent of any simple historical determinism'.[22] It is precisely this disengagement that permits Foucault to deploy spatial metaphors so extensively in his studies of power. Spatial imagery, liberated from its roots in any social determination, becomes a means to depict the forces of social determination. It is a short step, however, from Foucault's metaphors to reinforcement of a political ideology that sees place and being with all its associated aesthetic qualities as a proper basis for social action. Geopolitics and the Heideggerian trap come not too far behind. Jameson,[23] for his part, views:

> The spatial peculiarities of post-modernism as symptoms and expressions of a new and historically original dilemma, one that involves our insertion as individual subjects into a multidimensional set of radically discontinuous realities, whose frames range from the still surviving spaces of bourgeois private life all the way to the unimaginable decentering of global capitalism itself. Not even Einsteinian relativity, or the multiple subjective worlds of the older modernists, is capable of giving any adequate figuration to this process, which in lived experience makes itself felt by the so-called death of the subject, or, more exactly, the fragmented and schizophrenic decentering and dispersion of this last ... And although you may not have realised it, I am talking about practical politics here: since the crisis of socialist internationalism, and the enormous strategic and tactical difficulties of coordinating local and grassroots or neighborhood political actions with national or international ones, such urgent political dilemmas are all immediately functions of the enormously complex new international space I have in mind.

Jameson exaggerates somewhat with respect to the uniqueness and newness of this experience. Stressful though the current condition undoubtedly is, it is qualitatively similar to that which led to Renaissance and various modernist reconceptualisations of space and time. Nevertheless, the dilemmas which Jameson depicts are exact and capture the drift of postmodern sensibility as to the meaning of space in contemporary political and cultural as well as economic life. If, however, we have lost the modernist faith in becoming, as Foucault's Sartrean critic argued, is there any way out except via the reactionary politics of an aestheticised spatiality? Are we sadly destined to end up on the track that Sine began with, in his turn to Wagnerian mythology as support for his assertion of the primacy of place and community in a world of changing spaces? Worse still, if aesthetic production has now been so thoroughly commodified and thereby become really subsumed within a political economy of cultural production, how can we possibly stop that circle closing onto a produced, and hence all too easily manipulated, aestheticisation of a globally mediatised politics?

This should alert us to the acute geopolitical dangers that attach to the rapidity of time–space compression in recent years. The transition from Fordism to flexible accumulation, such as it has been, ought to imply a transition in our mental maps, political attitudes and political institutions. But political thinking does not necessarily undergo such easy transformations, and is in any case subject to the contradictory pressures that derive from spatial integration and differentiation. There is an omnipresent danger that our mental maps will not match current realities. The serious diminution of the power of individual nation-states over fiscal and monetary policies, for example, has not been matched by any parallel shift towards an internationalisation of politics. Indeed, there are abundant signs that localism and nationalism have become stronger precisely because of the quest for the security that place always offers in the midst of all the shifting that flexible accumulation implies. The resurgence of geopolitics and of faith in charismatic politics (Thatcher's Falklands War, Reagan's invasion of Grenada) fits only too well with a world that is increasingly nourished intellectually and politically by a vast flux of ephemeral images.

Time–space compression always exacts its toll on our capacity to grapple with the realities unfolding around us. Under stress, for example, it becomes harder and harder to react accurately to events. The erroneous identification of an Iranian Airbus, ascending within an established commercial flight corridor, with a fighter-bomber descending towards a targeted US warship – an incident that resulted in many civilian deaths – is typical of the way that reality gets created rather than interpreted under conditions of stress and time–space compression. The parallel with Kern's account of the outbreak of World War I is instructive. If 'seasoned negotiators cracked under the pressure of tense confrontations and sleepless nights, agonising over the probable disastrous consequences of their snap judgements and hasty actions', then how much more difficult must decision-making now be? The difference this time is that there is not even time to agonise. And the problems are not confined to the realms of political and military decision-making, for the world's financial markets are on the boil in ways that make a snap judgement here, an unconsidered word there, and a gut reaction somewhere else the slip that can unravel the whole skein of fictitious capital formation and of interdependency.

The conditions of postmodern time–space compression exaggerate in many respects the dilemmas that have from time to time beset capitalist procedures of modernisation in the past (1848 and the phase just before World War I spring particularly to mind). While the economic, cultural and political responses may not be exactly new, the range of those responses differs in certain important respects from those which have occurred before. The intensity of time–space compression in Western capitalism since the 1960s, with all of its congruent features of excessive ephemerality and fragmentation in the political and private as well as in the social realm, does seem to indicate an experiential context that makes the condition of postmodernity somewhat special. But by putting this condition into its historical context, as part of a history of successive waves of time–space compression generated out of the pressures of capital accumulation with its perpetual search to annihilate space through time and reduce turnover time, we can at least pull the condition of postmodernity into the range of conditions accessible to historical materialist analysis and interpretation.

Commentary

I was surprised at the initial reception and sustained popularity of *The Condition of Postmodernity* because I wrote the book fairly fast and freely, making use of the materials and insights I had assembled during my earlier political, economic and urban studies. I was familiar, for example, with the cultural shifts that occurred in Second Empire Paris and had read widely in urban history. I also felt free to incorporate the observations of novelists and painters, and as an urbanist the whole question of architecture and the role of planning was never far from the surface of my thinking. So when the postmodern wave, fashion or whatever it was, swept over academia in the 1980s I felt well placed to offer a critical response, particularly as it appeared to leave so many people in a confused state while those committed to and excited by it seemed to mean quite different things by it. This all happened to coincide with a move to Oxford from Johns Hopkins in Baltimore (where I was stagnating in midlife crisis mode) to take up a professorship of geography named after the reactionary imperialist apologist Halford Mackinder. It seemed a good moment to strike out and do something new.

There were, within the postmodern mix of ideas, a number I was definitely at odds with. The frequent dismissal of Marxist thinking I found irritating and the dogma that all hints of metatheory (with Marx as exhibit A) must be expunged from everyone's heads did not appeal to me at all. The belated discovery that the spatial dimension in social relations was an important attribute of our world was being used to dismantle and undermine meta-theories. This was particularly galling: my own work sought to integrate the production of space into Marx's political economy. It is clear, however, that around 1975 major shifts took place in how capital was working. Many people misinterpreted these shifts as emancipatory when flexible accumulation, deindustrialisation, the growing power of international finance, globali-sation and strong currents of what I called time–space compression were all being mobilised to destroy the power of working-class institutions and cultures. At the time I could only see the half of this; the full story I later told in *A Brief History of Neoliberalism*, published in 2005. But the half I did get plainly struck a chord. *The Condition of Postmodernity* identified the new ideas and showed how capital was involved in their production.

Chapter 6
From Managerialism to Entrepreneurialism

The Transformation in Urban Governance in Late Capitalism

A centrepiece of my academic concerns these last two decades has been to unravel the role of urbanisation in social change, in particular under conditions of capitalist social relations and accumulation. This project has necessitated deeper enquiry into the manner in which capitalism produces a distinctive historical geography. When the physical and social landscape of urbanisation is shaped according to distinctively capitalist criteria, constraints are put on the future paths of capitalist development. This implies that though urban processes under capitalism are shaped by the logic of capital circulation and accumulation, they in turn shape the conditions and circumstances of capital accumulation at later points in time and space. Put another way, capitalists, like everyone else, may struggle to make their own historical geography but, also like everyone else, they do not do so under historical and geographical circumstances of their own individual choosing, even when they have played an important and even determinant collective role in shaping those circumstances. This two-way relation of reciprocity and domination (in which capitalists, like workers, find themselves dominated and constrained by their own creations) can best be captured theoretically in dialectical terms. It is from such a standpoint that I seek more powerful insights into that process of city-making that is both product and condition of ongoing social processes of transformation in the most recent phase of capitalist development.

Enquiry into the role of urbanisation in social dynamics is, of course, nothing new. From time to time, the issue flourishes as a focus of major debates, though more often than not with regard to particular historical-geographical circumstances in which, for some reason or other, the role of urbanisation and of cities appears particularly salient. The part that city formation played in the rise of civilisation has long been discussed, as has the role of the city in classical Greece and Rome. The significance of cities to the transition from feudalism to capitalism is an arena of continuing controversy, having sparked a remarkable and revealing literature over the years. A vast array of evidence can now likewise be brought to bear on the significance of urbanisation to nineteenth-century industrial, cultural and political development as well as to the subsequent spread of capitalist social relations to lesser developed countries (which now support some of the most dramatically growing cities in the world).

All too frequently, however, the study of urbanisation becomes separated from that of social change and economic development, as if it can somehow be regarded either as a sideshow or as a passive side-product to more important and fundamental social changes. The successive revolutions in technology, space relations, social relations, consumer habits, lifestyles and the like that have so characterised capitalist history can, it is sometimes suggested, be understood without any deep enquiry into the roots and nature of urban processes. True, this judgement is by and large made tacitly, by virtue of sins of omission rather than commission. But the anti-urban bias in studies of macroeconomic and macrosocial change is rather too persistent for comfort. It is for this reason that it seems worthwhile to enquire what role the urban process might be playing in the quite radical restructuring going on in geographical distributions of human activity and in the political-economic dynamics of uneven geographical development in most recent times.

The shift to entrepreneurialism in urban governance
A colloquium held at Orléans in 1985 brought together academics, businessmen and policy-makers from eight large cities in seven advanced capitalist countries.[1] The charge was to explore the lines of action open to urban governments in the face of the widespread erosion of the economic and fiscal base of many large cities in the advanced capitalist world. The colloquium indicated a strong consensus: that urban governments had to be much more innovative and entrepreneurial, willing to explore all kinds of avenues through which to alleviate their distressed condition and thereby secure a better future for their populations. The only realm of disagreement concerned how this best could be done. Should urban governments play some kind of supportive or even direct role in the creation of new enterprises and if so of what sort? Should they struggle to preserve or even take over threatened employment sources and, if so, which ones? Or should they simply confine themselves to the provision of those infrastructures, sites, tax baits and cultural and social

attractions that would shore up the old and lure in new forms of economic activity?

I quote this case because it is symptomatic of a reorientation in attitudes to urban governance that has taken place these past two decades in the advanced capitalist countries. Put simply, the 'managerial' approach so typical of the 1960s has steadily given way to initiatory and 'entrepreneurial' forms of action in the 1970s and 1980s. In recent years in particular, there seems to be a general consensus emerging throughout the advanced capitalist world that positive benefits are to be had by cities taking an entrepreneurial stance to economic development. What is remarkable is that this consensus seems to hold across national boundaries and even across political parties and ideologies.

Both Boddy and Cochrane[2] agree, for example, that since the early 1970s local authorities in Britain 'have become increasingly involved in economic development activity directly related to production and investment', while Rees and Lambert[3] show how 'the growth of local government initiatives in the economic field was positively encouraged by successive central administrations during the 1970s' in order to complement central government attempts to improve the efficiency, competitive powers and profitability of British industry. David Blunkett, leader of the Labour council in Sheffield for several years, has recently put the seal of approval on a certain kind of urban entrepreneurialism:

> From the early 1970s, as full employment moved from the top of government priorities, local councils began to take up the challenge. There was support for small firms; closer links between the public and private sectors; promotion of local areas to attract new business. They were adapting the traditional economic role of British local government which offered inducements in the forms of grants, free loans, and publicly subsidised infrastructure, and no request for reciprocal involvement with the community, in order to attract industrial and commercial concerns which were looking for suitable sites for investment and trading ... Local government today, as in the past, can offer its own brand of entrepreneurship and enterprise in facing the enormous economic and social change which technology and industrial restructuring bring.[4]

In the United States, where civic boosterism and entrepreneuralism had long been a major feature of urban systems,[5] the reduction in the flow of federal redistributions and local tax revenues after 1972 (the year in which

President Nixon declared the urban crisis to be over, signalling that the federal government no longer had the fiscal resources to contribute to their solution) led to a revival of boosterism to the point where Robert Goodman[6] was prepared to characterise both state and local governments as 'the last entrepreneurs'. An extensive literature now exists dealing with how the new urban entrepreneurialism has moved centre stage in urban policy formulation and urban growth strategies in the USA.[7]

The shift towards entrepreneurialism has by no means been complete. Many local governments in Britain did not respond to the new pressures and possibilities, at least until relatively recently, while cities like New Orleans in the USA continue to remain wards of the federal government and rely fundamentally on redistributions for survival. And the history of its outcomes, though yet to be properly recorded, is obviously chequered, pockmarked with as many failures as successes and not a little controversy as to what constitutes 'success' anyway (a question to which I shall later return). Yet beneath all this diversity, the shift from urban managerialism to some kind of entrepreneurialism remains a persistent and recurrent theme in the period since the early 1970s. Both the reasons for and the implications of such a shift are deserving of some scrutiny.

There is general agreement, of course, that the shift has something to do with the difficulties that have beset capitalist economies since the recession of 1973. Deindustrialisation, widespread and seemingly 'structural' unemployment, fiscal austerity at both the national and local levels, all coupled with a rising tide of neoconservatism and much stronger appeal (though often more in theory than in practice) to market rationality and privatisation, provide a backdrop to understanding why so many urban governments, often of quite different political persuasions and armed with very different legal and political powers, have all taken a broadly similar direction. The greater emphasis on local action to combat these ills also seems to have something to do with the declining powers of the nation-state to control multinational money flows, so that investment increasingly takes the form of a negotiation between international finance capital and local powers doing the best they can to maximise the attractiveness of the local site as a lure for capitalist development. By the same token, the rise of urban entrepreneurialism may have had an important role to play in a general transition in the dynamics of capitalism from a Fordist–Keynesian regime of capital accumulation to a regime of 'flexible accumulation'.[8] The transformation of urban governance these last two decades has had, I shall argue, substantial macroeconomic roots and implications. And if Jane Jacobs[9] is only half right, that the city is the relevant unit for understanding how the wealth of nations is created, then the shift from urban managerialism to urban entrepreneurialism could have far-reaching implications for future growth prospects.

If, for example, urban entrepreneurialism (in the broadest sense) is embedded in a framework of zero-sum inter-urban competition for resources, jobs and capital, then even the most resolute and avant-garde municipal socialists will find themselves, in the end, playing the capitalist game and performing as agents of discipline for the very processes they are trying to resist. It is exactly this problem that has dogged the Labour councils in Britain.[10] They had on the one hand to develop projects which could 'produce outputs which are directly related to working people's needs, in ways which build on the skills of labour rather than de-skilling them',[11] while on the other hand recognising that much of that effort would go for naught if the urban region did not secure relative competitive advantages. Given the right circumstances, however, urban entrepreneurialism and even inter-urban competition may open the way to a non-zero-sum pattern of development. This kind of activity has certainly played a key role in capitalist development in the past. And it is an open question as to whether or not it could lead towards progressive and socialist transitions in the future.

Conceptual issues

There are conceptual difficulties to such an enquiry that deserve an initial airing. To begin with, the reification of cities when combined with a language that sees the urban process as an active, rather than passive, aspect of political-economic development poses acute dangers. It makes it seem as if 'cities' can be active agents when they are mere things. Urbanisation should, rather, be regarded as a spatially grounded social process in which a wide range of different actors with quite different objectives and agendas interact through a particular configuration of interlocking spatial practices. In a class-bound society such as capitalism, these spatial practices acquire a definite class content, which is not to say that all spatial practices can be so interpreted. Indeed, as many researchers have shown, spatial practices can and do acquire gender, racial and bureaucratic-administrative contents (to list just a subset of important possibilities). But under capitalism, it is the broad range of class practices connected to the circulation of capital, the reproduction of labour power and class relations, and the need to control labour power, that remains hegemonic.

The difficulty is to find a way of proceeding that can deal specifically with the relation between *process* and *object* without itself falling victim to unnecessary reification. The spatially grounded set of social processes that I call urbanisation produce innumerable artefacts: a built form, produced spaces and resource systems of particular qualities organised into a distinctive spatial configuration. Subsequent social action must take account of these artefacts, since so many social processes (such as commuting) become physically channelled by them. Urbanisation also throws up certain institutional arrangements, legal forms, political and administrative systems, hierarchies of power, and the like. These, too, give a 'city' objectified qualities that may dominate daily practices and confine subsequent courses of action. And, finally, the consciousness of urban inhabitants is affected by the environment of experience out of which perceptions, symbolic readings and aspirations arise. In all of these respects, there is a perpetual tension between form and process, between object and subject, between activity and thing. It is as foolish to deny the role and power of objectifications, the capacity of things we create to return to us as so many forms of domination, as it is to attribute to such things the capacity for social action.

Given the dynamism to which capitalism is prone, we find that these 'things' are always in the course of transformation, that activities are constantly escaping the bounds of fixed forms, that the objectified qualities of the urban are chronically unstable. So universal is this capitalist condition that the conception of the urban and of 'the city' is likewise rendered unstable, not because of any conceptual definitional failing, but precisely because the concept has itself to reflect changing relations between form and process, between activity and thing, between subjects and objects. When we speak, therefore, of a transition from urban managerialism towards urban entrepreneurialism these last two decades, we have to take cognisance of the reflexive effects of such a shift, through the impacts on urban institutions as well as urban built environments.

The domain of spatial practices has, unfortunately, changed in recent years, making any firm definition of the urban as a distinctive spatial domain even more problematic. On the one hand, we witness the greater fragmentation of the urban social space into neighbourhoods, communities and a multitude of street corner societies, while on the other telecommuting and rapid transport make nonsense of some concept of the city as a tightly walled physical unit or even a coherently organised administrative domain. The 'megalopolis' of the 1960s has suffered even further fragmentation and dispersal, particularly in the USA, as urban deconcentration gathers pace to produce a 'spread city' form. Yet the spatial grounding persists in some form with specific meanings and effects. The production of new ecological patterns and structures within a spread city form has significance for how production, exchange and consumption are organised, how social relationships are established, how power (financial and political) is exercised, and how the spatial integration of social action is achieved. I hasten to add that presentation of the urban problematic in such ecological terms in no way presumes ecological explanations. It simply insists that ecological patterns are important for social organisation and action. The shift towards entrepreneurialism in urban governance has to be examined, then, at a variety of spatial scales: local neighbourhood and community, central city and suburb, metropolitan region, region, nation-state, and the like.

It is likewise important to specify who is being entrepreneurial and about what. I want here to insist that urban 'governance' means much more than urban 'government'. It is unfortunate that much of the literature (particularly in Britain) concentrates so much on the latter when the real power to reorganise urban life so often lies elsewhere, or at least within a broader coalition of forces within which urban government and administration have only a facilitative and coordinating role to play. The power to organise space derives from a whole complex of forces mobilised by diverse social agents. It is a conflictual process, the more so in the ecological spaces of highly variegated social density. Within a metropolitan region as a whole, we have to look to the formation of coalition politics, to class alliance formation, as the basis for any kind of urban entrepreneurialism at all. Civic boosterism has, of course, often been the prerogative of the local chamber of commerce, some cabal of local financiers, industrialists and merchants, or some 'round table' of business leaders and real-estate and property developers. The latter frequently coalesce to form the guiding power in 'growth machine' politics.[12] Educational and religious institutions, different arms of government (varying from the military to research or administrative establishments), local labour organisations (the building and construction trades in particular) as well as political parties, social movements and the local state apparatuses (which are multiple and often quite heterogeneous) can also play the game of local boosterism though often with quite different goals.

Coalition and alliance formation are so delicate and difficult a task that the way is open here for a person of vision, tenacity and skill (such as a charismatic mayor, a clever city administrator or a wealthy business leader) to put a particular stamp upon the nature and direction of urban entrepreneurialism, perhaps to shape it, even, to particular political ends. Whereas it was a public figure like Mayor Schaefer who played the central role in Baltimore, in cities like Halifax or Gateshead in Britain it has been private entrepreneurs

139

who have taken the lead. In other instances, it has been a more intricate mix of personalities and institutions that have put a particular project together.

I raise these problems not because they are insurmountable or intractable – they are resolved daily within the practices of capitalist urbanisation – but because we have to attend to their manner of practical resolution with a requisite care and seriousness. I shall, however, venture three broad assertions which I know to be true for a city like Baltimore (the case study which underpins much of the argument I offer here) and which may be more generally applicable.

First, the new entrepreneurialism has, as its centrepiece, the notion of a 'public–private partnership' in which a traditional local boosterism is integrated with the use of local governmental powers to try and attract external sources of funding, new direct investments or new employment sources. The Orléans colloquium[13] was full of references to the importance of this public–private partnership and it was, after all, the kinds of economic projects (housing, education, and so on) that are precisely the aim of local government reforms in Britain in the 1970s to facilitate their formation (or in the end to bypass local resistance by setting up the urban development corporations). In the USA, the tradition of federally backed and locally implemented public–private partnership faded during the 1960s as urban governments struggled to regain social control of restive populations through redistributions of real income (better housing, education, healthcare and the like, all targeted towards the poor) in the wake of urban unrest. The role of the local state as facilitator for the strategic interests of capitalist development (as opposed to stabiliser of capitalist society) declined. The same dismissiveness towards capitalist development has been noted in Britain:

> The early 1970s was a period of resistance to change: motorway protest groups, community action against slum clearance, opponents of town centre redevelopment. Strategic and entrepreneurial interests were sacrificed to local community pressures. Conceivably, however, we are moving into a different period in which the entrepreneurial role becomes dominant.[14]

In Baltimore the transition point can be dated exactly. A referendum narrowly passed in 1978, after a vigorous and contentious political campaign, sanctioned the use of city land for the private development that became the highly spectacular and successful Harborplace. Thereafter, the policy of public–private partnership had a popular mandate as well as an effective subterranean presence in almost everything that urban governance was about.[15]

Secondly, the activity of that public–private partnership is entrepreneurial precisely because it is speculative in execution and design and therefore dogged by all the difficulties and dangers which attach to speculative as opposed to rationally planned and coordinated development. In many instances, this has meant that the public sector assumes the risk and the private sector takes the benefits, though there are enough examples where this is not the case (think, for example, of the private risk taken in Gateshead's Metrocentre development) to make any absolute generalisation dangerous. But I suspect it is this feature of risk-absorption by the local (rather than the national or federal) public sector which distinguishes the present phase of urban entrepreneurialism from earlier phases of civic boosterism in which private capital seemed generally much less risk-averse.

Thirdly, the entrepreneurialism focuses much more closely on the political economy of place rather than of territory. By the latter, I mean designed primarily to improve conditions of living or working within a particular jurisdiction. The construction of place (a new civic centre, an industrial park) or the enhancement of conditions within a place (intervention, for example, in local labour markets by retraining schemes or downward pressure on local wages), on the other hand, can have impacts either smaller or greater than the specific territory within which such projects happen to be located. The upgrading of the image of cities like Baltimore, Liverpool, Glasgow or Halifax, through the construction of cultural, retail, entertainment and office centres, can cast a seemingly beneficial shadow over the whole metropolitan region. Such projects can acquire meaning at the metropolitan scale of public–private action and allow for the formation of coalitions which leap over the kinds of city–suburb rivalries that dogged metropolitan regions in the managerial phase. On the other hand, a rather similar development in New York City – Southstreet Seaport – constructs a new place that has only local impacts, falling far short of any metropolitan-wide influence, and generating a coalition of forces that is basically local property developers and financiers.

The construction of such places may, of course, be viewed as a means to procure benefits for populations within a particular jurisdiction, and indeed this is a primary claim made in the public discourse developed to support them. But for the most part, their form is such as to make all benefits indirect and potentially either wider or smaller in scope than the jurisdiction within which they lie. Place-specific projects of this sort also have the habit of becoming such a focus of public and political attention that they divert concern and even resources from the broader problems that may beset the region or territory as a whole.

The new urban entrepreneurialism typically rests, then, on a public–private partnership focusing on investment and economic development with the speculative construction of place rather than amelioration of conditions within a particular territory as its immediate (though by no means exclusive) political and economic goal.

Alternative strategies for urban governance

There are four basic options for urban entrepreneurialism. Each warrants some separate consideration, even though it is the combination of them that provides the clue to the recent rapid shifts in the uneven development of urban systems in the advanced capitalist world.

First, competition within the international division of labour means the creation of exploitation of particular advantages for the production of goods and services. Some advantages derive from the resource base (the oil that allowed Texas to boom in the 1970s) or location (for example, favoured access to the vigour of Pacific Rim trading in the case of Californian cities). But others are created through public and private investments in the kinds of physical and social infrastructures that strengthen the economic base of the metropolitan region as an exporter of goods and services. Direct interventions to stimulate the application of new technologies, the creation of new products, or the provision of venture capital to new enterprises (which may even be cooperatively owned and managed) may also be significant, while local costs may be reduced by subsidies (tax breaks, cheap credit, procurement of sites). Hardly any large-scale development now occurs without local government (or the broader coalition of forces constituting local governance) offering a substantial package of aids and assistance as inducements. International competitiveness also depends upon the qualities, quantities and costs of local labour supply. Local costs can most easily be controlled when local replaces national collective bargaining and when local governments and other large institutions, like hospitals and universities, lead the way with reductions in real wages and benefits (a series of struggles over wage rates and benefits in the public and institutional sector in Baltimore in the 1970s was typical).

Labour power of the right quality, even though expensive, can be a powerful magnet for new economic development so that investment in highly trained and skilled workforces suited to new labour processes and their managerial requirements can be well rewarded. There is, finally, the problem of agglomeration economies in metropolitan regions. The production of goods and services is often dependent not on single decisions of economic units (such as the large multinationals to bring a branch plant to town, often with very limited local spillover effects), but upon the way in which economies can be generated by bringing together diverse activities within a restricted space of interaction so as to facilitate highly efficient and interactive production systems.[16] From this standpoint, large metropolitan regions like New York, Los Angeles, London and Chicago possess some distinctive advantages that congestion costs have by no means yet offset. But, as the case of Bologna[17] and the surge of new industrial development in Emilia-Romagna illustrates, careful attention to the industrial and marketing mix backed by strong local state action (communist-led in this instance) can promote powerful growth of new industrial districts and configurations, based on agglomeration economies and efficient organisation.

Under the second option, the urban region can also seek to improve its competitive position with respect to the spatial division of consumption. There is more to this than trying to bring money into an urban region through tourism and retirement attractions. The consumerist style of urbanisation after 1950 promoted an ever-broader basis for participation in mass consumption. While recession, unemployment and the high cost of credit have rolled back that possibility for important layers in the population, there is still a lot of consumer power around (much of it credit-fuelled). Competition for that becomes more frenetic while consumers who do have the money have the opportunity to be much more discriminating. Investments to attract the consumer dollar have paradoxically grown apace as a response to generalised recession. They increasingly focus on the quality of life. Gentrification, cultural innovation and physical upgrading of the urban environment (including the turn to postmodernist styles of architecture and urban design), consumer attractions (sports stadia, convention and shopping centres, marinas, exotic eating places) and entertainment (the organisation of urban spectacles on a temporary or permanent basis) have all become much more prominent facets of strategies for urban regeneration. Above all, the city has to appear as an innovative, exciting, creative and safe place to live in or to visit, to play and consume in. Baltimore, with its dismal reputation as 'the armpit of the east coast' in the early 1970s, has, for example, expanded its employment in the tourist trade from under one to over fifteen thousand in less than two decades of massive urban redevelopment. More recently, thirteen ailing industrial cities in Britain (including

Leeds, Bradford, Manchester, Liverpool, Newcastle and Stoke-on-Trent) put together a joint promotional effort to capture more of Britain's tourist trade. Here is how the *Guardian*[18] reports this quite successful venture:

> Apart from generating income and creating jobs in areas of seemingly terminal unemployment, tourism also has a significant spin-off effect in its broader enhancement of the environment. Facelifts and facilities designed to attract more tourists also improve the quality of life for those who live there, even enticing new industries. Although the specific assets of the individual cities are obviously varied, each is able to offer a host of structural reminders of just what made them great in the first place. They share, in other words, a marketable ingredient called industrial and/or maritime heritage.

Festivals and cultural events likewise become the focus of investment activities. 'The arts create a climate of optimism – the "can do" culture essential to developing the enterprise culture,' says the introduction to a recent Arts Council of Great Britain report, adding that cultural activities and the arts can help break the downward spiral of economic stagnation in inner cities and help people 'believe in themselves and their community'.[19] Spectacle and display become symbols of the dynamic community, as much in communist-controlled Rome and Bologna as in Baltimore, Glasgow and Liverpool. This way, an urban region can hope to cohere and survive as a locus of community solidarity while exploring the option of exploiting conspicuous consumption in a sea of spreading recession.

Thirdly, entrepreneurialism has also been strongly coloured by a fierce struggle over the acquisition of key control and command functions in high finance, government or information gathering and processing (including the media). Functions of this sort need particular and often expensive infrastructural provision. Efficiency and centrality within a worldwide communications net are vital in sectors where personal interactions of key decision-makers are required. This means heavy investments in transport and communications (airports and teleports, for example) and the provision of adequate office space equipped with the necessary internal and external linkages to minimise transactions times and costs. Assembling the wide range of supportive services, particularly those that can gather and process information rapidly or allow quick consultation with 'experts', calls for other kinds of investments, while the specific skills required by such activities put a premium on metropolitan regions with certain kinds of education provision (business and law schools, high-tech production sectors, media skills, and the like). Inter-urban competition in this realm is very expensive and peculiarly tough because this is an area where agglomeration economies remain supreme and the monopoly power of established centres, like New York, Chicago, London and Los Angeles, is particularly hard to break. But since command functions have been a strong growth sector these last two decades (employment in them doubled in Britain in less than a decade), so pursuit of them has more and more appealed as the golden path to urban survival. The effect, of course, is to make it appear as if the city of the future is going to be a city of pure command and control functions, an informational city, a post-industrial city in which the export of services (financial, informational, knowledge-producing) becomes the economic basis for urban survival.

Fourthly, competitive edge with respect to redistributions of surpluses through central (or, in the USA, state) governments is still of tremendous importance since it is somewhat of a myth that central governments do not redistribute to the degree they used to do. The channels have shifted so that in both Britain (take the case of Bristol) and the USA (take the case of Long Beach–San Diego), it is military and defence contracts that provide the sustenance for urban prosperity, in part because of the sheer amount of money involved but also because of the type of employment and the spin-offs it may have into so-called 'high-tech' industries.[20] And even though every effort may have been made to cut the flow of central government support to many urban regions, there are many sectors of the economy (health and education, for example) and even whole metropolitan economies (see Smith and Keller's[21] study of New Orleans) where such a cut-off was simply impossible. Urban ruling-class alliances have had plenty of opportunity, therefore, to exploit redistributive mechanisms as a means to urban survival.

These four strategies are not mutually exclusive and the uneven fortunes of metropolitan regions have depended upon the nature of the coalitions that have formed, the mix and timing of entrepreneurial strategies, the particular resources (natural, human, locational) with which the metropolitan region can work, and the strength of the competition. But uneven growth has also resulted from the synergism that leads one kind of strategy to be facilitative for another. For example, the growth of the Los Angeles–San Diego–Long Beach–Orange County megalopolis appears to have been fuelled by inter-action effects between strong governmental redistributions to the defence industries and rapid accrual of command and control functions that have further stimulated consumption-oriented activities to the point where there has been a considerable revival of certain types of manufacturing. On the other hand, there is little evidence that the strong growth of consumption-oriented activity in Baltimore has done very much at all for the growth of other functions save, perhaps, the relatively mild proliferation of banking and financial services. But there is also evidence that the network of cities and urban regions in, say, the Sunbelt or southern England has generated a stronger collective synergism than would be the case for their respective northern counterparts. Noyelle and Stanback[22] also suggest that position and function within the urban hierarchy have had an important role to play in the patterning of urban fortunes and misfortunes. Transmission effects between cities, and within the urban hierarchy, must also be factored in to account for the pattern of urban fortunes and misfortunes during the transition from managerialism to entrepreneurialism in urban governance.

Urban entrepreneurialism implies, however, some level of inter-urban competition. We here approach a force that puts clear limitations upon the power of specific projects to transform the lot of particular cities. Indeed, to the degree that inter-urban competition becomes more potent, it will almost certainly operate as an 'external coercive power' over individual cities to bring them closer into line with the discipline and logic of capitalist development. It may even force repetitive and serial reproduction of certain patterns of development (such as the serial reproduction of 'world trading centres' or of new cultural and entertainment centres, of waterfront development, of postmodern shopping malls, and the like). The evidence for serial reproduction of similar forms of urban redevelopment is quite strong and the reasons behind it are worthy of note.

With the diminution in transport costs and the consequent reduction in spatial barriers to movement of goods, people, money and information, the significance of the qualities of place has been enhanced and the vigour of inter-urban competition for capitalist development (investment, jobs, tourism, and so on) has strengthened considerably. Consider the matter, first of all, from the standpoint of highly mobile multinational capital. With the reduction of spatial barriers, distance from the market or from raw materials has become less relevant to locational decisions. The monopolistic elements in spatial competition, so essential to the workings of Löschian location theory, disappear. Heavy, low-value items (like beer and mineral water), which used to be locally produced, are now traded over such long distances that concepts such as the 'range of a good' make little sense. On the other hand, the ability of capital to exercise greater choice over location highlights the importance of the particular production conditions prevailing at a particular place. Small differences in labour supply (quantities and qualities), in infrastructures and resources, in government regulation and taxation, assume much greater significance than was the case when high transport costs created 'natural' monopolies for local production in local markets. By the same token, multinational capital now has the power to organise its responses to highly localised variations in market taste through small-batch and specialised production designed to satisfy local market niches. In a world of heightened competition – such as that which has prevailed since the post-war boom came crashing to a halt in 1973 – coercive pressures force multinational capital to be much more discriminating and sensitive to small variations between places with respect to both production and consumption possibilities.

Consider matters, in the second instance, from the standpoint of the places that stand to improve or lose their economic vitality if they do not offer enterprises the requisite conditions to come to or remain in town. The reduction of spatial barriers has, in fact, made competition between localities, states and urban regions for development capital even more acute. Urban governance has thus become much more oriented to the provision of a 'good business climate' and to the construction of all sorts of lures to bring capital into town. Increased entrepreneurialism has been a partial result of this process, of course. But we here see that increasing entrepreneurialism in a different light precisely because the search to procure investment capital confines innovation to a very narrow path built around a favourable package for capitalist development and all that entails. The task of urban governance is, in short, to lure highly mobile and flexible production, financial and consumption flows into its space. The speculative qualities of urban investments simply derive from the inability to predict exactly which package will succeed and which will not, in a world of considerable economic instability and volatility.

It is easy to envisage, therefore, all manner of upward and downward spirals of urban growth and decline under conditions where urban entrepreneurialism and inter-urban competition are strong. The innovative and competitive responses of many urban ruling-class alliances have engendered more rather than less uncertainty and in the end made the urban system more rather than less vulnerable to the uncertainties of rapid change.

The macroeconomic implications of inter-urban competition

The macroeconomic as well as local implications of urban entrepreneurialism and stronger inter-urban competition deserve some scrutiny. It is particularly useful to put these phenomena into relation with some of the more general shifts and trends that have been observed in the way capitalist economies have been working since the first major post-war recession of 1973 sparked a variety of seemingly profound adjustments in the paths of capitalist development.

To begin with, the fact of inter-urban competition and urban entrepreneurialism has opened up the urban spaces of the advanced capitalist countries to all kinds of new patterns of development, even when the net effect has been the serial reproduction of science parks, gentrification, world trading centres, cultural and entertainment centres, large-scale interior shopping malls with postmodern accoutrements, and the like. The emphasis on the production of a good local business climate has emphasised the importance of the locality as a site of regulation of infrastructural provision, labour relations, environmental controls, and even tax policy vis-à-vis international capital.[23] The absorption of risk by the public sector, and in particular the stress on public-sector involvement in infrastructural provision, has meant that the cost of locational change has diminished from the standpoint of multinational capital, making the latter more, rather than less, geographically mobile. If anything, the new urban entrepreneurialism adds to, rather than detracts from, the geographical flexibility with which multinational firms can approach their locational strategies. To the degree that the locality becomes the site of regulation of labour relations, so it also contributes to increased flexibility in managerial strategies in geographically segmented labour markets. Local, rather than national, collective bargaining has long been a feature of labour relations in the USA, but the trend towards local agreements is marked in many advanced capitalist countries over the past two decades.

There is, in short, nothing about urban entrepreneurialism which is antithetical to the thesis of some macroeconomic shift in the form and style of capitalist development since the early 1970s. Indeed, a strong case can be made[24] that the shift in urban politics and the turn to entrepreneurialism have had an important facilitative role in a transition from locationally rather rigid Fordist production systems backed by Keynesian state welfarism to a much more geographically open and market-based form of flexible accumulation. A further case can be made that the trend away from urban-based modernism in design, cultural forms and lifestyle towards postmodernism is also connected to the rise of urban entrepreneurialism. In what follows I shall illustrate how and why such connections might arise.

Consider, first, the general distributive consequences of urban entrepreneurialism. Much of the vaunted 'public–private partnership' in the USA, for example, amounts to a subsidy for affluent consumers, corporations and powerful command functions to stay in town at the expense of local collective consumption for the working class and poor. The general increase in problems of impoverishment and disempowerment, including the production of a distinctive 'underclass', has been documented beyond dispute for many of the large cities in the USA. Levine,[25] for example, provides abundant details for Baltimore in a setting where major claims are made for the benefits to be had from public–private partnership. Boddy[26] likewise reports that what he calls 'mainstream' (as opposed to socialist) approaches to local development in Britain have been 'property-led, business and market-oriented and competitive, with economic development rather than employment the primary focus, and with an emphasis on small firms'. Since the main aim has been 'to stimulate or attract in private enterprise by creating the preconditions for profitable investment', local government 'has in effect ended up underpinning private enterprise, and taking on part of the burden of production costs'. Since capital tends to be more, rather than less, mobile these days, it follows that local subsidies to capital will likely increase while local provision for the underprivileged will diminish, producing greater polarisation in the social distribution of real income.

The kinds of jobs created in many instances likewise militate against any progressive shift in income distributions since the emphasis upon small businesses and subcontracting can even spill over into direct encouragement of the 'informal sector' as a basis for urban survival. The rise of informal production activities in many cities, particularly in the USA,[27] has been a marked feature in the past two decades and is increasingly seen as either a necessary evil or a dynamic growth sector capable of reimporting some level of manufacturing activity back into otherwise declining urban centres. By the same token, the kinds of service activities and managerial functions which get consolidated in urban regions tend to be either low-paying jobs (often held exclusively by women) or very high-paying positions at the top end of the managerial spectrum. Urban entrepreneurialism consequently contributes to increasing disparities in wealth and income as well as to that increase in urban impoverishment which has been noted even in those cities (like New York) that have exhibited strong growth. It has, of course, been exactly this result that Labour councils in Britain (as well as some of the more progressive urban administrations in the USA) have been struggling to resist. But it is by no means clear that even the most progressive urban government can resist such an outcome when embedded in the logic of capitalist spatial development in which competition seems to operate not as a beneficial hidden hand, but as an external coercive law forcing the lowest common denominator of social responsibility and welfare provision within a competitively organised urban system.

Many of the innovations and investments designed to make particular cities more attractive as cultural and consumer centres have quickly been imitated elsewhere, thus rendering any competitive advantage within a system of cities ephemeral. How many successful convention centres, sports stadia, Disney Worlds, harbour places and spectacular shopping malls can there be? Success is often short-lived or rendered moot by parallel or alternative innovations arising elsewhere. Local coalitions have no option, given the coercive laws of competition, except to keep ahead of the game, thus engendering leapfrogging innovations in lifestyles, cultural forms, products and service mixes, even institutional and political forms if they are to survive. The result is a stimulating if often destructive maelstrom of urban-based cultural, political, production and consumption innovations. It is at this point that we can identify an albeit subterranean but nonetheless vital connection between the rise of urban entrepreneurism and the postmodern penchant for design of urban fragments rather than comprehensive urban planning, for ephemerality and eclecticism of fashion and style rather than the search for enduring values, for quotation and fiction rather than invention and function, and, finally, for medium over message and image over substance.

In the USA, where urban entrepreneurialism has been particularly rife, the result has been instability within the urban system. Houston, Dallas and Denver, boom towns in the 1970s, suddenly dissolved after 1980 into morasses of excess capital investment, bringing a host of financial institutions to the brink of, if not to actual, bankruptcy. Silicon Valley, once the high-tech wonder of new products and new employment, suddenly lost its lustre, but New York, on the edge of bankruptcy in 1975, rebounded in the 1980s with the immense vitality of its financial services and command functions, only to find its future threatened once more with the wave of lay-offs and mergers which rationalised the financial services sector in the wake of the stock market crash of October 1987. San Francisco, the darling of Pacific Rim trading, suddenly finds itself with excess office space in the early 1980s, only to recover almost immediately. New Orleans, already struggling as a ward of federal government redistribution, sponsors a disastrous World Fair that drives it deeper into the mire, while Vancouver, already booming, hosts a remarkably successful World Exposition. The shifts in urban fortunes and misfortunes since the early 1970s have been truly remarkable and the strengthening of urban entrepreneurialism and inter-urban competition has had a lot to do with it.

But there has been another rather more subtle effect that deserves consideration. Urban entrepreneurialism encourages the development of those kinds of activities and endeavours that have the strongest *localised* capacity to enhance property values, the tax base, the local circulation of revenues, and (most often as a hoped-for consequence of the preceding list) employment growth. Since increasing geographical mobility and rapidly changing technologies have rendered many forms of production of goods highly suspect, so the production of those kinds of services that are (1) highly localised and (2) characterised by rapid if not instantaneous turnover time appears as the most stable basis for urban entrepreneurial endeavour. The emphasis upon tourism, the production and consumption of spectacles, the promotion of ephemeral events within a given locale, bear all the signs of being favoured remedies for ailing urban economies. Urban investments of this sort may yield quick though ephemeral fixes to urban problems. But they are often highly speculative. Gearing up to bid for the Olympic Games is an expensive exercise, for example, which may or may not pay off. Many cities in the USA (Buffalo, for example) have invested in vast stadium facilities in the hope of landing a Major League Baseball team and Baltimore is similarly planning a new stadium to try and recapture a football team that went to a superior stadium in Indianapolis some years ago (this is the contemporary US version of that ancient cargo cult practice in Papua New Guinea of building an airstrip in the hope of luring a jetliner to earth). Speculative projects of this sort are part and parcel of a more general macroeconomic problem. Put simply, credit-financed shopping malls, sports stadia and other facets of conspicuous high consumption are high-risk projects that can easily fall on bad times and thus exacerbate, as the 'over-malling of America' only too dramatically illustrates,[28] the problems of overaccumulation and overinvestment to which capitalism as a whole is so easily prone.

The instability that pervades the US financial system (forcing something of the order of $100 billion in public moneys to stabilise the largely bankrupt savings and loan industry) is partly due to bad loans to energy, agriculture and urban real-estate development. Many of the 'festival market places' that looked like an 'Aladdin's lamp for cities fallen on hard times' just a decade ago, ran a recent report in the *Baltimore Sun*,[29] have now themselves fallen on hard times. Projects in Richmond, Virginia, Flint, Michigan, and Toledo, Ohio, managed by Rouse's Enterprise Development Co., are losing millions of dollars, and even the South Street Seaport in New York and Riverwalk in New Orleans have encountered severe financial difficulties. Ruinous inter-urban competition on all such dimensions bids fair to produce a quagmire of indebtedness.

Even in the face of poor economic performance, however, investments in these last kinds of projects appear to have both a social and political attraction. To begin with, the selling of the city as a location for activity depends heavily upon the creation of an attractive urban imagery. City leaders can look upon the spectacular development as a 'loss leader' to pull in other forms of development. Part of what we have seen these last two decades is the attempt to build a physical and social imagery of cities suited for that competitive purpose. The production of an urban image of this sort also has internal political and social consequences. It helps counteract the sense of alienation and anomie that Simmel long ago identified as such a problematic feature of modern city life. It particularly does so when an urban terrain is opened for display, fashion and the 'presentation of self' in a surrounding of spectacle and play. If everyone, from punks and rap artists to the 'yuppies' and the haute bourgeoisie, participates in the production of an urban image through their production of social space, then all can at least feel some sense of belonging to that place. The orchestrated production of an urban image can if successful also help create a sense of social solidarity, civic pride and loyalty to place, and even allow the urban image to provide a mental refuge in a world that capital treats as more and more place-less. Urban entrepreneurialism (as opposed to the much more faceless bureaucratic managerialism) here meshes with a search for local identity and, as such, opens up a range of mechanisms for social control. Bread and circuses was the famous Roman formula that now stands to be reinvented and revived, while the ideology of locality, place and community becomes central to the political rhetoric of urban governance which concentrates on the idea of togetherness in defence against a hostile and threatening world of international trade and heightened competition.

The radical reconstruction of the image of Baltimore through the new waterfront and inner-harbour development is a good case in point. The redevelopment put Baltimore on the map in new way, earned the city the title of 'renaissance city' and put it on the front cover of *Time* magazine, shedding its image of dreariness and impoverishment. It appeared as a dynamic go-getting city, ready to accommodate outside capital and to encourage the movement in of capital and of the 'right' people. No matter that the reality is one of increased impoverishment and overall urban deterioration, that a thorough local enquiry based on interviews with community, civic and business leaders identified plenty of 'rot beneath the glitter',[30] that a Congressional Report of 1984 described the city as one of the 'seediest' in the USA, and that a thorough study of the renaissance by Levine[31] showed again and again how partial and limited the benefits were and how the city as a whole was accelerating rather than reversing its decline. The image of prosperity conceals all that, masks the underlying difficulties and projects an imagery of success that spreads internationally so that the British newspaper the *Sunday Times*[32] can report, without a hint of criticism, that:

> Baltimore, despite soaring unemployment, boldly turned its derelict harbour into a playground. Tourists meant shopping, catering and transport, this in turn meant construction, distribution, manufacturing – leading to more jobs, more residents, more activity. The decay of old Baltimore slowed, halted, then turned back. The harbour area is now among America's top tourist draws and urban unemployment is falling fast.

Yet it is also apparent that putting Baltimore on the map in this way, giving it a stronger sense of place and of local identity, has been successful politically in consolidating the power of influence of the local public–private partnership that brought the project into being. It has brought development money into Baltimore (though it is hard to tell if it has brought more in than it has taken out, given the absorption of risk by the public sector). It also has given the population at large some sense of place-bound identity. The circus succeeds even if the bread is lacking. The triumph of image over substance is complete.

The entrepreneurial turn in urban governance

There has been a good deal of debate in recent years over the 'relative autonomy' of the local state in relation to the dynamics of capital accumulation. The turn to entrepreneurialism in urban governance seems to suggest considerable autonomy of local action. The notion of urban entrepreneurialism, as I have here presented it, does not in any way presume that the local state or the broader class alliance that constitutes urban governance is automatically (or even in the famous 'last instance') captive of solely capitalist class interests or that its decisions are prefigured directly in terms reflective of the requirements of capital accumulation. On the surface, at least, this seems to render my account inconsistent with that Marxist version of local state theory put forward by, say, Cockburn,[33] and strongly dissented from by a range of other non-Marxist or neo-Marxist writers such as Mollenkopf, Logan and Molotch, Gurr and King, and Smith.[34] Consideration of inter-urban competition, however, indicates a way in which a seemingly autonomous urban entrepreneurialism can be reconciled with the albeit contradictory requirements of continuous capital accumulation while guaranteeing the reproduction of capitalist social relations on ever wider scales and at deeper levels.

Marx advanced the powerful proposition that competition is inevitably the 'bearer' of capitalist social relations in any society where the circulation of capital is a hegemonic force. The coercive laws of competition force individual or collective agents (capitalist firms, financial institutions, states, cities) into certain configurations of activities which are themselves constitutive of the capitalist dynamic. But the 'forcing' occurs after the action rather than before. Capitalist development is always speculative – indeed, the whole history of capitalism can best be read as a whole series of minuscule and sometimes grandiose speculative thrusts piled historically and geographically one upon another. There is, for example, no exact prefiguring of how firms will adapt and behave in the face of market competition. Each will seek its own path to survival without any prior understanding of what will or will not succeed. Only after the event does the 'hidden hand' (Adam Smith's phrase) of the market assert itself as 'an a posteriori necessity imposed by nature, controlling the unregulated caprice of the producers'.[35]

Urban governance is similarly and liable to be equally, if not even more, lawless and capricious. But there is also every reason to expect that such 'lawless caprice' will be regulated after the fact by inter-urban competition. Competition for investments and jobs, particularly under conditions of generalised unemployment, industrial restructuring and in a phase of rapid shifts towards more flexible and geographically mobile patterns of capital accumulation, will presumably generate all kinds of ferments concerning how best to capture and stimulate development under particular local conditions. Each coalition will seek out its distinctive version of what Jessop[36] calls 'accumulation strategies and hegemonic projects'. From the standpoint of long-run capital accumulation, it is essential that different paths and different packages of political, social and entrepreneurial endeavours get explored. Only in this way is it possible for a dynamic and revolutionary social system, such as capitalism, to discover new forms and modes of social and political regulation suited to new forms and paths of capital accumulation. If this is what is meant by the 'relative autonomy' of the local state, then there is nothing about it which makes urban entrepreneurialism in principle in any way different from the 'relative autonomy' which all capitalist firms, institutions and enterprises possess in exploring different paths to capital accumulation. Relative autonomy understood in this way is perfectly consistent with, and indeed is constitutive of, the general theory of capital accumulation to which I would subscribe.[37] The theoretical difficulty arises, however, as in so many issues of this type, because Marxian as well as non-Marxian theory treats the relative autonomy argument as if it can be considered outside of the controlling power of space relations and as if inter-urban and spatial competition are either non-existent or irrelevant.

In the light of this argument, it would seem that it is the managerial stance under conditions of weak inter-urban competition that would render urban governance less consistent with the rules of capital accumulation. Consideration of that argument requires, however, an extended analysis of the relations of the welfare state and of national Keynesianism (in which local state action was embedded) to capital accumulation during the 1950s and 1960s. This is not the place to attempt such an analysis, but it is important to recognise that it was in terms of the welfare state and Keynesian compromise that much of the argument over the relative autonomy of the local state emerged. Recognising that as a particular interlude, however, helps understand why civic boosterism and urban entrepreneurialism are such old and well-tried traditions in the historical geography of capitalism (starting, of course, with the Hanseatic League and the Italian city-states). The recovery and reinforcement of that tradition, and the revival of inter-urban competition these past two decades, suggest that urban governance has moved more rather than less into line with the naked requirements of capital accumulation. Such a shift required a radical reconstruction of central to local state relations and the cutting-free of local state activities from the welfare state and the Keynesian compromise (both of which have been under strong attack these past two decades). And, needless to say, there is strong evidence of turmoil in this quarter in many of the advanced capitalist countries in recent years.

It is from this perspective that it becomes possible to construct a critical perspective on the contemporary version of urban entrepreneurialism. To begin with, enquiry should focus on the contrast between the surface vigour of many of the projects for regeneration of flagging urban economies and the underlying trends in the urban condition. It should recognise that behind the mask of many successful projects there lie some serious social and economic problems and that in many cities these are taking geographical shape in the form of a dual city of inner-city regeneration and a surrounding sea of increasing impoverishment. A critical perspective should also focus on some of the dangerous macroeconomic consequences, many of which seem inescapable given the coercion exercised through inter-urban competition. The latter include regressive impacts on the distribution of income, volatility within the urban network and the ephemerality of the benefits which many projects bring. Concentration on spectacle and image rather than on the substance of economic and social problems can also prove deleterious in the long run, even though political benefits can all too easily be had.

Yet there is something positive also going on here that deserves close attention. The idea of the city as a collective corporation, within which democratic decision-making can operate, has a long history in the pantheon of progressive doctrines and practices (the Paris Commune being, of course, the paradigm case in socialist history). There have been some recent attempts to revive such a corporatist vision both in theory[38] as well as in practice.[39] While it is possible, therefore, to characterise certain kinds of urban entrepreneurialism as purely capitalistic in method, intent and result, it is also useful to recognise that many of the problems of collective corporatist action originate not with the fact of some kind of civic boosterism, or even by virtue of who, in particular, dominates the urban class alliance, what form or what projects they devise. For it is the generality of inter-urban competition within an overall framework of uneven capitalist geographical development which seems so to constrain the options that 'bad' projects drive out 'good' and well-intended and benevolent coalitions of class forces find themselves obliged to be 'realistic' and 'pragmatic' to a degree which has them playing to the rules of capitalist accumulation rather than to the goals of meeting local needs or maximising social welfare. Yet even here, it is not clear that the mere fact of inter-urban competition is the primary contradiction to be addressed. It should be regarded, rather, as a condition which acts as a 'bearer' (to use Marx's phrase) of the more general social relations of any mode of production within which that competition is embedded.

Socialism within one city is not, of course, a feasible project even under the best of circumstances. Yet cities are important power bases from which to work. The problem is to devise a geopolitical strategy of inter-urban linkage that mitigates inter-urban competition and shifts political horizons away from the locality and into a more generalisable challenge to capitalist uneven development. Working-class movements, for example, have proved historically to be quite capable of commanding the politics of place, but they have always remained vulnerable to the discipline of space relations and the more powerful command over space (militarily as well as economically) exercised by an increasingly internationalised bourgeoisie. Under such conditions, the trajectory taken through the rise of urban entrepreneurialism these past few years serves to sustain and deepen capitalist relations of uneven geographical development and thereby affects the overall path of capitalist development in intriguing ways. But a critical perspective on urban entrepreneurialism indicates not only its negative impacts but its potentiality for transformation into a progressive urban corporatism, armed with a keen geopolitical sense of how to build alliances and linkages across space in such a way as to mitigate if not challenge the hegemonic dynamic of capitalist accumulation to dominate the historical geography of social life.

Commentary

This is by far my most cited article (rather oddly my most cited book and most cited article appeared in the same year as the Berlin Wall came down). As should be clear from the references, this was not because I was writing about an unusual topic. Anyone working in urban studies in the 1980s would be familiar with the trends in urban governance then emerging in the wake of deindustrialisation and the economic restructuring going on under Thatcher and Reagan. The massive job losses in manufacturing in the older industrial cities of Europe and North America were having dramatic and destructive impacts on social structures and community solidarities. Much of the opposition to neoliberalisation – and not a few hopes for an alternative future – were concentrated in the cities (with the Greater London Council under Ken Livingstone in his very Marxist phase being emblematic). So there was nothing politically unusual about the piece. It was helpful, of course, to have a synthetic statement to bring it all together. But I think what made the article special was its emphasis on the macroeconomic and general roots and consequences of the trend towards urban entrepreneurialism and, for example, its contribution to burgeoning social inequalities. It showed how local processes, when aggregated and coordinated through the power of spatial competition, constituted a global process of immense significance that would be very hard to resist through local mobilisations alone. The article highlighted in no uncertain terms how what Marx called 'the coercive laws of competition' were working through decentralisation and inter-urban competition. And, finally, it emphasised the seductive role of autonomous decision-making under conditions of liberty and freedom which has produced the coercive and unfree results we now have to live with.

In 1978/79 Michel Foucault, in a course of lectures at the Collège de France on *The Birth of Biopolitics*, enunciated another way to think of the consequences of this transition. He postulated a turn towards a neoliberal form of governmentality in which economic rationality shifts from the relatively narrow economic sphere of the market to the sphere of self-regulation and we all became entrepreneurs in ourselves and responsible for our own 'human capital' formation. His ideas played no role in constructing the transition I describe but they do provide an interesting interpretation of the potential and highly negative political consequences of changing political subjectivities. When I wrote this piece I did not use the term neoliberalism, preferring the term 'flexible accumulation', which had also framed my thinking in *The Condition of Postmodernity*. In 2005, in *A Brief History of Neoliberalism*, I rewrote the story of the political-economic shifts behind the rise of urban entrepreneurialism under neoliberalism. It is easier to interpret what happened in retrospect than to understand what's going on at the time. I often wonder how we will think of our present confusions when we look back in a few years. This is where the intuitions of a Marxist (liberated from dogmatism) might prove helpful.

Chapter 7
The Nature of Environment

The Dialectics of Social and Environmental Change

Around 'Earthday' 1970, I recall reading a special issue of the business journal *Fortune* on the environment. It celebrated the rise of the environmental issue as a 'non-class issue' and President Nixon, in an invited editorial, opined that future generations would judge us entirely by the quality of environment they inherited. On 'Earthday' itself, I attended a campus rally in Baltimore and heard several rousing speeches, mostly by middle-class white radicals, attacking the lack of concern for the qualities of the air we breathed, the water we drank, the food we consumed and lamenting the materialist and consumerist approach to the world which was producing all manner of resource depletion and environmental degradation. The following day I went to the Left Bank Jazz Society, a popular spot frequented by African-American families in Baltimore. The musicians interspersed their music with inter-active commentary over the deteriorating state of the environment. They talked about lack of jobs, poor housing, racial discrimination, crumbling cities, culminating in the claim, which sent the whole place into paroxysms of cheering, that their main environmental problem was President Richard Nixon.

What struck me at the time, and what continues to strike me, is that the 'environmental issue' necessarily means such different things to different people, that in aggregate it encompasses quite literally everything there is. Business leaders worry about the political and legal environment, politi-cians worry about the economic environment, city dwellers worry about the social environment and, doubtless, criminals worry about the environment of law enforcement and polluters worry about the regulatory environment. That a single word should be used in such a multitude of ways testifies to its fundamental incoherence as a unitary concept. Yet, like the word 'nature', the idea of which 'contains, though often unnoticed, an extraordinary amount of human history ... both complicated and changing, as other ideas and experiences change',[1] the uses to which a word like environment is put prove instructive. The 'unnoticed' aspect of this poses particular difficulties, however, because it is always hard to spot the 'incompletely explicit *assumptions*, or more or less *unconscious mental habits*, operating in the thought of an individual or generation', but which define 'the dominant intellectual tendencies of an age'. Lovejoy[2] continues:

> It is largely because of their ambiguities that mere words are capable of independent action as forces in history. A term, a phrase, a formula, which gains currency or acceptance because one of its meanings, or of the thoughts which it suggests, is congenial to the prevalent beliefs, the standards of value. The tastes of a certain age may help to alter beliefs, standards of value, and tastes, because other meanings or suggested implications, not clearly distinguished by those who employ it, gradually become the dominant elements of signification. The word 'nature,' it need hardly be said, is the most extraordinary example of this.

The contemporary battleground over words like 'nature' and 'environment' is more than a matter of mere semantics, but a leading edge of political conflict, albeit in the realm of ideology where 'we become conscious of political matters and fight them out'. The fight arises precisely because words like 'nature' and 'environment' convey a commonality and universality of concern that is, precisely because of their ambiguity, open to a great diversity of interpretation. 'Environment' is whatever surrounds or, to be more precise, whatever exists in the surroundings of some being that is *relevant* to the state of that being at a particular moment. Plainly, the 'situatedness' of a being and its internal conditions and needs have as much to say about the definition of environment as the surrounding conditions themselves, while the criteria of relevance can also vary widely. Yet each and every one of us is situated in an 'environment' and all of us therefore have some sense of what an environmental issue is all about.

Over recent years a rough convention has emerged, however, which circumscribes environmental issues to a particular subset of possible meanings, primarily focusing on the relationship between human activity and (a) the condition or 'health' of the bio- or ecosystem which supports that activity, (b) specific qualities of that ecosystem such as air, water, soil and landscapes and (c) the quantities and qualities of the natural resource base for human activity, including both reproducible and exhaustible assets. But even mildly biocentric interpretations would quite properly challenge the implicit division between 'nature' and 'culture' in this convention. The consequent division between 'environmentalists' who adopt an external and often managerial stance towards the environment and 'ecologists' who view human activities as embedded in nature is becoming politically contentious.[3] In any case, there is increasing public acceptance of the idea that much of what we call 'natural', at least as far as the surface ecology of the globe and its atmosphere is concerned, has been significantly modified by human action.[4] The distinction between built environments of cities and the humanly modified environments of rural and even remote regions then appears arbitrary except as a particular manifestation of a rather long-standing ideological distinction between the country and the city.[5] We ignore the ideological power of that distinction at our peril, however, since it underlies a pervasive anti-urban bias in much ecological rhetoric.

In what follows I shall try to establish a theoretical position from which to try and make sense of environmental issues in the rather circumscribed sense which we now attribute to that term.

The issue
I begin with two quotations.

> We abuse land because we regard it as a commodity belonging to us. When we see land as a community to which we belong, we may begin to use it with love and respect.[6]

> Where money is not itself the community, it must dissolve the community ... It is the elementary precondition of bourgeois society that labour should directly produce exchange value, money; and similarly that money should directly purchase labour, and therefore the labourer, but only insofar as he alienates his activity in the exchange ... Money thereby directly and simultaneously becomes the real community, since it is the general substance for the survival of all, and at the same time the social product of all.[7]

From Marx's perspective, the land ethic that Leopold has in mind looks a hopeless quest in a bourgeois society where the community of money prevails. Leopold's land ethic would necessarily entail the construction of an alternative mode of production and consumption to that of capitalism. The clarity and self-evident qualities of that argument have not, interestingly, led to any immediate rapprochement between ecological/environmentalist and socialist politics; the two have by and large remained antagonistic to each other and inspection of the two quotations reveals why. Leopold defines a realm of thinking and action outside of the narrow constraints of the economy; his is a much more biocentric way of thinking. Working-class politics and its concentration on revolutionising political economic processes comes then to be seen as a perpetuation rather than a resolution of the problem as Leopold defines it. The best that socialist politics can achieve, it is often argued, is an environmental (instrumental and managerial) rather than ecological politics. At its worst, socialism stoops to so-called 'Promethean' projects in which the 'domination' of nature is presumed both possible and desirable.

My concern in this essay is to see if there are ways to bridge this antagonism and turn it into a creative rather than destructive tension. Is there or ought there to be a place for a distinctively 'ecological' angle to progressive socialist politics? And, if so, what should it be? I begin with the question as to how 'nature' might be socially valued.

Money values

Can we put money values on 'nature' and if so how and why? There are three arguments in favour of so doing:

1. Money is the means whereby we all, in daily practice, value significant and very widespread aspects of our environment. Every time we purchase a commodity, we engage with a train of monetary and commodity transactions through which money values are assigned (or, equally importantly, not assigned to zero-priced free goods) to natural resources or significant environmental features used in production and consumption. We are all (no matter whether we are ecologically minded or not) implicated in putting monetary valuations on nature by virtue of our daily practices.

2. Money is the only well-understood and universal yardstick of value that we currently possess. We all use it and possess both a practical and intellectual understanding as to what it means. It serves to communicate our wants, needs, desires as well as choices, preferences and values, including those to be put specifically upon nature, to others. The comparability of different ecological projects

162

(from the building of dams to wildlife or biodiversity conservation measures) depends on the definition of a common yardstick (implicit or acknowledged) to evaluate whether one is more justifiable than another. No satisfactory or universally agreed upon alternative to money has yet been devised. Money, as Marx noted, is a leveller and cynic, reducing a wondrous multidimensional ecosystemic world of use values, of human desires and needs, as well as of subjective meanings, to a common denominator which everyone can understand.

3. Money in our particular society is the basic (though by no means the only) language of social power and to speak in money terms is always to speak in a language which the holders of that power appreciate and understand. To seek action on environmental issues often requires that we not only articulate the problem in universal (money) terms that all can understand, but also that we speak in a voice that is persuasive to those in power. The discourse of 'ecological modernisation' is precisely about trying to represent environmental issues as profitable enterprise. Environmental economics is also a useful and pragmatic tool for getting environmental issues on the agenda. I cite here E. P. Odum's struggle to gain wetland protection in his home state of Georgia, which fell upon deaf ears until he put some plausible but rather arbitrary money values on the worth of wetlands to the state economy.[8] This persuaded the legislature to formulate, at a relatively early date, extensive wetland protection legislation. There are enough parallel instances (such as Margaret Thatcher's sudden conversion to a shade of green politics in 1988) to make it quite evident that political clout attaches to being able to articulate environmental issues in raw money terms.

Exactly how to do that poses difficulties. Pearce et al.,[9] for example, operationalise the widely accepted Brundtland Report[10] view that 'sustainable' development means that present actions should not compromise the ability of future generations to meet their needs, by arguing that the value of the total stack of assets, both humanly produced (e.g. roads and fields and factories) and given in 'nature' (e.g. minerals, water supplies, etc.), must remain constant from one generation to another. But how can this stock be quantified? It cannot be measured in non-comparable physical terms (i.e. in actual or potential use values), let alone in terms of inherent qualities, so money values (exchange values) provide the only common (universal) denominator.

The difficulties with such a procedure are legion.

1. What, for example, is money? Itself dead and inert, it acquires its qualities as a measure of value by means of a social process. The social processes of exchange which give rise to money, Marx concluded, show that money is a representation of socially necessary labour time and price is 'the money name of value'. But the processes are contradictory and money is therefore always a slippery and unreliable representation of value as social labour. Debasement of the coinage, extraordinary rates of inflation in certain periods and places, speculative rages, all illustrate how money can itself be seriously unstable as a representation of value. Money, we say, 'is only worth what it will buy' and we even talk of 'the value of money', which means that we vest in whatever is designated as money some social qualities inherent in everything else that is exchanged. Furthermore, money appears in multiple guises – gold and silver, symbols, tokens, coins, paper (should we use dollars, pounds, sterling, yen, cruzeiros, marks?). There have, furthermore, been instances when formal moneys have been so discredited that chocolate, cigarettes or other forms of tangible goods become forms of currency. To assess the value of 'nature' or 'the flow of environmental goods and services' in these terms poses acute problems that have only partial recompense by way of sophisticated methods of calculation of 'constant prices', 'price deflators' and noble attempts to calculate constant rates of exchange in a world of remarkable currency volatility.

2. It is difficult to assign anything but arbitrary money values to assets independently of the market prices actually achieved by the stream of goods and services which they provide. This condemns economic valuation to a tautology in which achieved prices become the only indicators we have of the money value of assets whose independent value we are seeking to determine. Rapid shifts in market prices imply equally rapid shifts in asset values. The massive devaluation of fixed capital in the built environment in recent years (empty factories, warehouses, and the like), to say nothing of the effects of the property market crash, illustrates

the intense volatility of asset valuation depending upon market behaviours and conditions. This principle carries over into valuing 'natural' assets in market economies (consider the value of a Texas oil well during the oil scarcity of 1973–5 versus its value in the oil glut of 1980). The attempt to hand on a constant stock of capital assets (both humanly constructed and naturally occurring) measured in such money terms then appears an unreliable if not counterproductive enterprise.

3. Money prices attach to particular things and presuppose exchangeable entities with respect to which private property rights can be established or inferred. This means that we conceive of entities as if they can be taken out of any ecosystem of which they are a part. We presume to value the fish, for example, independently of the water in which they swim. The money value of a whole ecosystem can be arrived at, according to this logic, only by adding up the sum of its parts, which are construed in an atomistic relation to the whole. This way of pursuing monetary valuations tends to break down, however, when we view the environment as being constructed organically, ecosystemically or dialectically[11] rather than as a Cartesian machine with replaceable parts. Indeed, pursuit of monetary valuations commits us to a thoroughly Cartesian–Newtonian–Lockean and in some respects 'anti-ecological' ontology of how the natural world is constituted (see below).

4. Money valuations presume a certain structure to time as well as to space. The temporal structure is defined through the procedure of discounting, in which present value is calculated in terms of a discounted flow of future benefits. There are no firmly agreed-upon rules for discounting and the environmental literature is full of criticism as well as defences of different discounting practices in relation to environmental qualities. Volatility in actual interest rates and the arbitrariness of interest rates assigned on, for example, public projects make valuation peculiarly difficult. Such valuation, furthermore, only makes sense if assets are exchangeable so that discounting the future value of, say, the state of energy fluxes in the ocean or the atmosphere is totally implausible. The multiple and often non-linear notions of time which attach to different ecological processes also pose deep problems. While, for example, it might be possible to discover something about

human time preferences (or at least make reasonable assertions about them), the multiple temporalities at work in ecosystems are often of a fundamentally different sort. McEvoy[12] cites the case of the (non-linear) reproductive cycle of sardine populations in Californian waters – the sardines adapted to 'ecological volatility' by individually 'living long enough to allow each generation to breed in at least one good year'. The stock suddenly collapsed when fishing 'stripped the stock of its natural buffer'. Of course, sensible policies and practices with respect to risk and uncertainty might have avoided such an outcome, but the point remains that the temporality defined by such ecological behaviours is antagonistic to the linear, progressive and very Newtonian conception of time we characteristically use in economic calculation. But even supposing some sort of valuation can be arrived at, profound moral questions remain, for while it may be, as Goodin[13] points out, 'economically efficient for us to short change the future', it might well be 'wrong for us to do so' because it 'would amount to unjust treatment of future generations'. For this, and other reasons, 'green value theory' (as Goodin calls it) is deeply antagonistic to discounting practices. 'The concern for the future should add up towards zero,' writes the deep ecologist Naess.[14] The effect of such a discount rate would be to preclude any investment in future project.

5. Property arrangements can be of various sorts. They look very different under conditions of, say, strong wetland preservation or land-use controls. It is the task of much of contemporary environmental policy to devise a regulatory framework with which to cajole or persuade those holding private property rights to use them in environmentally benign ways, perhaps even paying attention to rather longer time horizons than those which the market discount rate dictates. Challenging though this theoretical, legal and political problem may be, it still presumes the environment has a clear enough structure so that some kind of cost–benefit argument concerning the relation between environmental goods and individualised property rights can be constructed. Appeal to money valuations condemns us, in short, to a world view in which the ecosystem is viewed as an 'externality' to be internalised in human action only via some arbitrarily chosen and imposed price structure or regulatory regime.

6. It is hard in the light of these problems not to conclude that there is something about money valuations that makes them inherently anti-ecological, confining the field of thinking and of action to instrumental environmental management. While the point of environmental economics (in both its theory and its practice) is to escape from a too-narrow logic of valuations and to seek ways to put money values on otherwise unpriced assets, it cannot escape from the confines of its own institutional and ontological assumptions (which may well be erroneous) about how the world is ordered as well as valued.

7. Money, lastly, hardly satisfies as an appropriate means to represent the strength or the manifold complexity of human wants, desires, passions and values. 'We see in the nature of money itself something of the essence of prostitution,' says Simmel,[15] and Marx[16] concurs. Freud took things even further, picking up on our penchant to describe money as something dirty and unclean ('filthy lucre' and 'filthy rich' are common expressions). 'It is possible the contrast between the most precious substance known to men and the most worthless ... has led to the specific identification of gold with faeces,' he wrote, and shocked his Victorian readers by treating gold as transformed excrement and bourgeois exchange relations as sublimated rituals of the anus. Money, wrote his friend Ferenczi, 'is nothing other than odourless, dehydrated filth that has been made to shine'.[17] We do not have to go so far as Freud and Ferenczi to recognise that there is something morally or ethically questionable or downright objectionable to valuing human life in terms of discounted lifetime earnings and 'nature' (for example, the fate of the grizzly bear and the spotted owl as species allowed to continue to dwell on earth) in monetary terms.

Capitalism is, from this last standpoint, beset by a central moral failing: money supplants all other forms of imagery (religion, traditional religious authority and the like) and puts in its place something that either has no distinctive image because it is colourless, odourless and indifferent in relation to the social labour it is supposed to represent or, if it projects any image at all, connotes dirt, filth, excrement and prostitution. The effect is to create a moral vacuum at the heart of capitalist society – a colourless self-image of value that can have zero purchase upon social identity. It cannot provide an image of social bonding or of community in the usual sense of that term (even though it is the real community in the sense that Marx meant it) and it fails as a central value system to articulate even the most mundane of human hopes and aspirations. Money is what we aspire to for purposes of daily reproduction and in this sense it does indeed become the community; but a community empty of moral passion or of humane meanings. The sentiment that Leopold tried to articulate is, from this standpoint, correct.

At this point, the critic of money valuations, who is nevertheless deeply concerned about environmental degradation, is faced with a dilemma: eschew the language of daily economic practice and political power and speak in the wilderness, or articulate deeply held non-monetisable values in a language (i.e. that of money) believed to be inappropriate or fundamentally alien. There is, it seems to me, no immediate solution to the paradox. Zola hit it right in *L'Argent* when he has Madame Caroline say that:

> Money was the dung-heap that nurtured the growth of tomorrow's humanity. Without speculation there could be no vibrant and fruitful undertakings any more than there could be children without lust. It took this excess of passion, all this contemptibly wasted and lost life to ensure the continuation of life ... Money, the poisoner and destroyer, was becoming the seed-bed for all forms of social growth. It was the manure to sustain great public works whose execution was bringing the peoples of the globe together and pacifying the earth ... Everything that was good came out of that which was evil.

Although the ultimate moral of Zola's novel is that acceptance of that thesis leads to speculative farce and personal tragedy, no less a theorist than Max Weber sternly and quite properly warned that it was an egregious error to think that only good could come out of good and only evil out of evil. Money may be profoundly inadequate, soulless and 'the root of all evil', but it does not necessarily follow that social and by extension all ecological ills result from market coordinations in which private property, individualism and money valuations operate. On the other hand, we also have sufficient evidence concerning the unrestrained consequences of what Kapp called *The Social Costs of Private Enterprise* to know that it is equally illusory to believe the Adam Smith thesis that good automatically arises out of the necessary evils of the hidden hand of market behaviours. Left to its own devices, Marx[18] argued, capitalistic progress 'is a progress in the art, not only of robbing the labourer, but of robbing the soil', while capitalist technology develops 'only by sapping the original sources of all wealth – the soil and the labourer'.

The conclusion is, then, rather more ambiguous than many might want to accept. First, all the time we engage in commodity exchanges mediated by money (and this proposition holds just as firmly for any prospective socialist society) it will be impossible in practice to avoid money valuations. Secondly, valuations of environmental assets in money terms, while highly problematic and seriously defective, are not an unmitigated evil. We cannot possibly know, however, how good the arbitrary valuations of 'nature' are (once we choose to go beyond the simple idea of an unpriced flow of goods and services) unless we have some alternative notion of value against which to judge the appropriateness or moral worth of money valuations. Nor can we avoid a deep connection between a Newtonian and Cartesian view of the biosphere (a view which many would now seriously challenge as inappropriate to confront ecological problems) and the very basis of economic thinking and capitalistic practices. It is important to stress that the Newtonian–Cartesian view is not in itself wrong, any more than is the parallel Smithian model of atomistic individualism, market behaviours and property rights. But both are severely limited in their purchase and we are now wise enough to know that there are many spheres of decision and action, such as quantum theory and ecological issues, which cannot be captured in such a format. Newtonian mechanics and Smithian economics may be adequate to building bridges, but they are totally inadequate in trying to determine the ecosystemic impact of such endeavours.

Do values inhere in nature?

There has been a long history within bourgeois life of resistance to and search for an alternative to money as a way to express values. Religion, community, family, nation have all been proffered as candidates, but the particular set of alternatives I here wish to consider are those which in some manner or other see values residing in nature – for romanticism, environmentalism and ecologism all have strong elements of that ethic built within them. And the idea is not foreign to Marxism either (at least in some of its renditions). When Marx[19] argued in 'On the Jewish question' that money has 'robbed the whole world – both the world of men and nature – of its specific value' and that 'the view of nature attained under the dominion of private property and money is a real contempt for and practical debasement of nature', he comes very close to endorsing the view that money has destroyed earlier and perhaps recoverable intrinsic natural values.

The advantage of seeing values as residing in nature is that it provides an immediate sense of ontological security and permanence. The natural world provides a rich, variegated and permanent candidate for induction into the hall of universal and permanent values to inform human action and to give meaning to otherwise ephemeral and fragmented lives.[20] 'It is inconceivable to me,' writes Leopold,[21] 'that an ethical relation to land can exist without love, respect and admiration for the land, and a high regard for its value. By value, I of course mean something far broader than mere economic value; I mean value in the philosophical sense,' so that 'a thing is right when it tends to preserve the integrity, stability and beauty of the biotic community. It is wrong when it tends otherwise.' But how do we know and what does it mean to say that 'integrity, stability and beauty' are qualities that inhere in nature?

This brings us to the crucial question: if values reside in nature, then how can we know what they are? The routes to such an understanding are many and varied. Intuition, mysticism, contemplation, religious revelation, metaphysics and personal introspection have all provided, and continue to provide, paths for acquiring such understandings. On the surface at least, these modes of approach contrast radically with scientific enquiry. Yet, I shall argue, they all necessarily share a commonality. All versions of revealed values in nature rely heavily upon particular human capacities and particular anthropocentric *mediations* (sometimes even upon the charismatic interventions of visionary individuals). Through deployment of highly emotive terms such as love, caring, nurturing, responsibility, integrity, beauty, and the like, they inevitably represent such 'natural' values in distinctively humanised terms, thus producing distinctively human discourses about intrinsic values. For some, this 'humanising' of values in nature is both desirable and in itself ennobling, reflecting the peculiarities of our own position in the 'great chain of being'.[22]

'Humanity is nature becoming conscious of itself' was the motto that the anarchist geographer Reclus adopted, clearly indicating that the knowing subject has a creative role to play at least in translating the values inherent in nature into humanised terms. But if, as Ingold[23] notes, 'the physical world of nature cannot be apprehended as such, let alone confronted and appropriated, save by a consciousness to some degree emancipated from it', then how can we be sure that human beings are appropriate agents to represent all the values that reside in nature?

The ability to discover intrinsic values depends, then, on the ability of human subjects endowed with consciousness and reflexive as well as practical capacities to become neutral mediators of what those values might be. This often leads, as in religious doctrines, to the strict regulation of human practices (e.g. asceticism or practices like yoga) so as to ensure the openness of human consciousness to the natural world. This problem of anthropocentric mediations is equally present within scientific enquiry. But here too the scientist is usually cast in the role of a knowing subject acting as a neutral mediator, under the strictest guidelines of certain methods and practices (which sometimes put to shame many a Buddhist), seeking to uncover, understand and represent accurately the processes at work in nature. If values inhere in nature, then science by virtue of its objective procedures should provide one reasonably neutral path for finding out what they might be. How neutral this turns out to be has been the subject of considerable debate. Consideration of two examples provide some insight into the difficulty.

1) The fable of the sperm and the egg

Feminist work has, over the years, revealed widespread resort to gendered metaphors in scientific enquiry. The effect is often to write social ideas about gender relations into scientific representations of the natural world and thereby make it appear as if those social constructions are 'natural'. Merchant[24] highlights, for example, the gendered imagery with which Francis Bacon approached nature (in essence as a female body to be explored and a female spirit to be dominated and tamed by ruse or force) in his foundational arguments concerning experimental method (an imagery which sheds great light on what is happening in Shakespeare's *The Taming of the Shrew*). These are not, however, isolated or singular examples. Haraway, in an insightful essay on 'Teddy Bear patriarchy' in the New York Museum of Natural History, points out how 'decadence – the threat of the city, civilisation, machine – was stayed in the politics of eugenics and the art of taxidermy. The Museum fulfilled its scientific purpose of conservation, preservation, and production of permanence in the midst of an urban world that even at the turn of this century seemed to be on the border of chaos and collapse.' It opposed to this world of troubled sociality a visual technology of exhibits deployed in part as a means to communicate to the outside world a sense of the true organicism of the natural order (founded on hierarchy, patriarchy, class and family) which ought to be the foundation of stability for any social order. In so doing, it explicitly used and continues to use primatology as a means to produce or promote race, class and gender relations of a certain sort.

Martin's[25] example of the fable of the egg and sperm as depicted in the extensive medical and biological literature on human fertility is particularly instructive. Not only is the female reproductive process (particularly menstruation) depicted as wasteful compared to the immensely productive capacity of men to generate sperm, but the actual process of fertilisation is depicted in terms of a passive female egg, tracked down, captured and claimed as a prize by an active, dynamic and thrusting male sperm after a difficult and arduous journey to claim its prize. The sperm sounds oddly like an explorer looking for gold or an entrepreneur competing for business (cf. Zola's parallel image cited above of financial speculation as the wasteful lust necessary to produce anything). It transpires, however, that the metaphor deployed in scientific studies of human fertility was fundamentally misleading; the sperm is by no means as directed, energetic and brave as it was supposed to be (it turns out to be rather listless and aimless when left to itself) and the egg turns out to play an active role in fertilisation. But it took time for researchers to lay their gendered predilections aside, and when they did so it was mainly by turning the egg into the equivalent of the aggressive femme fatale who ensnares, entraps and victimises the male (sperm) in an elaborate spider's web as 'an engulfing, devouring mother'. New data, Martin[26] suggests, 'did not lead scientists to eliminate gender stereotypes in their descriptions of egg and sperm. Instead, scientists simply began to describe egg and sperm in different, but no less damaging terms.' We plainly cannot draw any inferences whatsoever as to the values inherent in nature by appeal to investigations and enquiries of this sort.

2) Darwin's metaphors

Consider, as a second example, the complex metaphors that play against and alongside each other in Darwin's *The Origin of Species*. There is, firstly, the metaphor of stock breeding practices (about which Darwin was very knowledgeable by virtue of his farm background). This, as Young[27] points out, took the artificial selection procedures which were well understood in stock breeding and placed them in a natural setting, posing the immediate difficulty of who was the conscious agent behind natural selection. There is, secondly, the Malthusian metaphor which Darwin explicitly acknowledged as fundamental to this theory. Entrepreneurial values of competition, survival of the fittest in a struggle for existence, then appeared in Darwin's work as 'natural' values to which social Darwinism could later appeal and which contemporary 'common sense' continues to deploy. Todes,[28] in a detailed examination of how Darwin's ideas were received in Russia, shows, however, that the Russians almost universally rejected the relevance of the Malthusian metaphor and downplayed specific struggle and competition as an evolutionary mechanism:

This unifying national style flowed from the basic conditions of Russia's national life – from the very nature of its class structure and political traditions and of its land and climate. Russia's political economy lacked a dynamic pro-laissez faire bourgeoisie and was dominated by landowners and peasants. The leading political tendencies, monarchism and a socialist-oriented populism, shared a cooperative social ethos and a distaste for competitive individualism widely with Malthus and Great Britain. Furthermore, Russia was an expansive, sparsely populated land with a swiftly changing and often severe climate. It is difficult to imagine a setting less consonant with Malthus's notion that organisms were pressed constantly into mutual conflict by population on limited space and resources … This combination of anti-Malthusian and non-Malthusian influences deprived Darwin's metaphor of commonsensical power and explanatory appeal.[29]

Though a great admirer of Darwin, this aspect of his work was not lost on Marx. 'It is remarkable,' he wrote to Engels, 'how Darwin recognises among beasts and plants his English society with its divisions of labour, competition, opening up of new markets, inventions and the Malthusian "struggle for existence".'[30]

Had Darwin (and Wallace) not been so struck, as were many Englishmen of that era, by the extraordinary fecundity of tropical environments and oriented their thinking to the sub-Arctic regions, and if they had been socially armed with images of what we now call 'the moral economy of the peasantry', they might well have downplayed, as the Russian evolutionists of all political persuasions did, the mechanisms of competition. They might have emphasised cooperation and mutual aid instead. When Prince Kropotkin arrived in London from Russia, armed with his theories of mutual aid as a potent force in both natural and social evolution, he was simply dismissed as an anarchist crank (in spite of his impressive scientific credentials), so powerful was the aura of social Darwinism at the time.

But there is another interesting metaphor which flows into Darwin's work, to some degree antagonistic to that of competition and the struggle for existence. This had to do with species diversification into niches. The guiding metaphor here seems to have been the proliferation of the divisions of labour and the increasing roundaboutness of production occurring within the factory system, about which Darwin was also very knowledgeable given that he was married to Emma, the daughter of industrialist Josiah Wedgwood II. In all of these instances, the interplay of socially grounded metaphors and scientific enquiry is such as to make it extremely difficult to extract from the scientific findings any non-socially tainted information on the values that might reside in nature. It is not surprising, therefore, to find Darwin's influential and powerful scientific views being appropriated by a wide range of political movements as a 'natural' basis for their particular political programmes.[31] Nor should we be surprised that others, such as Allee and his ecologist colleagues at the University of Chicago in the interwar years, could use their scientific work on (in this case) animal ecology as a vehicle to support and even promote their communitarian, pacifist and cooperative views.[32]

The conclusion, it seems to me, is inescapable. If values reside in nature we have no scientific way of knowing what they are independently of the values implicit in the metaphors deployed in mounting specific lines of scientific enquiry. Even the names we use betray the depth and pervasiveness of the problem. 'Worker bees' cannot understand the *Communist Manifesto* any more than the 'praying mantis' goes to church; yet the terminology helps naturalise distinctive social power relations and practices.[33] The language of 'the selfish gene' or 'the blind watchmaker' provides equally vivid social referents of scientific arguments. Rousseau,[34] interestingly, spotted the ruse long ago when he wrote of 'the blunder made by those who, in reasoning on the state of nature, always import into it ideas gathered in a state of society'. Ecologists concerned, for example, to articulate conceptions of equilibrium, plant succession and climax vegetation as properties of the natural world have reflected as much about the human search for permanence and security as the quest for an accurate and neutral description or theorisation of ecological processes. And the idea of harmony with nature not as a human desire but as a nature-imposed necessity likewise smacks of the view that to be natural is to be harmonious rather than conflictual. We have loaded upon nature, often without knowing it, in our science as in our poetry, much of the alternative desire for value to that implied by money.

The choice of values lies within us and not in nature. We see, in short, only those values which our value-laden metaphors allow us to see in our studies of the natural world. Harmony and equilibrium; beauty, integrity and stability; cooperation and mutual aid; ugliness and violence; hierarchy and order; competition and the struggle for existence; turbulence and unpredictable dynamic change; atomistic causation; dialectics and principles of complementarity; chaos and disorder; fractals and strange attractors; all of them can be identified as 'natural values' not because they are arbitrarily assigned to nature, but because no matter how ruthless, pristine and rigorously 'objective' our method of enquiry may be, the framework of interpretation is given in the metaphor rather than in the evidence. From contemporary

reproductive and cell biology we will learn that the world is necessarily hiera-
chically ordered into command and control systems that look suspiciously
like a Fordist factory system, while from contemporary immunology we will
conclude that the world is ordered as a fluid communications system with
dispersed command-control-intelligence networks which look much more
like contemporary models of flexible industrial and commercial organisation.[35] When, therefore, it is claimed that 'nature teaches', what usually
follows, Williams[36] remarks, 'is selective, according to the speaker's general
purpose'.

The solution, here, cannot be to seek scientific enquiry without metaphors.
Their deployment (like the parallel deployment of models) lies at the root
of the production of all knowledge. 'Metaphoric perception', say Bohm and
Peat,[37] is 'fundamental to all science' both in extending existing thought
processes as well as in penetrating into 'as yet unknown domains of reality,
which are in some sense implicit in the metaphor'. We can, therefore, only
reflect critically upon the properties of the metaphors in use. And then we
find that the values supposedly inherent in nature are always properties of
the metaphors rather than inherent in nature. 'We can never speak about
nature,' says Capra,[38] 'without, at the same time, speaking about ourselves.'

The moral community and environmental values

Deep ecologists have tended to abandon the idea of values purely intrinsic to
nature in recent years.[39] They have in part done so because of their readings in
quantum theory and the translation of the ideas of Bohr and Heisenberg into
a distinctive form of ecological discourse in Capra's highly influential *Tao of
Physics* and *The Turning Point*. The parallel turn to metaphysics, hermeneu-
tics and phenomenology as means to present and discover the values that
should attach to nature emphasises the powers of the knowing subject. Fox,[40]
for example, writes:

> The appropriate framework of discourse for describing and presenting
> deep ecology is not one that is fundamentally to do with the value of the
> non-human world, but rather one that is fundamentally to do with the
> nature and possibilities of the self or, we might say, the question of who we
> are, can become and should become in the larger scheme of things.

The word 'should' here suggests that values do attach to the broader biotic
community of which we are a part, but the means by which we discover
them depend fundamentally on the human capacity for 'self-realisation'

(as opposed to the narrower sense of 'ego-fulfilment' or 'self-realisation' as understood in bourgeois society) within rather than without nature. The 'deep ecology' literature here tacitly appeals to the notion of a 'human essence' or a 'human potentiality' (or, in Marx's language, a 'species being' whose qualities have yet to be fully realised) from which humanity has become fundamentally alienated (both actually and potentially) through separation from 'nature'. The desire to restore that lost connection (severed by modern technology, commodity production, a Promethean or utilitarian approach to nature, the 'community' of money flows, and the like) then lies at the root of an intuitive, contemplative and phenomenological search for 'self-realisation'. If values are 'socially and economically anchored,' Naess[41] argues, then the philosophical task is to challenge those instrumental values which alienate. Through 'elaboration of a philosophical system' we can arrive at a 'comprehensive value clarification and disentanglement', so as to spark a collective movement that can achieve 'a substantial reorientation of our whole civilisation'.

All sorts of philosophical, metaphysical and religious 'clarifications' are here available to us. Heidegger, for example, offers considerable sustenance to contemporary ecological thinking.[42] Interestingly, his fundamental objections to modernity not only echo arguments against the fetishism of commodities, but also capture much of the sensibility that informs a broad spectrum of ecological metaphysics:

> The object-character of technological dominion spreads itself over the earth ever more quickly, ruthlessly, and completely. Not only does it establish all things as producible in the process of production: it also delivers the products of production by means of the market. In self-assertive production, the humanness of man and the thingness of things dissolve into the calculated market value of a market which not only spans the whole earth as a world market, but also, as the will to will, trades in the nature of Being and thus subjects all beings to the trade of a calculation that dominates most tenaciously in those areas where there is no need of numbers.[43]

Heidegger's response to this condition, as indeed is characteristic of much of this wing of the ecological movement, is to withdraw entirely into a metaphysics of *Being* as a way of *dwelling* that unfolds into a form of *building* that cultivates, cherishes, protects, preserves and nurtures the environment so as to bring it closer to us. The political project is to recover that 'rootedness' of 'man' which 'is threatened today as its core'. Instead of nature becoming 'a gigantic gasoline station' it must be seen as 'the serving bearer, blossoming and fruiting, spreading out in rock and water, rising up into plant and animal'. Mortals, Heidegger concludes, 'dwell in that they save the earth' but 'saving does not only snatch something from danger. To save really means to set something free into its own presenting.' The slogans of Earth First (e.g. 'set the rivers free!'), while they do not derive from Heidegger, appeal to exactly such sentiments. All genuine works of art, Heidegger[44] goes on to argue, depend upon their rootedness in native soil and the way in which they are constructed in the spirit of dwelling. We are, he says, 'plants which – whether we like to admit it to ourselves or not – must with our roots rise out of the earth in order to bloom in the ether and bear fruit'. Dwelling is the capacity to achieve a spiritual unity between humans and things. Place construction should be about the recovery of roots, the recovery of the art of dwelling with nature.

Heidegger's 'ontological excavations' focus attention on 'a new way to speak about and care for our human nature and environment', so that 'love of place and the earth are scarcely sentimental extras to be indulged only when all technical and material problems have been resolved. They are part of being in the world and prior to all technical matters.'[45] The relationship proposed here is active not passive. 'Dwelling', writes Norberg-Schulz,[46] 'above all presupposes *identification* with the environment' so that the 'existential purpose of building (architecture) is therefore to make a site become a place, that is to uncover the meanings potentially present in the given environment'. Human beings 'receive' the environment and 'make its character manifest' in a place that simultaneously acquires and imprints back on us a particular identity.

Heidegger's ideas are paralleled by movements in North America towards a bioregional ethic, in which Leopold's recommendation that we enlarge the boundaries of community 'to include soils, waters, plants, and animals, or collectively: the land' is taken quite literally as a programme for living with nature in place. The ideals of a place-bound environmental identity are strong. Berg and Dasmann[47] say this means:

> Learning to live-in-place in an area that has been disrupted and injured through past exploitation. It involves becoming native to a place through becoming aware of particular ecological relationships that operate within and around it. It means understanding activities and evolving social behaviour that will enrich the life of that place, restore its life-supporting systems, and establish an ecologically and socially sustainable pattern of

existence within it. Simply stated it involves becoming fully alive in and with a place. It involves applying for membership in a biotic community and ceasing to be its exploiter.

Bioregionalism as a cultural movement therefore 'celebrates the particular, the unique and often indescribable features of a place. It celebrates this through the visual arts, music, drama and symbols which convey the feeling of place.'[48]

We arrive here at the core of what Goodin[49] calls a green theory of value. It is a set of sentiments and propositions which provides a 'unified moral vision' running, in various guises, throughout almost all ecological and green political thinking. It has radical, liberal and quite conservative manifestations as we shall shortly see. And by virtue of its strong attachment of moral community to the experience of place, it frequently directs environmental politics towards a preservation and enhancement of the achieved qualities of places.

But the notion of a moral community also proves problematic. Consider, for example, how it plays in the work of an otherwise thoroughly liberal commentator like Sagoff.[50] While individuals often act as purely self-interested and atomistically constituted economic agents selfishly pursuing their own goals, he argues they not only can but frequently do act in completely different ways as members of a 'moral community', particularly with respect to environmental issues. In the American case he concludes that:

> Social regulation most fundamentally has to do with the identity of a nation – a nation committed historically, for example, to appreciate and preserve a fabulous natural heritage and to pass it on reasonably undisturbed to future generations. This is not a question of what we want, it is not exactly a question of what we believe in; it is a question of what we are. There is no theoretical way to such a question: the answer has to do with our history, our destiny, and our self-perception as a people.[51]

A variety of points can be made here. First, this is a strongly communitarian version of the 'self-realisation' thesis advanced by Fox (see above). Secondly, it has as much to say about the construction of a nation's identity as it does about the environment. And here we immediately hit upon a difficulty with the moral suasion and political implications of distinctively green values. For they are inevitably implicated in the construction of particular kinds of 'moral community' that can just as easily be nationalist, exclusionary and in some instances violently fascistic as they can be democratic, decentralised and anarchist. Bramwell,[52] for example, points out the Nazi connection, not only via Heidegger (whose role is more emblematic than real) but also via the building of a distinctively fascist tradition around German romanticism, themes about 'Blood and Soil' and the like, incidentally noting the extensive and often innovative conservation and afforestation programmes that the Nazis pursued. Even if Bramwell overstates the case, it is not hard to see how distinctive attitudes to particular environments can become powerfully implicated in the building of any sense of nationalist or communitarian identity. Sagoff's insensitivity in using the term America when he means the United States and his tendency to depopulate the continent of indigenous peoples and to ignore its class, gender and racial structure in his account of the nation's encounter with the environment contains many of the same disturbing exclusions.

Environmental politics then becomes caught up in handing down to future generations a sense of national identity grounded in certain environmental traits. Put the other way round, nationalism without some appeal to environmental imagery and identity is a most unlikely configuration. If the forest is a symbol of the German nation, then forest die-back is a threat to national identity. This fact played a role in sparking the contemporary German Green movement but it has also posed considerable difficulty for that movement in pointing up the way contemporary ecological sensibilities have their roots in traditions that also prompted the Nazis to be the first 'radical environmentalists in charge of a state'.[53] Even an ecological radical like Spretnak[54] is then forced to recognise that 'the spiritual dimension of Green politics is an extremely charged and problematic area in West Germany'.

The point here is not to see all ideas about 'moral community', regionalism or place-bound thinking (e.g. nationalism and imagined community) as necessarily exclusionary or neo-Nazi. Raymond Williams, for example, builds elements of such thinking into his socialism. In his novels the whole contested terrain of environmental imagery, place-bound ideals and the disruption of both by contemporary capitalism become meaningful arguments about the roots of alienation and the problematics of the human relation to nature. The task, then, is to try and articulate the social, political, institutional and economic circumstances that transform such place-bound sentiments concerning a special relation to 'nature' into exclusionary and sometimes radical neo-Nazi directions. The evocation of the Nazi connection by Bramwell (though itself a manifestation of conservative hostility to the Greens as 'new authoritarians antagonistic to market liberalism') is here very helpful, since it raises the question of the degree to which strong leanings towards reactionary rather than progressive trajectories might always in the last instance be implicated in green theories of value. In any case, it quickly becomes apparent that environmental values drawn from a moral community have as much to say about the politics of community as they do about the environment.

Political values and environmental-ecological issues

One of the more interesting exercises to undertake in enquiring into the environmental-ecological debate is to inspect arguments not for what they have to say about the environment, but for what it is they say about the 'community' and political-economic organisation. In so doing, an impressive array of alternative forms of social organisation is invoked as seemingly 'necessary' to solve the issues at hand, along with an extraordinary display of disparate culprits and villains needing to be overthrown if our present ecodrama is to have a happy rather than tragic ending. 'Environmentalists', notes Paehlke,[55] not only 'occupy almost every position on the traditional right-to-left ideological spectrum', but also can adapt to diverse political positions while simultaneously claiming they are beyond politics in the normal sense. Yet, again and again, 'the authority of nature and her laws' is claimed either to justify the existing condition of society or 'to be the foundation stone of a new society that will solve ecological problems'.[56] What is often at stake in ecological and environmentalist arguments, Williams[57] suggests, 'is the ideas of different kinds of societies'.

Part of the problem here is that environmental-ecological arguments precisely because of their diversity and generality are open to a vast array of uses to which environmentalists and ecologists would almost certainly object. Their rhetoric gets mobilised for a host of special purposes, ranging from advertisements for Audi cars, toothpastes and supposedly 'natural' flavours (for foods) and 'natural' looks (mainly for women) to more specific targets of social control and investment in 'sustainable development' or 'nature conservation'. But the other side of that coin is that ecologists and to some degree even environmentalists of a more managerial persuasion tend to leave so many loopholes in their arguments, litter their texts with so many symptomatic silences, ambiguities and ambivalences, that it becomes almost impossible to pin down their socio-political programmes with any precision even though their aim may be 'nothing less than a revolution to overthrow our whole polluting, plundering and materialistic industrial society and, in its place, to create a new economic and social order which will allow human beings to live in harmony with the planet'.[58]

My intention in what follows is not to provide some firm classification or indeed to engage in critical evaluation of any particular kind of politics (all of them are open to serious objections), but to illustrate the incredible political diversity to which environmental-ecological opinion is prone.

1) Authoritarianism

Ophuls[59] writes: 'whatever its specific form, the politics of the sustainable society seem likely to move us along the spectrum from libertarianism towards authoritarianism', and we have to accept that 'the golden age of individualism, liberty and democracy is all but over'. Faced with escalating scarcities, Heilbroner[60] likewise argues, there is only one kind of solution: a social order 'that will blend a "religious" orientation and a "military" discipline [that] may be repugnant to us, but I suspect it offers the greatest promise for bringing about the profound and painful adaptations that the coming generations must make'. While their personal commitments are overtly liberal (and in Heilbroner's case socialistic) both authors reluctantly concede the necessity of some kind of centralised authoritarianism as a 'realistic' response to natural resource limits and the painful adaptations that such limits will inevitably force upon us. In the case of the strongly Malthusian wing of the ecological movement, and Garrett Hardin is probably the best representative, the appeal to authoritarian solutions is explicit as the only possible political solution to the 'tragedy of the commons'. Most of the writing in this genre presumes that resource scarcities (and consequent limits to growth) and population pressure lie at the heart of the environmental-ecological issue. Since these issues were paramount in the early 1970s, this style of argument was then also at its height. In recent years, however, authoritarian solutions to the environmental crisis have been abandoned by the movement.[61] But there is always an authoritarian edge somewhere in ecological politics.

2) Corporate and state managerialism

A weak version of the authoritarian solution rests upon the application of techniques of scientific-technical rationality within an administrative state armed with strong regulatory and bureaucratic powers in liaison with 'big' science and big corporate capital. The centrepiece of the argument here is that our definition of many ecological problems such as acid rain, the ozone hole, global warming, pesticides in the food chain, etc., is necessarily science-led and that solutions equally depend upon the mobilisation of scientific expertise and corporate technological skills embedded within a rational (state-led) process of political-economic decision-making. 'Ecological modernisation'[62] is the ideological watchword for such a politics. Conservation and environmental regulation (at global as well as at national scale) would here be interpreted as both rational and efficient resource management for a sustainable future. Certain sectors of corporate capital, particularly those who stand to benefit from providing the technology necessary for global monitoring of planetary health, find the imagery of global management or 'planetary medicine' very attractive. For example, IBM has taken the lead in the 'greening' of corporate politics, since it will likely play a leading role in providing the technology for global monitoring. 'Sustainability' here applies, it seems, as much to corporate power as to the ecosystem.

3) Pluralistic liberalism

Democratic rights and freedoms (particularly of speech and opinion) are sometimes regarded as essential to ecological politics precisely because of the difficulty of defining in any omniscient or omnipotent way what a proper environmental-ecological policy might be. Open and perpetual negotiation over environmental-ecological issues in a society where diverse pressure groups (such as Greenpeace) are allowed to flourish is seen as the only way to assure that the environmental issue is always kept on the agenda. Whoever wants to speak for or about 'nature' can, and institutions are created (such as environmental impact statements and environmental law) to permit contestation over the 'rights of trees and owls'. Consensus about environmental issues, and therefore the best bet for environmental protection, can best be reached only after complex negotiation and power plays between a variety of interest groups. But consensus is at best only a temporary moment in a deeply contested and pluralistic politics concerning the values to be attributed to nature and how to view ecological change.

4) Conservativism

In some of the ecological literature the principle of prudence and respect for tradition plays a leading role. Human adaptations to and of natural environments have been arrived at over centuries and should not be unnecessarily disturbed. Conservation and preservation of existing landscapes and usages, sometimes argued for by explicit appeal to aesthetic judgements, give such a framework a conservative ring.[63] But arguments of this sort have a radical edge. They can be strongly anti-capitalist (against development) and, when placed in an international setting, they can also be strongly anti-imperialist. Tradition ought presumably to be respected everywhere, so that all-out modernisation is always regarded as problematic. Considerable sympathy can then be extended towards, say, indigenous peoples under siege from commodification and exchange relations. All of this has its romantic side, but it can also produce a hard-headed politics of place that is highly protective of a given environment. The issue is not non-intervention in the environment, but preservation of traditional modes of social and environmental interaction precisely because these have been found in some sense or other to work, at least for some (usually but not always elite) groups. The preservation of the political power and values of such groups is just as important here, of course, as environmental considerations.

5) Moral community

The complex issues which arise when ideals of 'moral community' are invoked have already been examined. Many 'communities' evolve some rough consensus as to what their moral obligations are with respect to modes of social relating as well as to ways of behaving with respect to the 'rights of nature'.[64] While often contested, by virtue of the internal heterogeneity of the community or because of pressure towards social change, these moral precepts concerning, for example, the relation to nature (expressed increasingly in the field of 'environmental ethics') can become an important ideological tool in the attempt to forge community solidarities (nationalist sentiments) and to gain empowerment. This is the space par excellence of moral debate[65] on environmental issues coupled with the articulation of communitarian politics and values that centre on ideals of civic virtues that carry over to certain conceptions of a virtuous relation to nature.

6) Ecosocialism

While there is a definite tendency in socialist circles to look upon environmentalism as a middle-class and bourgeois issue and to regard proposals for zero growth and constraints on consumption with intense suspicion[66] there are enough overlaps in enough areas to make ecosocialism a feasible political project (though it is still a relatively minor current within most mainstream socialist movements). Some environmental issues, such as occupational health and safety, are of intense concern to workers, while many ecological groups accept that environmental problems can be 'traced back to the capitalist precept that the choice of production technology is to be governed solely by private interest in profit maximisation of market share'.[67] 'If we want ecological sanity,' assert Haila and Levins,[68] 'we have to struggle for social justice.' This means social control of production technology and the means of production, control over the 'accumulation for accumulation's sake, production for production's sake' capitalist system which lies at the root of many environmental issues, and a recognition that 'the future of humanity simply cannot build on pleasant life for a few and suffering for the majority'.[69] This places the environmental issue firmly within the socialist orbit. Those socialists[70] who accept that there is an ecological crisis then argue that a second route to socialism is available; one that highlights the contradiction between the social organisation of production and the (ecological) conditions of production, rather than class contradictions. The necessity for socialism is then in part given because only in such a society can thorough, enduring and socially just solutions be found to environmental issues.

7) Ecofeminism
The nature–nurture controversy has been nowhere more thoroughly debated than in the feminist movement, and in ecofeminism we find a diverse set of opinions on how to connect the environmental-ecological issue with feminist politics. In radical ecofeminism, for example, the devaluation and degradation of nature are seen as deeply implicated in the parallel devaluation and degradation of women. The political response is to celebrate rather than deny the web-like interrelations between women and nature through the development of rituals and symbolism as well as an ethic of caring, nurturing and procreation. In this equation, the feminism is as prominent, if not more so, than the ecology, and solutions to ecological problems are seen as dependent upon the acceptance of feminist principles.

8) Decentralised communitarianism
Most contemporary ecological movements, Dobson[71] argues, eschew authoritarian solutions on principle and 'argue for a participatory form of society in which discussion takes place and explicit consent is asked for and given across the widest possible range of political and social issues'. Their politics generally derive inspiration from 'the self-reliant community modelled on anarchist lines',[72] and writers like Bookchin, Goldsmith and a host of others (including the German Green party) have tried to articulate the form of social relations which should prevail within such self-reliant communities that could become, by virtue of their scale, 'closer' to nature. Egalitarianism, non-hierarchical forms of organisation and widespread local empowerment and participation in decision-making are depicted as the political norm.[73] Decentralisation and community empowerment, coupled with a certain degree of bioregionalism, are then seen as the only effective solution to an alienated relation to nature and alienation in social relationships.

The array of ecological politics I have here outlined must be supplemented, however, by an ever vaster and much more complex array of special pleading, in which environmental-ecological issues or requirements are invoked for very particular social purposes. Scientists, for example, hungry for funding as well as for attention, may create environmental issues that reflect as much about the political economy and sociology of science as they do about the condition of the environment. Robert May,[74] a Royal Society Research Professor writing on the evident urgency of taking measures to conserve biological diversity, focuses, for example, as much on the underfunding of taxonomy (relative to physics) as on how to define the importance of, or deal with, loss of biodiversity. While on the one hand scientific ignorance is clearly a barrier to proper identification of what the relevant issues or solutions might be, self-serving claims for more funding deservedly provoke scepticism.

Jacks and Whyte[75] provide another and even more insidious example. Writing in 1939, these two highly respected soil scientists, deeply concerned about soil erosion in Africa, argued that:

> A feudal type of society in which the native cultivators would be to some extent tied to the lands of their European overlords seems the most generally suited to meet the needs of the soil in the present state of African development. Africa cannot be expected to accept feudalism without a struggle: in parts of British Africa it would mean jettisoning the promising experiment of Indirect Rule, everywhere it would mean denying to the natives some of the liberty and opportunities for material advancement to which their labours should entitle them. But it would enable the people who have been the prime cause of erosion and who have the means and ability to control it to assume responsibility for soil. Self-interest, untrammelled by fears of native rivalry, would ensure that responsibility was carried out in ultimate interests of soil. At present, humanitarian considerations for natives prevent Europeans from winning the attainable position of dominance over the soil. Humanity may perhaps be the higher ideal, but the soil demands a dominant, and if white men will not and black men cannot assume the position, the vegetation will do so, by process of erosion finally squeezing out the whites.

Both blunt and startling, this statement illustrates how, in the name of the environment, all kinds of restrictions should be put upon the rights of 'others' while conferring rights (and obligations) on those who supposedly have the knowledge and the high technology to control the problem. While few would now dare to be so blatant, there is a strong strain of this kind of thinking in World Bank arguments and even in such a seemingly progressive document as the Brundtland Report. Control over the resources of others, in the name of planetary health, sustainability of preventing environmental degradation, is never too far from the surface of many Western proposals for global environmental management. Awareness of precisely that potentiality stimulates a good deal of resistance in developing countries to any form of environmentalism emanating from the West.

Similar issues arise whenever the environmental-ecological issues get converted into aesthetic questions. The special issue of *Fortune* devoted to the environment in 1970, for example, contained a strong argument for the redevelopment of the downtowns of the USA, along what we would now call 'postmodern' lines, invoking environmental quality (usually depicted as user-friendly and as tree-lined or waterfront spaces) as its primary goal. The whole contemporary 'culture of nature', as Wilson[76] calls it, is a very culti-vated and hard-sold taste, that is in the end all about nature as a commodity.

A cynical observer might be tempted to conclude that discussion of the envi-ronmental issue is nothing more than a covert way of introducing particular social and political projects by raising the spectre of an ecological crisis or of legitimising solutions by appeal to the authority of nature-imposed necessity. I would want, however, to draw a somewhat broader conclusion: all ecological projects (and arguments) are simultaneously political-economic projects (and arguments) and vice versa. Ecological arguments are never socially neutral any more than socio-political arguments are ecologically neutral. Looking more closely at the way ecology and politics interrelate then becomes impera-tive if we are to get a better handle on how to approach questions.

The political economy of socio-ecological projects

There is an extraordinarily rich record of the historical geography of socio-ecological change that sheds much light on the ways in which socio-political and ecological projects intertwine with and at some point become indistin-guishable from each other. The archive of such materials from archaeology,[77] anthropology,[78] geography[79] and more recently history[80] is extensive indeed. Yet much of the contemporary debate on environmental-ecological issues, for all of its surface devotion to ideals of multidisciplinarity and 'depth', operates as if these materials either do not exist or, if they do, exist only as a repository of anecdotal evidence in support of particular claims. Systematic work is relatively rare and that which does exist[81] has not been anywhere near as central to discussion as it should. The debate now arising within Marxism – between, for example, Benton[82] and Grundmann[83] – operates at a level of historical-geographical abstraction that is most un-Marxist. Even a journal like *Capitalism, Socialism, Nature*, set up to explore green issues from a socialist perspective, is long on theory and anecdotal evidence and short on attempts to systematise across the historical-geographical record.

An impressionistic survey illustrates well how societies strive to create ecological conditions for themselves which are not only conducive to their own survival but also both manifestations and instanciations 'in nature' of their particular social relations. Since no society can accomplish such a task without encountering unintended ecological consequences, the contradiction between social and ecological change can become highly problematic, even from time to time putting the very survival of the society concerned at risk. This latter point was made long ago by Engels:

> Let us not, however, flatter ourselves overmuch on account of our human victories over nature. For each such victory nature takes its revenge on us. Each victory, it is true, in the first place brings about the results we expected, but in the second and third places it has quite different, unforeseen effects which only too often cancel the first ... Thus at every step we are reminded that we by no means rule over nature like a conqueror a foreign people, like someone standing outside of nature – but that we, with flesh, blood and brain, belong to nature, and exist in its midst, and that all our mastery of it consists in fact that we have the advantage over all other creatures of being able to learn its laws and apply them correctly.

This implies the sheer necessity of always taking the duality of social and ecological change seriously. The historian Cronon[84] argues, for example, that:

> An ecological history begins by assuming a dynamic and changing relationship between environment and culture, one as apt to produce contradictions as continuities. Moreover, it assumes that the interactions of the two are dialectical. Environment may initially shape the range of choices available to a people at a given moment but then culture reshapes environment responding to those choices. The reshaped environment presents a new set of possibilities for cultural reproduction, thus setting up a new cycle of mutual determination. Changes in the way people create and re-create their livelihood must be analysed in terms of changes not only in their social relations but in their ecological ones as well.

All of which is another way of stating Marx and Engels's[85] adage that the 'antithesis between nature and history is created' only when 'the relation of man to nature is excluded from history'. Cronon's study of colonial settlements in New England raises another issue, however. It shows how an environment that was the product of more than 10,000 years of Indian occupation and forest use (promoting, through burning, the forest edge conditions which tend to be so species diverse and rich) was misread by the settlers as pristine, virginal, rich and underutilised by indigenous peoples. The implantation of European institutions of governance and property rights (coupled with distinctively European aspirations towards accumulation of wealth) wrought, furthermore, an ecological transformation of such enormity that indigenous populations were deprived of the ecological basis for their way of life. The annihilation of that way of life (and thereby of Indian peoples) was, therefore, as much an ecological as a military or political event. In part this had to do with the introduction of new disease regimes (smallpox in particular) but changes in and on the land also make it impossible to sustain a nomadic and highly flexible indigenous mode of production and reproduction.

One path towards consolidation of a particular set of social relations, therefore, is to undertake an ecological transformation which requires the reproduction of those social relations in order to sustain it. Worster[86] doubtless exaggerates in his flamboyant projection onto the American West of Wittfogel's theses on the relation between large-scale irrigation schemes and despotic forms of government, but his basic argument is surely correct. Once the original proposals for a communitarian, decentralised, 'bio-regional', river-basin-confined settlement system for the American West, drawn up by the geologist John Wesley Powell at the end of the nineteenth century, were rejected by a Congress dominated by large-scale corporate interests (Powell being thoroughly vilified in the process), those interests sought to assure their own reproduction through construction of dams, mega-water projects of all sorts and vast transformations of the Western ecosystem. Sustaining such a grandiose ecological project came to depend crucially upon the creation and maintenance of centralised state powers and certain class relations (the formation and perpetuation, for example, of large-scale agribusiness and an oppressed landless agrarian proletariat). The consequent subversion of the Jeffersonian dream of agrarian democracy has ever since created intense contradictions in the body politic of states like California.[87] But here another implication (notably absent in much of Cronon's work) follows: contradictions in the social relations (in Worster's case of class, but gender, religion, etc., can also be just as significant) entail social contradictions on the land

and within ecosystemic projects themselves. Not only do the rich occupy privileged niches in the habitat while the poor tend to work and live in the more toxic and hazardous zones, but the very design of the transformed ecosystem is redolent of its social relations. Conversely, projects set up in purely ecological terms – one thinks of the so-called 'green revolution', for example – have all manner of distributive and social consequences (in the green revolution case the concentration of landholdings in a few hands and the creation of a landless agrarian proletariat).

Created ecosystems tend to both instanciate and reflect, therefore, the social systems that gave rise to them. They do so, however, in contradictory and unstable ways. This simple principle ought to weigh much more heavily than it does upon all angles of environmental-ecological debate. It is a principle which Lewontin[88] argues has been forgotten as much in biology as in social science:

> We cannot regard evolution as the 'solution' by species of predetermined environmental 'problems' because it is the life activities of the species themselves that determine both the problems and solutions simultaneously ... Organisms within their individual lifetimes and in the course of their evolution as a species do not adapt to environments; they construct them. They are not simply objects of the laws of nature, altering themselves to the inevitable, but active subjects transforming nature according to its laws.

It is pure idealism, for example, to suggest that we can somehow abandon in a relatively costless way the immense existing ecosystemic structures of, say, contemporary capitalistic urbanisation in order to 'get back close to nature'. The systems that now exist are a reworked form of 'second nature' that cannot be allowed to deteriorate or collapse without courting ecological disaster for our own species. Their proper management (and in this I include their long-term socialistic or ecological transformation into something completely different) may require transitional political institutions, hierarchies of power relations and systems of governance that could well be anathema to both ecologists and socialists alike. But this occurs because, in a fundamental sense, there is nothing unnatural about New York City and sustaining such an ecosystem even in transition entails an inevitable compromise with the forms of social organisation and social relations which produced it.

To term urbanisation a 'created ecosystem' may sound somewhat odd.

But human activity cannot be viewed as external to ecosystemic projects. To view it so makes no more sense than trying to study pollination without bees or the pre-colonial ecosystem of the north-eastern USA without the beaver. Human beings, like all other organisms, are 'active subjects transforming nature according to its laws' and are always in the course of adapting to the ecosystems they themselves construct. It is fundamentally mistaken, therefore, to speak of the impact of society on the ecosystem as if these are two separate systems in interaction with each other. The typical manner of depicting the world around us in terms of a box labelled 'society' in interaction with a box labelled 'environment' not only makes little intuitive sense (try drawing the boundary between the boxes in your own daily life) but it also has no fundamental theoretical or historical justification.

Money flows and commodity movements, for example, have to be regarded as fundamental to contemporary ecosystems, not only because of the accompanying geographical transfer of plant and animal species from one environment to another[89] but also because these flows form a coordinating network that keeps contemporary ecosystems reproducing and changing in the particular way they do. If these flows ceased tomorrow, then the disruption within the world's ecosystems would be enormous. And as the flows shift and change their character, so the creative impulses embedded in any socio-ecological system will also shift and change in ways that may be stressful, contradictory or harmonic as the case may be. Here, too, Cronon's[90] consideration of Chicago as a city operating as a fundamental exchange point between and transformative influence within the ecosystems of North America provides an interesting case study. It in effect translates and extends Smith's theses[91] concerning 'the production of nature' through commodity exchange and capital accumulation into a detailed historical-geographical narrative.

The category 'environmental or ecological movement' may also for this reason be a misnomer, particularly when applied to resistances of indigenous peoples to ecological change. Such resistances may not be based, as many in the West might suppose, upon some deep inner need to preserve a distinctive and unalienated relation to nature or to keep intact valued symbols of ancestry and the like, but upon a much clearer recognition that an ecological transformation imposed from outside (as happened in colonial New England or as has more recently happened to rubber tappers in the Amazon) will destroy indigenous modes of production as well as their distinctive forms of social organisation. Guha,[92] for example, in his study of the Chipko 'tree-hugging' movement in the Himalayas against commercial logging and high-tech forest yield management, shows that the 'most celebrated "environmental" movement in the Third World is viewed by its participants as being above all a *peasant* movement in defence of traditional rights in the forest, and only secondarily, if at all, an "environmental" or "feminist" movement'. Yet, to the degree that a 'homogenising urban-industrial culture' is generating its own distinctive forms of ecological and cultural contradictions and crises, the Chipko, precisely by virtue of their ecological practices, 'represent one of the most innovative responses to the ecological and cultural crisis of modern society'.[93]

Indigenous groups can, however, also be totally unsentimental in their ecological practices. It is largely a Western construction, heavily influenced by the romantic reaction to modern industrialism, which leads many to the view that they were and continue to be somehow 'closer to nature' than we are (even Guha, it seems to me, at some point falls into this trap). Faced with the ecological vulnerability often associated with such 'proximity to nature', indigenous groups can transform both their practices and their views of nature with startling rapidity. Furthermore, even when armed with all kinds of cultural traditions and symbolic gestures that indicate deep respect for the spirituality in nature, they can engage in extensive ecosystemic transformations that undermine their ability to continue with a given mode of production. The Chinese may have ecologically sensitive traditions of Tao, Buddhism and Confucianism (traditions of thought which have played an important role in promoting an 'ecological consciousness' in the West) but the historical geography of de-forestation, land degradation, river erosion and flooding in China contains not a few environmental events which would be regarded as catastrophes by modern-day standards. Archaeological evidence likewise suggests that late-ice-age hunting groups hunted many of their prey to extinction, while fire must surely rate as one of the most far-reaching agents of ecological transformation ever acquired, allowing very small groups to exercise immense ecosystemic influence, not always, as Sauer[94] points out, for the better.

The point here is not to argue that there is nothing new under the sun about the ecological disturbance generated by human activities, but to assess what exactly is new and unduly stressful, given the unprecedented rapidity and scale of contemporary socio-ecological transformations. But historical-geographical enquiries of this sort also put in perspective those claims typically advanced by some ecologists that once upon a time 'people everywhere knew how to live in harmony with the natural world'[95] and lead us to view with scepticism Bookchin's[96] equally dubious claim that 'a relatively self-sufficient community, visibly dependent on its environment for the means of life, would gain a new respect for the organic interrelationships that sustain it'. Much contemporary 'ecologically conscious' rhetoric pays far too much attention to what indigenous groups say without looking at what they do. We cannot conclude, for example, that native Indian practices are ecologically superior to ours from statements such as those of Luther Standing Bear that:

> We are of the soil and the soil of us. We love the birds and the beasts that grew with us on this soil. They drank the same water as we did and breathed the same air. We are all one in nature. Believing so, there was in our hearts a great peace and a welling kindness for all living, growing things.[97]

Such an inference would require belief in either some external and spiritual guidance to ensure ecologically 'right' outcomes, or an extraordinary omniscience in indigenous or pre-capitalistic judgements and practices in a dynamic field of action that is plagued by all manner of unintended consequences. 'The possibility of over-exploitation of a resource is perfectly compatible with our notion of peoples living close to nature, observing and acting accordingly.'[98] Furthermore, 'comparative studies have suggested that all high civilisations that incorporated intensification strategies were metastable and that their growth trajectories can be interpreted as those of accelerating energy extraction, to the point that both the ecosystem and the socioeconomic structures were stretched to capacity, with steady or declining absolute caloric productivity and input-output ratios'.[99] How capitalism has hitherto escaped such a fate is a long drawn-out story. All societies have had their share of ecologically based difficulties and, as Butzer goes on to assert, we have much to learn from studying them.

Indigenous or pre-capitalist practices are not, therefore, necessarily superior or inferior to our own just because such groups espouse respect for nature rather than the modern 'Promethean' attitude of domination or mastery.[100] Grundmann[101] is surely correct in his argument *contra* Benton[102] that the thesis of 'mastery over nature' (laying aside its gendered overtones for the moment) does not necessarily entail destructiveness; it can just as easily lead to loving, caring and nurturing practices. Uncritical acceptance of 'ecologically conscious'-sounding statements can, furthermore, be politically misleading. Luther Standing Bear prefaced the thoughts cited above with the very political argument that 'this land of the great plains is claimed by the

Lakota as their very own'. Native Indians may well have strong claims to land rights, but the creation of an 'ecologically conscious' rhetoric to support them is, as we have already argued, a familiar but dangerous practice of special pleading for another purpose.

We can, in the same vein, turn a critical eye upon the ideological, aesthetic and 'ecologically conscious' traditions through which the whole relation to nature is approached. Glacken's[103] monumental *Traces on the Rhodian Shore* well illustrates some of the twists and turns that the history of the idea of nature has taken in a variety of geographical contexts from the Greeks until the end of the eighteenth century. While he is not directly interested in how changes in such ideas connected to or might even have shaped the actual course of political-economic change, the connection is always tacitly present. In this regard even Marx was willing to countenance the way in which ideas could become a 'material force' for historical change when embedded in social practices. For this reason it appears vital to look upon ideas as well as practices in terms of the conflation of ecological and social projects.

In recent years, for example, we find Wordsworth at the centre of an interesting debate. On the one hand Bate[104] interprets him as a pioneer of 'romantic ecology', a purely 'green' writer whose concerns for restoring a relation to nature have been written out of discussion by those like McGann[105] who see him solely as an apologist for certain class relations. In a sense, the debate misses the point. Wordsworth was seriously both at the same time. Even Bate is in no doubt that Wordsworth sought to recover or reconstitute as part and parcel of his ecologism a certain set of social relations. His tourist-guide genre of writing invited nature to be paternalistically consumed (in ultimately destructive ways, as contemporary visitors to the Lake District soon find) through the production of what Urry[106] calls 'the tourist gaze'. Contemporary British practices in relation to the consumption of nature as a cultural spectacle owe a great deal to the ideas and practices that Wordsworth pioneered.

Inspection of the historical-geographical record thus reveals much about why words like 'nature' and 'environment' contain 'such an extraordinary amount of human history'.[107] The intertwinings of social and ecological projects in daily practices as well as in the realms of ideology, representations, aesthetics and the like are such as to make every social (including literary or artistic) project a project about nature, environment and ecosystem, and vice versa. Such a proposition should not, surely, be too hard for those working in the historical materialist tradition to swallow. Marx argued, after all, that we can discover who and what we are (our species potential, even) only through transforming the world around us and in so doing put the dialectics of social and ecological change at the centre of all human history. But how should that dialectic be understood?

The Cartesian trap

There are manifest dangers in imposing, as Engels did, a simple dialectical logic upon 'nature'. Yet the contemporary ecological literature is full of dialectical and quasi-dialectical modes of argumentation that parallel those that Marx practised. For this reason, there is, as Eckersley[108] points out, 'a much greater potential for theoretical synthesis' between 'ecocentrism and communitarian and socialist political philosophies than there is between ecocentrism and individualistic political philosophies such as liberalism'. I here want to take up briefly the implications of the vigorous denunciations within the ecological literature of the ontological presuppositions of Descartes, Newton and Locke and the reductionist (non-dialectical) forms of natural and social science (particularly economics) to which those ontological presuppositions give rise.[109] Ecological theory typically turns to quantum theory (Heisenberg, Bohr and David Bohm figure large in their writings) and various forms of ecological science for a quite different set of ontological propositions.

The Cartesian system to which ecologists object presupposes that there can be a strict separation between *res cogitans* and *res extensa* (between mind and body, fact and value, 'is' and 'ought') and that the materiality scientists study is no more affected by the scientific knowledge generated in the mind than the mind is affected in its capacity to represent 'objectively' by the materiality studied. Cartesianism, furthermore, builds a detailed picture of a universe structured according to certain basic principles. It presumes the existence of a 'natural' and self-evident set of entities (individuals or things) that 'are homogeneous within themselves, at least insofar as they affect the whole of which they are parts'. Such entities can be individuated (identified) in terms of an externally given and absolute space and time (this is the Newtonian presumption which carries over, as we have already seen, to the social theory of John Locke and contemporary economics). The entities are, furthermore, 'ontologically prior to the whole' and parts (individuals) 'have intrinsic properties, which they possess in isolation'. The whole (a society or an ecosystem) is nothing but the sum (or in complex cases a multiple) of its parts. Relations between entities are, furthermore, clearly separable from the entities themselves. The study of relations is then a study of the contingent way in which entities (e.g. billiard balls or people) collide. This poses the problem of the 'prime cause' and leads to the Cartesian–Newtonian vision of the universe as a clock-like mechanism which God wound up and set in motion. In this mode of thought, 'causes are separate effects, causes being the properties of subjects, and effects the properties of objects. While causes may respond to information coming from effects (so-called "feedback loops"), there is no ambiguity about which is causing subject and which is caused object.'[110]

This Cartesian view is widespread and it has proved an extraordinarily powerful device for generating knowledge and understanding of how the universe works. It also has intuitive appeal. We encounter 'things' (e.g. individuals) and systems (e.g. transport and communication nets) which appear to have a stable and self-evident existence so that it appears perfectly reasonable to build knowledge upon categorisations of them and upon the pattern of causal relations between them.

From the dialectical point of view, however, this is to look at matters in an unduly restrictive one-sided way. Levins and Lewontin call the Cartesian view 'alienated' because it depicts a world in which 'parts are separated from wholes and reified as things in themselves, causes separated from effects, subjects separated from objects'. Marx was similarly critical of the 'common sense' view which whenever 'it succeeds in seeing a distinction it fails to see a unity, and where it sees a unity it fails to see a distinction'.[111] He would, doubtless, be equally scathing about the atomistic and causative reasoning which dominates in contemporary economics and sociology, the methodological individualism which pervades much of current political (including Marxist) philosophy, and the like.

Perhaps the most characteristic form that Cartesian thinking takes in the environmental field is to view 'society' as a bounded system in interaction with another bounded system called the 'biosphere'. Our present sense of environmental problems is then defined broadly in terms of the complex and problematic relations between these two systems. It is, in practice, hard to see where 'society' begins and 'nature' ends (try looking around you and figuring where the boundary lies), but even as an act of abstraction this configuration of thought looks precisely to be the product of alienated reason, having no historical or well-grounded scientific justification. And there is a strong consensus in the ecological literature that this convention together with its basis in a Cartesian form of reasoning is not only profoundly anti-ecological in itself but also, through its effects on social practices, the root of many of our ecological problems. If this is so, then analytical and rational-choice Marxism, methodological individualism and perhaps even Marxist realism (though Bhaskar is now seeking to incorporate dialectics into his arguments) are also profoundly anti-ecological by virtue of their broadly Cartesian ontology. The debate between Grundmann and Benton on Marxism and ecology would then appear to be an argument based on fundamentally flawed ontological presuppositions.

Dialectics

The alternative to the Cartesian–Newtonian–Lockean view is a dialectical ontology which can unify the Marxist tradition with the emerging consensus about appropriate ontology in ecological theory. This might be through elaboration of the following propositions:

1. Dialectical thinking prioritises the understanding of processes, flows, fluxes and relations over the analysis of elements, things, structures and organised systems. The latter do not exist outside of the processes that support, give rise to or create them. Money – a thing – cannot be understood outside of the processes of exchange and capital flow that support it, any more than organisms can be understood outside of the environmental relationships that constitute them.[112] Capital in Marx's definition is both the process of circulation and the stock of assets ('things' like commodities, money, production apparatus). Quantum theory similarly states that 'the same entity (e.g. an electron) behaves under one set of circumstances as a wave, and in another set of circumstances as a particle'.[113] Yet it took many years for physicists to recognise that these two conceptions were not incommensurable or mutually exclusive. Only when they did so could modern quantum theory begin to take shape. It has likewise proved very difficult for social scientists to abandon what Ollman[114] calls the 'common sense view' erected into a philosophical system by Locke, Hume and others – that 'there are things and there are relations, and that neither can be subsumed in the other'.

2. 'Things' are as a consequence always assumed 'to be internally heterogeneous at every level' by virtue of the processes and relations that constitute them.[115] A number of consequences then follow. Firstly, any 'thing' can be decomposed into a collection of 'other things' which are in some relation to each other. For example, a city can be considered a 'thing' in interrelation with other cities, but it can also be broken down into neighbourhoods which can in turn be broken down into people, houses, schools,

factories, etc., which can in turn be broken down ad infinitum. There are, consequently, no irreducible building blocks of 'things' for any theoretical reconstruction of how the world works. What looks like a system at one level (e.g. a city or a pond) becomes a part at another level (e.g. a global network of world cities or a continental ecosystem). There can be, as Levins and Lewontin[116] put it, 'no basement' to enquiry since experience shows that 'all previously proposed undecomposable "basic units" turn out to be decomposable, and the decomposition has opened up new domains for investigation and practice'. The implication is that it is legitimate to investigate 'each level of organisation without having to search for fundamental units'. But this then poses a particular problem for enquiry: it is crucial to establish the scale (usually spatial and temporal) at which processes, things and systems are operative, for what is relevant at one scale (e.g. the pond) may not be so at another (e.g. the continent). Secondly, if all 'things' are internally heterogeneous by virtue of the complex process (or relations) which constitute them, then the only way we can understand the qualitative and quantitative attributes of 'things' is by understanding the very processes and relations which they internalise. We here find a very strong identity between Ollmann's[117] construction of the Marxian dialectic as internal relations and the ecological arguments set out by Eckersley,[118] Birch and Cobb,[119] Naess[120] and Zimmerman.[121] There is, however, a limitation to be put upon this argument. I, as an individual, do not in practice internalise everything in the universe, but absorb mainly what is relevant to me through my relationships (metabolic, social, political, cultural, etc.) to processes operating over a relatively bounded field (my ecosystem, economy, culture, etc.). There is no fixed or a priori boundary to this system. Where my relevant environment begins and ends is itself a function of what I do and the ecological, economic and other processes which are relevant to that. Here, too, setting boundaries with respect to space, time, scale and environment becomes a major strategic consideration in the development of concepts, abstractions and theories.

3. Space and time are neither absolute nor external to processes but are contingent and contained within them. There are multiple spaces and times (and space-times) implicated in different physical,

biological and social processes. The latter all produce – to use Lefebvre's[122] terminology – their own forms of space and time. Processes do not operate in but actively construct space and time and in so doing define distinctive scales for their development.

4. Parts and wholes are mutually constitutive of each other. There is more to this than a mere feedback loop between thing-like entities. As, for example, I capture powers that reside in those ecological and economic systems that are relevant to me, I actively reconstitute or transform them within myself even before I project them back to reconstitute or transform the system from which they were initially derived (again, to take a trivial example, I breathe in, I reconstitute myself by virtue of the oxygen I transform within me, and I breathe out and transform the atmosphere around me). Reductionist practices 'typically ignore this relationship, isolating parts as preexisting units of which wholes are then composed' while some holistic practices reverse the preferential treatment.[123]

5. The interdigitation of parts and wholes entails 'the interchangeability of subject and object, of cause and effect'.[124] Organisms, for example, have to be looked at as both the subjects and the objects of evolution in exactly the same way that individuals have to be considered as both subjects and objects of processes of social change. The reversibility of cause and effect renders causally specified models (even when endowed with feedback loops) suspect. In practice, dialectical reasoning, precisely by virtue of its embeddedness in and representation of the flow of continuous processes, makes limited appeal to cause and effect argument.

6. 'Change is a characteristic of all systems and all aspects of all systems.'[125] This is perhaps the most important of all dialectical principles and one which Ollman[126] prioritises above all else. The implication is that change and instability are the norm and that the stability of 'things' or systems is what has to be explained. In Ollman's[127] words, 'given that change is always a part of what things are, [our] research problem [can] only be how, when, and into what [things or systems] change and why they sometimes appear not to change'.

7. Transformative behaviour – 'creativity' – arises out of the complementarities and contradictions which attach both to the internalised heterogeneity of 'things' and out of the more obvious

heterogeneity present within systems. It is therefore omnipresent within the physical, biological and social worlds. This does not mean, however, that all moments within some continuous process are equally significant at a particular scale for understanding change or stability. The theoretical and empirical research task is to identify those characteristic 'moments', 'forms' and 'things' embedded within continuous flows which can produce radical transformations or, on the other hand, give a system qualities of identity, integrity and relative stability. The question of 'agency' in social and biological as well as in physical systems has to be formulated broadly in these terms.

8. Dialectical enquiry is not itself outside of its own form of argumentation but subject to it. Dialectical enquiry is a process that produces things in the form of concepts, abstractions, theories and all manner of institutionalised forms of knowledge which stand in their own right only to be supported or undermined by the continuing processes of enquiry. There is, furthermore, a certain relationship implied between the researcher and the researched, a relationship which is not construed in terms of an 'outsider' (the researcher) looking in on the researched as an object, but one between two subjects each of which necessarily internalises something from the other by virtue of the processes that operate. Observation of the world is, Heisenberg argued, inevitably intervention in the world, in much the same way that deconstructionists will argue that the reading of a text is fundamental to its production. Marx similarly insisted that only by transforming the world could we transform ourselves and that it is impossible to understand the world without simultaneously changing it as well as ourselves. This principle renders the duality of anthropocentrism and ecocentrism into a false opposition (in exactly the same way that feminist theory, perpetually forced back to discuss the relation between nature and nurture, has broadly concluded – see Fuss[128] – that the supposed opposition between essentialism and social constructivism is false because both are essential to each other). Dialectics cannot be superimposed on the world as an act of mind over matter (this was Engels's critical mistake, unfortunately replicated by Levins and Lewontin). The underlying unity of theory and praxis can, it seems, never be broken, only attenuated or temporarily alienated. Here lies, I would

suggest, the true path towards that transcendence of the opposition that Benton[129] seeks.

9. Eduction – the exploration of potentialities for change, for realisation, for the construction of new totalities (e.g. social ecosystems) and the like – rather than deduction or induction is, as Bookchin insists, the central motif of dialectical praxis. Dialectical enquiry necessarily incorporates, therefore, the building of ethical, moral and political choices into its own process and sees the constructed knowledges that result as discourses situated in a play of power. Values, for example, are not imposed as universal abstractions from outside but arrived at through a process of enquiry embedded in forms of praxis and plays of power attaching to the exploration of this or that potentiality (in ourselves as well as in the world we inhabit). To the degree that a distinctively 'green value theory' has arisen in recent years, it must be seen as the product of ecological processes and plays of power.

There is, evidently, a remarkable commonality of the dialectics (as both ontology and epistemology) present in Marx's argumentation in, say, *Capital* (and as set out by Ollman[130]) and those proffered, in one form or another, across a fairly wide spectrum of ecological writings. This commonality has not passed unnoticed,[131] nor can it be regarded as unproblematic.[132] But it has not been creatively worked upon. In the same way that Marxian theory can be extended dialectically to understand the production of both space and time – which are fundamental attributes of 'nature' after all – so the theoretical task of constructing a fuller and more coherent Marxian theory of the production of nature[133] cries out for attention. There is, plainly, nothing in principle anti-ecological about Marx's dialectics. The prospects for creating a political economic ecology are therefore good, provided the dialectical imagination can be restored to that central position in Marxian theory from which it has been dislodged by many countervailing neo-Marxist currents of thought.

Towards an ecosocialist politics

Benton[134] has recently argued that 'the basic ideas of historical materialism can without distortion be regarded as a proposal for an ecological approach to the understanding of human nature and history'. The difficulty, he asserts, is that there is a hiatus, 'internal to' the mature writings between this general commitment and Marx's political-economic conception of the labour process. I want to propose that a more dialectical reading of Marx, in which the labour *process* is seen as 'a form-giving fire' perpetually modifying other *processes* while passing through and giving rise to distinctive '*things*', eliminates much of that hiatus. Not only does it then become possible to explore the commonalities between Marx's project and some sectors of contemporary ecological thinking, but it also allows us to begin to construct more adequate languages with which to reflect upon the nature of socio-ecological activities and projects.

It is at this point useful to reflect for a moment upon the multiple languages – scientific, poetic, mythic, moral and ethical, economistic and instrumental, emotive and effective – in which ecological issues are typically addressed. For it is often argued that some kind of transdisciplinary language is required to better represent and resolve ecological problems and that the very existence of multiple discourses about 'nature' is a fundamental part of the problem. On the other hand, there is a deep reluctance to try to cram everything we want to say about 'nature' and our relation to it into one singular and homogeneous language. I want here to argue that a limited case can be made for both positions.

On the one hand we certainly need a much more unified language for the social and biological/physical sciences than we currently possess. The question of the unity of science has, of course, been broached many times – not least by Marx.[135] But serious problems have arisen on the social theory side whenever a biological basis has been invoked (familiar examples include the way social Darwinism founded Nazism, the profound social antagonisms generated in the debate over sociobiology). The response on the social science side has often been to retreat from any examination of the ecological side of social projects and act either as if these did not matter or as if they had to be construed as something 'external' to enquiry. I want to argue that this is not a satisfactory way to go about things and that ways have to be found to create a more common language. This is, however, dangerous territory – an open field for organicist or holistic rather than dialectical modes of thinking – and it may require deep shifts in ontological and epistemological stances on both the social and natural scientific sides, if it is to succeed.

On the other hand, the heterogeneity of discourses about 'nature' has to be accepted as not only an inevitable but also a very constructive and creative feature of ecological argumentation, provided that it is read not as fragmented and separate modes of thought and action embedded in isolated communities, but as the internalised heterogeneity, the play of difference, which all of us must surely feel and experience in our interaction with 'others' in both the human and non-human world. The pleasure of meaningful work and engagement with others is not irrelevant to the worker's life and the celebration of that in poetry and song has as much to convey as the more alienated representations of the world which science purveys.

Yet there is in this an omnipresent danger. Not only do different discourses lie uneasily side by side so that it becomes hard to spot the unity within the difference. But the careful analysis of the way power relations get embedded in distinctive discourses suggests that the vast conceptual muddle and cacophony of discourses is far from innocent in the reproduction of capitalism. Critical engagement with that is no trivial political task. If all socio-political projects are ecological projects and vice versa, then some conception of 'nature' and of 'environment' is omnipresent in everything we say and do. If, furthermore, concepts, discourses and theories can operate, when internalised in socio-ecological practices and actions, as 'material forces' that shape history,[136] then the present battles being waged over the concepts of 'nature' and of 'environment' are of immense importance. All critical examinations of the relation to nature are simultaneously critical examinations of society. The incredible vigour with which ruling interests have sought to contain, shape, mystify and muddy the contemporary debate over nature and environment (for the most part within discourses of 'ecological modernisation', 'sustainability', 'green consumerism' or the commodification and sale of 'nature' as a cultural spectacle) testifies to the seriousness of that connection.

The danger here is of accepting, often without knowing it, concepts that preclude radical critique. Consider, for example, the way in which 'scarcity' (and its cognate term of 'overpopulation') plays out in contemporary debate.[137] The emphasis is on the 'natural limits' to human potentialities. In Lee's[138] case, the narrative proceeds as if the rules of human behaviour should be derived from the second law of thermodynamics and the inherent sustaining power of ecosystems (neither of which is helpful at all in explaining the shifting history of human social organisation, let alone the genesis of life). But if we view 'natural resources' in the rather traditional geographical manner, as 'cultural, technological and economic appraisals of elements residing in nature and mobilised for particular social ends',[139] then 'ecoscarcity' means that we have not the will, wit or capacity to change our social goals, cultural modes, our technological mixes, or our form of economy and that we are powerless to modify 'nature' according to human requirements. Even the short history of capitalism surely proves that none of these features are fixed, that all of them are dynamic and changing. It is one thing to say that capitalism, given its narrow fixations and rules of capital accumulation, is encountering a condition of ecoscarcity and overpopulation. Indeed, it can be argued with some force, *pace* Marx, that capitalism as a mode of production produces scarcity so that to focus on universal limitations is to completely elide the political-ecological point. In this regard at least, Benton[140] has it right:

> What is required is the recognition that each form of social/economic life has its own specific mode and dynamic of interrelation with its own specific contextual conditions, resource materials, energy sources and naturally mediated unintended consequences (forms of 'waste', 'pollution' etc.). The ecological problems of any form of social and economic life … have to be theorised as the outcome of this specific structure of natural/social articulation.

Many of the terms used in contemporary environmental debates, it turns out, incorporate capitalist values without knowing it. While 'sustainability', for example, means entirely different things to different people,[141] the general drift of the term's use situates it against the background of sustaining a particular set of social relations by way of a particular ecological project. Imagine, for example, a highly simplified ecological-economic situation (along the lines of Lovelock's Daisyworld on Gaia) in which New York City has two species, international bankers and cockroaches. International bankers are the endangered species and so 'sustainability' gets defined in terms of organising the use of the earth (e.g. organising 'sustainable' agriculture in Malawi to facilitate debt repayments) to keep them in business. The model, though far-fetched, is illuminating, since it indicates why and how it is that international finance, via the World Bank, is these days so interested in ecological sustainability. The duality of ecological and social projects here takes some interesting twists, for while it is true that debt repayment, as ecologists argue, is at the root of many ecological problems it is precisely the threat of debt default that forces international finance to recognise that such ecological problems exist.

But for exactly the same reasons that we cannot afford to limit options by internalising a capitalistic logic in which concepts of sustainability, ecoscarcity and overpopulation are deeply implicated, so socialists cannot simply be content to try and co-opt the critical language of ecological discontent. The task is, rather, to both define and fight for a particular kind of ecosocialist project that extricates us from the peculiar oppressions and contradictions that capitalism is producing. Marx long ago summarised these succinctly enough:

In our days, everything seems pregnant with its contrary. Machinery, gifted with the wonderful power of shortening and fructifying human labour, we behold starving and overworking it. The new-fangled sources of wealth, by some strange weird spell, are turned into sources of want. The victories of art seem bought by the loss of character. At the same pace that mankind masters nature, man seems to become enslaved to other men or to his own infamy. Even the pure light of science seems unable to shine but on the dark background of ignorance. All our invention and progress seem to result in endowing material forces with intellectual life and in stultifying human life into a material force.[142]

It is then tempting , but not sufficient, to cite Engels's path towards an effective resolution to ecological as well as social dilemmas:

By long and often cruel experience and by collecting and analysing histor-ical material, we are gradually learning to get a clear view of the indirect, more remote, social effects of our production activities and so are afforded an opportunity to control and regulate these effects as well ... This regula-tion, however, requires something more than mere knowledge. It requires a complete revolution in our hitherto existing mode of production, and simultaneously a revolution in our whole contemporary social order.

I say this is insufficient because it leaves unresolved far too many dilemmas concerning the actual direction any ecosocialist project might take. And here the debate between Marxists and ecologists of all stripes has much to offer. That debate is largely a matter of articulating fixed positions, of course, but there are other, more dialectical ways, to go about reading it. 'One-sided representations are always restrictive and problematic,' Marx argued, and the best way to proceed when faced with a difficulty is 'to rub together conceptual blocks in such a way that they catch fire'. In that spirit I will conclude with the five key areas in which such a 'rubbing' might help ecosocialist conceptual politics catch fire:

1) Alienation, and self-realisation
Ideals of 'self-realisation' are widespread in the ecological literature. They parallel in certain ways Marx's concerns, particularly in *The Economic and Philosophic Manuscripts of 1844* but also in later works such as the *Grun-drisse*, for human emancipation and self-development through the working out of our creative powers. In the Marxist tradition, however, quite properly

concerned as it has been with impoverishment and deprivation, the liberation of the productive forces came to be seen as the privileged and to some degree exclusive means towards the broader goal of human self-realisation and emancipation.[143] As such, it became a goal in itself.

The ecologists' critique of socialist 'productivism' is here helpful, since it forces Marxists to re-examine the problematics of alienation.[144] Under capitalism, private property, class relations, wage labour and the fetishisms of market exchange separate and alienate us from any sensuous and immediate contact (except in those fragmented and partial senses achievable under class-ordered divisions of labour) from 'nature' as well as from other human beings. But if 'man lives on nature' then 'that nature is his *body* with which he must remain in continuous interchange if he is not to die'. The health of that body is fundamental to our health. To 'respect' nature is to respect ourselves. To engage with and transform nature is to transform ourselves. This forms one side of Marx's theses. But estrangement from immediate sensuous engagement with nature is an essential moment in consciousness formation. It therefore is a step on a path towards emancipation and self-realisation.[145] But herein lies a paradox. This never-ending estrangement of consciousness permits reflexivity and the construction of emancipatory forms of knowledge (such as science); but it also poses the problem of how to return to that which consciousness alienates us from. How to recuperate an unalienated relation to nature (as well as unalienated forms of social relations) in the face of contemporary divisions of labour and technological-social organisation then becomes part of a common project that binds Marxists and ecologists ineluctably together. Where they split asunder is in the way that such a recuperation might be sought.

For Marxists, there can be no going back, as many ecologists seem to propose, to an *unmediated* relation to nature (or a world built solely on face-to-face relations), to a pre-capitalist and communitarian world of non-scientific understandings with limited divisions of labour. The only path is to seek political, cultural and intellectual means that 'go beyond' the mediations such as scientific knowledge, organisational efficiency and technical rationality, money and commodity exchange, while acknowledging the significance of such mediations. The emancipatory potential of modern society, founded on alienation, must continue to be explored. But this cannot be, as it so often is, an end in itself, for that is to treat alienation as the end point, the goal. The ecologists' and the early Marx's concern to recuperate the alienation from nature (as well as from others) that modern-day capitalism instanciates must be a fundamental goal of any ecosocialist project. The quest for meaningful work as well as meaningful play (making sure, for example, that 'victories of art' are not bought by 'loss of character') becomes a central issue through which the labour movement can grasp the nettle of ecological argumentation concerning alienation from nature, from others and, in the last instance, from ourselves.

This does not deny the relevance or power of phenomenological approaches in exploring the potentialities of more intimate and immediate relations to nature or to others. The depth and intensity of feeling implicit even in Heidegger's approach is not irrelevant, any more than is the search for adequate poetic languages, representations, symbolic systems. Sartre's existentialism owes as much, after all, to Marx as to Heidegger. The danger arises when such modes of thought are postulated as the sole basis of politics (in which case they become inward-looking, exclusionary and even neo-fascist), when it was surely Marx's intent to search for unity within the difference. Exploring that duality has to be at the centre of ecosocialist politics, implying an uncomfortable but instructive duality of values between the purely instrumental (mediated) and the existential (unmediated).

2) Social relations and ecological projects

Explorations of our 'species potential' and our capacity for realisation require that we take cognisance of the relation between ecological projects and the social relations needed to initiate, implement and manage them. Nuclear power, for example, requires highly centralised and non-democratic power relations coupled with hierarchical command and control structures if it is to work successfully. Objections to it therefore focus as much on the social relations it implies as on the ecological problems of health and long-term hazardous wastes. The nature of many of the ecological projects undertaken in the Soviet Union likewise required social relations that were fundamentally at odds with the theoretical project of constructing a new society founded on egalitarianism and democracy. But this sort of critique is the easy part. For if we turn the equation around, and state that the only kinds of ecological projects to be undertaken are those which are consistent with non-hierarchical, decentralised, highly democratic and radically egalitarian social relations, then the range of possible ecological projects becomes highly restricted, perhaps even life-threatening for substantial numbers of people. Adoption of such a stance certainly does not accord with the open exploration of our species potentiality and would probably militate against the alleviation of the tangible material misery in which much of the world's population lives.

There is, here, no resolution to what will always be a contradictory situation, save that of recognising fully the nature of the tension and seeking political ways to live with it. More immediately, we have also to recognise the effects that arise from the instanciation 'in nature' of certain kinds of social relations. If, for example, we view, as I think we must, contemporary ecosystems as incorporating the built environments of cities and the capital and commodity flows that sustain them, and if these ecosystems are instanciations of capitalist social relations, then what feasible (as opposed to catastrophically destructive) social and ecological transformations are available to us?

3) *The question of technology*

'Technology discloses man's mode of dealing with nature, the process of production whereby he sustains his life, and thereby also lays bare the mode of formation of his social relations, and of the mental conceptions that flow from them.'[146]

While it is plainly wrong to attribute any technological determinism to Marx ('discloses' cannot be read as 'determines'), the centrality of technology and of technological choices in embedding social relations in ecological projects (and vice versa) means that careful attention has to be paid to this issue. Grundmann[147] is here surely on very strong ground when he points to some of the deep tensions in Marx's own approach. If, for example, machinery not only dispossesses workers of their surplus value but also deprives them of their skill and virtuosity while mediating their relations to nature in alienating ways, then self-realisation (however much we insist on the collectivity of the project) may be in jeopardy for technological reasons. Some kinds of technologies run counter even to the aim of exercising greater control over nature. But the problem goes even deeper. The technological mixes that capitalism bequeaths us (with its particular mixes of socio-ecological projects) either have to be roundly rejected (as many ecologists now suggest) or gradually transformed in ways that better accord with socialist social relations, and the mental conceptions (such as those concerning the relation to nature) that flow from them. Arguments over 'appropriate technology' and 'small-is-beautiful' here come into play, not as necessary technological principles or trajectories for the construction of socialism, but as a set of questions marks over the future technological organisation of a socialist society.[148]

4) The dialectics of commonality and difference, of centralisation and decentralisation

Since much of the radical ecological critique now in vogue has its roots in anarchism, it has typically taken the path of emphasising community, locality, place, proximity to 'nature', particularity and decentralisation (deeply antagonistic to state powers) as opposed to the more traditional socialistic concerns with the universality of proletarian struggles and the overthrow of capitalism as a world-historical system of domination. Any ecosocialist project has to confront that opposition. Here I think a more *geographical* historical materialism, one that is more ecologically sensitive, has much to offer, in terms of analysis as well as in terms of prospective transformations. The *general* struggle against capitalist forms of domination is always made up of *particular* struggles against the specific kinds of socio-ecological projects in which capitalists are engaged and the distinctive social relations they presuppose (against commercial forestry and timber management in the Himalayas as against large-scale water projects in California or nuclear power in France). The articulation of socialist principles of struggle therefore varies greatly with the nature and scale of the socio-ecological project to be confronted. And by the same token, the nature of the socialist transformation sought depends crucially upon the socio-ecological possibilities that exist in relation to particular projects, looking very different in Nicaragua or Zimbabwe from how they look in Sweden and very different in terms of multinational finance from how they look in terms of medical wastes dumped next to housing projects. But it is at this point that the *general* presumptions of the transition to socialism deserve to be reflected upon.

Socialism is not necessarily about the construction of homogeneity. The exploration of our species' potentiality can presumably also be about the creative search for and exploration of diversity and heterogeneity. Socio-ecological projects, much more in tune with resolving questions of alienation and opening up diverse possibilities for self-realisation, can be regarded as fundamentally part of some socialist future. The failures of capitalism to produce anything other than the uneven geographical development of bland, commoditised homogeneity is, surely, one of the most striking features of its failures.

The radical ecological literature that focuses on place construction, bioregionalism, and the like here has something creative to offer, partly as an excellent ground for the critique of capitalism's production of waste (do we really need to ship British beer to Australia and Australian beer to Britain?) as well as its production of serial conformity in urban design and the like.

Mumford wishfully depicted the region, for example, 'like its corresponding artifact, the city, [as] a collective work of art' not found 'as a finished product in nature, not solely the creation of human will and fantasy'. Embedded in a socialist project of ecological transformation, such a way of thinking turns on the 'production of nature' as diverse localised works of art coupled with the creation of ecosystemic differences which can respect diversity as much of culture and of places as of ecosystems. The richness of human capacity for complexity and diversity in a context of the free exploration of the richness, complexity and diversity encountered in the rest of nature can become a vital part of any ecosocialist project. 'Each of us', says a bioregionalist like Berg,[149] 'inhabits a 'terrain of consciousness' determined in large part by the place we dwell in, the work we do, and the people with whom we share our lives. And there is absolutely no reason not to follow him in arguing that 'the re-creation of caring and sustainable human cultures' ought to become 'part of the "real work" of our time'. In so doing he is echoing something that derives as much from Raymond Williams as from Heidegger.

But we also hit here the point of departure of ecosocialism from pure bioregionalism, place and local communitarian politics. The problem is that there is more than a hint of authoritarianism, surveillance and confine-ment in the enforced localism of such a decentralised politics and a naive belief that (1) respect for human diversity is compatible with the belief that all decentralised societies will necessarily construct themselves 'upon the [Enlightenment!] values of democracy, liberty, freedom, justice and other such like desiderata'[150] rather than in terms of slavery, sexual oppression, and the like;[151] (2) that the 'impoverishment' which often attaches to communal autarky and strong restrictions on foreign trade can be overcome; and (3) that restrictions on population movements coupled with exclusions of disruptive 'foreigners' can somehow be squared with ideals of maximising individual freedoms, democracy and openness to 'others'. Young's[152] salutary warnings concerning the nightmare of communitarian politics in which community is defined as against others and therefore formulated in an entirely exclusion-ary, chauvinistic and racist way is not that easily avoided. When Goldsmith condescendingly writes,[153] for example, that 'a certain number of foreigners could be allowed to settle', but that they would not 'partake in the running of the community until such time as the citizens elected them to be of their number', the leaning towards a politics of exclusion that is neo-fascist becomes rather too close for comfort. The 'ecologism' of the right-wing Lombardy Leagues in northern Italy, for example, shares exactly such a perspective not only with respect to the immigration of non-Italians but also with respect to movements from southern Italy. Furthermore, there is in this thinking a presumption that bioregions are given, by nature or by history, rather than that they are made by a variety of intersecting processes operating at quite different temporal and spatial scales. In other words, bioregions get thought about, in a most undialectical fashion, as things rather than as unstable products of shifting processes. This then provokes the question: at what scale should a *bioregion, place* or *human community* be defined?

Ecosocialist politics must, we can conclude, pay attention to a politics in which 'universality' has a dual meaning. This is best expressed in Young's[154] rule that 'universality in the sense of the participation and inclusion of everyone in moral and social life does not imply universality in the sense of adoption of a general point of view that leaves behind particular affiliations, feelings, commitments, and desires'. The perpetual negotiation of the relation between those two senses of universality, whether read across differences of gender, ethnicity or other social affiliation or across the diversity of socio-ecological projects that might be explored under socialism, must therefore remain at the heart of ecosocialist thinking.

5) The question of temporal and spatial scales

At first sight, the question of scale appears as a purely technical matter. Where, for example, do ecosystems (or socio-ecological projects) begin and where do they end, how does a pond differ from the oceans, how is it that processes which operate with profound effect at one scale become irrelevant at another, and so on? 'Issues of appropriate scaling', Haila and Levins[155] argue, 'are among the fundamental theoretical challenges in the understanding of society–nature interactions.' There is, they say, 'no single "correct" way' to define temporal and spatial scales: these are constituted by the organisms considered so that different scales are simultaneously present at any particular site in nature. If, as is the case in the dialectical view (see above), there are no basic units to which everything can be reduced, then the choice of scale at which to examine processes becomes both crucial and problematic. The difficulty is compounded by the fact that the temporal and spatial scales at which human beings operate as ecological agents have also been changing. Cronon[156] notes, for example, how even before colonial settlement began in New England, long-distance trade from Europe was bringing two hitherto largely isolated ecosystems into contact with one another in such a way as to commercialise the Indians' material culture and dissolve their earlier ecological practices. If we think these days of the scale defined by the commodity and money flows that put our breakfasts upon the table, and how that scale

210

has changed over the last hundred years, then immediately it becomes apparent that there is an instability in the definition of scale which arises out of practices of capital accumulation, commodity exchange, and the like.

Yet, as Smith[157] remarks, 'the theory of the production of geographical scale' (to which I would add also the production of temporalities) 'is grossly underdeveloped'. It seems to imply the production of a nested hierarchy of scales (from global to local) leaving us always with the political-ecological question of how to 'arbitrate and translate between them'. The ecological argument is incredibly confused on exactly this point. On the one hand the Gaian planetary healthcare specialists think globally and seek to act globally, while the bioregionalist and social anarchists want to think and act locally, presuming, quite erroneously, that whatever is good for the locality is good for the continent or the planet. But at this point the issue becomes profoundly political as well as ecological, for the political power to act, decide upon socio-ecological projects and to regulate their unintended consequences has also to be defined at a certain scale (and in the contemporary world the nation-states mostly carved out over the last hundred years maintain a privileged position even though they make no necessary politico-ecological sense). But this also says something very concrete about what any ecosocialist project must confront. On the one hand there will presumably be continuing transformations in human practices that redefine temporal and spatial scales, while on the other hand political power structures must be created that have the capacity to 'arbitrate and translate between' the different scales given by different kinds of projects. Here, too, it seems that an ecosocialist perspective has enormous impact for socialist thinking on how human potentialities are to be explored and what kinds of political institutions and power structures can be created that are sensitive to the ecological dimensions of any socialist project.

Epilogue

'At the end of every labour process', Marx[158] once observed, 'we get a result that already existed in the imagination of the labourer at its commencement.' The purpose of the kind of labour that I have here engaged in is to try and produce conceptual clarifications that might enter into the political practices of socialism. But to be realised, as Eckersley so acutely points out, the aspirations released by analyses of this sort 'must be critically related to one's knowledge of the present, thereby uniting desire with analysis and [lead on] to informed cultural, social, and political engagement'. To bring my argument full circle, that means developing ways to conceptualise and represent ecological issues in ways that speak to the aspirations of the working-class movement, certain segments of the women's and ecologists' movements, as well as to those African-Americans who, in the Left Bank Jazz Society in Baltimore those many years ago, quite correctly defined their main environmental problem as the presidency of Richard Nixon.

Commentary

Space, place and environment are central to geographical thinking. Approaching them via Marx's political economy and historical materialism has been a central mission of radical geography. The production of spaces, places and environments is not a mere by-product of capital accumulation and class struggle but an active moment in the evolutionary dynamics of capitalism. Consider, for example, the massive investment and circulation of capital in the built environments required to sustain capitalist production and consumption on an ever-expanding scale. Uneven geographical development consequent upon such investments can be an active element in crisis formation and resolution (as has been the case with housing over the last decade or so). There is also a powerful inner connection between urban processes and environmental change. Everything from habitat loss to ozone concentrations to pollution to global warming is profoundly affected by urbanisation. There can be no answer to some of the major questions of our time – those of environmental degradation and burgeoning social inequality – without radical transformations in an urbanisation dynamic powered by the need to absorb more and more surplus capital.

My former colleague Neil Smith advanced thinking on these topics in his seminal book on *Uneven Development: Nature, Capital and the Production of Space*. In the early 1990s what he called 'the production of nature' moved to the forefront of social movement activism. This was the one sector of anti-capitalist sentiment that grew rather than stagnated or diminished during these years. The quest for environmental justice was even supplanting that for social justice.

Integrating environmental issues and the relation to nature posed not a few methodological problems. The meaning of 'the political' in political economy had to be redefined, and it was not immediately clear how the relational approach to dialectics that I had always favoured (based on Bertell Ollman's works) could work at the interface between social and natural phenomena. Plainly, the approach that Engels had favoured in *The Dialectics of Nature* was not appropriate. What was needed, I concluded, was a process-based approach to dialectics that drew more on Alfred North Whitehead's *Process and Reality* rather than Hegel's *Science of Logic*.

This chapter, first published in the *Socialist Register* in 1993, explores these questions. *Justice, Nature and the Geography of Difference,* published three years later, elaborates them further. The incorporation of relations to nature into the analysis confused and disrupted some of the certainties of Marx's political economy (in much the same way as the incorporation of space had done earlier). But it led to a huge enrichment of perspectives and an open-ended version of Marx's evolutionism that gained in realism even as it lost in logical coherence. This piece and the book that followed signalled a major shift in the way I thought about nature and our place in the world. This is where I first sought to define the principles of a historical-geographical materialism.

Chapter 8
Militant Particularism and Global Ambition

In 1988, shortly after taking up a position in Oxford, I became involved in a research project concerning the fate of the Rover car plant in that city. Oxford, particularly for outsiders, is usually imagined as a city of dreaming spires and university grandeur, but as late as 1973 the car plant at Cowley in East Oxford employed some 27,000 workers, compared to less than 3,000 in the employ of the University. The insertion of the Morris Motors car plant into the medieval social fabric of the city early in the century had had enormous effects upon the political and economic life of the place, paralleling almost exactly the three-stage path to socialist consciousness set out in *The Communist Manifesto*. Workers had steadily been massed together over the years in and around the car plant and its ancillary installations; they had become conscious of their own interests and built institutions (primarily the unions) to defend and promote those interests. During the 1930s and again in the 1960s and early 1970s, the car plant was the focus of some of the most virulent class struggles over the future of industrial relations in Britain. The workers' movement simultaneously created a powerful political instrument in the form of a local Labour Party that ultimately assumed continuous control of the local council after 1980. But by 1988 rationalisations and cutbacks had reduced the workforce to around 10,000, and by 1993 it was down to less than 5,000 (as opposed to the 7,000 or so then in the employ of the University). The threat of total closure of the car plant was never far away.

A book on the Cowley story, edited by Teresa Hayter and me and entitled *The Factory and the City: The Story of the Cowley Auto Workers in Oxford*, was published late in 1993. It originated in research work conducted in support of a campaign against closure that began in 1988, when British Aerospace (BAe) acquired the Rover car company in a sweetheart privatisation deal from the Thatcher government. Partial closure and rationalisation at the plant was immediately announced and the prospect of total closure loomed. Land values in Oxford were high and BAe, with the property boom in full flood, acquired a property development company specialising in the creation of business parks (Arlington Securities) in 1989. The fear was that work would be transferred to Longbridge (Birmingham) or, worse still, to a greenfield non-union site in Swindon (where Honda was already involved in co-production arrangements with Rover), releasing the Oxford land for lucrative redevelopment that would offer almost no prospects for employment to a community of several thousand people that had evolved over many years to serve the car plant.

An initial meeting to discuss a campaign against closure drew representatives from many sectors. It was there agreed to set up a research group to provide information on what was happening and what the effects of any moves by BAe might be on the workforce and on the Oxford economy. The Oxford Motor Industry Research Project (OMIRP) was formed and I agreed to chair it. Shortly thereafter, the union leadership in the plant withdrew its support for both the campaign and the research, and most of the Labour members on the city council followed suit. The research was then left to a small group of dissident shop stewards within the plant and a group of independent researchers, some of whom were based at Oxford Polytechnic (now Oxford Brookes University) and Oxford University.

For personal reasons, I was not active in the campaign, nor did I engage much with the initial research. I did help to publicise the results and to mobilise resources for the research project which the union leadership and the majority of the local Labour Party actively tried to stop – they did not want anything to 'rock the boat' in the course of their 'delicate negotiations' with BAe over the future of the plant and the future of the site. Fortuitously, OMIRP produced a pamphlet, *Cowley Works*, at the very moment when BAe announced another wave of rationalisations that would cut the workforce in half and release half of the land for redevelopment. The history of the plant together with the story of the struggle to launch a campaign and the dynamics of the subsequent run-down are well described in the book.

Teresa Hayter, the coordinator of OMIRP, received a three-year research fellowship at St Peter's College in 1989 to pull together a book about the history of Cowley, the failed campaign and the political problems of mobilising resistance to the arbitrary actions of corporate capital. The book entailed the formation of a broad-based group (including academics as well as political activists), with each member producing chapters on topics with which they were most familiar. Each chapter was read by others and comments went back and forth until a final version was arrived at. I agreed, partly for purposes of making the book more attractive to prospective publishers, to be a co-editor of the book with Teresa Hayter. This meant that in addition to the one chapter I co-authored, I spent quite a lot of time, along with Hayter, editing, commissioning new segments to ensure full coverage, and generally trying to keep the book as a whole in view while attending to the parts.

The book is a fascinating document. It brings together radically different positionalities – varying from an unnamed shop steward and others who had worked in the plant or had been long-term residents of East Oxford, to academics, planners and independent leftists. The language differs drastically from one chapter to another. The activist voice emanating from the plant experience (what I will later, following Raymond Williams, call 'militant particularism') contrasts sharply with the more abstract judgements of the academics, for example, while the perspective from the community often reads rather differently from the perspective of the production line. The heterogeneity of voices and of styles is a particular strength of the book.

It was evident early, however, that the many contributors had quite different political perspectives and interpretations. Initially these were negotiated, in the sense that everyone trod warily through a minefield of differences in order to get to the other side with a completed book. The difficulties arose with the conclusion. I originally proposed that we should write two conclusions, one by Hayter and one by myself, so that readers might get a better handle on the political differences and be left to judge for themselves. This, however, was rejected. And so I undertook to draft a conclusion based on the various ideas that had been put forward by several members of the group. That draft conclusion succeeded in exploding almost every mine that had been negotiated in the writing of the book. Matters became extremely tense, difficult and sometimes hostile between Hayter and me, with the group to some degree polarised around us.

In the midst of these intense arguments, I recall a lunch in St Peter's College at which Hayter challenged me to define my loyalties. She was very clear about hers. They lay with the militant shop stewards in the plant, who were not only staying on and labouring under the most appalling conditions but daily struggling to win back control from a reactionary union leadership so as to build a better basis for socialism. By contrast, she saw me as a free-floating Marxist intellectual who had no particular loyalties to anyone. So where did my loyalties lie?

It was a stunning question and I have had to think about it a great deal since. At the time I recall arguing that while loyalty to those still employed in the plant (and perhaps to the Socialist Outlook Trotskyists, who formed the core of the opposition but whose views were in a minority) was important, there were many more people in East Oxford who had been laid off or who had no prospects for employment (for example, alienated and discontented young people, some of whom had taken to joyriding and thus had left criminalisation and police oppression for the whole community in their wake) who deserved equal time. All along, I noted, Hayter had treated my concerns for the politics of community as a parallel force to the politics of the workplace with scepticism. I further thought that some consideration had to be given to the future of socialism in Oxford under conditions in which the working-class solidarities that had been built around the plant were plainly weakening and even threatened with elimination. This meant the search for some broader coalition of forces both to support the workers in the plant and to perpetuate the socialist cause. I also thought it would be disloyal in a general sense not to put a critical distance between us and what had happened in order to better understand why the campaign had failed to take off. Hayter refused to countenance anything that sounded even remotely critical of the strategy of the group that had tried to mobilise sentiments behind a campaign. Likewise, she rejected any perspective that did not accept as its basis the critical struggle for power on the shop floor of the plant.

But all sorts of other issues divided us. Deteriorating work conditions in the plant, for example, made it hard to argue unequivocally for the long-term preservation of what were in effect 'shit jobs', even though it was plainly imperative to defend such jobs in the short run because there were no reasonable alternatives. The issue here was not to subordinate short-term actions to long-term pipe-dreams, but to point to how difficult it is to move on a long-term trajectory when short-term exigencies demand something quite different. I was also concerned about the incredible overcapacity in the automobile industry in Britain, and in Europe in general. Something had to give somewhere, and we had to find some way to protect workers' interests in general without falling into the reactionary politics of the 'new realism' then paralysing official union politics. But across what space should that generality be calculated? Britain? Europe? The world? I found myself arguing for at least a European-wide perspective on adjustments in automobile production capacity, but found it hard to justify stopping at that scale when pressed. There were also important ecological issues to be considered deriving not only from the plant itself (the paint shop was a notorious pollution source), but also from the nature of the product. Making Rover cars for the ultra-rich and so contributing to ecological degradation hardly seemed a worthy long-term socialist objective. The ecological issue ought not to be ducked, I felt, even though it was plain that the bourgeois North Oxford heritage interests would likely use it to get rid of the car plant altogether if given the chance. Again, the problem of time horizon and class interests needed to be explicitly debated rather than buried. Furthermore, while I would in no way defend the appalling behaviour of BAe, I did think it relevant to point out that the company had lost about a third of its stock market value in the first few months of 1992 and that its hopes for a killing on the property market had been seriously diminished in the property crash of 1990. This posed questions of new forms of public or community control over corporate activity (and in this case the turn to property speculation as an alternative to production) that would not repeat the bitter history of nationalisation (such as the disastrous rationalisations and reordering of job structures already suffered by Rover, when it was British Leyland in the 1970s, for example).

I felt that it would be disloyal to the conception of socialism as some real alternative not to talk about all of these issues in the conclusion to the book. Not, I hasten to add, with the idea that they could be resolved, but because they defined an open terrain of discussion and debate that seemed to me at least to flow out of the materials assembled in the book. Such a conclusion would keep options open and so help readers to consider active choices across a broad terrain of possibilities while paying proper attention to the complexities and difficulties. But Hayter felt, even when she partially agreed on the long-term significance of such ideas, that raising matters of this sort would dilute the immediate struggle to keep jobs in Cowley and prevent their transfer to a greenfield non-union site in Swindon. The issues which I wanted to raise could be attended to, she held, only when the workforce and the progressive stewards had regained their strength and power in the workplace.

I was operating, it became plain, at a different level and with different kinds of abstraction. But the impetus for the campaign, the research and the book did not come from me. It arose out of the extraordinary strength and power of a tradition of union militancy emanating from the plant. This tradition had its own version of internationalism and presumptions to universal truth, although a case could be made that its capture and ossification by a rather narrow Trotskyist rhetoric was as much a part of the problem as the more fundamental conflict between Hayter's and my perspective. But it would be wrong to depict the argument solely in sectarian terms. For the issue of a purely plant-based versus a more encompassing politics was always there. I could not abandon my own loyalty to the belief that the politics of a supposedly unproblematic extension outwards from the plant of a prospective model of total social transformation is fundamentally flawed. The view that what is right and good from the standpoint of the militant shop stewards at Cowley is right and good for the city and, by extension, for society at large is far too simplistic. Other levels and kinds of abstraction have to be deployed if socialism is to break out of its local bonds and become a viable alternative to capitalism as a working mode of production and social relations. But there is something equally problematic about imposing a politics guided by abstractions upon people who have given their lives and labour over many years in a particular way in a particular place.

So what level and what kinds of abstraction should be deployed? And what might it mean to be loyal to abstractions rather than to actual people? Beneath those questions lie others. What is it that constitutes a privileged claim to knowledge and how can we judge, understand, adjudicate and perhaps negotiate different knowledges constructed at very different levels of abstraction under radically different material conditions?

Raymond Williams and the politics of abstraction

These were questions that preoccupied Raymond Williams, erupting again and again in his work; though, for reasons that will shortly become apparent, they are far better articulated in his novels than in his cultural theorising. My purpose here is not, I should make plain, to hold up Williams as some paragon of virtue on these matters. Indeed, I accept the criticism that the nearer he steers in his theorising to what might be called 'cultural holism' – the view that culture must be understood as a 'whole way of life' and that social practices have to be construed as 'indissoluble elements of a continuous social material process' – the closer he comes to an organicist view of the social order that cannot help but be exclusionary with respect to outsiders and in some respects oppressive for insiders, too. The critical interventions of Said[1] and of Gilroy[2] strongly point to the difficulty with respect to outsiders, the latter accusing Williams of complicity with a metropolitan colonialism and imperialism by virtue of his situatedness within the 'structures of feeling' that were associated with working-class support for the British Empire. A purely organicist view makes it equally difficult to examine multiple forces of oppression and domination within a cultural configuration. Williams, it is generally acknowledged, is nowhere near sensitive enough on the gender issue, for example (though, again, he felt he handled such questions much more firmly in his novels than in his theorising). Roman's[3] sympathetic and constructive critique of some of the pitfalls into which Williams sometimes seems to fall exposes some of the dangers as well as opportunities that Williams creates from both a feminist and a more racially sensitive perspective. There is no doubt, either, that Williams's reluctance to let go of 'lived experience' leads him to accept, as Hall[4] has remarked, a rather 'empiricist notion of experience' as if there were nothing problematic about taking daily experience as a direct basis for theory construction. Williams's reticence in this regard has even led some critics to conclude, erroneously I believe, that Williams made no real theoretical contributions at all, save giving Gramsci's notions of hegemony a new and somewhat more nuanced lease of life. Yet there is a certain paradox at work here, for it is also true that Williams's influence, in spite of all his supposed defects, 'remains powerful in contemporary cultural studies, with their emphasis on the counter-hegemonies of feminist, Third World, and working-class movements'.[5]

I shall not here try either to defend or offer a systematic critique of Williams's controversial stances on politics and culture.[6] But there are two crucial points concerning his work which may explain why so many of his most trenchant critics so often find themselves returning to his formulations. The first concerns the dialectical way in which his concepts get formulated. Consider, for example, the following passage:

> In most description and analysis, culture and society are expressed in an habitual past tense. The strongest barrier to the recognition of human cultural activity is this immediate and regular conversion of experience into finished products. What is defensible as a procedure in conscious history, where on certain assumptions many actions can be definitively taken as having ended, is habitually projected, not only into the always moving substance of the past, but into contemporary life, in which relationships, institutions and formations in which we are still actively involved are converted, by this procedural mode, into formed wholes rather than forming and formative processes. Analysis is then centred on relations between these produced institutions, formations, and experiences, so that now, as in that produced past, only the fixed explicit forms exist, and living presence is always, by definition, receding.[7]

Williams is not immune from the tendency to produce alienated conceptions that instantiate 'formed wholes' as dominants over 'forming and formative processes'. But certainly in this passage he declares a strong preference for dialectical readings that prioritise the understanding of processes over things, so that any organicist notion of community, for example, is tempered by the knowledge of the complicated flows and processes that sustain it. Williams here charts a terrain of theoretical possibilities in which the reduction of relations between people into relations between concepts can be continuously challenged, while our understanding of relationships, institutions and forms can be brought alive by focusing attention on the processes that work to produce, sustain or dissolve them.

The second point is that the manner of 'embeddedness' (as contemporary sociologists [such as Granovetter[8]] refer to it) of political action in what anthropologists like to term 'intimate culture'[9] is simultaneously empowering and problematic. But it also follows that the abstractions to which we appeal cannot be understood independently of whatever it is that political and theoretical activity is embedded in and whatever it is that social life is being intimate about. A study of some of Williams's formulations can here be extremely helpful, since he both uses and systematically questions the notion of embeddedness and intimate culture. In what follows, I shall pay particular attention to the way Williams treats environment, space and place as framing concepts that help define what these ideas might mean.

The novel as environmental history

> Press your fingers close on this lichened sandstone. With this stone and this grass, with this red earth, this place was received and made and remade. Its generations are distinct but all suddenly present.[10]

So ends the opening statement of both volumes of Williams's last and unfinished novel, *People of the Black Mountains*. The story begins in 23,000 BC and passes across periods of vast environmental and social change. The second story, for example, is set at the edge of the great ice sheet that surrounded the Black Mountains at the maximum point of glaciation in 16,000 BC. Subsequent episodes take up the advent of settled agriculture, writing and other key moments of transformation of both the physical and social environment through human action. The earlier reconstructions draw heavily on archaeological, palaeological and environmental history (the list of sources furnished at the end of volume 2 is extensive), while the later periods lean much more heavily on the works of economic, social and cultural historians, making this a fictional account deeply rooted in those material realities identified through research across a wide range of disciplines. In episode after episode, the people who have traversed and struggled in that place are imagined into life.

So why was one of Britain's most eminent socialist thinkers, in the very last fictional work he undertook, writing the social and environmental history of the Black Mountains? One partial answer to that question presumably lies in Williams's insistence that social beings can never escape their embeddedness in the world of nature and that no conception of political action could, in the final analysis, afford abstractions that did not encompass that fact. 'Nature' was, thus, a key word for Williams[11] – perhaps 'the most complex word in the language' since the idea of it 'contains, though often unnoticed, an extraordinary amount of human history … both complicated and changing, as other ideas and experiences change'.[12] An enquiry into environmental history as well as into changing conceptions of nature therefore provided a privileged and powerful way to enquire into and understand social and cultural change. Williams construes the social and environmental dialectically, as different faces of the same coin.

Williams's close attention to the environmental side was, however, bound to throw into relief certain features that might otherwise be missed. His materialism and critical realism always see to it that work (or what he elsewhere calls 'livelihood') – broadly understood as a simultaneously life-giving and culturally creative activity – is the fundamental process through which our relation to and understanding of the world of nature get constituted. 'Once we begin to speak of men mixing their labour with the earth, we are in a whole world of new relations between man and nature and to separate natural history from social history becomes extremely problematic.'[13] Such a dialectical and transformative view of how specific social relations connect to new ways of mixing labour with the land is not unique to Williams. It echoes, for example, the views of Marx and Engels that 'as long as men exist, the history of nature and the history of men are mutually conditioned' because 'through this movement he acts upon external nature and changes it, and in this way he simultaneously changes his own nature'.[14] The environmental historian William Cronon[15] similarly argues:

> An ecological history begins by assuming a dynamic and changing relationship between environment and culture, one as apt to produce contradictions as continuities. Moreover, it assumes that the interactions of the two are dialectical. Environment may initially shape the range of choices available to a people at a given moment but then culture reshapes environment responding to those choices. The reshaped environment presents a new set of possibilities for cultural reproduction, thus setting up a new cycle of mutual determination. Changes in the way people create and recreate their livelihood must be analysed in terms of changes not only in their social relations but in their ecological ones as well.

But the environmental history of the Black Mountains is not something that evolves purely in place. The novel is also a story of wave after wave of migratory influences and colonisations that situate the history of the Black Mountains in a matrix of spatiality, constituted by the flows and movements pulsing across Europe and beyond. The distinctiveness, or what Williams affectionately calls the 'sweetness of the place', gets constructed through the working out in that place of interventions and influences from outside. The three themes of place, space and environment are tightly interwoven in this particular novel as inseparable elements in complex processes of social and environmental transformation.

Why choose the novel as a vehicle to explore these themes? Why not write straight environmental history, or rest content with the abundant source materials upon which Williams draws? I think there are two reasons. The first is explicitly laid out again and again in the novels as key characters reflect on the nature of the knowledge and understandings they hold. In *People of the Black Mountains*[16] we find Glyn – the person through whom the voices and tales of the past become historically present – looking for his uncle lost on the mountains, reflecting thus on the vast literatures assembled by different disciplines about the place:

> Yet the kinds of scrutiny that were built into these disciplines had their own weaknesses ... They would reduce what they were studying to an internal procedure; in the worst cases to material for an enclosed career. If lives and places were being seriously sought, a powerful attachment to lives and to places was entirely demanded. The polystyrene model and its textual and theoretical equivalents remained different from the substance they reconstructed and simulated ... At his books and maps in the library, or in the house in the valley, there was a common history which could be translated anywhere, in a community of evidence and rational inquiry. Yet he had only to move on the mountains for a different kind of mind to assert itself: stubbornly native and local, yet reaching beyond to a wider common flow, where touch and breadth replaced record and analysis; not history as narrative but stories as lives.

This is a familiar theme in all of Williams's novels (and it is interesting to note how it presages the move within history of a shift from narrative to story form). In *Border Country*, we similarly encounter Matthew Price, like Williams, a Cambridge-educated son of a railway signalman from a rural Welsh community, but now fictionally placed as a university lecturer in economic history in London. His work on population movements in Wales in the nineteenth century has hit an impasse. The data are all there but something is missing:

> The techniques I have learned have the solidity and precision of ice cubes, while a given temperature is maintained. But it is a temperature I can't really maintain: the door of the box keeps flying open. It's hardly a population movement from Glynmawr to London, but it's a change of substance, as it must have been for them, when they left their villages. And the ways of measuring this are not only outside my discipline. They are somewhere else altogether, that I can feel but not handle, touch but not grasp.[17]

The implication is clear enough and applies with great force to Williams's own work. Concerned as he always was with the lived lives of people, the novel form allows him to represent the daily qualities of those lives in ways that could not be handled or grasped by other means. So while on the one hand Williams insists that his novels should not be treated as separate from his cultural theorising, he also freely admits that he found some themes far easier to explore in his novels than in his theoretical work.[18]

There is another reason behind the choice of the novel form. He wants always to emphasise the ways in which personal and particular choices made under given conditions are the very essence of historical-geographical change. The novel is not subject to closure in the same way that more analytic forms of thinking are. There are always choices and possibilities, perpetually unresolved tensions and differences, subtle shifts in structures of feeling, all of which stand to alter the terms of debate and political action, even under the most difficult and dire of conditions. It was for precisely this reason that Williams admired Brecht's theatre. Brecht, he says, discovered 'ways of enacting genuine alternatives: not so much as in traditional drama, through the embodiment of alternatives in opposing characters, but by their embodiment in one person, who lives through this way and then that and invites us to draw our own conclusions'.[19] This means, he goes on to point out, that 'there is no imposed resolution – the tension is there to the end, and we are invited to consider it'. All of Williams's central characters live that tension. The stories of the people of the Black Mountains are precisely about that. Politically, this allows Williams to remind us of the way in which these people, by virtue of the choices they made and the ways they lived their lives, are 'all historically present'. His aim is empowerment in the present through celebrating the strength and capacity to survive. But it is not only that:

The crisis which came to me on the death of my father, who was a socialist and a railway worker – I haven't been able to explain this to people properly, perhaps I explained it partly in my novel *Border Country* – was the sense of a kind of defeat for an idea of value. Maybe this was an unreasonable response. All right, he died, he died too early, but men and women die. But it was very difficult not to see him as a victim at the end. I suppose it was this kind of experience which sent me back to the historical novel I'm now writing, *People of the Black Mountains*, about the movements of history over a very long period, in and through a particular place in Wales. And this history is a record of ... defeat, invasion, victimisation, oppression. When one sees what was done to the people who are physically my ancestors, one feels it to be almost incredible ... The defeats have occurred over and over again, and what my novel is then trying to explore is simply the condition of anything surviving at all. It's not a matter of the simple patriotic answer: we're Welsh, and still here. It's the infinite resilience, even deviousness, with which people have managed to persist in profoundly unfavourable conditions, and the striking diversity of beliefs in which they've expressed their autonomy. A sense of value which has won its way through different kinds of oppression of different forms ... an ingrained and indestructible yet also changing embodiment of the possibilities of common life.[20]

The embeddedness that Williams here wants to celebrate is the ability of human beings, as social beings, to perpetuate and nurture in their daily lives and cultural practices the possibility of that sense of value that seeks a commonality to social life even in the midst of a striking heterogeneity of beliefs. But the maintenance of such a sense of value depends crucially upon a certain kind of interpersonal relating that typically occurs in particular places.

The dialectics of space and place
So what were people building in the Black Mountains? It was a place that was being 'received and made and remade'. But what did 'place' mean to Williams? It is not one of his key words (though 'community', which is generally given a place-bound connotation in his work, is). Nevertheless:

A new theory of socialism must now centrally involve place. Remember the argument was that the proletariat had no country, the factor which differentiated it from the property-owning classes. But place has been shown to be a crucial element in the bonding process – more so perhaps for the working class than the capital-owning classes – by the explosion of the international economy and the destructive effects of deindustrialisation upon old communities. When capital has moved on, the importance of place is more clearly revealed.[21]

The embeddedness of working-class political action is, according to this account, primarily in 'place'. In his novels, however, the meaning of place becomes particularly clear, since it is almost as if the processes of place creation and dissolution – again a very dialectical conception as compared to the formed entity of an actual place – become active agents in the action. But the constitution of place cannot be abstracted from the shifting patterns of space relations. This is well established in *People of the Black Mountains* and was, of course, the guiding principle that allowed Williams to construct the incredibly rich literary analysis deployed in *The Country and the City*. But this material relation is rendered even more vivid in the strike episode in *Border Country*: political consciousness in a rural Welsh village community, traversed by a railway line along which goods and information flow, gets transformed by virtue of its relation to the miners' strike in South Wales, only in the end to be sold out by decisions taken in London. In an essay on the general strike of 1926 Williams[22] makes clear how the episode in *Border Country* was shaped only after long conversations with his father. He then reflects on the structure of the problem as follows:

> These men at that country station were industrial workers, trade unionists, in a small group within a primarily rural and agricultural economy. All of them, like my father, still had close connections with that agricultural life ... At the same time, by the very fact of the railway, with the trains passing through, from the cities, from the factories, from the ports, from the collieries, and by the fact of the telephone and the telegraph, which was especially important for the signalmen, who through it had a community with other signalmen over a wide social network, talking beyond their work with men they might never actually meet but whom they knew very well through voice, opinion and story, they were part of a modern industrial working class.

The point of the strike episode is to show how something special is achieved – in this case a realisation of class consciousness and an understanding of the possibility (and this word is always lurking in the margins of all of Williams's discussions) of a real alternative. But this possibility is arrived at precisely through the internalisation within that particular place and community of impulses originating from outside. How those external impulses were transformed and internalised as a very local 'structure of feeling' is a crucial part of the story. Something very special occurred in the fictional Glynmawr (the strike, he narrates, had raised the prospects of common improvement 'to an extraordinary practical vividness'[23]) and in the actual Pandy, giving a meaning to socialism that was of a peculiarly high order, thus making the tragedy of its sell-out from afar particularly devastating.

There is a counterflow at work here. After the collapse of the strike, one of its dynamic leaders, Morgan Prosser, takes to doing business deals until he ultimately becomes the biggest businessman in the valley, only in the end to be bought out by corporate capital. Says Morgan:

'This place is finished, as it was. What matters from now on is not the fields, not the mountains, but the road. There'll be no village, as a place on its own. There'll just be a name you pass through, houses along the road. And that's where you'll be living, mind. On a roadside.'[24]

While Morgan always professes his willingness to give up his business ways if another genuine alternative for common betterment can be found, he pushes home relentlessly the view that the only choice is either to 'settle' in place and take what comes or to internalise whatever can be had from the external forces at play and use them to particular, personal or place-bound advantage.

In *The Fight for Manod*, this local place-bound internalisation of capitalistic values becomes even more apparent. Says Peter Owen, the radical sociologist co-opted to look at what a new town built in the rural backwater of Manod in Wales might mean, 'the actual history is back there in the bloody centre: the Birmingham–Dusseldorf axis, with offices in London, Brussels, Paris, Rome'. 'What always breaks us up is this money from outside,' complains local resident Gwen.[25] As the tale of secret land company procurements comes to light, we see how a faceless capitalism exercises a deeply corrupting influence on everyone:

The companies. And then the distance, the everyday obviousness of the distance, between that lane in Manod, all the immediate problems of Gwen and Ivor and Trevor and Gethin and the others: the distance from them to this register of companies, but at the same time the relations are so solid, so registered. The transactions reach right down to them. Not just as a force from outside but as a force they've engaged with, are now part of. Yet still a force that cares nothing about them, that's just driving its own way.[26]

What follows for Matthew is the bitter realisation that: 'To follow what seem our own interests, as these farmers are doing in Manod, isn't against [this process] but is part of it; is its local reproduction.' All of this poses acute problems of political identity depending upon the spatial range across which political thought and action is construed as possible:

'This is Tom Meurig,' Peter said. 'He lives in Llanidloes or in Europe, I can't remember which.' Tom Meurig laughed ... 'He can't make up his mind,' Peter said, 'whether to proclaim an immediate federation of the Celtic Peoples, with honorary membership for the Basques, or whether simply to take over Europe, with this new communal socialism they've been dreaming up in the hills.' 'Either of those,' Meurig said, 'or the third possibility: getting one of our people on to the District Council.'[27]

The humour of that exchange conceals an incredible tension. It turns out that the internalisation of these external forces in Manod depends crucially upon a farmer on the District Council having privileged knowledge of plans being hatched elsewhere. The relevant place and range of political action (as well as action in the novel) cannot get resolved outside of a particularly dialectical way of defining loyalties to place across space. And within such loyalties we will always find a peculiar tension between resistance and complicity.

The place of socialist politics

Williams tries to incorporate 'place' more directly into socialist theorising. The key phrase here is what Williams calls 'militant particularism'. I want to pay particular attention to this idea since it captures something very important about both the history and prospects for socialism, at least insofar as Williams saw them. Williams[28] reflects as follows:

The unique and extraordinary character of working-class self-organisation has been that it has tried to connect particular struggles to a general struggle in one quite special way. It has set out, as a movement, to make real what is at first sight the extraordinary claim that the defence and advancement of certain particular interests, properly brought together, are in fact the general interest.

Ideals forged out of the affirmative experience of solidarities in one place get generalised and universalised as a working model of a new form of society that will benefit all of humanity. This is what Williams means by 'militant particularism', and he sees it as deeply ingrained in the history of progressive socialism in Britain as well as 'a most significant part of the history of Wales'. It is not hard to generalise the point, even though Williams himself was reluctant to let go of the particularities and specificities of actual places as the fundamental basis for his thinking. The French revolutionaries, after all, proclaimed doctrines of 'the rights of man'; the international workers' movement proclaimed the global transition to socialism for the benefit of all; the Civil Rights movement in the United States articulated a politics of universal racial justice; certain wings of contemporary feminism and the ecology movement project their militant particularism as the basis for a wide-ranging social reconstruction that will benefit, if not save, us all.

Williams appears to suggest that many if not all forms of political engagement have their grounding in a militant particularism based in particular structures of feeling of the sort I encountered in Cowley. But the difficulty is:

> That because it had begun as local and affirmative, assuming an unproblematic extension from its own local and community experience to a much more general movement, it was always insufficiently aware of the quite systematic obstacles which stood in the way.[29]

Such obstacles could only be understood through abstractions capable of confronting processes not accessible to direct local experience. And here is the rub. The move from tangible solidarities understood as patterns of social life organised in affective and knowable communities to a more abstract set of conceptions that would have universal purchase involves a move from one level of abstraction – attached to place – to another level of abstractions capable of reaching out across space. And in that move, something was bound to be lost. 'In came,' Williams ruefully notes, 'necessarily, the politics of negation, the politics of differentiation, the politics of abstract analysis. And these, whether we liked them or not, were now necessary even to understand what was happening.' Even the language changes, shifting from words like 'our community' and 'our people' in the coalfields to 'the organised working class', the 'proletariat' and the 'masses' in the metropolis, where the abstractions are most hotly debated.[30]

The shift from one conceptual world, from one level of abstraction to another, can threaten that sense of value and common purpose that grounds the militant particularism achieved in particular places:

This was my saddest discovery: when I found that in myself ... that most crucial form of imperialism had happened. That is to say, where parts of your mind are taken over by a system of ideas, a system of feelings, which really do emanate from the power centre. Right back in your own mind, and right back inside the oppressed and deprived community, there are reproduced elements of the thinking and the feeling of that dominating centre ... If that negative politics is the only politics then it is the final victory of a mode of thought which seems to me the ultimate product of capitalist society. Whatever its political label it is a mode of thought which really has made relations between men into relations between things or relations between concepts.[31]

The tension between the different levels and kinds of abstractions to which individuals necessarily appeal in order to understand their relation to the world is particularly vivid in his novels, often internalised within the conflicting emotions of the protagonists. In *Border Country*, Matthew takes that name given by his father into the wider world, but in Glynmawr he is always known as Will, the name his mother wanted. The duality of that identity – who is he, Matthew or Will? – is perpetually at work throughout the novel. Caught in that duality it becomes almost impossible to find a language with which to speak:

He was trained to detachment: the language itself, consistently abstracting and generalising, supported him in this. And the detachment was real in another way. He felt, in this house, both a child and a stranger. He could not speak as either; could not speak really as himself at all, but only in the terms that this pattern offered.[32]

The tension is registered even in the way in which a familiar landscape gets remembered:

It was one thing to carry its image in his mind, as he did, everywhere, never a day passing but he closed his eyes and saw it again, his only landscape. But it was different to stand and look at the reality. It was not less beautiful; every detail of the land came up with its old excitement. But it was not still, as the image had been. It was no longer a landscape or a view, but a valley that people were using. He realised as he watched, what had happened in going away. The valley as landscape had been taken, but its work forgotten. The visitor sees beauty: the inhabitant a place where he works and has friends. Far away, closing his eyes, he had been seeing this valley, but as a visitor sees it, as the guide book sees it: this valley, in which he had lived more than half his life.[33]

This distinction between a 'tourist gaze' and lived lives in place is vital to Williams. Lived lives and the sense of value that attaches thereto are embedded in an environment actively moulded and achieved through work, play and a wide array of cultural practices. There is a deep continuity here between the environmental ambience of *Border Country* and the more explicit environmental history of *People of the Black Mountains*. Only at the end of the former novel can Matthew/Will come together, perhaps to reconcile the different structures of feeling that arise through the mind that asserts itself walking on the mountains and the knowledge achieved through the 'polystyrene models and their theoretical equivalents':

Now it seems like the end of exile. Not going back, but the feeling of exile ending. For the distance is measured, and that is what matters. By measuring the distance, we come home.[34]

Again and again, the same duality erupts in Williams's novels. The battle between different levels of abstraction, between distinctively understood particularities of places and the necessary abstractions required to take those understandings into a wider realm, the fight to transform militant particularism into something more substantial on the world stage of capitalism – all of these elements become central lines of contradiction and tension that power the storyline of the novels. *Loyalties* turns crucially on such tensions. And in that novel we get a far more profound exploration of certain dilemmas than comes from any of the theoretical work.

A question of loyalties
The story of *Loyalties* begins with a meeting in 1936 between Welsh miners and Cambridge University students on a farmstead in Wales to work out common means to fight fascism in Spain. Out of that meeting comes a brief passionate liaison between a Welsh girl, Nesta, who has striking artistic talents, and Norman, a young Cambridge student from an upper-class background. The question of their distinctive places, both materially and in the structure of society, is raised immediately. She maintains that the place – Danycapel – has made her what she is; he graciously concedes that it must therefore be a good place but then urges her not to get stuck in it. She remains there for the rest of

her life – the woman embedded in the particular place that has both nurtured her and which she continues to nurture – while he, the man, returns to a more cosmopolitan, internationalist and seemingly rootless world of international political intrigue and scientific enquiry. Though the two never talk again after their brief initial encounters, the novel turns on the continuance of the tension between them, primarily in the figure of Gwyn, the son born out of wedlock between two class and gender positions – the one closely place-bound and the other ranging more widely across space – within a supposedly common politics defined largely through the Communist Party. Gwyn, like Matthew Price in *Border Country*, internalises the tension: raised in that place where Nesta dwells, he eventually goes to Cambridge to study, in part at the insistence of Norman's sister, who performs a crucial link role nurturing a familial connection to Gwyn that Norman broadly ignores.

The place-bound politics arising out of the experience of class solidarities and gender relations in Wales is radically different from the more abstract conceptions held by academics and party leaders. The difference is not, it should be noted, between parochialism and universalism. The miner, Bert, who ultimately marries Gwyn's mother and becomes Gwyn's real father, fights in Spain alongside other workers and students. When the student who was close to Norman at Cambridge is killed in action, Bert acquires his binoculars (a symbolic terrain of vision?) only on his deathbed to hand them on to Gwyn. Bert also fights in World War II (billed as 'the ultimate war against fascism'), and suffers a hideous injury in Normandy that permanently disfigures his face – Bert forever carries the marks of his internationalist commitments on his body.

Norman, Gwyn's biological father, dwells in a different world and fashions loyalties to the Party and to the cause in a radically different way. Perhaps modelled on Burgess, Maclean, Philby and Blunt (the Cambridge group who became Soviet agents during the 1930s), Norman is involved in passing on scientific knowledge to the communist powers, suffering interrogation and perpetual mental pressures, acquiring internal mental scars as he anguishes over whether to sustain loyalties contracted in one era when they made sense, in a Cold War world where conscience might dictate another course of action. Williams does not, interestingly, condemn Norman, though Bert's bitter deathbed judgement is powerfully registered against these 'runaways from their class' – 'they used us … we know now we got to do it by ourselves'. Gwyn echoes this judgement – Norman and his ilk were the very worst 'because they involved in their betrayal what should have been the alternative: their own working-class party, their socialism'.

But Gwyn's final angry confrontation with Norman (see below) is paralleled by an extraordinary outburst directed against Gwyn by his mother, Nesta. The occasion arises when she reveals to him two sketch portraits she has hidden away – one of the young Norman, fair-haired and ethereal, and the other of a now-deceased Bert, drawn after his return from the war, a portrait that 'was terrible beyond any likeness, as if the already damaged face was still being broken and pulled apart'. Gwyn is deeply moved but can only say how 'intensely beautiful' the latter portrait is:

> She was staring at him angrily. Her face and body seemed twisted with sudden pain. He was bewildered because he had never seen her in even ordinary anger. She had been always so contained and quiet and pleasant, always younger than her age, self-possessed and slightly withdrawn.
> 'It is not beautiful!' she screamed, in a terrible high voice.
> 'Mam, please, I didn't mean that,' Gwyn struggled to say.
> 'Do you understand nothing?' she screamed. 'Do you know nothing? Have you learned nothing?'
> 'Mam, all I meant—'
> 'It is not beautiful!' she cried again. 'It's ugly. It's destroying! It's human flesh broken and pulped!'
> 'Yes. Yes in him. But the truth, that you saw the truth—'
> 'It's ugly, it's ugly!' she screamed now past all control.[35]

The violent clash of sensibilities, of 'structures of feeling' as Williams puts it, says it all. The problem here is not only the level of abstraction at which the world view of socialist politics gets constituted, but of the very different structures of feeling that can attach to those different levels of abstraction. Gwyn has acquired the distance to look upon the portrait of his father as a work of art, as an aesthetic event, as a thing of beauty precisely because it can capture and represent the awfulness of disfigurement with an elemental truth. But for Nesta it is not the representation that matters, but what is being represented; the sheer pain of that always remains fundamental and elemental.

The difficulties posed by the search for any kind of critical distance then come more clearly into focus. In *Border Country*, for example, Matthew/Will takes to climbing the nearby mountain, the Kestrel, and admiring the view from on high. Looking at 'the patch' where he had been raised, he knew it:

> was not only a place, but people, yet from here it was as if no one lived there, no one had ever lived there, and yet, in its stillness, it was a memory

of himself ... The mountain had this power, to abstract and to clarify, but in the end he could not stay here: he must go back down where he lived.[36]

And then:

On the way down the shapes faded and the ordinary identities returned. The voice in his mind faded and the ordinary voice came back. Like old Blakely asking, digging his stick in the turf. What will you be reading, Will? Books, sir? No better not. History, sir. History from the Kestrel, where you sit and watch memory move, across the wide valley. That was the sense of it: to watch, to interpret, to try and get clear. Only the wind narrowing the eyes, and so much living in you, deciding what you will see and how you will see it. Never above, watching. You'll find what you're watching is yourself.[37]

But it is only partly the level of abstraction at which different representations operate that is vital here. For there is something else going on in these interchanges that derives from the kind of abstraction achievable given different ways of acquiring knowledge of the world. And here there is a definite polarisation in Williams's argument. Ingold,[38] in a rather different context, describes the opposition as that between a vision of the world as a sphere which encompasses us or as a globe upon which we can gaze:

The local is not a more limited or narrowly focused apprehension than the global, it is one that rests on an altogether different mode of apprehension – one based on an active, perceptual engagement with components of the dwelt-in world, in the practical business of life, rather than on the detached, disinterested observation of a world apart. In the local perspective the world is a sphere ... centred on a particular place. From this experiential centre, the attention of those who live there is drawn ever deeper into the world, in the quest for knowledge and understanding.

Both Bert and Nesta seem always to be reaching out from their centred place – Danycapel – whereas Norman always tries to understand the world in a more detached way en route to arriving at his political commitments. Gwyn internalises both perspectives and is riven with conflicting thoughts and feelings. Yet, Williams seems to be saying, we cannot do without both kinds of abstraction any more than we can do without the conflicting modes of representation that necessarily attach thereto. Williams tries to define a complementary, even dialectical relation between the two visions, though I think it is evident on what side of that opposition he feels most comfortable. We should, he again and again insists, never forget the brute ugliness of the realities of lived experience for the oppressed. We should not aestheticise or theorise those lived realities out of existence as felt pains and passions. To do so is to diminish or even to lose the raw anger against injustice and exploitation that powers so much of the striving for social change. The formulaic view that 'truth is beauty', for example, deserves to be treated with the wrath that Nesta metes out.

The question of loyalties is defined, then, by both the level and the kind of abstraction through which political questions are formulated. As an affective and emotive political force, loyalties always attach to certain definite structures of feeling. The richest characters in all of Williams's novels are precisely those who internalise different and conflicting loyalties to radically different structures of feeling – Gwyn in *Loyalties* or Matthew Price in *Border Country* and Owen Price in *Second Generation*. And it is no accident here that Williams turns to the novel form to explore the conflicts and tensions. The Brechtian strategy is everywhere apparent and suggests not only that the tensions can never be resolved but that we should never expect them to be. By perpetually keeping them open, we keep open a primary resource for the creative thinking and practices necessary to achieve progressive social change.

This is a telling formulation of a problem that many of us can surely recognise. I certainly recognise it not only as someone who, like Williams, went from an English state school to a Cambridge education, but also more immediately in the contested politics of the Cowley project. Where did my loyalties lie? Williams's warnings are salutary. The possibility of betrayal looms, in our heads as well as in our actions, as we move from one level of abstraction or from one kind of epistemology to another. The dissident shop stewards in the Cowley car plant probably said unkind words about me of exactly the sort that Bert said of 'the class runaways' in *Loyalties*. Interestingly, Hayter (though herself even more of a 'class runaway' than me) inserted into the conclusion the very strong words of a shop steward in the plant: 'Betrayal is a process, not an individual act, and it is not always conscious.' While the comment was not directed at me, it could well have been in the light of our discussions.

But betrayal is a complex as well as a bitter term. Let me go back to the fictional account in *Loyalties* for a moment. Here is how Norman's close associate defends him to Gwyn:

'There are genuine acts of betrayal of groups to which one belongs. But you have only to look at the shifts of alliance and hostility, both the international shifts and within them the complex alliances and hostilities of classes, to know how dynamic this definable quantity becomes. There are traitors within a class to a nation, and within a nation to a class. People who live in times when these loyalties are stable are more fortunate than we were.'

'Not only in times. In places,' Gwyn said.[39]

In any case, Norman was involved in scientific research that had a completely different domain of reference. This entailed:

a dynamic conflict within a highly specialised field. It was vital to prevent it, through imbalance, reaching that exceptionally dangerous stage in which, by its own logic, it passed beyond nations and classes and beyond all the loyalties that any of us had known. Except, perhaps, in the end, a simple loyalty to the human species.[40]

Nothing of such moment was involved in the Cowley case, of course. Although there is one minor twist at the end of *Loyalties* that would make the connection. Norman, allowed to retire without disgrace, has bought a wood to save it from development. In the face of Gwyn's accusation of class betrayal, of betrayal of 'the morality of shared existence' that underlies the militant particularism of a community like Danycapel, Norman argues:

'You abuse what you call my class but what you are really abusing is knowledge and reason. By the way the society is, it is here, with us, that ideas are generated. So it has been with socialism: at once the good ideas and the errors. Yet we have begun to correct them, and this is all that can be done. In reason and in conscience our duty now is not to something called socialism, it is to conserving and saving the earth. Yet nothing significant for either is generated among what you call your fellow countrymen. Indeed, that is, precisely, their deprivation. It is also their inadequacy, and then what are you asking of me. That I should be loyal to ignorance, to shortsightedness, to prejudice, because these exist in my fellow countrymen? That I should stay still and connive in the destruction of the earth because my fellow countrymen are taking part in it? And that I should do this because of some traditional scruple, that I am bound to inherit a common inadequacy, a common ignorance, because its bearers speak the same tongue, inhabit the same threatened island? What morality, really, do you propose in that?'

Gwyn's response is sharp:

'What you thought about communism, what you now think about nature, is no more than a projection of what suited you. The fact that for others each belief is substantial merely enabled you to deceive them.'[41]

The argument in *Loyalties* is not, of course, resolved. And I think Williams's point is to insist that it will never be. Loyalties contracted at one scale, in one place and in terms of a particular structure of feeling, cannot easily or simply be carried over without transformation or translation into the kinds of loyalties required to make socialism a viable movement either elsewhere or in general. But in the act of translation something important necessarily gets lost, leaving behind a bitter residue of always unresolved tension.

Loyalties, identities and political commitments

Accepting this leads to some uncomfortable political reflections. Let me depict them at their starkest. The socialist cause in Britain has always been powered by militant particularisms of the sort that Williams described in Wales, and that I encountered in Cowley. A good deal of historical evidence could, I believe, be assembled in support of that argument. A recent volume of essays, *Fighting Back in Appalachia*,[42] documents the point brilliantly within the United States. But those militant particularisms – even when they can be brought together into a national movement, as they have been at various historical moments by the Labour Party in Britain – are in some senses profoundly conservative because they rest on the perpetuation of patterns of social relations and community, of solidarities and loyalties, achieved under a certain kind of oppressive and uncaring industrial order. While ownership may change (through nationalisation, for example), the mines and assembly lines must be kept going, for these are the material bases for the ways of social relating and mechanisms of class solidarity embedded in particular places and communities. Socialist politics acquires its conservative edge because it cannot easily be about the radical transformation and overthrow of old modes of working and living – it must in the first instance be about keeping the coal mines open and the assembly lines moving at any cost (witness the tangled industrial policy of successive British Labour governments in the 1960s and 1970s). Should the struggle at Cowley be to keep the increasingly oppressive jobs in the car plant going, or to seek out different, better, healthier, more satisfying jobs in some quite different and more ecologically sensitive system of production? At a time of weakness and no alternatives, the Cowley struggle necessarily focused on the former objective, but I had the distinct impression that even in the long run and under the best of circumstances it would always be thus for those working on the shop floor, for those most strongly imbued with the militant particularism associated with working in the plant.

There is another way of putting this. Can the political and social identities forged under an oppressive industrial order of a certain sort operating in a certain place survive the collapse or radical transformation of that order? The immediate answer I shall proffer is 'no' (and again I think a good deal of evidence can be marshalled to support that conclusion). If that is the case, then perpetuation of those political identities and loyalties requires perpetuation of the oppressive conditions that gave rise to them. Working-class movements may then seek to perpetuate or return to the conditions of oppression that spawned them, in much the same way that those women who have acquired their sense of self under conditions of male violence return again and again to living with violent men.

That parallel is instructive here. It is, as many feminists have argued and many women have shown, possible to break the pattern, to come out of the dependency. Working-class movements can similarly retain a revolutionary impulse while taking on new political identities under transformed conditions of working and living. But it is a long, hard process that needs a lot of careful work. Williams recognises this difficulty explicitly in his discussion of the ecological issue:

> It is no use simply saying to South Wales miners that all around them is an ecological disaster. They already know. They live in it. They have lived in it for generations. They carry it with them in their lungs ... But you cannot just say to people who have committed their lives and their communities to certain kinds of production that this has all got to be changed. You can't just say: come out of the harmful industries, come out of the dangerous industries, let us do something better. Everything will have to be done by negotiation, by equitable negotiation, and it will have to be taken steadily along the way.[43]

The worry at the end of that road of negotiation is that socialist parties and governments will only succeed in undermining the social and political identities and loyalties that provide the seedbed of their own support (again, quite a bit of evidence can be marshalled for that proposition in Western Europe since World War II). Socialism, it could be argued, is always about the negation of the material conditions of its own political identity. But it so happens that capitalism has fortuitously taken a path these last twenty years towards the elimination of many of the militant particularisms that have traditionally grounded socialist politics – the mines have closed, the assembly lines have been cut back or shut down, the shipyards turned silent. We then either take the position that Hayter voiced to me – that the future of socialism in Oxford depended on the outcome of a struggle to get mass employment in car production back into Cowley (a view I could not accept) – or else have to search for new combinations of both old and new forms of militant particularism to ground rather different version of socialist politics. I see no option except to take the latter path, however difficult and prob-lematic it may be. This does not entail abandoning class politics for those of the 'new social movements', but exploring different forms of alliances that can reconstitute and renew class politics. Put pragmatically, class politics in Oxford could survive the total closure of the Cowley plant, but only if it secures a new basis.

There is still another dimension to all this, which has to do with the question of spatial scale and temporal horizon. With respect to the former, Neil Smith[44] has recently remarked how we have done a very bad job of learning to negotiate between and link across different spatial scales of social theorising and political action. He emphasises what I see as a central confusion in contemporary constructions of socialism arising out of 'an extensive silence on the question of scale':

The theory of geographical scale – more correctly the theory of the pro-duction of geographical scale – is grossly underdeveloped. In effect, there is no social theory of geographical scale, not to mention an historical materialist one. And yet it plays a crucial part in our whole geographi-cal construction of material life. Was the brutal repression of Tiananmen Square a local event, a regional or national event, or was it an international event? We might reasonably assume that it was all four, which immedi-ately reinforces the conclusion that social life operates in and constructs some sort of nested hierarchical space rather than a mosaic. How do we critically conceive of these various nested scales, how do we arbitrate and translate between them?

Capitalism as a social system has managed not only to negotiate but often to actively manipulate such dilemmas of scale in its forms of class struggle. This has been particularly true of its penchant for achieving uneven sectoral and geographical development so as to force a divisive competitiveness between places defined at different scales. But where does 'place' begin and end? And is there a scale beyond which 'militant particularism' becomes impossible to ground, let alone sustain? The problem for socialist politics is to find ways to answer such questions, not in any final sense, but precisely through defining modes of communication and translation between different kinds and levels of abstraction.

On conclusions

I let Hayter write the conclusion to *The Factory and the City*. The book, after all, was largely the result of her efforts. The result reads very oddly. Broadly 'workerist' assertions that focus exclusively on the struggle to regain radical control in the plant are ameliorated here and there by questions about over-capacity, community involvement and the environment. The effect is strange since it does not, I think, arrive at any sort of identifiable or productive inter-nalised tension. I think this a pity. For there was an opportunity here not to seek closure of an argument but to use the materials in the book to reflect upon and learn from what had happened, to open up a terrain of discus-sion and debate. Our failure helps explain, I think, why Williams resorted to the novel form to explore certain dilemmas. The closure that we often seem compelled to search for in a piece of cultural or political economic research can more easily remain perpetually open for reflection in the novel form, even when, as happens to Matthew Price, some sort of reconciliation becomes possible once 'the distance is measured'. Dual conclusions to the Cowley book would have gone some way towards keeping issues open and the tensions alive, at the same time highlighting the question of different levels and kinds of abstractions.

In view of all this, I was quite startled to read Williams's novel *Second Generation*, some time after the Cowley book was finished. This novel was published in 1964 and set in Oxford at around that time. It revolves around the tensions between a university-based socialism on the one hand and the contested politics within the car plant on the other. The opening paragraph sets the scene for the problem of socialist politics in a divided city:

If you stand, today, in between Town Road, you can see either way: west to the spires and towers of the cathedral and colleges; east to the yards and sheds of the motor works. You see different worlds, but there is no frontier between them; there is only the movement and traffic of a single city.[45]

Kate Owen, a local Labour Party organiser and wife of a union leader in the plant, is torn between loyalty to family and community and the sexual freedom that beckons from the other side of the class divide within a university-based socialism. Peter Owen, her son, is likewise caught in between. He is studying for his doctorate in industrial sociology at an Oxford college in the midst of violent shop floor struggle in the car plant that wears his father down. All the themes that Williams develops elsewhere concerning the kinds of knowledge that it is possible to acquire and hold are richly developed here, including the interplays of gender and class within the 'structures of feeling' that get incorporated into a socialist politics.

But, interestingly, many of the substantive issues that arose in the work on the Cowley project actually crop up, without resolution, in *Second Generation*. Had I read it before rather than after becoming associated with the Cowley research, I think my approach might well have been different. I would on the one hand have insisted much more strongly on the Brechtian strategy of keeping the conclusions open. But on the other I would have taken much more careful notice of Williams's[46] injunction that 'everything will have to be done by negotiation, equitable negotiation, and it will have to be taken steadily along the way'.

Evaluations and possibilities

The three words *space, place* and *environment* encompass much of what geographers do. Their meaning has been contested within geography over the years in fierce debates (particularly in the radical journal *Antipode*) over, for example, how and why localities and places might be said to matter and how properly to view relations between place and space.[47] And in the course of this discussion, the question of level of abstraction and scale has again and again been raised.[48] But geographers are not the only ones to deal in such matters. In recent years the meanings to be attributed to space, place and nature have become a crucial matter of debate in social, cultural and literary theory[49] – a debate in which geographers have certainly participated.[50] These sorts of concerns and interests have been impelled in part by the question of the relations between what appears to be an emergent global capitalist culture on the one hand and the reassertion of all sorts of reactionary as well as potentially progressive 'militant particularisms' based in particular places on the other, coupled with a seemingly serious threat of global environmental degradation. But the concerns have also in part been produced by a burgeoning tradition of cultural studies that Raymond Williams helped to define, with its emphasis upon structures of feeling, values, embeddedness, difference and the particularities of the counter-hegemonic discourses and social relations oppositional groups construct.

Williams thought a great deal about questions of space, place and environment and evidently worried as to how they might be brought into play both in his cultural theory and in his views on how socialism might be constructed. The social transformations of space, place and environment are neither neutral nor innocent with respect to practices of domination and control. Indeed, they are fundamental framing decisions, replete with multiple possibilities, that govern the conditions (often oppressive) over how lives can be lived.[51] Such issues cannot, therefore, be left unaddressed in struggles for liberation. Furthermore, such struggles must internalise a certain reflexivity, if not an unresolvable tension, concerning both the levels and kinds of abstractions they must necessarily embrace as part and parcel of their working tools for practical action.

The fact that Williams's dealings and concerns over space, place and environment are voiced primarily in his novels suggests, however, a certain hesitancy on his part if not an outright difficulty in getting this tripartite conceptual apparatus into the very heart of cultural theory. The conclusion is not, however, that space, place and environment cannot be incorporated into social and cultural theory, but that practices of theorising have to be opened up to the possibilities and dilemmas that such an incorporation requires. By treating Williams at his word, and seeing his novels and his critical cultural theory as complementary aspects within a unified field of endeavour, we find him opening up a terrain of theorising far more profound than that of many of the high theorists of contemporary culture who ignore such dimensions. Theory cannot be construed as a pure achievement of abstraction; more importantly, theoretical practice must be constructed as a continuous dialectic of the militant particularism of lived lives on the one hand, and the struggle to achieve sufficient critical distance and detachment on the other. In this regard, the problematic that Williams defines is surely universal enough to bring its own rewards. The search for a critical materialist and thoroughly grounded, as opposed to a confined metaphorical and purely idealist, incorporation of place, space and environment into cultural and social theory is on. And the stakes are high. The return of theory to the world of daily political practices across a variegated and hierarchically structured geographical space of social and ecological variation can then become both the aim and the reward of a particular kind of theoretical practice.

One of the most moving chapters in *Fighting Back in Appalachia* is entitled 'Singing across dark spaces'. It is a personal account by Jim Sessions and Fran Ansley of the union/community takeover of Pittston's Moss 3 Plant in the bitter coal strike of 1989 in Appalachia – a takeover that proved crucial in resolving the strike on terms much more acceptable to the miners. Jim Sessions, who was on the inside of the plant during the takeover as 'an unaffiliated witness', and Fran Ansley, who remained on the outside, recorded their day-by-day experiences. Wrote the latter, after two days of the occupation, 'there are moments of transcendence that are capable of teaching us, of making us *feel* the possibilities that reside in us, in the people around us, and in the groups of which we are or can be part'.[52] Theorists can also learn to sing across the dark spaces of increasingly violent and bitter social and cultural conflict. But only if we open ourselves to the sorts of possibilities that Williams created. I should have learned to listen more closely to the workers on the shop floor and the lifelong residents of Cowley without abandoning my loyalties to modes of analysis and of theorising that shed light on the uncaring ways and evolutionary directions of capital in general.

Commentary

The theoretical problem all geographers face is how to put together the three themes of space, place and environment in ways that are expressive of a unity without suppressing difference. One Marxist way to do this is to say that unities are always 'contradictory unities', which is helpful provided we have a good idea of the nature of the contradictions and how they work singly or in combination. This is the focus of my last book, *Seventeen Contradictions and the End of Capitalism*. Marx approached this question in an interesting way. We need to recognise, he says in the *Grundrisse*,[53] that 'the concrete is concrete because it is the concentration of many determinations, hence unity of the diverse'. We geographers typically deal with the concrete, such as the building of the Basilica of Sacré-Coeur. The question for me in Chapter 4 was what were the 'many determinations' involved in its construction? The follow-up question is how do we determine the many determinations? It is, says Marx, 'the abstract determinations' that 'lead towards a reproduction of the concrete by way of thought'. In the case of Sacré-Coeur, for example, the abstraction of class struggle (among many others) plainly plays such a role. But what legitimises the deployment of such an abstraction? The answer, says Marx, is that we have to begin with the concrete 'as the point of departure for observation and conception', such that the method of enquiry 'has to appropriate the material in detail, to analyse its different forms of development and to track down their inner connection. Only after this work has been done can the real movement be appropriately presented. If this is done successfully, if the life of the subject-matter is now reflected back in the ideas, then it may appear as if we have before us an a priori construction.'[54] This goes to the heart of Marx's dialectical method. The preparatory work uncovers the 'many abstractions' which then operate as the 'many determinations' of the concrete. My account of the building of Sacré-Coeur may appear as a prior construction precisely because it shows how important class conflicts were in the building of Haussmann's Paris.

In the 1980s a fierce controversy arose among geographers over the role of locality in shaping geographical research. I stood on the side of those who said that locality studies were a vital part of what we should be doing but if they became an end in themselves they would imperil the radical project. The celebration of locality as particularity, of difference as somehow inimical to unity, and of local politics as the exclusive terrain for fighting the abstractions of globalisation all seemed highly problematic to me. It may sometimes have seemed as if those of us who were concerned about such things were totally opposed to locality studies: the defenders of locality studies (and in particular a very large project generously funded by the Economic and Social Research Council in Britain) often portrayed the rest of us as insensitive to the multiple differences (in everything from gender relations to racial, religious and ethnic discriminations) which came more clearly into view at local levels. But this was simply not the case. Everything depended upon how such studies articulated 'the unity in the diverse'.

I wrote 'Militant particularism' – a positive concept for me as it was derived from the work of Raymond Williams – in order to find a way out of the thicket of misunderstandings that surrounded the localities debate. It coincided with my move to Oxford and involvement in the Cowley project to protect the jobs of the Rover car workers. No one would accuse Williams of being insensitive to local 'structures of feeling', though many find his writings on the topic problematic. I was primarily fascinated by how he addressed the contradictory unity of local and global forces in his novels. The intensity of debate has subsided in geography, but the foundational issue has not gone away. The political questions have in fact intensified because so much anti-capitalist politics is now grounded in local action. The discussion deserves to be brought back to centre-stage.

Chapter 9
The 'New' Imperialism

Accumulation by Dispossession

The survival of capitalism for so long in the face of multiple crises and reorganisations accompanied by dire predictions, from both the left and the right, of its imminent demise, is a mystery that requires illumination. Lefebvre,[1] for one, thought he had found the key in his celebrated comment that capitalism survives through the production of space, but he did not explain exactly how this might be so. Both Lenin and Luxemburg, for quite different reasons and utilising quite different arguments, considered that imperialism – a certain form of the production of space – was the answer to the riddle, though both argued that this solution was finite because of its own terminal contradictions.

The way I sought to look at this problem in the 1970s was to examine the role of 'spatiotemporal fixes' to the inner contradictions of capital accumulation.[2] This argument makes sense only in relation to a pervasive tendency of capitalism to produce crises of overaccumulation. Such crises are registered as surpluses of capital and of labour power side by side without there apparently being any means to bring them profitably together to accomplish socially useful tasks. If system-wide devaluations (and even destruction) of capital and of labour power are not to follow, then ways must be found to absorb these surpluses. Geographical expansion and spatial reorganisation provide one such option. But this cannot be divorced from temporal fixes either, since geographical expansion often entails investment in long-lived physical and social infrastructures (in transport and communications networks and education and research, for example) that take many years to return their value to circulation through the productive activity they support (see Chapter 3).

Global capitalism has experienced a chronic and enduring problem of overaccumulation since the 1970s. I find the empirical materials Robert Brenner[3] assembles to document this point generally convincing. I interpret the volatility of international capitalism during these years, however, as a series of temporary spatiotemporal fixes that failed even in the medium run to deal with problems of overaccumulation. It was, as Peter Gowan[4] argues, through the orchestration of such volatility that the United States sought to preserve its hegemonic position within global capitalism. The apparent shift in the late 1990s in the 'Project for a New American Century' towards an open imperialism backed by military force on the part of the USA may then be seen as a sign of the weakening of that hegemony. In the administration of President George W. Bush, the even more explicit embrace of the politics of imperialism seemed to derive from the need for a political antidote to the threat of recession and widespread devaluation at home. Prior to that, various bouts of devaluation had been inflicted elsewhere, such as Latin America in the 1980s and early 1990s, and, even more seriously, through the crisis that consumed East and South-East Asia in 1997 and then engulfed Russia before moving on to Turkey, Brazil and Argentina in the early 2000s.[5] But I also want to argue that the inability to accumulate through expanded reproduction on a sustained basis has been paralleled by a rise in attempts to 'accumulate by dispossession'. This, I then conclude, is the hallmark of what some like to call 'the new imperialism' is actually about.[6]

The spatiotemporal fix and its contradictions

The basic idea of the spatiotemporal fix is simple enough. Overaccumulation within a given territorial system means a condition of surpluses of labour (rising unemployment) and surpluses of capital (registered as a glut of commodities on the market that cannot be disposed of without a loss, as idle productive capacity, and/or as surpluses of money capital lacking outlets for productive and profitable investment). Such surpluses may be absorbed by: (a) temporal displacement through investment in long-term capital projects (e.g. in the built environment) or social expenditures (such as education and research) that defer the re-entry of current excess capital values into circulation well into the future, (b) spatial displacements through opening up new markets, new production capacities and new resource, social and labour possibilities elsewhere, or (c) some combination of (a) and (b).

The combination of (a) and (b) is particularly important when we focus on fixed capital of an independent kind embedded in the built environment. This provides the necessary physical infrastructures for production and consumption to proceed over space and time (everything from industrial parks, ports and airports, transport and communications systems, to sewage and water provision, housing, hospitals, schools). Plainly, this is not a minor sector of the economy and it is capable of absorbing massive amounts of capital and labour, particularly under conditions of rapid geographical expansion and intensification.

The reallocation of capital and labour surpluses to such investments requires the mediating help of financial and/or state institutions. These have the capacity to generate credit. A quantity of 'fictitious capital' is created that can be allocated away from current consumption to future-oriented projects in, say, highway construction or education, thereby reinvigorating the economy (including, perhaps, augmenting the demand for surplus commodities like shirts and shoes by teachers and construction workers). If the expenditures on built environments or social improvements prove productive (i.e. facilitative of more efficient forms of capital accumulation later on) then the fictitious values are redeemed (either directly by retirement of debt or indirectly in the form of, say, higher tax returns to pay off state debt). If not, overaccumulations of values in built environments or education can become evident with attendant devaluations of these assets (housing, offices, industrial parks, airports, etc.) or difficulties in paying off state debts on physical and social infrastructures (a fiscal crisis of the state).

The role of such investments in stabilising and destabilising capitalism has been significant. I note, for example, that the starting point of the crisis of 1973 was a worldwide collapse of property markets (beginning with the Herstatt Bank in Germany which brought down the Franklin National in the United States), followed shortly thereafter by the virtual bankruptcy of New York City in 1975 (a classic case of social expenditures outrunning tax revenues). It was also notable that the decade-long stagnation in Japan began in 1990 with a collapse of a speculative bubble in land, property and other asset markets, putting the whole banking system in jeopardy, and that the beginning of the Asian collapse in 1997 was the bursting of the property bubbles in Thailand and Indonesia. The most important prop to the US and British economies after the onset of general recession in all other sectors from mid-2001 onwards has been the speculative vigour in property markets. Since 1998, the Chinese have kept their economy growing and sought to absorb their labour surpluses (and curb the threat of social unrest) by debt-financed investment in huge mega-projects that dwarf the already huge Three Gorges Dam (8,500 miles of new railroads, superhighways and urbanisation projects, massive engineering works to divert water from the Yangtze to Yellow rivers, new airports, etc.). It is, I think, passing strange that most accounts of capital accumulation (including Brenner's) either ignore these matters entirely or treat them as epiphenomal.

The term 'fix' has, however, a double meaning. A certain portion of the total capital becomes literally fixed in some physical form for a relatively long period of time (depending on its economic and physical lifetime). There is a sense in which social expenditures also become territorialised and rendered geographically immobile through state commitments. (In what follows, however, I will exclude social infrastructures from explicit consideration since the matter is complicated and would take too much text to elucidate.) Some fixed capital is geographically mobile (such as machinery that can easily be unbolted from its moorings and taken elsewhere) but the rest is fixed in the land such that it cannot be moved without being destroyed. Aircraft are mobile but the airports to which they fly are not.

The spatiotemporal 'fix', on the other hand, is a metaphor for solutions to capitalist crises through temporal deferment and geographical expansion. The production of space, the organisation of wholly new territorial divisions of labour, the opening up of new and cheaper resource complexes, of new dynamic spaces of capital accumulation, and the penetration of pre-existing social formations by capitalist social relations and institutional arrange-ments (such as rules of contract and private property arrangements) provide multiple ways to absorb surplus capital and labour. Such geographical expan-sions, reorganisations and reconstructions often threaten, however, the values fixed in place but not yet realised elsewhere. Vast quantities of capital fixed in place act as a drag upon the search for a spatial fix elsewhere. The values of the fixed assets that constitute New York City were and are not trivial and the threat of their massive devaluation in 1975 (and then again in 2003) was (and is) viewed by many as a major threat to the future of capitalism. If capital does move out, it leaves behind a trail of devastation (the deindustri-alisation experienced in the 1970s and 1980s in the heartlands of capitalism, like Pittsburgh and Sheffield, as well as in many other parts of the world, such as Bombay, illustrates the point). If overaccumulated capital does not or cannot move, on the other hand, then it stands to be devalued directly. The summary statement of this process I usually offer is this: capital necessarily creates a physical landscape in its own image at one point in time only to have to destroy it at some later point in time as it pursues geographical expansions and temporal displacements as solutions to the crises of overaccumulation to which it is regularly prone. Thus is the history of creative destruction (with all manner of deleterious social and environmental consequences) written into the evolution of the physical and social landscape of capitalism.

Another series of contradictions arises within the dynamics of spatiotemporal transformations more generally. If the surpluses of capital and labour power exist within a given territory (such as a nation-state) and cannot be absorbed internally (by either geographical adjustments or social expenditures) then they must be sent elsewhere to find a fresh terrain for their profitable realisation if they are not to be devalued. This can happen in a number of ways. Markets for commodity surpluses can be found elsewhere. But the spaces to which the surpluses are sent must possess means of payment such as gold or currency (e.g. dollar) reserves or tradable commodities. Surpluses of commodities are sent out and money or commodities flow back. The problem of overaccumulation is alleviated only in the short term; it merely switches the surplus from commodities to money or into different commodity forms, though if the latter turn out, as is often the case, to be cheaper raw materials or other inputs they can relieve the downward pressure on the profit rate at home temporarily. If the territory does not possess reserves or commodities to trade back, it must either find them (as Britain forced India to do by opening up the opium trade with China in the nineteenth century and thus extracting Chinese silver via Indian trade) or be given credit or aid. In the latter case a territory is lent or donated the money with which to buy back the surplus commodities generated at home. The British did this with Argentina in the nineteenth century and Japanese trade surpluses during the 1990s were largely absorbed by lending to the United States to support the consumerism that purchased Japanese goods. Plainly, market and credit transactions of this sort can alleviate problems of overaccumulation at least in the short term. They function very well under conditions of uneven geographical development in which surpluses available in one territory are matched by lack of supply elsewhere. But resort to the credit system simultaneously makes territories vulnerable to flows of speculative and fictitious capitals that can both stimulate and undermine capitalist development and even, as in recent years, be used to impose savage devaluations upon vulnerable territories.

The export of capital, particularly when accompanied by the export of labour power, works rather differently and typically has longer-term effects. In this case, surpluses of (usually money) capital and labour are sent elsewhere to set capital accumulation in motion in the new space. Surpluses generated in Britain in the nineteenth century found their way to the United States and to the settler colonies like South Africa, Australia and Canada, creating new and dynamic centres of accumulation in these territories which generated a demand for goods from Britain. Since it may take many years for capitalism to mature in these new territories (if it ever does) to the point where they, too, begin to produce overaccumulations of capital, the originating country can hope to benefit from this process for a considerable period of time. This is particularly the case when the goods demanded elsewhere are fixed physical infrastructures (such as railroads and dams) required as a basis for future capital accumulation. But the rate of return on these long-term investments in the built environment eventually depends upon the evolution of a strong dynamic of accumulation in the receiving country. Britain lent to Argentina in this way during the last part of the nineteenth century. The United States, via the Marshall Plan for Europe (Germany in particular) and Japan, clearly saw that its own economic security (leaving aside the political and military aspect dependent on the Cold War) rested on the active revival of capitalist activity in these spaces.

Contradictions arise, because new dynamic spaces of capital accumulation ultimately generate surpluses and have to absorb them through geographical expansions. Japan and Germany became competitors with US capital from the late 1960s onwards, much as the USA overwhelmed British capital (and helped pull down the British Empire) as the twentieth century dragged on. It is always interesting to note the point at which strong internal development spills over into a search for a spatiotemporal fix. Japan did so during the 1960s, first through trade, then through the export of capital as direct investment first to Europe and the United States and more recently through massive investments (both direct and portfolio) in East and South-East Asia, and finally through lending abroad (particularly to the United States). South Korea suddenly switched outwards in the 1980s, shortly followed by Taiwan in the 1990s, in both cases exporting not only financial capital but some of the most vicious labour management practices imaginable as subcontractors to multinational capital throughout the world (in Central America, in Africa, as well as throughout the rest of South and East Asia). Even recently successful adherents to capitalist development have, therefore, quickly found themselves in need of a spatiotemporal fix for their overaccumulating capital. The rapidity with which certain territories, like South Korea, Singapore, Taiwan and now even China, moved from being net receiving to net capital-exporting territories has been quite startling relative to the slower rhythms characteristic of former periods. But by the same token these successful territories have to adjust fast to the blowbacks from their own spatiotemporal fixes. China, absorbing surpluses in the form of foreign direct investments from Japan, Korea and Taiwan, is rapidly supplanting those countries in many lines of production and export (particularly of the lower-value-added and labour-intensive sort, but it is quickly moving up to the higher-value-added commodities as well). The generalised overcapacity that Brenner identifies can in this way be disaggregated into a cascading and proliferating series of spatiotemporal fixes primarily throughout South and East Asia but with additional elements within Latin America – Brazil, Mexico and Chile in particular – supplemented now by Eastern Europe and Turkey. And in an interesting reversal, explicable in large part by the role of the dollar as a secure global reserve currency which confers the power of seigniorage, the USA has in recent years with its huge increase in indebtedness absorbed surplus capitals chiefly from East and South-East Asia but also from elsewhere.[7]

The aggregate result, however, is increasingly fierce international competition as multiple dynamic centres of capital accumulation emerge to compete on the world stage in the face of strong currents of overaccumulation occurring in many different spaces of the global economy. Since they cannot all succeed in the long run, either the weakest territories succumb and fall into serious crises of devaluation, or geopolitical confrontations erupt in the form of trade wars, currency wars and even military confrontations (of the sort that gave us two world wars between capitalist powers in the twentieth century). In this case it is devaluation and destruction (of the sort that the US financial institutions visited on East and South-East Asia in 1997/98) that is being exported, and the spatiotemporal fix takes on much more sinister forms. There are, however, some further points to make about this process in order to better understand how it actually occurs.

Inner contradictions

In *The Philosophy of Right*, Hegel[8] notes how the inner dialectic of bourgeois society, producing an overaccumulation of wealth at one pole and a rabble of paupers at the other, drives it to seek solutions through external trade and colonial/imperial practices. He rejects the idea that there might be ways to solve the problem of social inequality and instability through internal mechanisms of redistribution. Lenin (1963) quotes Cecil Rhodes as saying that colonialism and imperialism abroad were the only possible way to avoid civil war at home. Class relations and struggles within a territorially bounded social formation drive impulses to seek a spatiotemporal fix elsewhere.

The evidence from the end of the nineteenth century is here of interest. Joseph Chamberlain ('Radical Joe' as he was known) was closely identified with the liberal manufacturing interests of Birmingham, and was initially opposed to imperialism (in the Afghan Wars of the 1850s, for example). He devoted himself to educational reform and improvements in the social and physical infrastructures for production and consumption in his home city of Birmingham. This provided, he thought, a productive outlet for surpluses that would be repaid in the long run. An important figure within the liberal conservative movement, he saw the rising tide of class struggle in Britain at first hand and in 1885 made a celebrated speech in which he called for the propertied classes to take cognisance of their responsibilities to society (i.e. to better the conditions of life of the least well off and invest in social and physical infrastructures in the national interest) rather than solely to promote their individual rights as property owners. The uproar that followed on the part of the propertied classes forced him to recant and from that moment on he became the most ardent advocate for imperialism (ultimately, as Colonial Secretary, leading Britain into the disaster of the Boer War). This career trajectory was quite common for the period. Jules Ferry in France, an ardent supporter of internal reform, particularly education, in the 1860s, took to colonial advocacy after the Commune of 1871 (leading France into the mire of South-East Asia that culminated in defeat at Dien Bien Phu in 1954); Crispi sought to solve the land problem in the Italian south through colonisation in Africa; and even Theodore Roosevelt in the United States turned, after Frederick Jackson Turner declared, erroneously, at least as far as investment opportunities were concerned, that the American Frontier was closed, to support imperial policies rather than internal reforms. The fascinating common history of this radical shift in European politics from internal to external solutions to political economic problems – in part dictated by the fearful state of class struggles after the Paris Commune – is beautifully laid out in a little-known collection of essays by Julien, Bruhat, Bourgin, Crouzet and Renovin.[9] The cases of Ferry, Chamberlain, Roosevelt, Crispi and others are there examined in comparative detail.

In all these instances, the turn to a liberal form of imperialism (and one that had attached to it an ideology of progress and of a civilising mission) resulted not from absolute economic imperatives but from the political unwillingness of the bourgeoisie to give up any of its class privileges, thus blocking the possibility of absorbing overaccumulation through social reform at home. The fierce opposition by the owners of capital to any politics of redistribution or internal social amelioration in the United States today likewise leaves the country no option but to look outwards for solutions to its economic difficulties. Internal class politics of this sort forced many European powers to look outwards to solve their problems from 1884 to 1945, and this gave a specific coloration to the forms that European imperialism then took. Many liberal and even radical figures became proud imperialists during these years and much of the working-class movement was persuaded to support the imperial project as essential to their well-being. This required, however, that bourgeois interests should thoroughly command state policy, ideological apparatuses and military power.

Hannah Arendt[10] interprets this Euro-centric imperialism, correctly in my view, as 'the first stage in political rule of the bourgeoisie rather than the last stage of capitalism', as Lenin depicted it. There are in fact many eerie resemblances between Arendt's analysis of the situation in the nineteenth century and our contemporary condition. Consider, for example, her following commentary:

> Imperialist expansion had been touched off by a curious kind of economic crisis, the overproduction of capital and the emergence of 'superfluous' money, the result of over saving, which could no longer find productive investment within the national borders. For the first time, investment of power did not pave the way for investment of money, but export of power followed meekly in the train of exported money, since uncontrolled investments in distant countries threatened to transform large strata of society into gamblers, to change the whole capitalist economy from a system of production into a system of financial speculation, and to replace the profits of production with profits in commissions. The decade immediately before the imperialist era, the seventies of the last century, witnessed an unparalleled increase in swindles, financial scandals and gambling in the stock market.

There are, as we shall see, several other ways in which Arendt's thinking is appropriate for the interpretation of contemporary imperialist practices.

Institutional arrangements for power over space

In a trenchant piece of comparative analysis, Henderson[11] shows that the difference in 1997/98 between Taiwan and Singapore (which both escaped the crisis relatively unscathed except for currency devaluation) and Thailand and Indonesia (which suffered almost total economic and political collapse) turned on differences in state and financial policies. The former territories were insulated from speculative flows into property markets by strong state controls and protected financial markets, whereas the latter were not. Differences of this sort plainly matter. The forms taken by the mediating institutions (the state in particular) are productive of, as well as products of, the dynamics of capital accumulation.

Clearly the whole pattern of turbulence in the relations between state, supra-state and financial powers on the one hand, and the more general dynamics of capital accumulation (through production and selective devaluations) on the other, has been one of the most signal, and most complex, elements in the narrative of uneven geographical development and imperialist politics to be told of the period since 1973. I think Gowan[12] is correct to see the radical restructuring of international capitalism after 1973 as a series of gambles on the part of the United States to try to maintain its hegemonic position in world economic affairs against Europe, Japan and later East and South-East Asia. This began during the crisis of 1973 with Nixon's double strategy of high oil pricing and financial deregulation. The US banks were then given the exclusive right to recycle the vast quantities of petro-dollars being accumulated in the Gulf region. This recentred global financial activity in the USA and incidentally helped, along with the deregulation of the financial sector within the USA, to rescue New York from its own local economic crisis. A powerful Wall Street/US Treasury financial regime was created, with controlling powers over global financial institutions (such as the IMF) and able to make or break many weaker foreign economies through credit manipulations and debt management practices. This monetary and financial regime was used, Gowan argues, by successive US administrations 'as a formidable instrument of economic statecraft to drive forward both the globalisation process and the associated neo-liberal domestic transformations'. The regime thrived on crises. 'The IMF covers the risks and ensures that the US banks don't lose (countries pay up through structural adjustments etc.) and flight of capital from localised crises elsewhere ends up boosting the strength of Wall Street ...'[13] The effect was to project US economic power outwards (in alliance with others wherever possible), to force open markets, particularly for capital and financial flows (now a requirement for membership in the IMF), and impose other neoliberal practices (culminating in the WTO) upon much of the rest of the world.

There are two major points to be made about this system. First, free trade in commodities is often depicted as opening up the world to free and open competition. But this whole argument fails, as Lenin long ago pointed out, in the face of monopoly or oligopoly power (in either production or consumption). The USA, for example, has repeatedly used the weapon of denial of access to the huge US market to force other nations to comply with its wishes. The most recent (and crass) example of this line of argument comes from the US Trade Representative Robert Zoellick to the effect that if Lula, the newly elected Workers' Party president of Brazil, does not go along with US plans for free markets in the Americas, he would find himself having 'to export to Antarctica'.[14] Taiwan and Singapore were forced to sign on to the WTO, and thereby open their financial markets to speculative capital, in the face of US threats to deny them access to the US market. At US Treasury insistence, South Korea was forced to do the same as a condition for an IMF bail-out in 1998. The USA now plans to attach a condition of financial institutional compatibility to the foreign aid it offers as 'challenge grants' to poor countries. On the production side, oligopolies, largely based in the core capitalist regions, effectively control the production of seeds, fertilisers, electronics, computer software, pharmaceutical products, petroleum products and much more. Under these conditions, the creation of new market openings does not open up competition but merely creates opportunities to proliferate monopoly powers with all manner of social, ecological, economic and political consequences. The fact that nearly two-thirds of foreign trade is now accounted for by transactions within and between the main transnational corporations is indicative of the situation. Even something as seemingly benevolent as the Green Revolution has, most commentators agree, paralleled the increased agricultural outputs with considerable concentrations of wealth in the agrarian sector and higher levels of dependency upon monopolised inputs throughout South and East Asia. The penetration of the China market by US tobacco companies is set fair to compensate for their losses in the US market at the same time as it will surely generate a public health crisis in China for decades to come. In all of these respects, the claims generally made that neoliberalism is about open competition rather than monopoly control or limited competition within oligopolistic structures turn out to be fraudulent, masked as usual by the fetish worship of market freedoms. Free trade does not mean fair trade.

There is also, as even advocates of free trade readily acknowledge, a huge difference between freedom of trade in commodities and freedom of movement for finance capital. This immediately poses the problem of what kind of market freedom is being talked about. Some, like Bhagwati,[15] fiercely defend free trade in commodities but resist the idea that this necessarily holds good for financial flows. The difficulty here is this. On the one hand credit flows are vital to productive investments and reallocations of capital from one line of production or location to another. They also play an important role in bringing consumption needs – for housing, for example – into a potentially balanced relationship with productive activities in a spatially disaggregated world marked by surpluses in one space and deficits in another. In all of these respects the financial system, with or without state involvement, is critical to coordinate the dynamics of capital accumulation through uneven geographical development. But finance capital also embraces a lot of unproductive activity in which money is simply used to make more money through speculation on commodity futures, currency values, debt, and the like. When huge quantities of capital become available for such purposes, then open capital markets become vehicles for speculative activity, some of which, as we saw during the 1990s with both the 'dot.com' and the stock market 'bubbles', become self-fulfilling prophecies, just as the hedge funds, armed with trillions of dollars of leveraged money, could force Indonesia and even South Korea into bankruptcy no matter what the strength of their underlying economies. Much of what happens on Wall Street has nothing to do with facilitating investment in productive activities. It is purely speculative (hence the descriptions of it as 'casino', 'predatory' or even 'vulture' capitalism – with the debacle of Long Term Capital Management needing a $2.3 billion bail-out reminding us that speculations can easily go awry). This activity has, however, deep impacts upon the overall dynamics of capital accumulation. Above all, it facilitated the recentring of political-economic power primarily in the United States but also within the financial markets of other core countries (Tokyo, London, Frankfurt).

How this occurs depends on the dominant form of the class alliances arrived at within the core countries, the balance of power between them in negotiating international arrangements (such as the new international financial architecture put in place after 1997/98 to replace the so-called Washington Consensus of the mid-1990s) and the political-economic strategies set in motion by dominant agents with respect to surplus capital. The emergence of a 'Wall Street–Treasury–IMF' complex within the United States, able to control global institutions and to project vast financial power across the world through a network of other financial and governmental institutions, has played a determinant and problematic role in the dynamics of global capitalism in recent years. But this power centre can only operate the way it does because the rest of the world is networked and successfully hooked into (and effectively 'hooked on') a structured framework of interlocking financial and governmental (including supra-national) institutions. Hence the significance of collaborations between, for example, central bankers of the G7 nations and the various international accords (temporary in the case of currency strategies and more permanent with respect to the WTO) designed to deal with particular difficulties.[16] And if market power is not sufficient to accomplish particular objectives and to bring recalcitrant elements or 'rogue states' into line, then unchallengeable US military power (covert or overt) is available to force the issue.

This complex of institutional arrangements should in the best of all possible capitalist worlds be geared to sustain and support expanded reproduction (growth). But, like war in relation to diplomacy, finance capital intervention backed by state power can frequently become accumulation by other means. An unholy alliance between state powers and the predatory aspects of finance capital forms the cutting edge of a 'vulture capitalism' dedicated to the appropriation and devaluation of assets, rather than to building them up through productive investments. But how are we to interpret these 'other means' to accumulation or devaluation?

Accumulation by dispossession

In *The Accumulation of Capital*, Luxemburg[17] focuses attention on the dual aspects of capitalist accumulation:

> One concerns the commodity market and the place where surplus value is produced – the factory, the mine, the agricultural estate. Regarded in this light accumulation is a purely economic process, with its most important phase a transaction between the capitalist and the wage labourer ... Here, in form at any rate, peace, property and equality prevail, and the keen dialectics of scientific analysis were required to reveal how the right of ownership changes in the course of accumulation into appropriation of other people's property, how commodity exchange turns into exploitation and equality becomes class rule. The other aspect of the accumulation of capital concerns the relations between capitalism and the non-capitalist modes of production which start making their appearance on the international stage. Its predominant methods are colonial policy, an international loan system – a policy of spheres of interest – and war. Force, fraud, oppression, looting are openly displayed without any attempt at concealment, and it requires an effort to discover within this tangle of political violence and contests of power the stern laws of the economic process.

These two aspects of accumulation, she argues, are 'organically linked' and 'the historical career of capitalism can only be appreciated by taking them together'.

Marx's general theory of capital accumulation is constructed under certain crucial initial assumptions which broadly match those of classical political economy and which exclude primitive accumulation processes. These assumptions are: freely functioning competitive markets with institutional arrangements of private property, juridical individualism, freedom of contract and appropriate structures of law and governance guaranteed by a 'facilitative' state which also secures the integrity of money as a store of value and as a medium of circulation. The role of the capitalist as a commodity producer and exchanger is already well established and labour power has become a commodity that trades generally at its value. 'Primitive' or 'original' accumulation has already occurred and accumulation now proceeds as expanded reproduction (albeit through the exploitation of living labour in production) within a closed economy working under conditions of 'peace, property and equality'. These assumptions allow us to see what will happen if the liberal project of the classical political economists, or, in our times, the neoliberal project of the neoclassical economists, is realised. The brilliance of Marx's dialectical method is to show that market liberalisation – the credo of the liberals and the neoliberals – will not produce a harmonious state in which everyone is better off. It will instead produce ever greater levels of social inequality, as indeed has been the global trend over the last thirty years of neoliberalism, particularly within those countries such as Britain and the United States that have most closely hewed to such a political line. It will also, Marx predicts, produce serious and growing instabilities culminating in chronic crises of overaccumulation of the sort we are now witnessing.

The disadvantage of these assumptions is that they relegate accumulation based upon predation, fraud and violence to an 'original stage' that is considered no longer relevant or, as with Luxemburg, as being somehow 'outside of' the capitalist system. A general re-evaluation of the continuous role and persistence of the predatory practices of 'primitive' or 'original' accumulation within the long historical geography of capital accumulation is, therefore, very much in order, as several commentators[18] have recently observed. There has also been an extensive debate in *The Commoner* (www.thecommoner.org) on the new enclosures and on whether primitive accumulation should be understood as a purely historical or a continuing process. Since it seems peculiar to call an ongoing process 'primitive' or 'original' I shall, in what follows, substitute these terms by the concept of 'accumulation by dispossession'.

A closer look at Marx's[19] description of primitive accumulation reveals a wide range of processes. These include the commodification and privatisation of land and the forceful expulsion of peasant populations; conversion of various forms of property rights – common, collective, state, etc. – into exclusive private property rights; suppression of rights to the commons; commodification of labour power and the suppression of alternative, indigenous, forms of production and consumption; colonial, neocolonial and imperial processes of appropriation of assets, including natural resources; monetisation of exchange and taxation, particularly of land; slave trade; and usury, the national debt and ultimately the credit system. The state, with its monopoly of violence and definitions of legality, plays a crucial role in both backing and promoting these processes and there is considerable evidence, which Marx suggests and Braudel[20] confirms, that the transition to capitalist development was vitally contingent upon the stance of the state – broadly supportive in Britain, weakly so in France and highly negative, until very recently, in China. The invocation of the recent shift towards primitive accumulation in the case of China indicates that this is an ongoing issue and the evidence is strong, particularly throughout East and South-East Asia, that state policies and politics (consider the case of Singapore) have played a critical role in defining both the intensity and the paths of new forms of capital accumulation. The role of the 'developmental state' in recent phases of capital accumulation has therefore been the subject of intense scrutiny. Wade and Veneroso[21] define the developmental state as one with 'high household savings, plus high corporate debt/equity ratios, plus bank-firm-state collaboration, plus national industrial strategy, plus investment incentives conditional on international competitiveness'. One only has to look back at Bismarck's Germany or Meiji Japan to recognise that this has long been the case. The recent cases of East Asia are of obvious relevance also.[22]

All the features that Marx mentions have remained powerfully present within capitalism's historical geography. Some of them have been fine-tuned to play an even stronger role now than in the past. The credit system and finance capital have, as Lenin, Hilferding and Luxemburg all remarked, been major levers of predation, fraud and thievery. Stock promotions, Ponzi schemes, structured asset destruction through inflation, asset stripping through mergers and acquisitions, the promotion of levels of debt encumbrancy that reduce whole populations, even in the advanced capitalist countries, to debt peonage, to say nothing of corporate fraud, dispossession of assets (the raiding of pension funds and their decimation by stock and corporate collapses) by credit and stock manipulations – all of these are central features of what contemporary capitalism is about. The collapse of Enron dispossessed many people of their livelihoods and their pension rights. But above all we have to look at the speculative raiding carried out by hedge funds and other major institutions of finance capital as the cutting edge of accumulation by dispossession in recent times. By creating a liquidity crisis throughout South-East Asia, the hedge funds forced profitable businesses into bankruptcy. These businesses could be purchased at fire-sale prices by surplus capitals in the core countries, thus engineering what Wade and Veneroso[23] refer to as 'the biggest peacetime transfer of assets from domestic (i.e. South-East Asian) to foreign (i.e. US, Japanese and European) owners in the past fifty years anywhere in the world'.

Wholly new mechanisms of accumulation by dispossession have also opened up. The emphasis upon intellectual property rights in the WTO negotiations (the so-called TRIPS agreement) points to ways in which the patenting and licensing of genetic materials, seed plasmas, and all manner of other products, can now be used against whole populations whose environmental management practices have played a crucial role in the development of those materials. Biopiracy is rampant and the pillaging of the world's stockpile of genetic resources is well under way, to the benefit of a few large multinational companies. The escalating depletion of the global environmental commons (land, air, water) and proliferating habitat degradations that preclude anything but capital-intensive modes of agricultural production have likewise resulted from the wholesale commodification of nature in all its forms. The commodification of cultural forms, histories and intellectual creativity entails wholesale dispossessions – the music industry is notorious for the appropriation and exploitation of grass-roots culture and creativity. The corporatisation and privatisation of hitherto public assets (like universities), to say nothing of the wave of privatisation of water and other public utilities that has swept the world, constitute a new wave of 'enclosing the commons'. As in the past, the power of the state is frequently used to force such processes through even against the popular will. As also happened in the past, these processes of dispossession are provoking widespread resistance, and this now forms the core of what the anti-globalisation movement is about.[24] The reversion to the private domain of common property rights won through past class struggles (the right to a state pension, to welfare or to national healthcare) has been one of the most egregious of all policies of dispossession pursued in the name of neoliberal orthodoxy. The Bush administration's plan to privatise social security (and make pensions subject to the vagaries of the stock market) is a clear case in point. Small wonder that much of the emphasis within the anti-globalisation movement in recent times has been focused on the theme of reclaiming the commons and attacking the joint role of the state and capital in their appropriation.

Capitalism internalises cannibalistic as well as predatory and fraudulent practices. But it is, as Luxemburg cogently observed, 'often hard to determine, within the tangle of violence and contests of power, the stern laws of the economic process'. Accumulation by dispossession can occur in a variety of ways and there is much that is both contingent and haphazard about its modus operandi. Yet it is omnipresent in no matter what historical period and picks up strongly when crises of overaccumulation occur in expanded reproduction, when there seems to be no other exit except devaluation. Arendt[25] suggests, for example, that for Britain in the nineteenth century, the depressions of the 1860s and 1870s initiated the push into a new form of imperialism in which the bourgeoisie realised 'for the first time that the original sin of simple robbery, which centuries ago had made possible "the original accumulation of capital" (Marx) and had started all further accumulation, had eventually to be repeated lest the motor of accumulation suddenly die down'. This brings us back to relations between the drive for spatiotemporal fixes, state powers, accumulation by dispossession and the forms of contemporary imperialism.

The 'new' imperialism

Capitalist social formations, often arranged in particular territorial or regional configurations and usually dominated by some hegemonic centre, have long engaged in quasi-imperialist practices in search of spatiotemporal fixes to their overaccumulation problems. It is possible, however, to periodise the historical geography of these processes by taking Arendt seriously when she argues that the European-centred imperialism of the period 1884 to 1945 constituted the first stab at global political rule by the bourgeoisie. Individual nation-states engaged in their own imperialist projects to deal with problems of overaccumulation and class conflict within their orbit. Initially stabilised under British hegemony and constructed around open flows of capital and commodities on the world market, this first system broke down at the turn of the century into geopolitical conflicts between major powers pursuing autarky within increasingly closed systems. It erupted in two world wars in much the way that Lenin foresaw. Much of the rest of the world was pillaged for resources during this period (just look at the history of what Japan did to Taiwan or Britain did to the Witwatersrand in South Africa) in the hope that accumulation by dispossession would compensate for a chronic inability, which came to a head in the 1930s, to sustain capitalism through expanded reproduction.

This system was displaced in 1945 by a US-led system that sought to establish a global compact among all the major capitalist powers to avoid internecine wars and find a rational way to deal collectively with the overaccumulation that had plagued the 1930s. For this to happen they had to share in the benefits of an intensification of an integrated capitalism in the core regions (hence US support for moves towards European union) and engage in systematic geographical expansion of the system (hence the US insistence upon decolonisation and 'developmentalism' as a generalised goal for the rest of the world). This second phase of global bourgeois rule was largely held together by the contingency of the Cold War. This entailed US military and economic leadership as the sole capitalist superpower. The effect was to construct a hegemonic US 'superimperialism' that was more political and military than it was a manifestation of economic necessity. The USA was not itself highly dependent upon external outlets or even inputs. It could even afford to open its market to others and thereby absorb through internal spatiotemporal fixes, such as the interstate highway system, sprawling suburbanisation and the development of its south and west, part of the surplus capacity that began to emerge strongly in Germany and Japan during the 1960s. Strong growth through expanded reproduction occurred throughout the capitalist world. Accumulation by dispossession was relatively muted, though countries with capital surpluses, like Japan and West Germany, increasingly needed to look outwards for markets, including by competing for control of post-colonial developing markets.[26] Strong controls over capital export (as opposed to commodities) were, however, kept in place in much of Europe and capital imports into East Asia remained restricted. Class struggles within individual nation-states over expanded reproduction (how it would occur and who would benefit) dominated. The main geopolitical struggles that arose were either those of the Cold War (with that other empire constructed by the Soviets) or residual struggles (more often than not cross-cut by Cold War politics that pushed the USA to support many reactionary post-colonial regimes) which resulted from the reluctance of European powers to disengage from their colonial possessions (the invasion of Suez by the British and French in 1956, not supported at all by the USA, was emblematic). Growing resentments of being locked into a spatiotemporal situation of perpetual subservience to the centre did, however, spark anti-dependency and national liberation movements. Third World socialism sought modernisation but on an entirely different class and political basis.

This system broke down around 1970. Capital controls became hard to enforce as surplus US dollars flooded the world market. Inflationary pressures resulting from the USA trying to have both guns and butter in the midst of the Vietnam War became very strong, while the level of class struggle in many of the core countries began to erode profits. The USA then sought to construct a different kind of system that rested upon a mix of new international and financial institutional arrangements to counter economic threats from Germany and Japan and to recentre economic power as finance capital operating out of Wall Street. The collusion between the Nixon administration and the Saudis to push oil prices sky high in 1973 did far more damage to the European and Japanese economies than it did to the USA, which at that time was little dependent upon Middle Eastern supplies.[27] US banks gained the privilege of recycling the petro-dollars into the world economy. Threatened in the realm of production, the USA countered by asserting its hegemony through finance. But for this system to work effectively, markets in general and capital markets in particular had to be forced open to international trade – a slow process that required fierce US pressure backed by use of international levers such as the IMF and an equally fierce commitment to neoliberalism as the new economic orthodoxy. It also entailed shifting the balance of power and interests within the bourgeoisie from production activities to institutions of finance capital. This could be used to attack the power of working-class movements within expanded reproduction either directly, by exerting disciplinary oversight on production, or indirectly by facilitating greater geographical mobility for all forms of capital. Finance capital was therefore central to this third phase of bourgeois global rule.

This system was much more volatile and predatory and visited various bouts of accumulation by dispossession – usually as structural adjustment programmes administered by the IMF – as an antidote to difficulties in the realm of expanded reproduction. In some instances, such as Latin America in the 1980s, whole economies were raided and their assets recovered by US finance capital. The hedge funds' attack upon the Thai and Indonesian currencies in 1997, backed up by the savage deflationary policies demanded by the IMF, drove even viable concerns into bankruptcy and reversed the remarkable social and economic progress that had been made in much of East and South-East Asia. Millions of people fell victim to unemployment and impoverishment as a result. The crisis also conveniently sparked a flight to the dollar, confirming Wall Street's dominance and generating an amazing boom in asset values for the affluent in the United States. Class struggles began to coalesce around issues such as IMF-imposed structural adjustment, the predatory activities of finance capital and the loss of rights through privatisation.

Debt crises could be used to reorganise internal social relations of production in each country on a case-by-case basis in such a way as to favour the penetration of external capitals. Domestic financial regimes, domestic product markets and thriving domestic firms were, in this way, prised open for takeover by American, Japanese or European companies. Low profits in the core regions could thereby be supplemented by taking a cut out of the higher profits being earned abroad. Accumulation by dispossession became a much more central feature within global capitalism (with privatisation as one its key mantras). Resistance to this became more central within the anti-capitalist and anti-imperialist movement. But the left, embedded as it was (and still in many respect is) in the politics of expanded reproduction, was slow to recognise the significance of anti-IMF riots and other movements against dispossession. Walton's[28] pioneering study on the pattern of anti-IMF riots stands out in retrospect. But it also seems right that we do a far more sophisticated analysis to determine which of the myriad movements against dispossession are regressive and anti-modernising in any socialist sense and which can be progressive or at least be pulled in a progressive direction by alliance formation. As ever, the way in which Gramsci analysed the Southern question seems to be a pioneering study of this sort. Petras[29] has recently emphasised this point in his critique of Hardt and Negri's *Empire* with its undifferentiated concept of an oppositional multitude battling decentred imperial power. Affluent peasants fighting against land reform are not the same as landless peasants fighting for the right to subsist.

But the system, while centred on the Wall Street–Treasury complex, had many multilateral aspects with the financial centres of Tokyo, London, Frankfurt and many other global cities participating. It was associated with the emergence of transnational capitalist corporations which, though they may have a basis in one or other nation-state, spread themselves across the map of the world in ways that were unthinkable in the earlier phases of impe-rialism (the trusts and cartels that Lenin described were all tied very closely to particular nation-states). This was the world that the Clinton White House, with an all-powerful Treasury Secretary, Robert Rubin, drawn from the spec-ulator side of Wall Street, sought to manage by a centralised multilateralism (epitomised by the so-called 'Washington Consensus' of the mid-1990s). It seemed, for a brief moment, that Lenin was wrong and that Kautsky's theory of a collaborative 'superimperialism' might be right. An ultra-imperialism based on a 'peaceful' collaboration between all the major capitalist powers, as symbolised by the grouping known as the G7 and the so-called 'new inter-national financial architecture', albeit under the hegemony of US leadership, was possible.[30]

This system has now run into serious difficulties. The sheer volatility and chaotic fragmentation of power conflicts make it hard, as Luxemburg earlier noted, to discern how the stern laws of economics are working behind all the smoke and mirrors (particularly those of the financial sector). But insofar as the crisis of 1997/98 revealed that the main centre of surplus productive capacity lay in East and South-East Asia (so that the USA targeted that region specifically for devaluation), the rapid recovery of some parts of East and South-East Asian capitalism has forced the general problem of overaccumulation back into the forefront of global affairs.[31] This poses the question of how a new form of the spatiotemporal fix (into China?) might be organised, or who will bear the brunt of a new round of devaluation. The gathering recession of 2001 within the United States after a decade or more of spectacular (even if 'irrational') exuberance indicates that the USA may not be immune. A major fault line of instability lies in the rapid deterioration in the balance of payments of the United States. 'The same exploding imports that drove the world economy' during the 1990s, writes Brenner,[32] 'brought US trade and current account deficits to record levels, leading to the historically unprecedented growth of liabilities to overseas owners' and 'the historically unprecedented vulnerability of the US economy to the flight of capital and a collapse of the dollar'. But this vulnerability exists on both sides. If the US market collapses then the economies that look to that market as a sink for their excess productive capacity will go down with it. The alacrity with which the central bankers of countries like Japan and Taiwan lend funds to cover US deficits has a strong element of self-interest. They thereby fund the US consumerism that forms the market for their products. They may now even find themselves funding the US war effort.

But the dominance of the USA is, once more, under threat and this time the danger seems more acute. If, for example, Braudel, followed by Arrighi and Silver,[33] is correct, and a powerful wave of financialisation is a likely prelude to a transfer of dominant power from one hegemon to another, then the US turn towards financialisation in the 1970s would appear to exemplify a self-destructive historical pattern. The deficits, both internal and external, cannot continue to spiral out of control indefinitely and the ability and willingness of others, primarily in Asia, to fund them, to the tune of $2.3 billion a day at current rates, is not inexhaustible. Any other country in the world that exhibited the macroeconomic condition of the US economy would by now have been subjected to ruthless austerity and structural adjustment procedures by the IMF. But, as Gowan[34] remarks: 'Washington's capacity to manipulate the dollar price and to exploit Wall Street's international financial dominance enabled the US authorities to avoid doing what other states have had to do; watch the balance of payments; adjust the domestic economy to ensure high levels of domestic savings and investment; watch levels of public and private indebtedness; ensure an effective domestic system of financial intermediation to ensure the strong development of the domestic productive sector.' The US economy has had 'an escape route from all these tasks' and has become 'deeply distorted and unstable' as a result. Furthermore, the successive waves of accumulation by dispossession, the hallmark of the new US-centred imperialism, are sparking resistance and resentments wherever they happen to break, generating not only an active worldwide anti-globalisation movement (quite different in form from class struggles embedded in processes of expanded reproduction) but also active resistance to US hegemony by formerly pliant subordinate powers, particularly in Asia (South Korea is a case in point), and now even in Europe.

The options for the United States are limited. The USA could turn away from its current form of imperialism by engaging in a massive redistribution of wealth within its borders and seek paths to surplus absorption through temporal fixes internally (dramatic improvements in public education and repair of ageing infrastructures would be good places to start). An industrial strategy to revitalise manufacturing would also help. But this would require even more deficit financing or higher taxation as well as heavy state direction, and this is precisely what the bourgeoisie will refuse to contemplate, as was the case in Chamberlain's Britain; any politician who proposes such a package will almost certainly be howled down by the capitalist press and their ideologists and lose any election in the face of overwhelming money power. Yet, ironically, a massive counter-attack within the USA as well as within other core countries of capitalism (particularly in Europe) against the politics of neoliberalism and the cutting of state and social expenditures might be one of the only ways to protect Western capitalism internally from its self-destructive tendencies.

Even more suicidal politically, within the USA, would be to try to enforce by self-discipline the kind of austerity programme that the IMF typically visits on others. Any attempt by external powers to do so (by capital flight and collapse of the dollar, for example) would surely elicit a savage US political, economic and even military response. It is hard to imagine that the USA would peacefully accept and adapt to the phenomenal growth of East Asia and recognise, as Arrighi suggests it should, that we are in the midst of a major transition towards Asia as the hegemonic centre of global power. Arrighi does not envisage any serious external challenge but he and his colleagues do conclude that the USA 'has even greater capabilities than Britain did a century ago to convert its declining hegemony into exploitative domination. If the system eventually breaks down, it will be primarily because of US resistance to adjustment and accommodation. And conversely,

US adjustment and accommodation to the rising economic power of the East Asian region is an essential condition for a non-catastrophic transition to a new world order.'[35]

It is unlikely that the USA will go quietly and peacefully into that good night. It would, in any case, entail a reorientation – some signs of which already exist – of East Asian capitalism away from dependency on the US market to the cultivation of an internal market within Asia itself. This is where the huge modernisation programme within China – an internal version of a spatiotemporal fix that is equivalent to what the USA did internally in the 1950s and 1960s through suburbanisation and development of the so-called Sun Belt – may have a critical role to play in gradually siphoning off the surplus capitals of Japan, Taiwan and South Korea and thereby diminishing the flows into the United States. Taiwan, for example, now exports more to China than to North America. The consequent diminution of the flow of funds for the USA could have calamitous consequences.

And it is in this context that we see elements within the US political establishment looking to flex military muscle as the only clear absolute power they have left, talking openly of empire as a political option (presumably to extract tribute from the rest of the world) and looking to control oil supplies as a means to counter the power shifts threatened within the global economy. The attempts by the USA to gain better control of Iraqi and Venezuelan oil supplies – in the former case by purportedly seeking to establish democracy and in the latter by overthrowing it – make a lot of sense. They reek of a rerun of what happened in 1973, since Europe and Japan, as well as East and South-East Asia, now crucially including China, are even more heavily dependent on Gulf oil than is the United States. If the US engineers the overthrow of Chávez as well as Saddam, if it can stabilise or reform an armed-to-the-teeth Saudi regime that is currently based on the shifting sands of authoritarian rule (and in imminent danger of falling into the hands of radicalised Islam – this was, after all, Osama bin Laden's primary objective), if it can move on, as seems likely, from Iraq to Iran and consolidate its position in Turkey and Uzbekistan as a strategic presence in relation to Caspian basin oil reserves, then the USA, through firm control of the global oil spigot, might hope to keep effective control over the global economy and secure its own hegemonic position for the next fifty years.

The dangers of such a strategy are immense. Resistance will be formidable, not least from Europe and Asia, with Russia not far behind. The reluctance to sanction US military invasion of Iraq in the United Nations, particularly by France and Russia, which already have strong connections to Iraqi oil exploitation, was a case in point. And the Europeans in particular are far more attracted to a Kautskyian vision of ultra-imperialism in which all the major capitalist powers will supposedly collaborate on an equal basis. An unstable US hegemony that rests on permanent militarisation and adventurism of a sort that could seriously threaten global peace is not an attractive prospect for the rest of the world. This is not to say that the European model is much more progressive. If Robert Cooper,[36] a Blair consultant, is to be believed, it resurrects nineteenth-century distinctions between civilised, barbarian and savage states in the guise of postmodern, modern and pre-modern states with the postmoderns, as guardians of decentred civilised behaviour, expected to induce by direct or indirect means obeisance to universal (read 'Western' and 'bourgeois') norms and humanistic (read 'capitalistic') practices across the globe. This was exactly the way that nineteenth-century liberals, like John Stuart Mill, justified keeping India in tutelage and exacting tribute from abroad while praising the principles of representative government at home. In the absence of any strong revival of sustained accumulation through expanded reproduction, this will entail a deepening politics of accumulation by dispossession throughout the world in order to keep the motor of accumulation from stalling entirely.

This alternative form of imperialism will hardly be acceptable to wide swathes of the world's population who have lived through (and in some instances begun to fight back against) accumulation by dispossession and the predatory forms of capitalism they have had to confront over the last few decades. The liberal ruse that someone like Cooper proposes is far too familiar to post-colonial writers to have much traction.[37] And the blatant militarism that the USA is increasingly proposing on the grounds that this is the only possible response to global terrorism is not only fraught with danger (including dangerous precedents for 'pre-emptive strikes'); it is increasingly recognised as a mask for trying to sustain a threatened hegemony within the global system.

But perhaps the most interesting question concerns the internal response within the United States itself. On this point Hannah Arendt[38] again makes a telling argument: imperialism abroad cannot for long be sustained without active repressions, even tyranny, at home. The damage done to democratic institutions domestically can be substantial (as the French learned during the Algerian struggle for independence). The popular tradition within the United States is anti-colonial and anti-imperial and it has taken a very substantive conjuring trick, if not outright deception, to mask the imperial role of the USA in world affairs or at least to clothe it in grand humanitarian intentions over the past few decades. It is not clear that the US population will generally support an overt turn to any long-term militarised empire (any more than it ended up supporting the Vietnam War). This has been a long-standing popular concern against imperial ventures on the part of the United States, as William Appleman Williams[39] has pointed out. Nor will the US public likely accept for long the price, already substantial given the repressive clauses inserted into the Patriot and the Homeland Security Acts, that has to be paid at home in terms of civil liberties, rights and general freedoms. If empire entails tearing up the Bill of Rights then it is not clear that this trade-off will easily be accepted. But the other side of the difficulty is that in the absence of any dramatic revival of sustained accumulation through expanded reproduction and with limited possibilities to accumulate by dispossession, the US economy will likely sink into a deflationary depression that will make the last decade or so in Japan fade into insignificance by comparison. And if there is a serious flight from the dollar, then the austerity will have to be intense – unless, that is, there emerges an entirely different politics of redistribution of wealth and assets (a prospect the bourgeoisie will contemplate with utter horror) which focuses on the complete reorganisation of the social and physical infrastructures of the nation to absorb idle capital and labour into socially useful, as opposed to purely speculative, tasks.

The shape and form any new imperialism will take is therefore up for grabs. The only thing that is certain is that we are in the midst of a major transition in how the global system works and that there is a variety of forces in motion which could easily tip the balance in one or another direction. The balance between accumulation by dispossession and expanded reproduction has already shifted towards the former and it is hard to see this trend doing anything other than deepening, making this the hallmark of what the new imperialism is all about (and making overt claims about the new imperialism and the necessity of empire of great ideological significance). We also know that the economic trajectory taken by Asia is key, but that military dominance still lies with the United States. This, as Arrighi remarks, is a unique configuration and we may well be seeing in Iraq the first stage of how it might play out geopolitically on the world stage under conditions of generalised recession. The United States, whose hegemony was based on production, finance and military power in the immediate post-war period, lost its superiority in production after 1970 and may well now be losing financial dominance, leaving it with military might alone. What happens within the United States is therefore a vitally important determinant of how the new imperialism might be articulated. And there is, to boot, a gathering storm of opposition to the deepening of accumulation by dispossession. But the forms of class struggle which this provokes are of a radically different nature from the classic proletarian struggles within expanded reproduction (which continue, though, in somewhat more muted forms) upon which the future of socialism was traditionally supposed to rest. The unities beginning to emerge around these different vectors of struggle are vital to nurture, for within them we can discern the lineaments of an entirely different, non-imperialistic, form of globalisation that emphasises social well-being and humanitarian goals coupled with creative forms of uneven geographical development, rather than the glorification of money power, stock market values and the incessant accumulation of capital across the variegated spaces of the global economy by whatever means, but always ending up heavily concentrated in a few spaces of extraordinary wealth. The moment may be full of volatility and uncertainties; but that means it is also a moment of the unexpected and consequently full of potential.

Commentary

This piece was written shortly before the invasion of Iraq but published after it. It is a summary of the general argument laid out in *The New Imperialism*, published in 2003. It was the first piece in which I argued for the importance of 'accumulation by dispossession' as a key concept through which to understand the shifting global dynamics of capital accumulation. The concept has since been widely taken up because of its relevance to the massive, ongoing land grabs and extraction taking place in many parts of the world. The wave of dispossession in US housing markets through the foreclosures after 2007 (to say nothing of widespread predatory practices in housing markets), and the resultant cross-class transfers of asset values, brought home the importance of accumulation by dispossession in the advanced capitalist countries. Intellectual property rights are another terrain where the politics of accumulation by dispossession is of paramount importance. The sense of instability in global capitalism at the time of writing comes through markedly in this piece, as does the obvious need to theorise what's going on. Marx's concept of a permanent tendency towards the overaccumulation of capital is particularly useful. While *The New Imperialism* does not foretell any crash in the property markets then emerging as a primary vehicle for the absorption of surplus capital in the United States, I did point to the possibility.

The continuing politics of accumulation by dispossession has been masked in recent years by the 'necessity' for the politics of austerity, which is nothing more than organised dispossession, as has been dramatically and sadly illustrated by Greece. In a civilised world nothing so barbaric should have ever been contemplated. But from the Mexican debt crisis of 1982 onwards, accumulation by dispossession has become standard politics within global capitalism under the name of 'structural adjustment and austerity' for the masses, while bailing out the bankers and handsomely rewarding them for their egregious errors.

Chapter 10
The Urban Roots of Financial Crises

Reclaiming the City for Anti-Capitalist Struggle

In an article in the *New York Times* on 5 February 2011, entitled 'Housing bubbles are few and far between', Robert Shiller,[1] the economist who many consider the great housing expert given his role in the construction of the Case-Shiller index of housing prices in the United States, reassured everyone that the recent housing bubble was a 'rare event, not to be repeated for many decades'. The 'enormous housing bubble' of the early 2000s 'isn't comparable to any national or international housing cycle in history. Previous bubbles have been smaller and more regional.' The only reasonable parallels, he asserted, were the land bubbles that occurred in the United States way back in the late 1830s and the 1850s. This is, as I shall show, an astonishingly inaccurate reading of capitalist history. The fact that it passed so unremarked testifies to a serious blind spot in contemporary economic thinking. Unfortunately, it also turns out to be an equally blind spot in Marxist political economy.

Conventional economics routinely treats investment in the built environment along with urbanisation as some sidebar to the more important affairs that go on in some fictional entity called 'the national economy'. The subfield of 'urban economics' is, thus, the arena where inferior economists go while the big guns ply their macroeconomic trading skills elsewhere. Even when the latter notice urban processes, they make it seem as if spatial reorganisations, regional development and the building of cities are merely some on-the-ground outcome of larger-scale processes that remain unaffected by that which they produce. Thus, in the 2009 *World Bank Development Report*, which, for the first time ever, took economic geography seriously, the authors did so without a hint that anything could possibly go so catastrophically wrong in urban and regional development as to spark a crisis in the economy as a whole. Written wholly by economists (without consulting geographers, historians or urban sociologists), the aim was supposedly to explore the 'influence of geography on economic opportunity' and to elevate 'space and place from mere undercurrents in policy to a major focus'.

The authors were actually out to show how the application of the usual nostrums of neoliberal economics to urban affairs (like getting the state out of the business of any serious regulation of land and property markets and minimising the interventions of urban, regional and spatial planning) was the best way to augment economic growth (i.e. capital accumulation). Though they did have the decency to 'regret' that they did not have the time or space to explore in detail the social and environmental consequences of their proposals, they did plainly believe that cities that provide 'fluid land and property markets and other supportive institutions – such as protecting property rights, enforcing contracts, and financing housing – will more likely flourish over time as the needs of the market change. Successful cities have relaxed zoning laws to allow higher-value users to bid for the valuable land – and have adopted land use regulations to adapt to their changing roles over time.'[2]

But land is not a commodity in the ordinary sense. It is a fictitious form of capital that derives from expectations of future rents. Maximising its yield has driven low- or even moderate-income households out of Manhattan and central London over the last few years, with catastrophic effects on class disparities and the well-being of underprivileged populations. This is what is putting such intense pressure on the high-value land of Dharavi in Mumbai (a so-called slum that the report correctly depicts as a productive human ecosystem). The World Bank report advocates, in short, the kind of free market fundamentalism that has spawned both macroeconomic disruptions such as the crisis of 2007–09 alongside urban social movements of opposition to gentrification, neighbourhood destruction and the eviction of low-income populations to make way for higher-value land uses.

Since the mid-1980s, neoliberal urban policy (applied, for example, across the European Union) concluded that redistributing wealth to less advantaged neighbourhoods, cities and regions was futile and that resources should instead be channelled to dynamic 'entrepreneurial' growth poles. A spatial version of 'trickle down' would then in the proverbial long run (which never comes) take care of all those pesky regional, spatial and urban inequalities. Turning the city over to the developers and speculative financiers redounds to the benefit of all! If only the Chinese had liberated land uses in their cities to free market forces, the World Bank report argued, their economy would have grown even faster than it did!

The World Bank plainly favours speculative capital and not people. The idea that a city can do well (in terms of capital accumulation) while its people (apart from a privileged class) and the environment do badly is never examined. Even worse, the report is deeply complicit with the policies that lay at the root of the crisis of 2007–09. This is particularly odd, given that the report was published six months after the Lehman bankruptcy and nearly two years after the US housing market turned sour and the foreclosure tsunami was clearly identifiable. We are told, for example, without a hint of critical commentary, that:

> since the deregulation of financial systems in the second half of the 1980s, market-based housing financing has expanded rapidly. Residential mortgage markets are now equivalent to more than 40 per cent of gross domestic product (GDP) in developed countries, but those in developing countries are much smaller, averaging less than 10 per cent of GDP. The public role should be to stimulate well-regulated private involvement ... Establishing the legal foundations for simple, enforceable, and prudent mortgage contracts is a good start. When a country's system is more developed and mature, the public sector can encourage a secondary mortgage market, develop financial innovations, and expand the securitisation of mortgages. Occupant-owned housing, usually a household's largest single asset by far, is important in wealth creation, social security and politics. People who own their house or who have secure tenure have a larger stake in their community and thus are more likely to lobby for less crime, stronger governance, and better local environmental conditions.[3]

These statements are nothing short of astonishing given subsequent events. Roll on the sub-prime mortgage business, fuelled by pablum myths about the benefits of homeownership for all and the filing away of toxic mortgages in highly rated CDOs to be sold to unsuspecting investors! Roll on endless suburbanisation that is both land and energy consuming way beyond what is reasonable for the sustained use of planet earth for human habitation! The authors might plausibly maintain that they had no remit to connect their thinking about urbanisation with issues of global warming. Along with Alan Greenspan, they could also argue that they were blindsided by the events of 2007–09, and that they could not be expected to have anticipated anything troubling about the rosy scenario they painted. By inserting the words 'prudent' and 'well-regulated' into the argument they had, as it were, 'hedged' against potential criticism.[4]

But since they cite innumerable 'prudentially chosen' historical examples to bolster their neoliberal nostrums, how come they missed that the crisis of 1973 originated in a global property market crash that brought down several banks? Did they not notice that the end of the Japanese boom in 1990 corresponded to a collapse of land prices (still ongoing); that the Swedish banking system had to be nationalised in 1992 because of excesses in property markets; that one of the triggers for the collapse in East and South-East Asia in 1997/98 was excessive urban development in Thailand; that the commercial property-led Savings and Loan Crisis of 1987–90 in the United States saw several hundred financial institutions go belly-up at the cost of some $200 billion to the US taxpayers, a situation that so exercised William Isaacs, then chairman of the Federal Deposit Insurance Corporation, that in 1987 he threatened the American Bankers Association with nationalisation unless they mended their ways.[5]

Where were the World Bank economists when all this was going on? There have been hundreds of financial crises since 1973 (compared to very few prior to that) and quite a few of them have been property or urban development led. And it was pretty clear to almost anyone who thought about it, including, it turns out, Robert Shiller, that something was going badly wrong in US housing markets after 2000 or so. 'Irrational exuberance' and the 'animal spirits' of the financiers were getting out of hand.[6] But he saw it as exceptional rather than systemic. Shiller could well claim, of course, that all of the above examples were merely regional events. But then so, from the standpoint of the people of Brazil or China, was the crisis of 2007–09. The geographical epicentre was the US south-west and Florida (with some spillover in Georgia) along with a few other hot spots (the grumbling foreclosure crises that began as early as 2005 in poor areas in older cities like Baltimore and Cleveland were too local and 'unimportant' because those affected were African-Americans and minorities). Internationally, Spain and Ireland were badly caught out, as was also, though to a lesser extent, Britain. But there were no serious problems in the property markets in France, Germany, the Netherlands, Poland or, at that time, throughout Asia.

A regional crisis centred in the United States went global, to be sure, in ways that did not happen in the cases of, say, Japan or Sweden in the early 1990s. But the Savings and Loan crisis centred on 1987 (the year of a serious stock crash that is still viewed as a totally separate incident) had global ramifications. The same was true of the much-neglected global property market crash of early 1973. Conventional wisdom has it that only the oil price hike in the autumn of 1973 mattered. But it turned out that the property crash preceded the oil price hike by six months or more and the recession was well under way by the autumn. The boom can be measured by the fact that Real Estate Investment Trust Assets in the USA grew from $2 billion in 1969 to $20 billion in 1973 and that commercial bank mortgage loans increased from $66.7 billion to $113.6 billion over the same period. The property market crash that then followed in the spring of 1973 spilled over (for obvious revenue reasons) into the fiscal crisis of local states (which would not have happened had the recession been only about oil prices). The subsequent New York City fiscal crisis of 1975 was hugely important because at that time it controlled one of the largest public budgets in the world (prompting pleas from the French president and the West German chancellor to bail New York City out to avoid a global implosion in financial markets). New York then became the centre for the invention of neoliberal practices of gifting moral hazard to the banks and making the people pay up through the restructuring of municipal contracts and services. The impact of the most recent property market crash has also carried over into the virtual bankruptcy of states like California, creating huge stresses in state and municipal government finance and government employment almost everywhere in the USA. The story of the New York City fiscal crisis of the 1970s eerily resembles that of the state of California, which today has the eighth-largest public budget in the world.[7]

The National Bureau of Economic Research (NBER) has recently unearthed yet another example of the role of property booms in sparking deep crises of capitalism. From a study of real estate data in the 1920s, Goetzmann and Newman[8] show how 'publicly issued real estate securities affected real estate construction activity in the 1920s and the breakdown in their valuation, through the mechanism of the collateral cycle, may have led to the subsequent stock market crash of 1929–30'. With respect to housing, Florida, then as now, was an intense centre of speculative development with the nominal value of a building permit increasing by 8,000 per cent between 1919 and 1925. Nationally, the estimates of increases in housing values were around 400 per cent over roughly the same period.[9] But this was a sideshow compared to commercial development, which was almost entirely centred on New York and Chicago, where all manner of financial supports and securitisation procedures were concocted to fuel a boom 'matched only in the mid-2000s'. Even more telling is the graph Goetzmann and Newman compile on tall-building construction in New York City. The property booms that preceded the crashes of 1929, 1973, 1987 and 2000 stand out like a pikestaff. The buildings we see around us in New York City, they poignantly note, represent 'more than an architectural movement; they were largely the manifestation of a widespread financial phenomenon'. Noting that real estate securities in the 1920s were every bit as 'toxic as they are now', they went on to conclude: 'The New York skyline is a stark reminder of securitisation's ability to connect capital from a speculative public to building ventures. An increased understanding of the early real estate securities market has the potential to provide a valuable input when modelling for worst-case scenarios in the future. Optimism in financial markets has the power to raise steel, but it does not make a building pay.'

Property market booms and busts are, clearly, inextricably intertwined with speculative financial flows and these booms and busts have serious consequences for the macroeconomy in general as well as all manner of externality effects upon resource depletion and environmental degradation. Furthermore, the greater the share of property markets in GDP, then the more significant the connection between financing and investment in the built environment becomes as a potential source of macro crises. In the case of developing countries such as Thailand, where housing mortgages, if the World Bank report is right, are equivalent to only 10 per cent of GDP, a property crash could certainly contribute to but not totally power a macroeconomic collapse (of the sort that occurred in 1997/98), whereas in the United States, where housing mortgage debt is equivalent to 40 per cent of GDP, then it most certainly could – and did in fact generate the crisis of 2007–09.

The Marxist perspective

With bourgeois theory, if not totally blind, at best lacking in insights relating urban developments to macroeconomic disruptions, one would have thought that Marxist critics with their vaunted historical materialist methods would have had a field day with fierce denunciations of soaring rents and the savage dispossessions characteristic of what Marx and Engels referred to as the secondary forms of exploitation visited upon the working classes in their living places by merchant capitalists and landlords. They would have set the appropriation of space within the city through gentrification, high-end condo construction and 'Disneyfication' against the barbaric homelessness, lack of affordable housing and degrading urban environments (both physical, as in air quality, and social, as in crumbling schools and so-called 'benign neglect' of education) for the mass of the population. There has been some of that in a restricted circle of Marxist urbanists (I count myself one). But in fact the structure of thinking within Marxism generally is distressingly similar to that within bourgeois economics. The urbanists are viewed as specialists while the truly significant core of macroeconomic Marxist theorising lies elsewhere. Again the fiction of a national economy takes precedence because that is where the data can most easily be found and, to be fair, some of the major policy decisions are taken. The role of the property market in creating the crisis conditions of 2007–09 and its aftermath of unemployment and austerity (much of it administered at the local and municipal level) is not well understood, because there has been no serious attempt to integrate an understanding of processes of urbanisation and built environment formation into the general theory of the laws of motion of capital. As a consequence, many Marxist theorists, who love crises to death, tend to treat the recent crash as an obvious manifestation of their favoured version of Marxist crisis theory (be it falling rates of profit, underconsumption or whatever).

Marx is to some degree himself to blame, though unwittingly so, for this state of affairs. In the introduction to the *Grundrisse*, he states his objective in writing *Capital* is to explicate the general laws of motion of capital. This meant concentrating exclusively on the production and realisation of surplus value while abstracting from and excluding what he called the 'particularities' of distribution (interest, rents, taxes and even actual wage and profit rates) since these were accidental, conjunctural and of the moment in space and time. He also abstracted from the specificities of exchange relations, such as supply and demand and the state of competition. When demand and supply are in equilibrium, he argued, they cease to explain anything, while the coercive laws of competition function as the enforcer rather than the determinant of the general laws of motion of capital. This immediately provokes the thought of what happens when the enforcement mechanism is lacking, as happens under conditions of monopolisation, and what happens when we include spatial competition in our thinking, which is, as has long been known, always a form of monopolistic competition (as in the case of inter-urban competition).

Finally, Marx depicts consumption as a 'singularity' (a very Spinoza-like conception that Hardt and Negri have been at pains recently to revive). As such it is chaotic, unpredictable and uncontrollable, and, therefore, in Marx's view, generally outside of the field of political economy (the study of use values, he declares on the first page of *Capital*, is the business of history and not of political economy). Marx also identified another level, that of the metabolic relation to nature, which is a universal condition of all forms of human society and therefore broadly irrelevant to an understanding of the general laws of motion of capital understood as a specific social and historical construct. Environmental issues have a shadowy presence throughout *Capital* for this reason (which does not imply that Marx thought them unimportant or insignificant, any more than he dismissed consumption as irrelevant in the grander scheme of things). Throughout most of *Capital*, Marx pretty much sticks to the framework outlined in the *Grundrisse*.[10] He lasers in on the generality of production of surplus value and excludes everything else. He recognises from time to time that there are problems in so doing. There is, he notes, some 'double positing' going on – land, labour, money, commodities are crucial facts of production while interest, rents, wages and profits are excluded from the analysis as particularities of distribution!

The virtue of Marx's approach is that it allows a very clear account of the general laws of motion of capital to be constructed in a way that abstracts from the specific and particular conditions of his time (such as the crises of 1847–48 and 1857–58). This is why we can still read him today in ways that are relevant to our own times. But this approach imposes costs. To begin with, Marx makes clear that the analysis of an actually existing capitalist society/ situation requires a dialectical integration of the universal, the general, the particular and the singular aspects of a society construed as a working organic totality. We cannot hope, therefore, to explain actual events (such as the crisis of 2007–09) simply in terms of the general laws of motion of capital (this is one of my objections to those who try to cram the facts of the present crisis into some theory of the falling rate of profit). But, conversely, we cannot attempt such an explanation without reference to the general laws of motion either (though Marx himself appears to do so in his account in *Capital* of the 'independent and autonomous' financial and commercial crisis of 1847–48 or even more dramatically in his historical studies of the *Eighteenth Brumaire* and *Class Struggles in France*, where the general laws of motion of capital are never mentioned).

Secondly, the abstractions within Marx's chosen level of generality start to fracture as the argument in *Capital* progresses. There are many examples of this, but the one that is most conspicuous, and in any case most germane to the argument here, relates to Marx's handling of the credit system. Several times in volume 1 and repeatedly in volume 2, Marx invokes the credit system only to lay it aside as a fact of distribution that he is not prepared yet to confront. The general laws of motion he studies in volume 2, particularly those of fixed capital circulation and working periods, production periods, circulation times and turnover times, all end up not only invoking but necessitating the credit system. He gets very explicit on this point. When commenting on how the money capital advanced must always be greater than that applied in surplus value production in order to deal with differential turnover times, he notes how changes in turnover times can 'set free' some of the money earlier advanced. 'This money capital that is set free by the mechanism of the turnover movement (together with the money capital set free by the successive reflux of the fixed capital and that needed for variable capital in every labour process) must play a significant role, as soon as the credit system has developed, *and must also form one of the foundations for this*.'[11] From this and other similar comments it becomes clear that the credit system becomes absolutely necessary for capital circulation and that some accounting of the credit system has to be incorporated into the general laws of motion of capital. This poses a serious problem because when we get to the analysis of the credit system in volume 3, we find that the interest rate is set by supply and demand and by the state of competition, two specificities that have been earlier totally excluded from the theoretical level of generality at which Marx works.

I mention this because the significance of the rules that Marx imposed upon his enquiries in *Capital* has largely been ignored. When these rules necessarily get not only bent but broken, as happens in the case of credit and interest, then new prospects for theorising are opened up that go beyond the insights that Marx has already produced. Marx actually recognises this might happen at the very outset of his endeavours. In the *Grundrisse*,[12] he thus says of consumption, the most recalcitrant of his categories for analysis given the singularities involved, that while it, like the study of use values, 'actually belongs outside of economics' the possibility exists for consumption to react 'in turn upon the point of departure (production) and initiate the whole process anew'. This is particularly the case with productive consumption, the labour process itself. Tronti and those who followed in his footsteps, such as Negri, are therefore perfectly correct to see the labour process as itself constituted as a singularity – chaotic, hard to discipline, unpredictable and therefore always potentially dangerous for capital – internalised within the general laws of motion of capital.[13] The legendary difficulties faced by capitalists as they seek to mobilise the 'animal spirits' of the workers to produce surplus value signals the existence of this singularity in the heart of the production process (this is nowhere more obvious than in the construction industry, as we will see). Internalising the credit system and the relation between the rate of interest and the rate of profit within the general laws of production, circulation and realisation of capital is likewise a disruptive necessity if we are to bring Marx's theoretical apparatus more acutely to bear on actual events.

The integration of credit into the general theory has to be carefully done, however, in ways that preserve, albeit in a transformed state, the theoretical insights already gained. With regards to the credit system, for example, we cannot treat it simply as an entity in itself, a kind of efflorescence located on Wall Street or in the City of London that is free-floating above the grounded activities on Main Street. A lot of credit-based activity may indeed be speculative froth and a disgusting excrescence of human lust for gold and pure money power. But much of it is fundamental and absolutely necessary to the functioning of capital. The boundaries between what is necessary and what is (a) necessarily fictitious (as in the case of state and mortgage debt) and (b) pure excess are not easy to define.

Clearly, to try to analyse the dynamics of the recent crisis and its aftermath without reference to the credit system (with mortgages standing at 40 per cent of GDP in the USA), consumerism (70 per cent of the driving force in the US economy compared to 35 per cent in China) and the state of competition (monopoly power in financial, real estate, retailing and many other markets) would be a ridiculous enterprise – $1.4 trillion in mortgages, many of them toxic, are sitting on the secondary markets of Fannie Mae and Freddy Mac in the United States, thus forcing the government to allocate $400 billion to a potential rescue effort (with around $142 billion already spent). To understand this, we need to unpack what Marx might mean by the category of 'fictitious capital' and its connectivity to land and property markets. We need a way to understand how securitisation, as Goetzmann and Newman[14] put it, connects 'capital from a speculative public to building ventures'. For was it not speculation in the values of land and housing prices and rents that played a fundamental role in the formation of this crisis?

Fictitious capital, for Marx, is not a figment of some Wall Street trader's cocaine-addled brain. It is a fetish construct which means, given Marx's characterisation of fetishism in volume 1 of *Capital*, that it is real enough but that it is a surface phenomenon that disguises something important about underlying social relations. When a bank lends to the state and receives interest in return, it appears as if there is something productive going on within the state that is actually producing value when most (but not all, as I shall shortly show) of what goes on within the state (like fighting wars) has nothing to do with value production. When the bank lends to a consumer to buy a house and receives a flow of interest in return, it makes it seem as if something is going on in the house that is directly producing value when that is not the case. When banks take up bond issues to construct hospitals, universities, schools and the like in return for interest it seems as if value is being directly produced in those institutions when it is not. When banks lend to purchase land and property in search of extracting rents, then the distributive category of rent becomes absorbed into the flow of fictitious capital circulation.[15] When banks lend to other banks or when the central bank lends to the commercial banks who lend to land speculators looking to appropriate rents, then fictitious capital looks more and more like an infinite regression of fictions built upon fictions. These are all examples of fictitious capital flows. And it is these flows that convert real into unreal estate.

Marx's point is that the interest that is paid comes from somewhere else – taxation or direct extractions on surplus value production or levies on revenues (wages and profits). And for Marx, of course, the only place where value and surplus value are created is in the labour process of production. What goes on in fictitious capital circulation may be socially necessary to sustaining capitalism. It may be part of the necessary costs of production and reproduction. Secondary forms of surplus value can be extracted by capitalist enterprises through the exploitation of workers employed by retailers, banks and hedge funds. But Marx's point is that if there is no value and surplus value being produced in production in general, then these sectors cannot exist by themselves. If no shirts and shoes are produced, what would retailers sell?

There is, however, a caveat that is terribly important. Some of the flow of fictitious capital can indeed be associated with value creation. When I convert my mortgaged house into a sweatshop employing illegal immigrants, the house becomes fixed capital in production. When the state builds roads and other infrastructures that function as collective means of production for capital, then these have to be categorised as 'productive state expenditures'. When the hospital or university becomes the site for innovation and design of new drugs, equipment and the like, it becomes a site of production. Marx would not be fazed by these caveats at all. As he says of fixed capital, whether something functions as fixed capital or not depends upon its use and not upon its physical qualities.[16] Fixed capital declines when textile lofts are converted into condominiums while micro-finance converts peasant huts into (far cheaper) fixed capital of production!

Much of the value and surplus value created in production is siphoned off to pass, by all manner of complicated paths, through fictitious channels. And when banks lend to other banks, it is clear that all manner of both socially unnecessary side-payments and speculative movements become possible, built upon the perpetually shifting terrain of fluctuating asset values. Those asset values depend upon a critical process of 'capitalisation'. A revenue stream from some asset, such as land, property, a stock, or whatever, is assigned a capital value at which it can be traded, depending upon the interest and discount rates determined by supply and demand conditions in the money market. How to value such assets when there is no market for them became a huge problem in 2008 and it has not gone away. The question of how toxic the assets held by Fannie Mae really are gives almost everyone a headache (there is an important echo here of the capital value controversy that erupted and got promptly buried, like all manner of other inconvenient truths, in conventional economic theory in the early 1970s).[17]

The problem that the credit system poses is that it is vital to the production, circulation and realisation of capital flows at the same time as it is the pinnacle of all manner of speculative and other 'insane forms'. It is this that led Marx to characterise Isaac Pereire, who, with his brother Emile, was one of the masters of the speculative reconstruction of urban Paris under Haussmann, as having 'the nicely mixed character of swindler and prophet'.[18]

Capital accumulation through urbanisation

I have argued at length elsewhere that urbanisation has been a key means for the absorption of capital and labour surpluses throughout capitalism's history.[19] I have long argued it has a very particular relation to the absorption of overaccumulating capital for very specific reasons that have to do with the long working periods, turnover times and the lifetimes of investments in the built environment. It also has a geographical specificity such that the production of space and of spatial monopolies becomes integral to the dynamics of accumulation, not simply by virtue of the changing patterns of commodity flows over space but also by virtue of the very nature of the created and produced spaces and places over which such movements occur. But precisely because all of this activity – which, by the way, is a hugely important site for value and surplus value production – is so long term, it calls for some combination of finance capital and state engagements as absolutely fundamental to its functioning. This activity is clearly speculative in the long term and always runs the risk of replicating, at a much later date and on a magnified scale, the very overaccumulation conditions that it initially helps relieve. Hence the crisis-prone character of urban and other forms of physical infrastructural investments (transcontinental railroads and highways, dams, and the like).

The cyclical character of such investments has been well documented for the nineteenth century in the meticulous work of Brinley Thomas.[20] But the theory of construction business cycles became neglected after 1945 or so, in part because state-led Keynesian-style interventions were deemed effective in flattening them out. The construction business cycle (circa eighteen years in the USA) effectively disappeared.[21] But the gradual breakdown of systemic

Keynesian contra-cyclical interventions after the mid-1970s would suggest that a return to construction business cycles was more than a little likely. The data suggest that while fluctuations in construction have remained muted, asset value bubbles have become much more volatile than in the past (though the NBER accounts of the 1920s might be taken as contrary evidence to that view). The cyclical movements have also come to exhibit a more complicated geographical configuration, even within countries (e.g. the US south and west exhibiting different rhythms to the north-east and Midwest).

Without a general perspective of this sort, we cannot even begin to understand the dynamics that led into the catastrophe of housing markets and urbanisation in 2008 in certain regions and cities of the United States as well as in Spain, Ireland and the United Kingdom. By the same token we cannot understand some of the paths that are currently being taken, particularly in China, to get out of the mess that was fundamentally produced elsewhere. For in the same way that Brinley Thomas documents contra-cyclical movements between Britain and the United States in the nineteenth century, such that a boom in residential construction in one place was balanced by a crash in the other, so we now see a crash in construction in the United States and much of Europe being counterbalanced by a huge urbanisation and infrastructural investment boom centred in China (with several offshoots elsewhere, particularly in the so-called BRIC countries). And just to get the macro-picture connection right, we should immediately note that the United States and Europe are mired in low growth while China is registering a 10 per cent growth rate as of 2011 (with the other BRIC countries not far behind).

The pressure for the housing market and urban development in the United States to absorb overaccumulating capital through speculative activity began to build in the mid-1990s and fiercely accelerated after the end of the high-tech bubble and the stock market crash of 2001. The political pressures put on respectable financial institutions, including Fannie Mae and Freddie Mac, to lower their lending standards to accommodate the housing boom, coupled with the low interest rates favoured by Greenspan at the Fed, unquestionably fuelled the boom. But as Goetzmann and Newman remark, finance (backed by the state) can build cities and suburbs but they cannot necessarily make them pay. So what fuelled the demand?

To understand the dynamics we have to understand how productive and fictitious capital circulation combine within the credit system in the context of property markets. Financial institutions lend to developers, landowners and construction companies to build, say, suburban tract housing around San Diego or condos in Florida and southern Spain. In boom times, construction accounts directly for some 7 per cent of employment and more than double that when building materials suppliers and all the legal/financial services that rotate around the real estate industry are counted in. The viability of this sector presumes, however, that value can be realised. This is where fictitious capital comes in. Money is lent to purchasers who presumably have the ability to pay out of their revenues (wages or profits).

The financial system thus regulates to a considerable degree both the supply of and demand for tract housing and condos. This difference is similar to that between what Marx identifies in *Capital*[22] as 'loan capital' for production and the discounting of bills of exchange which facilitates the realisation of values in the market. In the case of housing in southern California, the same finance company often furnished the finance to build and the finance to buy what had been built. As happens with labour markets, capital has the power to manipulate both supply and demand, which is totally at odds with the idea of the freely functioning markets that the World Bank report supposes to be in place.[23]

But the relationship is lopsided. While bankers, developers and construction companies easily combine to forge a class alliance – one that often dominates what is called 'the urban growth machine'[24] both politically and economically – consumer mortgages are singular and dispersed and often involve loans to those who occupy a different class or, particularly in the United States but not in Ireland, racial or ethnic position. With securitisation of mortgages, the finance company could simply pass any risk on to someone else, which is, of course, precisely what they did, after having creamed off all the origination and legal fees that they could. If the financier has to choose between the bankruptcy of a developer because of failures of realisation or the bankruptcy of and foreclosure on the purchaser of housing (particularly if the purchaser is from the lower classes or from a racial or ethnic minority) then it is fairly clear which way the financial system will lean. Class and racial prejudices are invariably involved.

Furthermore, the asset markets constituted by housing and land inevitably have a Ponzi character even without a Bernie Madoff at the top. I buy a property and the property prices go up and a rising market encourages others to buy. When the pool of truly creditworthy buyers dries up, then why not go further down the income layers to higher-risk consumers, ending up with no income and no asset buyers who might gain by 'flipping' the property as prices rise (a property dealer would buy a run-down house cheaply, put in a few cosmetic repairs – much overvalued – and arrange 'favourable' mortgage finance for the unsuspecting buyer, who lived in the house only so long as the roof did not fall in or the furnace blow up)? And so it goes until the bubble pops. Financial institutions have tremendous incentives to sustain the bubble as long as they can. The problem is that they often can't get off the train before it wrecks because the train is accelerating so quickly. This is where the disparate turnover times, which Marx so cannily analyses in volume 2 of *Capital*, also become crucial. Contracts that finance construction are drawn up long before sales can begin. The time-lags are often substantial. The Empire State Building in New York opened on May Day 1931, almost two years after the stock market crash and more than three years after the real estate crash. The Twin Towers opened shortly after the crash of 1973 (and for years could find no private tenants) and now the downtown rebuilding on the 9/11 site is about to come online when commercial property values are depressed! Since the realisation of the values produced is so crucial to the recuperation of the initial loans then finance companies will go to any lengths to stimulate the market beyond its real capacity.

But there are longer-term issues here that also need to be taken into account. If the NBER papers are correct, the collapse of the construction boom after 1928, which was manifest as a $2 billion drop-off (huge for the time) in housing construction and a collapse of housing starts to less than 10 per cent of their former volume in the larger cities, played an important but still not well-understood role in the 1929 crash. A Wikipedia entry notes: 'devastating was the disappearance of 2 million high paying jobs in the construction trades, plus the loss of profits and rents that humbled many landlords and real estate investors'.[25] This surely had implications for confidence in the stock market more generally. Small wonder that there were desperate subsequent attempts by the Roosevelt administration to revive the housing sector. To that end a raft of reforms in housing mortgage finance was implemented, culminating in the creation of a secondary mortgage market through the founding of the Federal National Mortgage Association (Fannie Mae) in 1938. The task of Fannie Mae was to insure mortgages and to allow banks and other lenders to pass the mortgages on, thus providing much-needed liquidity to the housing market. These institutional reforms were later to play a vital role in financing the suburbanisation of the United States after World War II.

While necessary, they were not sufficient to put housing construction onto a different plane in US economic development. All sorts of tax incentives (such as the mortgage interest tax deduction) along with the GI Bill and a very positive Housing Act of 1947, which declared the right of all Americans to live in 'decent housing in a decent living environment', were devised to promote home ownership for political as well as economic reasons. Home ownership was widely promoted as central to the 'American Dream' and it rose from just above 40 per cent of the population in the 1940s to more than 60 per cent by the 1960s and close to 70 per cent at its peak in 2004 (as of 2010 it had fallen to 66 per cent). Home ownership may be a deeply held cultural value in the United States but cultural values of this sort always flourish best when promoted and subsidised by state policies. The stated reasons for such policies are all those that the World Bank report cites. But the political reason is rarely now acknowledged: as was openly noted in the 1930s, debt-encumbered homeowners do not go on strike![26] The military personnel returning from service in World War II would have constituted a social and political threat had they returned to unemployment and depression. What better way to kill two birds with one stone: revive the economy through massive housing construction and suburbanisation and co-opt the better-paid workers into conservative politics by home ownership!

During the 1950s and the 1960s these policies worked, both from the political and the macroeconomic viewpoints, since they underpinned two decades of very strong growth in the United States and the effects of that growth spilled over globally. The problem was that the urbanisation process was as geographically uneven as were the income streams that flowed to different segments of the working class. While the suburbs flourished, the inner cities stagnated and declined. While the white working class flourished, in relative terms the impacted inner-city minorities – African-American in particular – did not. The result was a whole sequence of inner-city uprisings – Detroit, Watts, culminating in spontaneous uprisings in some forty cities across the United States in the wake of the assassination of Martin Luther King in 1968. Something that came to be known as 'the urban crisis' was there for all to see and easily name (even though it was not, from the macroeconomic standpoint, a crisis of urbanisation). Massive federal funds were released to deal with it after 1968 until Nixon declared the crisis over (for fiscal reasons) in the recession of 1973.[27]

The sidebar to all of this was that Fannie Mae became a government-sponsored private enterprise in 1968 and, after it was provided with a 'competitor', the Federal Home Mortgage Corporation (Freddie Mac), in 1972, both institutions played a hugely important and eventually destructive role in promoting home ownership and sustaining housing construction over nearly fifty years. Home mortgage debt now accounts for some 40 per cent of the accumulated private debt of the United States, much of which, as we have seen, is toxic. And both Fannie Mae and Freddie Mac have passed back into government control. What to do about them is an intensely debated political question (as are the subsidies to home ownership) in relation to US indebtedness more generally. Whatever happens will have major consequences for the future of the housing sector in particular and urbanisation more generally in relation to capital accumulation within the United States.

The current signs in the United States are not encouraging. The housing sector is not reviving. There are signs it is heading for a dreaded 'double-dip' recession as federal monies dry up and unemployment remains high. Housing starts have plunged for the first time to below pre-1940s levels. As of March 2011, the unemployment rate in construction stood above 20 per cent compared to a rate of 9.7 per cent in manufacturing that was very close to the national average. In the Great Depression, more than a quarter of construction workers remained unemployed as late as 1939. Getting them back to work was a crucial target for public interventions (such as the WPA). Attempts by the Obama administration to create a stimulus package for infrastructural investments have largely been frustrated by Republican opposition. To make matters worse, the condition of state and local finances in the USA is so dire as to result in lay-offs and furloughs as well as savage cuts in urban services. The collapse of the housing market and the fall of housing prices by 20 per cent or more nationwide have put a huge dent in local finances, which rely heavily on property taxes. An urban fiscal crisis is brewing as state and municipal governments cut back and construction languishes.

On top of all this comes a class politics of austerity that is being pursued for political and not for economic reasons. Radical right-wing Republican administrations at the state and local levels are using the so-called debt crisis to savage government programmes and reduce state and local government employment. This has, of course, been a long-standing tactic of a capital-inspired assault on government programmes more generally. Reagan cut taxes on the wealthy from 72 per cent to around 30 per cent and launched a debt-financed arms race with the Soviet Union. The debt soared under Reagan as a result. As his budget director, David Stockman, later noted, running up the debt became a convenient excuse to go after government regulation (e.g. the environment) and social programmes, in effect externalising the costs of environmental degradation and social reproduction. President Bush Jnr faithfully followed suit, with his vice-president, Dick Cheney, proclaiming that 'Reagan taught us that deficits do not matter'.[28] Tax cuts for the rich, two unfunded wars in Iraq and Afghanistan, and a huge gift to big pharma through a state-funded prescription drug programme turned what has been a budget surplus under Clinton into a sea of red ink, enabling the Republican Party and conservative Democrats later to do big capital's bidding, and go as far as possible in externalising those costs that capital never wants to bear: the costs of environmental degradation and social reproduction.

The assault on the environment and the well-being of the people is palpable and it is taking place for political and class, not economic, reasons. It is inducing, as David Stockman has very recently noted, a state of plain class war. As Warren Buffett also put it, 'sure there is class war, and it is my class, the rich, who are making it and we are winning'.[29] The only question is: when will the people start to wage class war back? And one of the places to start would be to focus on the rapidly degrading qualities of urban life, through foreclosures, the persistence of predatory practices in urban housing markets, reductions in services and above all the lack of viable employment opportunities in urban labour markets almost everywhere, with some cities (Detroit being the sad poster child) utterly bereft of employment prospects. The crisis now is as much an urban crisis as it ever was.

Predatory urban practices

In *The Communist Manifesto*, Marx and Engels[30] note in passing that no sooner does the worker receive 'his wages in cash, than he is set upon by the other portions of the bourgeoisie, the landlord, the shopkeeper, the pawnbroker, etc.' Marxists have traditionally relegated such forms of exploitation, and the class struggles (for such they are) that inevitably arise around them, to the shadows of their theorising as well as to the margins of their politics. But I here want to argue that they constitute, at least in the advanced capitalist economies, a vast terrain of accumulation by dispossession through which money is sucked up into the circulation of fictitious capital to underpin the vast fortunes made from within the financial system.

The predatory practices that were omnipresent within the sub-prime lending field before the crash were legendary in their proportions. Before the crisis broke, the low-income African-American population of the United States was estimated to have lost somewhere between $71 and $93 billion in asset values through predatory sub-prime practices. Contemporaneously, the bonuses on Wall Street were soaring on unheard-of profit rates from pure financial manipulations, particularly those associated with the securitisation of mortgages. The inference is that by various hidden channels massive transfers of wealth from the poor to the rich were occurring, beyond those since documented in the plainly shady practices of mortgage companies like Countrywide, through financial manipulations in housing markets.[31]

What has happened since is even more astonishing. Many of the foreclosures (over a million during the last year) turn out to have been illegal if
not downright fraudulent, leading a Congressman from Florida to write to
the Florida Supreme Court Justice that 'if the reports I am hearing are true,
the illegal foreclosures taking place represent the largest seizure of private
property ever attempted by banks and government entities'.[32] Attorneys
General in all fifty states are now investigating the problem, but (as might be
expected) they all seem anxious to close out the investigations in as summary
a way as possible at the price of a few financial settlements (but no restitutions
of illegally seized properties). Certainly, no one is likely to go to jail for it,
even though there is clear evidence of systematic forgery of legal documents.

Predatory practices of this sort have been long-standing. So let me give
some instances from Baltimore. Shortly after arriving in the city in 1969, I
became involved in a study of inner-city housing provision that focused on the
role of different actors – landlords, tenants and homeowners, the brokers and
lenders, the Federal Housing Administration, the city authorities (Housing
Code Enforcement in particular) – in the production of the terrifying rat-
infested inner-city living conditions in the areas racked by uprisings in the
wake of the assassination of Martin Luther King. The vestiges of redlining of
areas of low-income African-American populations denied credit was etched
into the map of the city, but exclusions were by then justified as a legitimate
response to high credit risk and not supposedly to race. In several areas of
the city, active blockbusting practices were to be found. This generated high
profits for ruthless real estate companies. But for this to work, African-Americans had also to somehow acquire access to mortgage finance when they were
all lumped together as a high credit risk population. This could be done by
way of something called the 'Land Installment Contract'. In effect, African-
Americans were 'helped' by property owners who acted as intermediaries to
the credit markets and took out a mortgage in their own names. After a few
years, when some of the principal plus the interest had been paid down, thus
proving the family's creditworthiness, the title was supposed to be passed on
to the resident with help from the friendly property owner and local mortgage
institution. Some takers made it (though usually in neighbourhoods that
were declining in value) but in unscrupulous hands (and there were many
in Baltimore, though not, it appears, so many in Chicago, where this system
was also common) this could be a particularly predatory form of accumulation by dispossession.[33] The property owner was permitted to charge fees
to cover property taxes, administrative and legal costs, and the like. These
fees (sometimes exorbitant) could be added to the principal of the mortgage.

After years of steady payment, many families found they owed more on the principal on the house than they did at the start. If they failed once to pay the higher payments after interest rates rose, the contract was voided and families were evicted. Such practices caused something of a scandal. A civil rights action was started against the worst landlord offenders. But it failed because those who had signed on to the Land Installment Contract had simply not read the small print or had their own lawyer (which poor people rarely have) to read it for them (the small print is in any case incomprehensible to ordinary mortals – have you ever read the small print on your credit card?).

Predatory practices of this sort never went away. The Land Installment Contract was displaced by practices of 'flipping' in the 1980s. And when the sub-prime market began to form in the 1990s, cities like Baltimore, Cleveland, Detroit, Buffalo and the like became major centres for a growing wave of accumulation by dispossession ($70 billion or more nationwide). Baltimore eventually launched a civil rights lawsuit after the crash of 2008 against Wells Fargo over its discriminatory sub-prime lending practices (reverse redlining in which people were steered into taking sub-prime rather than conventional loans) in which African-Americans and single-headed households – women – were systematically exploited. Almost certainly the suit will fail (although at the third iteration it has been allowed to go forward in the courts) since it will be almost impossible to prove intent based on race as opposed to credit risk. As usual, the incomprehensible small print allows for a lot (consumers beware!). Cleveland took a more nuanced path: sue the finance companies for the creation of a public nuisance because the landscape was littered with foreclosed houses that required city action to board them up!

The China story

Insofar as there has been any exit from the crisis this time, it is notable that the housing and property boom in China, along with a huge wave of debt-financed infrastructural investments there, has taken a leading role not only in stimulating their internal market (and mopping up unemployment in the export industries) but also in stimulating the economies that are tightly integrated into the China trade, such as Australia and Chile with their raw materials and Germany with its high-speed rail and automotive exports. (In the United States, on the other hand, construction has been slow to revive, with the unemployment rate in construction, as I earlier noted, more than twice the national average.) Urban investments typically take a long time to produce and an even longer time to mature. It is always difficult to determine, therefore, when an overaccumulation of capital has been or is about to be transformed into an overaccumulation of investments in the built environment. The likelihood of overshooting, as regularly happened with the railways in the nineteenth century and as the long history of building cycles and crashes shows, is very high.

The fearlessness of the pell-mell urbanisation and infrastructural investment boom that is completely reconfiguring the geography of the Chinese national space rests in part on the ability of the central government to intervene arbitrarily in the banking system if anything goes wrong. A relatively mild (by comparison) recession in property markets in the late 1990s in leading cities such as Shanghai left the banks holding title to a vast array of 'non-earning assets' ('toxic' we call them). Unofficially, estimates ran as high as 40 per cent of bank loans being non-earning.[34] The response of the central government was to use their abundant foreign exchange reserves to recapitalise the banks (a Chinese version of what later became known as the controversial Troubled Asset Relief Program – TARP – in the United States). It is known that the state used some $45 billion of its foreign exchange reserves for this purpose in the late 1990s and it may have indirectly used much more. But as China's institutions evolve in ways more consistent with global financial markets, so it becomes harder for the central government to control what is happening in the financial sector.

The reports now available from China make it seem rather too similar for comfort to the American south-west and Florida in the 2000s, or Florida in the 1920s. Since the general privatisation of housing in China in 1998, housing construction has taken off in a spectacular (and speculative) fashion. Housing prices are reported to have risen 140 per cent nationwide since 2007 and as much as 800 per cent in the main cities such as Beijing and Shanghai over the last five years. In the latter city property prices are reputed to have doubled over the last year alone. The average apartment price there now stands at $500,000 and even in second-tier cities a typical home 'costs about 25 times the average income of residents', which is clearly unsustainable. One consequence is the emergence of strong inflationary pressures. 'Too much of the country's growth continues to be tied to inflationary spending on real estate development and government investment in roads, railways and other multibillion dollar infrastructure projects. In the first quarter of 2011, fixed asset investment – a broad measure of building activity – jumped 25 per cent from the period a year earlier, and real estate investment soared 37 per cent,' according to government statements.[35]

Extensive land acquisitions and displacements of legendary proportions in some of the major cities (as many as 3 million people displaced in Beijing over the last ten years) indicate an active economy of dispossession booming alongside this huge urbanisation push throughout the whole of China. The forced displacements and dispossessions are probably the single most important cause of a rising tide of popular and sometimes violent protests. On the other hand, the land sales to developers have been providing a lucrative cash cow to fill local government coffers. Only in early 2011 did the central government demand they be curbed in order to stifle what many commentators saw as the out-of-control property market. The result, however, was to plunge many municipalities into fiscal difficulties.

Whole new cities, with hardly any residents or real activities as yet, can now be found in the Chinese interior, prompting a curious advertising programme in the United States business press to attract investors and companies to this new urban frontier of global capitalism.[36] And as happened in the post-World War II suburbanisation boom in the United States, when all the ancillary housing appliances and appurtenances are added in, it becomes clear that the Chinese urbanisation boom is playing a highly significant if not driving role in stimulating the revival of global economic growth. 'By some estimates, China consumes up to 50 per cent of key global commodities and materials such as cement, iron ore, steel and coal, and Chinese real estate is the main driver of that demand.'[37] Since at least half of the steel consumption ends up in the built environment, this means that a quarter of the global steel output is now absorbed by this activity alone. China is not the only place where such a property boom can be identified. All of the so-called BRIC countries seem to be following suit. Property prices thus doubled in both São Paulo and Rio last year and in India and Russia similar conditions prevail. But all of these countries are experiencing high aggregate growth rates.

Attempts by the Chinese central government to control their boom and quell inflationary pressures by raising stepwise the reserve requirements of the banks have not been too successful. A 'shadow banking system' is rumoured to have emerged, strongly connected to land and property investments. The result of accelerating inflation has been proliferating unrest. Reports are now coming in of work actions by taxi drivers and truckers (in Shanghai), alongside sudden full-blown factory strikes in the industrial areas of Guangdong in response to low wages, poor working conditions and escalating prices. Official reports of unrest have risen dramatically and wage adjustments have been occurring along with government policies designed to confront the swelling unrest, and, perhaps, stimulate the internal market as a substitute for riskier and stagnant export markets (Chinese consumerism currently accounts for only 35 per cent of GDP as opposed to 70 per cent in the United States).

All of this has to be understood, however, against the background of the concrete steps the Chinese government took to deal with the crisis of 2007–09. The main impact of the crisis on China was the sudden collapse of export markets (particularly that of the United States) and a 20 per cent fall-off in exports in early 2008. Several reasonably reliable estimates put the number of jobs lost in the export sector in the 20 million range over a very short period in 2008. Yet the IMF could report that the net job loss in China as of fall 2009 was only 3 million.[38] Some of the difference between gross and net job losses may have been due to the return of unemployed urban migrants to their rural base. But the rest of it was almost certainly due to the government's implementation of a massive Keynesian-style stimulus programme of urban and infrastructural investment. Nearly $600 billion was made available by the central government while the centrally controlled banks were instructed to lend extensively to all manner of local development projects (including the property sector) as a way to mop up surplus labour. This massive programme was designed to lead the way towards economic recovery. And it appears to have been at least minimally successful in its immediate objectives if the IMF figures on net job loss are correct.

The big question, of course, is whether or not these state expenditures fall in the category of 'productive' or not, and, if so, productive of what and for whom? There is no question that the Chinese national space could benefit from deeper and more efficient spatial integration and on the surface at least the vast wave of infrastructural investments and urbanisation projects would appear to do just that, linking the interior to the wealthier coastal regions and the north with the south. At the metropolitan level, the processes of urban growth and urban regeneration would also appear to bring modernist techniques to urbanisation along with a diversification of activities (including all the mandatory cultural and knowledge industry institutions, exemplified by the spectacular Shanghai Expo, that are so characteristic of neoliberal urbanisation in the United States and Europe). The absorption of surplus liquidity and overaccumulated capital at a time when profitable opportunities are otherwise hard to come by has certainly sustained capital accumulation, not only in China but also around much of the rest of the globe.

In some ways, China's development mimics that of the post-World War II United States, where the interstate highway system integrated the south and the west and this, coupled with suburbanisation, then played a crucial role in sustaining both employment and capital accumulation. But the parallel is instructive in other ways. United States development after 1945 was not only profligate in its use of energy and land, but also generated, as we have seen, a distinctive crisis for marginalised and excluded urban populations that elicited a raft of policy responses during the late 1960s. All of this faded after the crash of 1973, when President Nixon declared in his State of the Union Address that the urban crisis was over and that federal funding would be withdrawn. The effect at the municipal level was to create a crisis in urban services with all of the terrifying consequences of degeneration in public schooling, public health and the availability of affordable housing from the late 1970s onwards.

The investment strategy in China is in danger also of falling into such a lopsided path. A high-speed train between Shanghai and Beijing is fine for the business people and the upper middle class but it does not constitute the kind of affordable transport system to take workers back to their rural origins for the Chinese New Year. Similarly, high-rise apartment blocks, gated communities and golf courses for the rich along with high-end shopping malls do not really help to reconstitute an adequate daily life for the impoverished masses. The same question is arising in India as well as in the innumerable cities around the world where there are high concentrations of marginalised populations, from the restive suburbs of Paris to social movements agitating in Argentina, South Africa or throughout North Africa. In fact the issue of how to deal with impoverished, insecure and excluded workers that now constitute a majoritarian and putatively dominant power block in many capitalist cities could (and in some instances has already) become a major political problem, so much so that military planning is now highly focused on how to deal with restive and potentially revolutionary urban-based movements.

But in the Chinese case there is one interesting wrinkle to this narrative. In some respects the trajectory of development since liberalisation began in 1979 rests on a simple thesis that decentralisation is one of the best ways to exercise centralised control. The idea was to liberate regional, local and even villages and townships to seek their own betterment within a framework of centralised control and market coordinations. Successful solutions arrived at through local initiatives then became the basis for the reformulation of central government policies. Reports emanating from China suggest that the power transition anticipated for 2012 is faced with an intriguing choice. Attention is focused on the city of Chongqing, where a shift away from market-based policies back onto a path of state-led redistribution has been under way for some time, accompanied by 'an arsenal of Maoist slogans'. In this model 'everything links back to the issue of poverty and inequality', as the municipal government 'has turned the market profits of state-owned enterprises toward traditional socialist projects, using their revenues to fund the construction of affordable housing and transportation infrastructure'.[39] The housing initiative entails a massive construction programme designed to provide cheap apartments to a third of the 30 million residents in the city region, where twenty satellite towns are expected to be built, each with a population of 300,000, of which 50,000 people will live in state-subsidised housing. The aim (contrary to World Bank advice) is to reduce the spiralling social inequalities that have arisen over the last two decades across China. It is an antidote to the private-developer-led projects of gated communities for the rich. This turn back to a socialist redistributive agenda, using the private sector for public purposes, is now providing a model for the central government to follow. It neatly solves the capital surplus absorption problem at the same time as it offers a way to both further urbanise the rural population and to dispel popular discontent by offering reasonable housing security to the less well off. There are echoes of US urban policies after 1945. Keep economic growth on track while co-opting potentially restive populations. The scale of land acquisition entailed in such a programme is, however, already sparking unrest and opposition from those being displaced.

Rival market-based paths exist elsewhere, particularly in the coastal and southern cities, such as Shenzhen. Here the emphasis is more upon political liberalisation and what sounds like bourgeois urban democracy alongside a deepening of free market initiatives. In this case, rising social inequality is accepted as a necessary cost of sustained economic growth and competitiveness. Which way the central government will lean is impossible at this point to predict. But the key point is the role of urban-based initiatives in pioneering the way towards different futures. How then might the left in general relate – both in theory and in political practices – to such a prospect?

Towards urban revolution?

The city is a terrain where anti-capitalist struggles have always flourished. The history of such struggles, from the Paris Commune through the Shanghai Commune, the Seattle General Strike, the Tucuman uprising and the Prague Spring to the more general urban-based movements of 1968 (which we now see faintly echoed in Cairo and Madison) is stunning. But it is a history that is also troubled by political and tactical complications that have led many on the left to underestimate and misunderstand the potential and the potency of urban-based movements, to often see them as separate from class struggle and therefore devoid of revolutionary potential. And when such events do take on iconic status, as in the case of the Paris Commune, they are typically claimed as one of 'the greatest proletarian uprisings' in world history, even as they were as much about reclaiming the right to the city as they were about revolutionising class relations in production.

Anti-capitalist struggle is about the abolition of that class relation between capital and labour in production that permits the production and appropriation of surplus value by capital. The ultimate aim of anti-capitalist struggle is, quite simply, the abolition of that class relation. Even and particularly when this struggle has to be seen, as it invariably does, through the prisms of race, ethnicity, sexuality and gender, it must eventually reach into the very guts of what a capitalist system is about and wrench out the cancerous tumour of class relations at its very centre.

It would be a truthful caricature to say that the Marxist left has long privileged the industrial workers of the world as the vanguard agent that leads class struggle through the dictatorship of the proletariat to a world where state and class wither away. It is also a truthful caricature to say that things have never worked out that way. Marx argued that the class relation of domination had to be displaced by the associated workers controlling their own production processes and protocols. From this derives a long history of political pursuit of worker control, autogestion, worker cooperatives and the like.[40] Most attempts of this sort have not proved viable in the long run, in spite of the noble efforts and sacrifices that kept them going in the face of often fierce hostilities and active repressions. The main reason for the long-run failure of these initiatives is simple enough. As Marx shows in the second volume of *Capital*, the circulation of capital comprises three distinctive circulatory processes, those of money, productive and commodity capitals. No one circulatory process can survive or even exist without the others: they intermingle and co-determine each other. By the same token, no one circulation process can be changed without changing the others. Workers' control in relatively isolated production units can rarely survive, in spite of all the hopeful autonomista and autogestion rhetoric, in the face of a hostile credit system and the predatory practices of merchant capital. The power of merchant capital (the Wal-Mart phenomenon) has been particularly resurgent in recent years (another arena of much neglected analysis in Marxist theory).

Recognising this difficulty, much of the left came to the view that struggle for proletarian command over the state apparatus was the only other path to communism. The state would be the agent to control the three circuits of capital and to tame the institutions, powers and class agents that managed the flows that supported the perpetuation of the class relation in production. The problem has always been, of course, that the lifeblood of the state comes from facilitating and tapping into the very flows that the state is supposed to control. That is as true for the socialist state as for the capitalist state. Centralised and top-down management does not work except by way of some liberation of the flows (as the Chinese have proved so expert at doing). And once the flows are liberated, all hell breaks loose because the capitalist genie is out of the bottle. So what are the political prospects for finding a middle path between autogestion and centralised state control when neither of them on its own works effectively as an antidote to the power of capital?

The problem with worker control has been that the focus of struggle has been the factory as a privileged site of production of surplus value and the privileging of the industrial working class as the vanguard of the proletariat, the main revolutionary agent. But it was not factory workers who produced the Paris Commune. So there is a dissident view of that event that says it was not a proletarian uprising or a class-based movement but an urban social movement that was reclaiming the right to the city rather than seeking a revolutionary path towards the building of an anti-capitalist alternative.[41]

But why could it not be both? Urbanisation is itself produced. Thousands of workers are engaged in its production and their work is productive of value and of surplus value. Why not reconceptualise the site of surplus value production as the city rather than as the factory? The Paris Commune can then be reconceptualised in terms of that proletariat that produced the city seeking to claim back the right to have and control that which they had produced. This is (and in the Paris Commune case was) a very different kind of proletariat to that which Marxists have typically favoured. But at this point in the history of those parts of the world characterised as advanced capitalism, the factory proletariat has been radically diminished. So we have a choice: mourn the passing of the possibility of revolution or change our conception of the proletariat to that of the hordes of unorganised urbanisation producers and explore their distinctive revolutionary capacities and powers.

So who are these workers who produce the city? The city builders, the construction workers in particular, are the most obvious candidate, even as they are not the only nor the largest labour force involved. As a political force the construction workers have in recent times in the United States (and possibly elsewhere) all too often been supportive of the large-scale and class-biased developmentalism that keeps them employed. They do not have to be so. The masons and builders played an important role in the Paris Commune. The 'Green Ban' construction union movement in New South Wales in the early 1970s banned working on projects they deemed environmentally unsound and were successful in much of what they did. They were ultimately destroyed by a combination of concerted state power and their own Maoist national leadership, who considered environmental issues a manifestation of flabby bourgeois sentimentality.[42]

But there is a seamless connection between those who mine the iron ore that goes into the steel that goes into the construction of the bridges across which the trucks carrying commodities travel to their final destinations of factories and homes for consumption. All of these activities (including spatial movement) are, according to Marx, productive of value and of surplus value. And if, again as Marx argues, maintenance, repairs and replacements (often difficult to distinguish in practice) are all part of the value-producing stream, then the vast army of workers involved in these activities in our cities is also contributing to value- and surplus-value-producing investment in the physical infrastructures that make our cities what they are. If the flow of commodities from place of origin to final destination is productive of value, then so are the workers who are employed on the food chain that links rural producers to urban consumers. Organised, those workers would have the power to strangle the metabolism of the city. Strikes of transport workers (e.g. France over the last twenty years and now in Shanghai) are extremely effective political weapons (used negatively in Chile in the coup year of 1973). The Bus Riders Union in Los Angeles and the organisation of taxi drivers in New York and LA are other examples.[43]

Consider the flows not only of food and other consumer goods, but also of energy, water and other necessities and their vulnerabilities to disruption too. The production and reproduction of urban life, while some of it can be 'dismissed' (an unfortunate word) as 'unproductive' in the Marxist canon, is nevertheless socially necessary, part of the '*faux frais*' of the reproduction of the class relations between capital and labour. Much of this labour has always been temporary, insecure, itinerant and precarious. New forms of organising are absolutely essential for this labour force that produces and sustains the city. The newly fledged Excluded Workers Congress in the United States is an example of the forms that are emerging – an alliance of workers bedevilled by temporary and insecure conditions of employment who are often, as with domestic workers, spatially scattered throughout the urban system.[44]

It is in this light too that the history of the politics of conventional labour struggles requires a rewrite. Most struggles that are depicted as focused solely on the factory-based worker turn out, on inspection, to have had a much broader base. Margaret Kohn[45] complains, for example, how left historians of labour laud the Turin Factory Councils in the early twentieth century while totally ignoring the fact that it was in the 'Houses of the People' in the community that much of the politics was shaped and from which much of the logistical support flowed. E. P. Thompson depicts how the making of the English working class depended as much upon what happened in chapels and in neighbourhoods as in the workplace. How successful would the Flint sit-down strike of 1937 have been were it not for the mass of unemployed people and the neighbourhood organisations outside the gates that unfailingly delivered their support, moral and material? And is it not interesting that in the British miners' strikes of the 1970s and 1980s, the miners that lived in diffuse urbanised areas such as Nottingham were the first to cave in while the tightly knit communities of Northumbria remained solidarious to the end? Organising the community has been just as important in prosecuting labour struggles as has organising the workplace. And to the degree that conventional workplaces are disappearing in many parts of the so-called advanced capitalist world (though not, of course, in China or Bangladesh), then organising around work in the community appears to be even more important.

In all these instances, as we alter the lens on the social milieu in which struggle is occurring, then the sense of who the proletariat might be and what their aspirations might be gets transformed. The gender composition of oppositional politics looks very different when relations outside of the factory are placed firmly in the picture. The social dynamics of the workplace are not homologous with those in the living space. In the latter space distinctions based on gender, race, ethnicity and religion are frequently more deeply etched into the social fabric, while issues of social reproduction play a more prominent, even dominant, role in the shaping of political subjectivities and consciousness. From this perspective the dynamics of class struggles along with the nature of political demands appear very different. But then when we look backward and reassess, we see that they always were rather different from how the Marxist imaginary wishfully depicted them.

Fletcher and Gapasin[46] thus argue that the labour movement should pay more attention to geographical rather than sectoral forms of organisation, that the movement should empower the central labour councils in cities in addition to organising sectorally.

To the extent that labor speaks about matters of class, it should not see itself as separate from the community. The term labor should denote forms of organisation with roots in the working class and with agendas that explicitly advance the class demands of the working class. In that sense, a community-based organisation rooted in the working class (such as a workers' centre) that addresses class-specific issues is a labor organisation in the same way that a trade union is. To push the envelope a bit more, a trade union that addresses the interests of only one section of the working class (such as a white supremacist craft union) deserves the label labor organisation less than does a community-based organisation that assists the unemployed or the homeless.[47]

They therefore propose a new approach to labour organising that

essentially defies current trade union practices in forming alliances and taking political action. Indeed, it has the following central premise: if class struggle is not restricted to the workplace, then neither should unions be. The strategic conclusion is that unions must think in terms of organising cities rather than simply organising workplaces (or industries). And organising cities is possible only if unions work with allies in metropolitan social blocks.

'How then', they go on to ask, 'does one organise a city?' This, it seems to me, is one of the key quetions that the left will have to answer if anti-capitalist struggle is to be revitalised in the years to come. And actually such struggles have a distinguished history. The inspiration drawn from 'Red Bologna' in the 1970s is a case in point.[48] And it is one of those curious ironies of history that the French Communist Party distinguished itself far more in municipal administration (in part because it had no dogmatic theory or instructions from Moscow to guide it) than it did in other arenas of political life from the 1960s even up until the present day. The struggles fought by the municipalities in Britain against Thatcherism in the early 1980s were not only rearguard but, as in the case of the Greater London Council, potentially innovative until Thatcher abolished that whole layer of governance. Even in the United States, Milwaukee for many years had a socialist administration and it is worth remembering that the only socialist ever elected to the US Senate began his career and earned the people's trust as mayor of Burlington, Vermont.

If the Parisian producers in the Commune were reclaiming their right to the city they had produced, then in what sense might we look to a slogan such as 'the right to city' as a 'cry and a demand' (as Lefebvre put it) around which political forces might rally as a key slogan for anti-capitalist struggle? The slogan is, of course, an empty signifier full of immanent but not transcendent possibilities. This does not mean it is irrelevant or politically impotent.

Everything depends on who gets to fill the signifier with revolutionary as opposed to reformist immanent meaning. That is bound to be contested and then, as Marx once put it, 'between equal rights force decides'.[49]

It is indeed often difficult to distinguish between reformist and revolutionary initiatives in urban settings. Participatory budgeting in Porto Alegre, ecologically sensitive programmes in Curitiba or living-wage campaigns in many US cities appear on the surface to be merely reformist (and rather marginal at that). The Chongqing initiative may, despite the Maoist rhetoric, more resemble redistributive Nordic social democracy than a revolutionary movement. But as their influence spreads, so the initiatives reveal other deeper layers of possibility for more radical conceptions and actions at the metropolitan scale. A spreading rhetoric (from Zagreb to Hamburg to Los Angeles) over the right to the city, for example, seems to suggest something more revolutionary might be at stake.[50] The measure of that possibility appears in the desperate attempts of existing political powers (e.g. the NGOs and international institutions, including the World Bank, assembled at the Rio World Urban Forum in 2010) to co-opt that language to their own purposes.

There is no point in complaining at the attempt to co-opt. The left should take it as a compliment and battle for our distinctive immanent meaning, which is simply that all those whose labours are engaged in producing and reproducing the city have a collective right not only to that which they produce but also to decide on what is to be produced where and how. Democratic vehicles (other than the existing democracy of money power) need to be constructed to decide how to revitalise urban life outside of dominant class relations and more after 'our' (the producers of urbanisation and urbanism) heart's desire.

One objection that immediately arises, of course, is why concentrate on the city when there are multiple rural, peasant and indigenous movements in motion that can also claim their own distinctive rights? In any case, has not the city as a physical object lost its meaning as an object of struggle? There is of course an obvious truth to these objections. Urbanisation has produced a highly differentiated mosaic of communities and interactive spaces which are hard to bring together around any kind of coherent political project. Indeed, there is plenty of rivalry and conflict between the spaces that constitute the city. It was, I suspect, for this reason that Lefebvre changed his focus from the urban revolution to the broader terrain of the production of space, or, as I might formulate it, to the production of uneven geographical development as the focus of theoretical analysis and political struggle.

In the pedestrian imaginations of literally minded academics, such objections sometimes produce the conclusion that the city has disappeared and that pursuit of the right to the city is therefore the pursuit of a chimera. But political struggles are animated by visions as much as by practicalities. And the term 'city' has an iconic and symbolic history that is deeply embedded in the pursuit of political meanings. The city of God, the city on a hill, the city as an object of utopian desire, the relationship between city and citizenship, of a distinctive place of belonging within a perpetually shifting spatiotemporal order, all give it a political meaning that mobilises a political imaginary that is lost in a slogan such as 'the right to produce space' or 'the right to uneven geographical development'!

The right to the city is not an exclusive right but a focused right. It is inclusive not only of construction workers but also of all those who facilitate the reproduction of daily life: the caregivers and teachers, the sewer and subway repair men, the plumbers and electricians, the hospital workers and the truck, bus and taxi drivers, the restaurant workers and the entertainers, the bank clerks and the city administrators. It seeks a unity from within an incredible diversity of fragmented social spaces. And there are many putative forms of organisation – from workers' centres and regional workers' assemblies (such as that of Toronto) to alliances (such as the Right to the City alliances and the Excluded Workers Congress and other forms of organisation of precarious labour) that have this objective upon their political radar. This is the proletarian force that must be organised if the world is to change. This is how and where we have to begin if we wish to organise the whole city. The urban producers must rise up and reclaim their right to the city they collectively produce. The transformation of urban life and above all the abolition of the class relations in the production of urbanisation will have to be one, if not the, path towards an anti-capitalist transition. This is what the left has to imagine as constituting the core of its political strategy in years to come.

Commentary

In January 2006 I took the high-speed train from Cordoba to Madrid in Spain. En route we passed by a place called Ciudad Real and as we raced through the fringes of the city, I recall thinking that I had never ever seen so many construction cranes in the same place at the same time. Plainly a speculative construction boom was going on which was almost certainly going to end badly. But it was not only housing that was being built. Almost every Spanish city at that time had some extravagant public infrastructure project most of which made little economic sense. Ciudad Real has a new airport that cost a billion or so euros (in a part of the country that has very little to attract industry or tourists). In July 2015 the empty airport was put up for auction. The top bid was 10,000 euros. In China whole newly built cities stand empty. Elsewhere, property markets that crashed in 2007/08 are exhibiting signs of forming yet another asset bubble, particularly in major metropolitan markets, with skyrocketing land and property prices in London, New York, Shanghai and Istanbul, just to name cities I have visited.

The key moment in the recent economic crisis we experienced is generally taken to be the collapse of Lehman Brothers on 15 September 2008. Since then much has been written about who said what to whom at the Fed and on Wall Street, the intricacies of the shadow banking system, the complexities of the new financial products and how the freezing up of credit markets and the collapse of consumer demand led to rising unemployment with contagious effects (though of a differing magnitude depending on the degree and form of exposure) for an increasingly integrated global capitalism. But for some reason or other very little attention has been paid to why it all began in the property markets of certain regions of the United States with outliers in countries such as Spain, Ireland, Latvia and Hungary.

Property markets and investments in built environments are a big part of the contemporary economy and the indebtedness involved forms a nontrivial threat to the stability of global capitalism. China's investments in the built environment have been, as I point out in this piece, the grand stabiliser of global capitalism since 2008. The recent slowing of the pace of urbanisation in China has had negative consequences for raw material producers (like Australia, Canada, Chile and Brazil) who now find themselves in or close to recession. So what kind of urbanisation are the Chinese now proposing? They are looking to build a continuous urban matrix across a region as large as Kansas (with Beijing at its centre) to accommodate some 130 million people linked together with high-speed transport and communications. Istanbul has a smaller-scale version already under way but is experiencing difficulties of funding. The risks of speculative collapse and/or environmental disasters from projects such as these are considerable. As of August 2015, the threat of a major global crisis looms. In addition, the sheer physicality of these investments is in itself problematic. Yet most analysts take no notice.

Considerable attention has been paid to the economic and wealth impacts of the property market collapse and its subsequent patchy revival. We have plenty of maps of foreclosures and they show a disproportionate loss of asset values for vulnerable and marginalised populations (blacks, Hispanic immigrants and single-headed households, mainly women, in the United States). We also know that much of the wealth of the top 1 per cent is stored in real estate and that capital seems far more interested in building cities for the affluent (and institutions like hedge funds) to invest in than cities with affordable housing for the mass of the population to live in. We also know that there are many signs of a bubbling discontent with the qualities of daily urban life, leading to riots and urban uprisings in many parts of the world (such as Gezi Park in Istanbul and Brazilian cities in July of 2013). The politics of daily urban life increasingly foster political activism.

I wrote this piece on the urban roots of the crisis and the subsequent book, *Rebel Cities: From the Right to the City to the Urban Revolution*, to draw attention to these features of our contemporary world. Even a casual knowledge of Marx's analytic tools for the study of the circulation and accumulation of capital suggests where the stress points and vulnerabilities as well as the temporary solutions (such as moving the crisis around) might lie. Beneath it all I have sought to be faithful to Marx's fundamental insight that a crisis of capital of the sort we experienced 2007–09 (and which in many respects is still going on) is nothing more nor less than a 'violent fusion of disconnected factors operating independently of one another yet correlated'. There are a lot of missing correlations in general accounts of the crisis that purportedly began in 2008. One of them entails a closer look at the circulation and accumulation of capital in the secondary circuit of capital. We need to ferret them out and put them together in easily comprehensible ways.

Chapter 11
Capital Evolves

The forces unleashed by the rise of capitalism have re-engineered the world many times over since 1750. Flying over central England in 1820, we would have seen a few compact industrialised towns (with small factory smokestacks belching forth noxious fumes) separated by large areas of agricultural activity where traditional forms of rural life were preserved in scattered villages and farmsteads, even as lords of the manor waxed poetic about the new agricultural practices that underpinned rising agricultural productivity (and rising money rents). Compact industrial centres with names like Manchester and Birmingham were linked with each other and to the main commercial port cities (Bristol and Liverpool), as well as to the teeming capital city of London, by threads of dirt turnpikes and skinny slivers of canals. Barges full of coal and raw materials were laboriously towed along the canals either by sweating horses or, as Marx records in *Capital*, by almost-starving women. Locomotion was slow.

Flying over the Pearl river delta in 1980, one would have seen tiny villages and towns with names like Shenzhen and Dongguan nestled in a largely self-sufficient agrarian landscape of rice, vegetable, livestock production and fish farming, socialised into communes ruled with an iron fist by local party officials who were also carrying an 'iron rice bowl' to guard against the threat of starvation. Flying over both these areas in 2008, the landscapes of sprawling urbanisation below would be totally unrecognisable, as would be the forms of production and transportation, the social relations, the technologies, the ways of daily life and the forms of consumption on the ground.

If, as Marx once averred, our task is not so much to understand the world as to change it, then, it has to be said, capitalism has done a pretty good job of following his advice. Most of these dramatic changes have occurred without bothering first to understand how the world worked or what the consequences might be. Again and again the unanticipated and the unexpected have happened, leaving behind a vast intellectual and practical industry of trying to clean up the messy consequences of what was unknowingly wrought.

The saga of capitalism is full of paradoxes, even as most forms of social theory – economic theory in particular – abstract entirely from consideration of them. On the negative side we have not only the periodic and often localised economic crises that have punctuated capitalism's evolution, including inter-capitalist and inter-imperialist world wars, problems of environmental degradation, loss of bio-diverse habitat, spiralling poverty among burgeoning populations, neocolonialism, serious dilemmas in public health, alienations and social exclusions galore and the anxieties of insecurity, violence and unfulfilled desires. On the positive side some of us live in a world where standards of material living and well-being have never been higher, where travel and communications have been revolutionised and physical (though not social) spatial barriers to human interactions have been much reduced, where medical and biomedical understandings offer for many a longer life, where huge, sprawling and in many respects spectacular cities have been built, where knowledge proliferates, hope springs eternal and everything seems possible (from self-cloning to space travel).

That this is the contradictory world in which we live, and that it continues to evolve at a rapid pace in unpredictable and seemingly uncontrollable ways, is undeniable. Yet the principles that underpin this evolution remain opaque in part because we humans have made so much of this history more in accord with the competing whims of this or that collective and sometimes individual human desire, rather than according to some governing evolutionary principles of the sort that Darwin uncovered in the realm of natural evolution. If we are to collectively change this world into a more rational and humane configuration through conscious interventions, then we must first learn to understand far better than is now the case the ways of this world, what we do in it and with what consequences.

The historical geography of capitalism cannot be reduced, of course, to questions of capital accumulation. Yet it also has to be said that capital accumulation along with population growth has lain at the core of human evolutionary dynamics since 1750 or so. Exactly how they do so is central to uncovering what the enigma of capital is all about. Are there some evolutionary principles at work here to which we can appeal for some sort of illumination?

Consider, first, capitalist development over time, laying aside for the moment the question of its evolving spatial organisation, its geographical dynamics and its environmental impacts and constraints. Imagine, then, a situation in which capital revolves through different but interrelated 'activity spheres' (as I shall call them) in search of profit. One crucial 'activity sphere' concerns the production of new technological and organisational forms. Changes in this sphere have profound effects on social relations as well as on the relation to nature. But we also know that both social relations and the relation to nature are changing in ways that are in no way determined by technologies and organisational forms. Situations arise, furthermore, in which scarcities of labour supply or in nature put strong pressures to come up with new technologies and organisational forms. These days, for example, the US media are full of commentary on the need for a range of new technologies to free the USA of dependency on foreign oil and to combat global warming. The Obama administration promises programmes to that end and is already pushing the auto industry towards making electric or hybrid cars (unfortunately the Chinese have got there first).

Production systems and labour processes are likewise deeply implicated in the way daily life is reproduced through consumption. Neither of these are independent of the dominant social relations, the relation to nature and the duly constituted technologies and organisational forms. But what we call 'nature', while clearly affected by capital accumulation (habitat and species destruction, global warming, new chemical compounds that pollute as well as soil structures and forests whose productivity has been enhanced by sophisticated management), is most certainly not determined by capital accumulation. Evolutionary processes on planet earth are independently occurring all the time. The emergence of a new pathogen – such as HIV/AIDS – has had, for example, an immense impact upon capitalist society (and calls forth technological, organisational and social responses that are embedded in capital circulation). The effects on the reproduction of daily life, on sexual relations and activities, and on reproductive practices are profound, but are mediated by medical technologies, institutional responses and social and cultural beliefs.

All of these 'activity spheres' are embedded in a set of institutional arrangements (e.g. private property rights and market contracts) and administrative structures (the state and other local and multinational arrangements). These institutions also evolve on their own account even as they find themselves forced to adapt to crisis conditions and to changing social relations. People act, furthermore, on their expectations, their beliefs and their understandings of the world. Social systems depend on trust (in experts), adequate knowledge and information on the part of those making decisions, acceptance as to reasonable social arrangements (of hierarchies or of egalitarianism) as well as constructions of ethical and moral standards (vis-à-vis, for example, our relations to animals and our responsibilities to the world we call nature as well as to others not like us). Cultural norms and belief systems (e.g. religion and political ideologies) are powerfully present but do not exist independently of social relations, production and consumption possibilities and dominant technologies. The contested interrelations between the evolving technical and social requirements for capital accumulation and the knowledge structures and the cultural norms and beliefs consistent with endless accumulation have all played a critical role in capitalism's evolution. For purposes of simplification, I collect together all of these last elements under the rubric of 'mental conceptions of the world'.

This way of thinking yields us seven distinctive 'activity spheres' within the evolutionary trajectory of capitalism: technologies and organisational forms, social relations, institutional and administrative arrangements, production and labour processes, relations to nature, the reproduction of daily life and of the species, and mental conceptions of the world. No one of the spheres dominates even as none of them are independent of the others. But none of them are determined even collectively by all of the others either. Each sphere evolves on its own account but always in dynamic interaction with the others. Technological and organisational changes arise for all manner of reasons (sometimes accidental), while the relation to nature is unstable and perpetually changing only in part because of human-induced modifications. Our mental conceptions of the world, to take another example, are usually unstable, contested, subject to scientific discoveries as well as whims, fashions and passionately held cultural and religious beliefs and desires. Changes in mental conceptions have all manner of intended and unintended consequences for acceptable technological and organisational forms, social relations, labour processes, relations to nature, as well as for institutional arrangements. The demographic dynamics that arise out of the sphere of reproduction and daily life are simultaneously autonomous but deeply affected by its relations to the other spheres.

The complex flows of influence that move between the spheres are perpetually reshaping all of them. Furthermore, these interactions are not necessarily harmonious. Indeed, we can reconceptualise crisis formation in terms of the tensions and antagonisms that arise between the different activity spheres as, for example, new technologies play against the desire for new configurations in social relations or disrupt the organisation of existing labour processes. But instead of examining these spheres sequentially as we typically do in the analysis of capital circulation, we here think of them as collectively co-present and co-evolving within the long history of capitalism.

In a given society at a particular point in space and time – Britain in 1850, or the Pearl river delta of China now, say – we can define its general character and its condition largely in terms of how these seven spheres are organised and configured in relation to each other. Something can also be said about the likely future development of the social order in such places given the tensions and contradictions between them, even as it is recognised that the likely evolutionary dynamic is not determinant but contingent.

Capital cannot circulate or accumulate without touching upon each and all of these activity spheres in some way. When capital encounters barriers or limits within a sphere or between spheres, then ways have to be found to circumvent or transcend the difficulty. If the difficulties are serious, then here too we find a source of crises. A study of the co-evolution of activity spheres therefore provides a framework within which to think through the overall evolution and crisis-prone character of capitalist society. So how can this rather abstract framework for analysis be put to work in concrete ways?

An anecdote may help here. Back in the autumn of 2005, I was co-chair of a jury to select ideas for the design of a completely new city in South Korea. The city then called the Multifunctional Administrative City (now called Sejong) was originally planned to be a new capital city but constitutional objections led to it being reduced to a satellite city, about halfway between Seoul and Busan, with many of the administrative functions of government to be placed there. The jury's task was to adjudicate on ideas rather than to select any final design. Those in charge of the project were tasked to undertake the final design, incorporating whatever we (and they) thought was useful from the submissions to the competition. The jury was half Korean and half foreign and weighted heavily with engineers, planners and some prominent architects. It had also become clear that the South Korean government, tired of the formulaic urbanisation that had hitherto dominated in South Korea and much of Asia, was interested in doing something different, perhaps generating a new worldwide model for an innovative urbanisation.

As prelude to our decision-making, we discussed the kind of criteria that would be most relevant in judging the many designs that had been submitted. The initial discussion focused around the differing views of the architects on the relative strengths of circles and cubes both as symbolic forms and as physical forms that could accommodate different kinds of development strategies. Looking at the various map-like designs, it was easy to see differences of this sort clearly displayed. But I intervened to suggest that we broaden the discussion and think of a number of different criteria such as: the proposed relation to nature and the technological mixes to be deployed in the city;

how the designs addressed the forms of production and employment to be generated and the associated social relations (how should we approach the problem that the city would be dominated by a scientific, technological and bureaucratic elite, for example); the qualities of daily life for differently positioned inhabitants and the mental conceptions of the world that would be entailed, including the political subjectivities that might arise from the experience of living in this new kind of city (would people become more individualistic or incline towards forms of social solidarity?). I concluded by saying that I thought it would be wrong to imagine that physical designs could answer to all of these issues but that we should do our best to think about building this new city in ways that were sensitive to these criteria.

There was considerable interest in this way of thinking. Debate over my ideas proceeded in the meeting for a while until one of the architects, evidently impatient with the complexity of the discussion, intervened to suggest that of all of these doubtlessly valid perspectives, there was one that stood out as paramount and that was mental conceptions. From this standpoint the most important question was one of symbolic meanings. In short order we were back to the discussion of the symbolic, conceptual and material potentialities of circles and squares in urban design!

It may sound utopian, but were I in charge of constructing a wholly new city, I would want to imagine one that could evolve into the future rather than a permanent structure that is fixed, frozen and completed. And I would want to imagine how the dynamics of relations between these different spheres might not only work but be consciously mobilised not so much to achieve some specific goal but to open up possibilities. To be sure, the city would have to be built in the first instance according to the dominant social relations, employment structures and the available technologies and organisational forms. But it could also be viewed as a site for the exploration of new technologies and organisational forms consistent with the development of more egalitarian social relations, respectful of gender issues, for example, and a more sensitive relation to nature than that demanded in pursuit of the increasingly unholy grail of endless capital accumulation at a 3 per cent compound rate.

This framework of thought does not originate with me. It derives, in fact, from elaboration upon a footnote in chapter 15 of Marx's *Capital*, volume 1. Marx there comments, interestingly after a brief engagement with Darwin's theory of evolution, that 'technology reveals the active relation of man to nature, the direct process of production of his life, and thereby it also lays bare the process of production of the social relations of his life and of the mental conceptions that flow from these relations'. Here Marx invokes five (perhaps six if 'the direct process of production of his life' refers both to the production of commodities and their consumption in daily life) of the different spheres of activity that I have identified. Only the institutional arrangements are missing.

The positioning of this footnote in the preamble to a lengthy examination of how the dominant technological and organisational forms of capitalism came into being is significant. Marx is concerned to understand the origins of the factory system and the rise of a machine-tool industry (producing machines by way of machines) as an autonomous business dedicated to the production of new technologies. This is the key industry that underpins 'the constant revolutionising of production, uninterrupted disturbance of all social conditions, everlasting uncertainty and agitation' identified in *The Communist Manifesto* as the hallmark of what capitalism has been and still is about.

In this long chapter on machinery, the different spheres co-evolve in ways that accommodate and consolidate the permanently revolutionary character of capitalism. Mental conceptions of production as an art were displaced by scientific understandings and the conscious design of new technologies. Class, gender and family relations shifted as workers were increasingly reduced to the status of flexible appendages to the machine rather than as individuals endowed with the unique skills of the artisan. At the same time, capitalists mobilised new technologies and organisational forms as weapons in the class struggle against labour (eventually using the machine to discipline the labouring body). The entry of a large number of women into the labour force, then as now, had all sorts of social ramifications. Public education (an institutional innovation) became necessary the more the flexibility and adaptability of labour to different tasks became a crucial requirement. This brought forth other institutional changes, notably the educational clauses in the Factory Acts passed by a state dominated by capitalists and landlords. The factory inspectors appointed by that state provided Marx with abundant ammunition with which to bolster his arguments. New organisational forms (the corporate factory) promoted new technologies under new institutional arrangements that had ramifications for social relations and the relation to nature. At no point does it seem as if any one of the spheres dominates the others.

Yet there are uneven developments between the spheres that create stresses within the evolutionary trajectory. At some crucial turning points these stresses redirect the trajectory in this direction rather than that. Could a new and 'higher' form of the family arise out of this dynamic in which more and more women were being absorbed into the labour force? Would the public education eventually required to produce a literate, flexible and well-trained workforce lead to popular enlightenment that would allow working-class movements to take command? Could technologies be devised that would lighten the load of labour rather than tie it more ruthlessly to the juggernaut of endless capital accumulation? Different possibilities were inherent in the situation even as the choices actually made pushed capitalism down ever more repressive paths. The British penchant for policies of free market 'laissez-faire' did not have to triumph in the nineteenth century. But once they did, the evolution of capitalism took a very particular and not particularly benevolent turn.

So let me summarise. The seven activity spheres co-evolve within the historical evolution of capitalism in distinctive ways. No one sphere prevails over the others even as there exists within each sphere the possibility for autonomous development (nature independently mutates and evolves, as do mental conceptions, social relations, forms of daily life, institutional arrangements, technologies, etc.). Each of the spheres is subject to perpetual renewal and transformation both in interaction with the others as well as through an internal dynamic that perpetually creates novelty in human affairs. The relations between the spheres are not causal but dialectically interwoven through the circulation and accumulation of capital. As such, the whole configuration constitutes a socio-ecological totality. This is not, I must emphasise, a mechanical totality, a social engine in which the parts strictly conform to the dictates of the whole. It is more like an ecological system made up of many different species and forms of activity, what the French philosopher/sociologist Henri Lefebvre refers to as an 'ensemble' or the French philosopher Gilles Deleuze calls an 'assemblage' of elements in dynamic relation with each other. In such an ecological totality, the interrelations are fluid and open even as they are inextricably interwoven with each other.

Uneven development between and among the spheres produces contingency as well as tensions and contradictions (in much the same way that unpredictable mutations produce contingency in Darwinian theory). Furthermore, it is entirely possible that explosive developments in one sphere, in a given time and place, can take on a vanguard role. The sudden development of new pathogens (e.g. HIV/AIDS, avian flu or SARS), or the rise of some strong social movement around labour rights, civil or women's and gay rights, a burst of technological innovation as in the recent rise of electronics and computer-chip-based technologies, or a heady burst of utopian politics, have all in various times and places got out in front of the co-evolutionary process, putting immense pressure on the other spheres either to play catch-up or to form centres of recalcitrance or active resistance. Once technology became a business in its own right (as it increasingly did from the mid-nineteenth century onwards) then a social need sometimes had to be created to use up the new technology rather than the other way around. In the pharmaceutical sector we see in recent times the creation of whole new diagnostics of mental and physical states to match new drugs (Prozac was the classic example). The existence of a dominant belief within the capitalist class and the social order more generally that there is a technological fix for every problem and a pill for every ailment produces all sorts of consequences. The 'fetish of technology' therefore does have an unduly prominent role in driving bourgeois history, defining both its astonishing achievements and its self-inflicted catastrophes. Problems in the relation to nature have to be solved by new technologies rather than by revolutions in social reproduction and daily life!

Historically it seems as if there are periods when some of the spheres get radically at odds with each other. In the United States, for example, where the pursuit of science and technology holds supreme, it is odd to find that so many people do not believe in the theory of evolution. While the science of global climate change is well established, many are convinced it is a hoax. How can the relation to nature be better understood in the face of overwhelming religious or political beliefs that give no credence to science? Situations of this kind typically lead either to phases of stasis or to radical reconstruction. Crises usually betoken the occurrence of such phases. Here, too, the crisis tendencies of capitalism are never resolved but merely moved around.

But there is a bottom line in all of this. No matter what innovation or shift occurs where, the survival of capitalism in the long run depends on the capacity to achieve 3 per cent compound growth. Capitalist history is littered with technologies which were tried and did not work, utopian schemes for the promotion of new social relations (like the Icarian communes in the nineteenth-century USA, the Israeli kibbutzim in the 1950s or today's 'green communes') only to be either co-opted or abandoned in the face of a dominant capitalist logic. But no matter what happens, by hook or by crook, capital must somehow organise the seven spheres to conform to the 3 per cent rule.

Capitalism seems in practice to have evolved in ways somewhat similar to Steven Gould's 'punctuated equilibrium' theory of natural evolution: periods of relatively slow but reasonably harmonic co-evolution between the spheres are punctuated by phases of disruption and radical reform. We are possibly now (2010) in the midst of such a disruptive phase. But there are also signs of a desperate attempt to restore the pre-existing order, to proceed as if nothing of consequence has really changed, nor should it.

Consider how this idea of punctuated equilibrium looks when we cast our eye backward over the last major phase of capitalist reconstruction that occurred during the crisis of 1973–82. In *A Brief History of Neoliberalism*, I attempted an account of capitalist restructuring that began during these years. Throughout the capitalist world but particularly in the United States (the undisputed dominant power of that time) capitalist class power was weakening relative to labour and other social movements and capital accumulation was lagging. The heads of leading corporations along with media barons and wealthy individuals, many of whom, like the Rockefeller brothers, were scions of the capitalist class, went on the counter-attack. They set in motion the radical reconstruction of the state–finance nexus (the national and then international deregulation of financial operations, the liberation of debt financing, the opening of the world to heightened international competition and the repositioning of the state apparatus with respect to social provision). Capital was re-empowered vis-à-vis labour through the production of unemployment and deindustrialisation, immigration, offshoring and all manner of technological and organisational changes (e.g. subcontracting). When later coupled with an ideological and political attack on all forms of labour organisation in the Reagan/Thatcher years, the effect was to solve the crisis of declining profitability and declining wealth by way of wage repression and the reduction in social provision by the state. Mental conceptions of the world and political subjectivities were reshaped as far as possible by appeal to neoliberal principles of individual liberty as necessarily embedded in free markets and free trade. This required the withdrawal of the state from social provision and the gradual dismantling of the regulatory environment that had been constructed in the early 1970s (e.g. environmental protection). New forms of niche consumerism and individualised lifestyles also suddenly appeared, built around a postmodern style of urbanisation (the Disneyfication of city centres coupled with gentrification), and the emergence of social movements around a mix of self-centred individualism, identity politics, multiculturalism and sexual preference.

Capital did not create these movements but it did figure out ways to exploit and manipulate them both in terms of fracturing hitherto important class solidarities and commodifying and channelling the affective and effective demands associated with these movements into niche markets. New electronic technologies with widespread applications in both production and consumption had a huge impact upon labour processes as well as on the conduct of daily life for the mass of the population (laptops, mobile phones and iPods are everywhere). That the new electronic technologies of the 1990s held the answer to all the world's problems became the fetish mantra of the 1990s. And all of this presaged an equally huge shift in mental conceptions of the world such that an even more intensive possessive individualism arose, along with moneymaking, indebtedness, speculation in asset values, privatisation and the widespread acceptance of personal responsibility as a cultural norm across social classes. Preliminary studies of those caught up in the foreclosure wave now indicate, for example, that many of them blame themselves, rather than systemic conditions, for not being able, for whatever reason, to live up to the personal responsibility entailed in home ownership. The view of the appropriate role of the state and of state power shifted dramatically during the neoliberal years only now to be challenged as the state has to step in with massive aid to deal with the current crisis.

Of course, the details were much more complicated than this, and the myriad forces at work flowed in all manner of cross-cutting directions. On the world stage, uneven geographical developments of neoliberalism were everywhere in evidence along with differentials of resistance. All I wish to illustrate here is how much the world changed, depending upon where one was, across all of these spheres between 1980 and 2010. The co-evolutionary movement has been palpable and obvious to anyone who has lived through it.

The danger for social theory as well as for popular understandings is to see one of the spheres as determinant. When the architect on the South Korean urban jury said only mental conceptions matter, he was making a very common move doubtless impelled by an understandable desire for simplification. But such simplifications are both unwarranted and dangerously misleading. We are, in fact, surrounded with dangerously over-simplistic mono-causal explanations. In a best-selling book, *The World is Flat*, the journalist Thomas Friedman shamelessly espouses a version of technological determinism (which he mistakenly attributes to Marx). Jared Diamond's best-selling book on *Guns, Germs and Steel* argues that the relation to nature is what counts, thus transforming human evolution into a tale of environmental determinism. Africa is poor for environmental reasons, not, he says, because of racial inferiorities or (what he does not say) because of centuries of imperialist plundering (beginning with the slave trade). Acemoglu et al. prove without doubt that innovations in institutional arrangements are what really account for the differential wealth of nations. In the Marxist and anarchist traditions there is a good deal of class struggle determinism. Others place social relations of gender, sexuality or racialisation in the vanguard of social evolution. Still others preach that the current problems arise out of an arrant individualism and universal human greed. Idealism, in which mental conceptions are placed in the vanguard of social change, has an immensely long tradition (most spectacularly represented by Hegel's theory of history). There are, however, many other versions in which the visions and ideas of powerful innovators and entrepreneurs or of religious leaders or utopian political thinkers (such as some versions of Maoism) are placed at the centre of everything. Changing beliefs and values are, it is said, what really matter. Change the discourses, it is sometimes said, and then the world will change.

The workerist wing in the Marxist tradition, on the other hand, treats the labour process as the only position from which truly revolutionary change can come because the real power to change the world lies exclusively in the activity of labouring. From this starting point and only from this starting point is it possible, claims John Holloway, to *Change the World without Taking Power*. In yet another popular text, *Blessed Unrest*, Paul Hawken makes it seem as if social change in our times can only emanate and already is emanating from the practical engagements of millions of people seeking to transform their daily lives in the particular places in which they live, casting aside all of those political ideologies and utopian mental conceptions (from communism to neoliberalism) that have proved so disastrous in the past. The left version of this now sees the politics of everyday life in particular locales as the fundamental seedbed for both political action and radical change. The creation of local 'solidarity economies' is the exclusive answer. On the other hand, there is a whole school of historians and political philosophers who, by choosing the title of 'institutionalists', signal their adherence to a theory of social change that privileges command over and reform of institutional and administrative arrangements as fundamental. Capture and smash state power is the revolutionary Leninist version of this. Another radical version derives from Michel Foucault's focus on questions of 'governmentality', which interestingly analyses the intersections between two spheres – institutional and administrative systems and daily life (construed as body politics).

Each position in this pantheon of possibilities has something important, albeit one-dimensional, to say about the socio-ecological dynamism of capitalism and the potentiality to construct alternatives. Problems arise, however, when one or other of these perspectives is exclusively and dogmatically viewed as the only source, and hence the primary political pressure point for change. There has been an unfortunate history within social theory of favouring some spheres of activity more than others. Sometimes this reflects a situation in which one or other of the spheres – such as class struggle or technological dynamism – seems to be in the forefront of the transformations then occurring. In such a situation it would be churlish not to acknowledge the forces that are in the vanguard of socio-ecological change in that place and time. The argument is not, therefore, that the seven spheres should always be given equal weight but that the dialectical tension within their uneven development should always be borne in mind.

What appears minor in one era or in one place can become major in the next. Labour struggles are not now in the forefront of the political dynamic in the way they were in the 1960s and early 1970s. Much more attention is now focused on the relation to nature than formerly. Contemporary interest in how the politics of daily life unfolds – the politics of the everyday – is clearly to be welcomed simply because it has not received the attention it should have commanded in the past. Right now we probably do not need yet another exposition on the social impacts of new technologies and organisational forms which have in the past too often been thoughtlessly prioritised.

Marx's whole account of the rise of capitalism out of feudalism can in fact be reconstructed and read in terms of a co-evolutionary movement across and between the seven different activity spheres here identified. Capitalism did not supplant feudalism by way of some neat revolutionary transformation resting on the forces mobilised within only one of these spheres. It had to grow within the interstices of the old society and bit by bit supplant it, sometimes through main force, violence, predation and seizures of assets but at other times with guile and cunning. And it often lost battles against the old order even as it eventually won the war. As it achieved a modicum of power, however, a nascent capitalist class had to build its alternative social forms at first on the basis of the technologies, social relations, administrative systems, mental conceptions, production systems, relations to nature and patterns of daily life as these had long been constituted under the preceding feudal order. It took a co-evolution and uneven development in the different spheres before capitalism found not only its own unique technological base but also its belief systems and mental conceptions, its unstable but clearly class-ridden configurations of social relations, its curious spatiotemporal rhythms and its equally special forms of daily life, to say nothing of its production processes and its institutional and administrative framework, before it was possible to say that this was truly capitalism.

Even as it did so, it carried within it multiple marks of the differential conditions under which the transformation to capitalism had been wrought. While too much has probably been made of the differentials between Protestant, Catholic and Confucian traditions in marking out significant differences in how capitalism works in different parts of the world, it would be foolhardy to suggest that such influences are irrelevant or even negligible. Furthermore, once capitalism found its own feet, so it engaged in a perpetual revolutionary movement across all the spheres to accommodate the inevitable stresses of endless capital accumulation at a compound rate of growth. Working-class habits and mores in Britain in the 1950s and 1960s bear little relationship to daily life habits and mental conceptions of the working classes (along with a redefinition of what constitutes a 'working-class' social relation in the first place) that emerged in the 1990s. The process of co-evolution that capitalism sets in motion has been perpetual.

Perhaps one of the biggest failures of past attempts to build socialism has been the reluctance to engage politically across all of these spheres and to let the dialectic between them open up possibilities rather than close them down. Revolutionary communism, particularly that of the Soviet sort, even more particularly after the period of revolutionary experimentation of the 1920s, was terminated by Stalin, who reduced the dialectic of relations between the spheres to a single-track programme in which productive forces (technologies) were placed in the vanguard of change. This approach inevitably failed. It led to stasis, stagnant administrative and institutional arrangements, turned daily life into monotony and froze the possibility to explore new social relations or mental conceptions. It paid no mind to the relation to nature with disastrous consequences. Lenin, of course, had no option except to strive to create communism on the basis of the configuration given by the preceding order (part feudal and part capitalist) and from this standpoint his embrace of the Fordist factory, its technologies and organisational forms, as a necessary step in the transition to communism is understandable. He plausibly argued that if the transition to socialism and then communism was to work then it had to be initially on the basis of the most advanced technologies and organisational forms that capitalism had produced. But there was no conscious attempt, particularly after Stalin took over, to imagine and begin to move towards the construction of truly socialist let alone communist technologies and organisational forms.

Mao's overwhelming dialectical sense of how contradictions worked, as well as his recognition, in principle at least, that a revolution had to be permanent or nothing at all, led him to consciously prioritise revolutionary transformation in different activity spheres in different historical

phases. The 'Great Leap Forward' emphasised production and technological and organisational change. It failed in its immediate objectives and
produced a massive famine but almost certainly had a huge impact upon
mental conceptions. The Cultural Revolution sought to radically reconfig-
ure social relations and mental conceptions of the world directly. While it
is contemporary received wisdom to say that he failed miserably in both
of these endeavours, the suspicion lurks that in many respects the astonishing economic performance and revolutionary transformation that have
characterised China since the shift towards institutional and administrative reforms from the late 1970s onwards have rested solidly on the real
achievements of the Maoist period (in particular the break with many
'traditional' mental conceptions and social relations within the masses as
the Party deepened its grasp over daily life). Mao completely reorganised
the delivery of healthcare in the 1960s, for example, by sending an army of
'barefoot doctors' out into the hitherto neglected and impoverished rural
regions to teach elementary preventive medicine, public health measures
and prenatal care. The dramatic reductions in infant mortality that resulted
just happened to produce the labour surpluses that fuelled China's growth
surge after 1980. China also enforced draconian limitations on reproductive activity through a one child per family policy. That all of this opened
the path towards a certain kind of capitalist development is an unintended
consequence of huge significance.

How, then, might revolutionary strategies be construed in the light of
this co-evolutionary theory of social change? It provides a framework for
enquiry that can have practical implications for thinking through everything
from grand revolutionary strategies to redesign of urbanisation and city
life. At the same time it signals that we perpetually confront contingencies,
contradictions and autonomous possibilities as well as a host of unintended
consequences.

As with the transition from feudalism to capitalism, there are plenty of
interstitial spaces in which to start alternative social movements that are
anti-capitalist. But there are also plenty of possibilities for well-intended
moves to be co-opted or go catastrophically wrong. Conversely, seemingly
negative developments may turn out surprisingly well. Should that deter
us? Since evolution in general and in human societies in particular (with or
without the capitalist imperative) cannot be stopped, then we have no option
but to be participants in the drama. The only choice is whether we seek to
be conscious of how our interventions are working or not and to be ready to
change course rapidly as conditions unfold or as unintended consequences

become more apparent. The evident adaptability and flexibility of capitalism here provide an important model worthy of emulation.

So where shall we start our revolutionary anti-capitalist movement? Mental conceptions? The relation to nature? Daily life and reproductive practices? Social relations? Technologies and organisational forms? Labour processes? The capture of institutions and their revolutionary transformation?

A survey of alternative thinking and of oppositional social movements would show different currents of thought (more often than not unfortunately posed as mutually exclusive) as to where it is most appropriate to begin. But the implication of the co-evolutionary theory here proposed is that we can start anywhere and everywhere as long as we do not stay where we start from! The revolution has to be a movement in every sense of that word. If it cannot move within, across and through the different spheres then it will ultimately go nowhere at all. Recognising this, it becomes imperative to envision alliances between a whole range of social forces configured around the different spheres. Those with a deep knowledge of how the relation to nature works need to ally with those deeply familiar with how institutional and administrative arrangements function, how science and technology can be mobilised, how daily life and social relations can most easily be reorganised, how mental conceptions can be changed, and how production and the labour process can be reconfigured.

Commentary

This chapter from *The Enigma of Capital* summarises my view of how Marx's evolutionary thinking can be put to work to grapple with the complexities of capitalism's current and future trajectories and to get an idea of how, why and when it might evolve into some other mode of production. Marx embeds other kinds of limited technical and economic enquiries (some of which take the form of mathematical models) into this grander evolutionary view of capital as a dynamic and perpetually changing totality of social and natural relations. It is vital to understand the fluidity of the processes by which capital gets reproduced and from time to time reconstituted into different configurations. The intersecting pressures for change in productive and social relations, consumption and distribution, our relations to nature, institutional arrangements and our daily lives, along with our conceptions of the world, form a totality that is evolving, always in motion, and perpetually crisis-prone. A finer-grained analysis, of the sort I presented in *Seventeen Contradictions and the End of Capitalism*, reveals the inner tensions within the capitalist system that form the mainsprings of change. A study of the multiple interlocking contradictions of capital allows us to see more clearly the impossibilities, the insanity and irrational consequences of the endless accumulation that capital demands. It is imperative that we begin to think through the political strategies required to confront the excesses of capital in the here and now and find openings for the construction of viable political-economic alternatives.

Notes

Chapter 1

1. Kuhn, *The Structure of Scientific Revolutions*, 1962.
2. Bernal, *Science in History*, 1971.
3. See ibid.; Rose and Rose, *Science and Society*, 1969.
4. See Kuhn, *The Structure of Scientific Revolutions*, 1962, p. 37; Nagel, *The Structure of Science*, 1961.
5. Johnson, 'The Keynesian revolution', 1971.
6. See Althusser and Balibar, *Reading Capital*, 1970.
7. Kuhn, *The Structure of Scientific Revolutions*, 1962, pp. 52–6.
8. Marx, *Capital*, vol. 2, 1978, pp. 97–8.
9. See Marx, *The Economic and Philosophic Manuscripts*, 1964, p. 164.
10. Park, Burgess and McKenzie, *The City*, 1925.
11. Ibid.
12. See Berry and Horton, *Geographic Perspectives*, 1970.
13. Engels, *The Condition of the English Working Class*, 1987, pp. 86–7.
14. Ibid., pp. 68–9.
15. Kerner Commission, *Report of the National Advisory Commission*, 1968.
16. Alonso, *Location and Land Use*, 1964; Muth, *Cities and Housing*, 1969.
17. Lave, 'Congestion and urban location', 1970.
18. *Wall Street Journal*, 27 November 1970.
19. Muth, *Cities and Housing*, 1969.
20. Valdès, 'Health and revolution in Cuba', 1971.
21. Ibid., p. 320.
22. Spoehr, 'Cultural differences', 1956.
23. Pearson, 'The economy has no surplus', 1957.
24. See Sternlieb, *The Tenement Landlord*, 1966; Grigsby et al., *Housing and Poverty*, 1971.
25. Marx, *Capital*, vol. 3, 1978; Marx, *Theories of Surplus Value*, Part 2, 1968.
26. Engels, *The Housing Question*, 1935, p. 23.
27. Ibid., p. 43.
28. Ibid., pp. 74–7.

Chapter 2

1. Marx and Engels, *The Communist Manifesto*, 2008, pp. 46–7.
2. Marx, *Capital*, vol. 1, 1976, p. 128.
3. Ibid., p. 183.
4. Marx, *Capital*, vol. 2, 1978, pp. 225–9.
5. Marx, *Capital*, vol. 1, 1976, p. 209.
6. Marx, *Capital*, vol. 2, 1978, ch. 6.
7. Marx, *Grundrisse*, 1973, pp. 533–4; Marx, *Capital*, vol. 2, 1978, pp. 226–7.
8. Marx, *Grundrisse*, 1973, pp. 533–4.
9. Ibid.
10. Marx, *Capital*, vol. 2, 1978, pp. 134–5.
11. Marx, *Grundrisse*, 1973, pp. 33–4.
12. Marx, *Capital*, vol. 1, 1976, p. 506.
13. Marx, *Grundrisse*, 1973, p. 524.
14. Ibid.
15. Marx, *Capital*, vol. 2, 1978, p. 327.
16. Marx, *Grundrisse*, 1973, p. 538.
17. Marx, *Capital*, vol. 2, 1978, pp. 327–8.
18. Marx, *Grundrisse*, 1973, p. 539.
19. Marx, *Capital*, vol. 2, 1978, pp. 249–50.
20. Ibid., p. 357.
21. Marx, *Grundrisse*, 1973, p. 535.
22. Marx, *Capital*, vol. 3, 1978, Part V.
23. Ibid., ch. 20.
24. Ibid., chs 16–19.
25. Ibid., pp. 52–3.
26. Marx, *Capital*, vol. 1, 1976, pp. 284–5, 647–50.
27. Ibid., p. 647.
28. Marx, *Capital*, vol. 3, 1978, pp. 784–7, 814–16, ch. 47.
29. Marx, *Capital*, vol. 1, 1976, p. 446.
30. Ibid., p. 464.
31. Marx, *Grundrisse*, 1973, p. 587; Marx and Engels, *The Communist Manifesto*, 2008, pp. 47–8.
32. Marx, *Capital*, vol. 1, 1976, p. 499.
33. Marx, *Capital*, vol. 2, 1978, pp. 328–9.
34. Ibid.
35. Ibid., p. 327.
36. Marx, *Capital*, vol. 1, 1976, p. 815.
37. Ibid., pp. 380, 848.
38. Marx and Engels, *Selected Correspondence*, 1955, pp. 236–7.
39. Marx, *Capital*, vol. 1, 1976, pp. 794–5.
40. Ibid., p. 718.

41. Ibid., p. 799.
42. Cf. Marx and Engels, *The Communist Manifesto*, 2008.
43. Marx, *Grundrisse*, 1973, pp. 407–10.
44. Marx, *Capital*, vol. 1, 1976, pp. 474, 579–80.
45. Marx, *Theories of Surplus Value*, Part 3, 1972, p. 288.
46. Marx, *Capital*, vol. 1, 1976, p. 474; Marx, *The German Ideology*, xxxx, p. 69.
47. Marx, *Grundrisse*, 1973, pp. 407–10.
48. Marx, *Capital*, vol. 2, 1978, pp. 327–8.
49. Marx, 'Results of the Immediate Process of Production', Marx, *Capital*, vol. 1, 1976, pp. 1013–14.
50. Marx, *Grundrisse*, 1973, p. 740.
51. Ibid., p. 728.
52. Marx, *Capital*, vol. 2, 1978, ch. 8.
53. Marx, *Grundrisse*, 1973, p. 703.
54. Ibid., pp. 739–40.
55. Marx, *Capital*, vol. 2, 1978, p. 351.
56. Marx, *Capital*, vol. 1, 1976, p. 133.
57. Ibid., p. 129.
58. Marx, *Grundrisse*, 1973, pp. 224–5.
59. Marx, *Capital*, vol. 3, 1978, pp. 448–9.
60. Marx, *Capital*, vol. 1, 1976, pp. 579–80.
61. Marx, *Theories of Surplus Value*, Part 2, 1968, pp. 302–3.
62. Marx, *Theories of Surplus Value*, Part 3, 1972, p. 243.
63. Marx, *Capital*, vol. 1, 1976, p. 931.
64. Ibid., p. 940.
65. Ibid., p. 647.
66. Ibid., p. 644.
67. Ibid., pp. 701–2.
68. Marx, *Wages, Price, and Profit*, 1965, pp. 72–3.
69. Marx, *Capital*, vol. 1, 1976, p. 702.
70. Marx, *Capital*, vol. 3, 1978, p. 345.
71. Marx, *Theories of Surplus Value*, Part 2, 1968, pp. 474–5.
72. Ibid., p. 201.
73. Marx, *Theories of Surplus Value*, Part 3, 1972, pp. 105–6.
74. Marx, *Capital*, vol. 1, 1976, p. 241.
75. Marx, *Theories of Surplus Value*, Part 3, 1972, p. 253.
76. Marx, *Capital*, vol. 3, 1978, pp. 448–9.

Chapter 4

1. Jonquet, *Montmartre Autrefois et Aujourd'hui*, 1892.
2. Ibid.; Dansette, *Histoire Religieuse*, 1965.

3. Price, *The Economic Modernisation of France*, 1975; Braudel and Labrousse, *Histoire Economique*, 1976.
4. Rohault de Fleury, *Historique de la Basilique de Sacré Coeur*, 1903–09.
5. Zeldin, *The Political System of Napoleon III*, 1958; Zeldin, *France, 1848–1945*, 1973.
6. Gaillard, *Paris, La Ville, 1852–1870*, 1977.
7. Lepidis and Jacomin, *Belleville*, 1975.
8. Pinkney, *Napoleon III and the Rebuilding of Paris*, 1958.
9. Rohault de Fleury, *Historique de la Basilique de Sacré Coeur*, 1903–09, pp. 10–13.
10. Ibid., pp. 10–13.
11. Guillemin, *Cette Curieuse Guerre de 70*, 1956.
12. Thomas, *Rossel 1844–71*, 1967.
13. Lissagary, *Histoire de la Commune*, 1976.
14. Bruhat et al., *La Commune de 1871*, 1971, p. 75.
15. Marx and Lenin, *The Civil War in France*, 1968.
16. Lazare, *La France et Paris*, 1872; Goncourt, *Paris under Siege, 1870–71*, 1969.
17. Bruhat et al., *La Commune de 1871*, 1971; Edwards, *The Paris Commune*, 1971.
18. Lissagaray, *Histoire de la Commune*, 1976, p. 75.
19. Guillemin, 1956; Bruhat et al., *La Commune de 1871*, 1971, pp. 104–5; Dreyfus, *Monsieur Thiers contre l'Empire*, 1928, p. 266.
20. Allison, *Monsieur Thiers*, 1932; Guillemin, 1956.
21. Rohault de Fleury, *Historique de la Basilique de Sacré Coeur*, 1903–09, p. 88.
22. Ibid., p. 264.
23. Marx and Lenin, *The Civil War in France*, 1968.
24. Foulon, *Eugène Varlin*, 1934.
25. Goncourt, *Paris under Siege, 1870–71*, 1969, p. 288.
26. Thomas, *The Women Incendiaries*, 1966.
27. Cited in Jellinek, *The Paris Commune of 1871*, 1937, p. 339.
28. Rohault de Fleury, *Historique de la Basilique de Sacré Coeur*, 1903–09, p. 13.
29. Cited in Jellinek, *The Paris Commune of 1871*, 1937.
30. Goncourt, *Paris under Siege, 1870–71*, 1969, p. 312.
31. Dansette, *Histoire Religieuse*, 1965, pp. 340–45.
32. Guillemin, 1956, pp. 295–6; Rohault de Fleury, *Historique de la Basilique de Sacré Coeur*, 1903–09, p. 365.
33. Rohault de Fleury, *Historique de la Basilique de Sacré Coeur*, 1903–09, p. 27.
34. Jonquet, *Montmartre Autrefois et Aujourd'hui*, 1892, pp. 85–7.
35. Pinkney, *Napoleon III and the Rebuilding of Paris*, 1958, pp. 85–7.
36. Rohault de Fleury, *Historique de la Basilique de Sacré Coeur*, 1903–09, p. 75.
37. Dansette, *Histoire Religieuse*, 1965, pp. 340–45.
38. Rohault de Fleury, *Historique de la Basilique de Sacré Coeur*, 1903–09, p. 88.
39. Ibid.

40. Abadie, *Paul Abadie, Architecte, 1812–1884*, 1988.
41. Rohault de Fleury, *Historique de la Basilique de Sacré Coeur*, 1903–09, p. 244.
42. Ibid., p. 269.
43. Ibid., p. 165.
44. Dansette, *Histoire Religieuse*, 1965, pp. 356–8; Lepidis and Jacomin, *Belleville*, 1975, pp. 271–2.
45. Ville de Paris, Conseil Municipal, Prods Verbaux, 3 August, 7 October and 2 December, 1880.
46. Rohault de Fleury, *Historique de la Basilique de Sacré Coeur*, 1903–09, pp. 71–3.
47. Ibid., pp. 71ff.
48. Lesourd, *Montmartre*, 1973, pp. 224–5.

Chapter 5

1. See, e.g., Gregory and Urry, *Social Relations and Spatial Structures*, 1985; Soja, *Postmodern Geographies*, 1988.
2. Mandel, *Late Capitalism*, 1975; Jameson, 1984.
3. Toffler, *Future Shock*, 1970.
4. Ibid., p. 40.
5. Ibid., pp. 326–9.
6. Baudrillard, *For a Critique*, 1981.
7. Taylor, *Modernism, Post-Modernism, Realism*, 1987, p. 77.
8. Bell, *The Cultural Contradictions of Capitalism*, 1978, p. 20.
9. Calvino, *If on a Winter's Night*, 1981, p. 8.
10. Baudrillard, *L'Amérique*, 1986.
11. Rochberg-Halton, *Meaning and Modernity*, 1986, p. 173.
12. Dicken, *Global Shift*, 1986, pp. 110–13.
13. Virilio, *L'Esthétique de la Disparition*, 1980.
14. Martin and Rowthorn, *The Geography of Deindustrialisation*, 1986; Bluestone and Harrison, *The Deindustrialisation of America*, 1982; Harrison and Bluestone, *The Great U-Turn*, 1988.
15. Boyer, 'The return of aesthetics', 1988.
16. Baudrillard, *L'Amérique*, 1986.
17. Jencks, *The Language of Post-Modern Architecture*, 1984, p. 127.
18. Chambers, 'Maps for the metropolis', 1987.
19. McHale, *Postmodernist Fiction*, 1987.
20. Cohen and Taylor, *Escape Attempts*, 1978, quoted in McHale, *Postmodernist Fiction*, 1987, p. 38.
21. Foucault, *The Foucault Reader*, 1984, p. 253.
22. Colquhoun, 1991.
23. Jameson, 'Cognitive mapping', 1988, p. 351.

Chapter 6

1. Bouinot, *L'Action Economique des Grands Villes*, 1987.
2. Boddy, 'Local economic and employment strategies', 1984; Cochrane, *Developing Local Economic Strategies*, 1987.
3. Rees and Lambert, *Cities in Crisis*, 1985, p. 179.
4. Blunkett and Jackson, *Democracy in Crisis*, 1987, pp. 108–42.
5. See Elkin, *City and Regime*, 1987.
6. Goodman, *The Last Entrepreneurs*, 1979.
7. See Judd and Ready, 'Entrepreneurial cities', 1986; Peterson, *City Limits*, 1981; Leitner, 'Cities in pursuit of economic growth', 1989.
8. For some elaboration and critical reflection on this controversial concept, see Gertler, 'The limits to flexibility', 1988; Harvey, *The Condition of Postmodernity*, 1989; Sayer, 'Post-Fordism in question', 1989; Schoenberger, 'From Fordism to flexible accumulation', 1988; Scott, *New Industrial Spaces*, 1988; Swyngedouw, 'The socio-spatial implications of innovations', 1986.
9. Jacobs, *Cities and the Wealth of Nations*, 1984.
10. See the excellent account by Rees and Lambert, *Cities in Crisis*, 1985.
11. Murray, 'Pension funds and local authority investments', 1983.
12. Molotch, 'The city as a growth machine', 1976.
13. Bouinot, *L'Action Economique des Grands Villes*, 1987.
14. Davies, 'The relevance of development control', 1980, p. 23, quoted in Ball, *Housing Policy and Economic Power*, 1983, pp. 270–71.
15. See Berkowitz, 'Economic development really works', 1984; Levine, 'Downtown redevelopment', 1987; Lyall, 'A bicycle built for two', 1982; Stoker, 'Baltimore: the self-evaluating city', 1986.
16. See Scott, *New Industrial Spaces*, 1988.
17. See Gundle, S., 1986.
18. *Guardian*, 9 May 1987.
19. See Bianchini, 'The arts and the inner cities', 1991.
20. Markusen, 'Defense spending', 1986.
21. Smith and Keller, 'Managed growth', 1983.
22. Noyelle and Stanback, 1984.
23. See Swyngedouw, 'The heart of the place', 1989.
24. See Harvey, *The Condition of Postmodernity*, 1989, ch. 8.
25. Levine, 'Downtown redevelopment', 1987.
26. Boddy, 'Local economic and employment strategies', 1984.
27. Sassen-Koob, *Global Cities*, 1988.
28. Green, 1988.
29. *Baltimore Sun*, 20 August 1987.
30. Szanton, *Baltimore 2000*, 1986.
31. Levine, 'Downtown redevelopment', 1987.
32. *Sunday Times*, 29 November 1987.

33. Cockburn, *The Local State*, 1977.
34. Mollenkopf, *The Contested City*, 1983; Logan and Molotch, *Urban Fortunes*, 1987; Gurr and King, *The State and the City*, 1987; Smith, *City, State and Market*, 1988.
35. Marx, *Capital*, vol. 1, 1976, p. 476.
36. Jessop, 'Accumulation strategies', 1983.
37. Harvey, *The Limits to Capital*, 1982.
38. See Frug, 'The city as a legal concept', 1980.
39. See Blunkett and Jackson, *Democracy in Crisis*, 1987.

Chapter 7

1. Williams, *Problems in Materialism and Culture*, 1980, p. 67.
2. Lovejoy, *The Great Chain of Being*, 1964, pp. 7–14.
3. See Dobson, *Green Political Thought*, 1990.
4. Marsh, *Man and Nature*, 1965; Thomas, *Man's Role*, 1956; Goudie, *The Human Impact*, 1986.
5. Williams, *The Country and the City*, 1973.
6. Leopold, *A Sand County Almanac*, 1968.
7. Marx, *Grundrisse*, 1973, pp. 224–6.
8. See Gosselink et al., *The Value of the Tidal Marsh*, 1974.
9. Pearce et al., *Blueprint for a Green Economy*, 1989.
10. Brundtland Report, *Our Common Future*, 1987.
11. Norgaard, 'Environmental economics', 1985.
12. McEvoy, 'Towards an interactive theory of nature and culture', 1988, p. 222.
13. Goodin, *Green Political Theory*, 1992, p. 67.
14. Naess, *Ecology, Community and Lifestyle*, 1989, p. 127.
15. Simmel, *The Philosophy of Money*, 1978, p. 377.
16. Marx, *Grundrisse*, 1973.
17. Borneman, *The Psychoanalysis of Money*, 1976, p. 86.
18. Marx, *Theories of Surplus Value*, Part 1, 1967, pp. 474–5.
19. Marx, 'On the Jewish question', 1971.
20. Cf. Goodin, *Green Political Theory*, 1992, p. 40.
21. Leopold, *A Sand County Almanac*, 1968, pp. 223–4.
22. Lovejoy, 1964.
23. Ingold, *The Appropriation of Nature*, 1986, p. 104.
24. Merchant, *The Death of Nature*, 1980.
25. Martin, 'The egg and the sperm', 1991.
26. Ibid., p. 498.
27. Young, *Darwin's Metaphor*, 1985.
28. Todes, *Darwin without Malthus*, 1989.
29. Ibid., p. 168.
30. Marx and Engels, *Selected Correspondence*, 1955, p. 128.

31. See Gerratana, 'Marx and Darwin', 1973.
32. Mitman, *The State of Nature*, 1992.
33. Cf. Bookchin, *Remaking Society*, 1990.
34. Rousseau, *The Social Contract and Discourses*, 1973.
35. Martin, 'The end of the body?', 1992.
36. Williams, *Problems in Materialism and Culture*, 1980, p. 70.
37. Bohm and Peat, *Science, Order and Creativity*, 1987, pp. 35–41.
38. Capra, *The Tao of Physics*, 1975, p. 77.
39. Cf. Dobson, *Green Political Thought*, 1990, pp. 57–63.
40. Cited in Naess, *Ecology, Community and Lifestyle*, 1989, p. 19.
41. Naess, *Ecology, Community and Lifestyle*, 1989, p. 45.
42. Steiner, *Heidegger*, 1992, p. 136.
43. Heidegger, *Poetry, Language, Thought*, 1991, pp. 114–15.
44. Heidegger, 1966, pp. 47–8.
45. Relph, 'Geographical experiences', 1989, pp. 27–9.
46. Norberg-Schulz, *Genius Loci*, 1980, pp. 15–21.
47. Cited in Alexander, 'Bioregionalism', 1990, p. 163.
48. Mills, cited in ibid.
49. Goodin, *Green Political Theory*, 1992, ch. 2.
50. Sagoff, *The Economy of the Earth*, 1988.
51. Ibid., p. 17.
52. Bramwell, *Ecology in the Twentieth Century*, 1989.
53. Cited in ibid., p. 11.
54. Spretnak, 'The spiritual dimension of Green politics', 1985, p. 232.
55. Paehlke, *Environmentalism and the Future of Progressive Politics*, 1989, p. 194.
56. Grundmann, *Marxism and Ecology*, 1991, p. 114.
57. Williams, *Problems in Materialism and Culture*, 1980, p. 71.
58. Porritt and Winner, cited in Dobson, *Green Political Thought*, 1990, p. 7.
59. Ophuls, *Ecology and the Politics of Scarcity*, 1977, p. 161.
60. Heilbroner, *An Inquiry into the Human Prospect*, 1974, p. 161.
61. Dobson, *Green Political Thought*, 1990, p. 26.
62. Hajer, 'The politics of environmental performance review', 1992; Weale, *The New Politics of Pollution*, 1992, ch. 3.
63. See, e.g., Collingwood, *The Idea of Nature*, 1960.
64. See Nash, *The Rights of Nature*, 1989.
65. See Attfield, *The Ethics of Environmental Concern*, 1991.
66. For a good summary, see Benton, 'Marxism and natural limits', 1989, p. 52.
67. Commoner, *Making Peace with the Planet*, 1990, p. 219.
68. Haila and Levins, *Humanity and Nature*, 1992, p. 251.
69. Ibid., p. 227.
70. See O'Connor, 'Capitalism, nature, socialism', 1988.
71. Dobson, *Green Political Thought*, 1990, p. 25.

72. O'Riordan, *Environmentalism*, 1981, p. 307.

73. Dauncey, *After the Crash*, 1988.

74. May, 'How many species inhabit the earth?', 1992.

75. Jacks and Whyte, *Vanishing Lands*, 1939.

76. Wilson, *The Culture of Nature*, 1992.

77. See, e.g., Butzer, *Archaeology as Human Ecology*, 1982.

78. See Bennett, *The Ecological Transition*, 1976; Ellen, *Environment, Subsistence and System*, 1982; Ingold, *The Appropriation of Nature*, 1986.

79. Thomas, *Man's Role*, 1956; Goudie, *The Human Impact*, 1986.

80. Cf. the debate in *Journal of American History*, 1990.

81. E.g. Butzer, *Archaeology as Human Ecology*, 1982.

82. Benton, 'Marxism and natural limits', 1989; Benton, 'Ecology, socialism and the mastery of nature', 1992.

83. Grundmann, 'The ecological challenge to Marxism', 1991; Grundmann, *Marxism and Ecology*, 1991.

84. Cronon, *Changes in the Land*, 1983, pp. 13–14.

85. Marx and Engels, 1975, p. 55.

86. Worster, *Rivers of Empire*, 1985.

87. See Gottlieb, *A Life of Its Own*, 1988, or Polanski's film *Chinatown*.

88. Lewontin, 1982.

89. See Crosby, *Ecological Imperialism*, 1986.

90. Cronon, *Nature's Metropolis*, 1991.

91. See Smith, *Uneven Development*, 1990, and Smith and O'Keefe, 'Geography, Marx and the concept of nature', 1985.

92. Guha, *The Unquiet Woods*, 1989, p. xii.

93. Ibid., p. 196.

94. Sauer, 'The agency of man on earth', 1956.

95. Goldsmith, *The Way*, 1992, p. xvii.

96. Bookchin, 'Ecology and revolutionary thought', 1985, p. 97.

97. Cited in Booth and Jacobs, 'Ties that bind', 1990, p. 27.

98. Haila and Levins, *Humanity and Nature*, 1992, p. 195.

99. Butzer, *Archaeology as Human Ecology*, 1982, p. 320.

100. See Leiss, *The Domination of Nature*, 1974.

101. Grundmann, 'The ecological challenge to Marxism', 1991.

102. Benton, 'Marxism and natural limits', 1989; Benton, 'Ecology, socialism and the mastery of nature', 1992.

103. Glacken, *Traces on the Rhodian Shore*, 1967.

104. Bate, *Romantic Ecology*, 1991.

105. McGann, *The Romantic Ideology*, 1983.

106. Urry, *The Tourist Gaze*, 1990.

107. Williams, *Problems in Materialism and Culture*, 1980, p. 67.

108. Eckersley, *Environmentalism and Political Theory*, 1992, p. 53.

109. See Capra, 1975.
110. All citations from Levins and Lewontin, *The Dialectical Biologist*, 1985.
111. Cited in Ollman, 'Putting dialectics to work', 1990, p. 44.
112. Eckersley, *Environmentalism and Political Theory*, 1992, p. 49.
113. Bohm and Peat, *Science, Order and Creativity*, 1987, p. 40.
114. Ollman, *Dialectical Investigations*, 1993, p. 34.
115. Levins and Lewontin, *The Dialectical Biologist*, 1985, p. 272.
116. Ibid., p. 278.
117. Ollman, *Alienation*, 1971; Ollman, *Dialectical Investigations*, 1993.
118. Eckersley, *Environmentalism and Political Theory*, 1992, pp. 49–55.
119. Birch and Cobb, *The Liberation of Life*, 1981.
120. Naess, *Ecology, Community and Lifestyle*, 1989, p. 79.
121. Zimmerman, 'Quantum theory', 1988.
122. Lefebvre, 1991.
123. Levins and Lewontin, *The Dialectical Biologist*, 1985.
124. Ibid., p. 274.
125. Ibid., p. 275.
126. Ollman, 1990; Ollman, *Dialectical Investigations*, 1993.
127. Ollman, 1990, p. 34.
128. See Fuss, 1989.
129. Benton, 'Ecology, socialism and the mastery of nature', 1992, p. 72.
130. Ollman, *Dialectical Investigations*, 1993.
131. Parsons, *Marx and Engels on Ecology*, 1977; Lee, 'On the Marxian view', 1980.
132. Clark, 'Marx's inorganic body', 1989; Dickens, *Society and Nature*, 1992, pp. 190–95.
133. See Smith, *Uneven Development*, 1990.
134. Benton, 'Marxism and natural limits', 1989, p. 55.
135. Marx, *The Economic and Philosophic Manuscripts*, 1964.
136. Cf. Lovejoy, cited above; Ollman, *Alienation*, 1971, pp. 23–4.
137. See, e.g., Benton, 'Marxism and natural limits', 1989; Benton, 'Ecology, socialism and the mastery of nature', 1992.
138. Lee, *Social Philosophy*, 1989.
139. See, e.g., Spoehr, 'Cultural differences', 1956; Firey, *Man, Mind and the Land*, 1960.
140. Benton, 'Marxism and natural limits', 1989, p. 77.
141. See Redclift, *Sustainable Development*, 1987.
142. Cited in Grundmann, *Marxism and Ecology*, 1991, p. 228.
143. See ibid., p. 54.
144. See, e.g., Meszaros, *Marx's Theory of Alienation*, 1970; Ollman, *Alienation*, 1971.
145. Cf. Ingold, *The Appropriation of Nature*, 1986, cited above.
146. Marx, *Theories of Surplus Value*, Part 1, 1967, p. 352.

147. Grundmann, *Marxism and Ecology*, 1991.

148. Cf. Commoner, *Making Peace with the Planet*, 1990.

149. Cited in Alexander, 'Bioregionalism', 1990, p. 170.

150. Sale, *Dwellers in the Land*, 1985.

151. See Dobson, *Green Political Thought*, 1990, p. 122.

152. Young, *Justice and the Politics of Difference*, 1990.

153. Cited in Dobson, *Green Political Thought*, 1990, p. 97.

154. Young, *Justice and the Politics of Difference*, 1990, p. 105.

155. Haila and Levins, *Humanity and Nature*, 1992, p. 236.

156. Cronon, *Changes in the Land*, 1983, p. 99.

157. Smith, 'Geography, difference and the politics of scale', 1992, p. 72.

158. Marx, *Theories of Surplus Value*, Part 1, 1967, p. 174.

Chapter 8

1. Said, 'Appendix', 1989.

2. Gilroy, *There Ain't No Black in the Union Jack*, 1987.

3. Roman, 'On the ground', 1993.

4. Hall, 'Politics and letters', 1989, p. 62.

5. Snedeker, 'Between humanism and social theory', 1993, p. 113.

6. For extended discussions, see the edited collections in Eagleton, *Raymond Williams*, 1989, and Dworkin and Roman, *Views beyond the Border Country*, 1993.

7. Williams, *Marxism and Literature*, 1977, pp. 128–9.

8. Granovetter, 'Economic action and social structure', 1985.

9. Lomnitz-Adler, 'Concepts for the study of regional culture', 1991.

10. Williams, *People of the Black Mountains*, 1990, p. 2.

11. Williams, *Keywords*, 1983, p. 219.

12. Williams, *Problems in Materialism and Culture*, 1980, p. 67.

13. Ibid., p. 76.

14. Marx, *Capital*, vol. 1, 1976, p. 173.

15. Cronon, *Changes in the Land*, 1983, pp. 13–14.

16. Williams, *People of the Black Mountains*, 1989, pp. 10–12.

17. Williams, *Border Country*, 1960, p. 10.

18. Williams, *People of the Black Mountains*, 1989, p. 319.

19. Williams, 'The achievement of Brecht', 1961, p. 157.

20. Williams, *Resources of Hope*, 1989, pp. 321–2.

21. Ibid., p. 242.

22. Ibid., pp. 165–6.

23. Ibid., p. 153.

24. Williams, *Border Country*, 1960, p. 242.

25. Williams, *The Fight for Manod*, 1979, p. 140.

26. Ibid., p. 153.

27. Ibid., p. 133.
28. Williams, *Resources of Hope*, 1989, pp. 249, 115.
29. Ibid., p. 115.
30. Williams, *Loyalties*, 1985, p. 293.
31. Williams, *Resources of Hope*, 1989, p. 117.
32. Williams, *Border Country*, 1960, p. 83.
33. Ibid., p. 75.
34. Ibid., p. 351.
35. Williams, *Loyalties*, 1985, pp. 347–8.
36. Williams, *Border Country*, 1960, p. 293.
37. Ibid.
38. Ingold, 1986, p. 41.
39. Williams, *Loyalties*, 1985, p. 317.
40. Ibid., pp. 317–19.
41. Ibid., p. 364.
42. Fisher, *Fighting Back in Appalachia*, 1993.
43. Williams, *Resources of Hope*, 1989, p. 220.
44. Smith, 'Geography, difference and the politics of scale', 1992, pp. 72–3.
45. Williams, *Second Generation*, 1964, p. 9.
46. Williams, *Resources of Hope*, 1989, p. 220.
47. See, e.g., Agnew and Duncan, *The Power of Place*, 1989; Cooke, *Localities*, 1989; Cooke, 1990; Massey, 'The political place of locality studies', 1991; Pred, 'Place as historically contingent process', 1984; Smith, 'Dangers of the empirical turn', 1987; Swyngedouw, 'The heart of the place', 1989; Swyngedouw, 'Territorial organisation', 1992.
48. See Cox and Mair, 'Levels of abstraction', 1989; Cooke, *Localities*, 1989; Duncan and Savage, 'Space, scale and locality', 1989; Horvath and Gibson, 'Abstraction in Marx's method', 1984; Merrifield, 'Place and space', 1993; Swyngedouw, 'The mammon quest', 1992; Smith, *Uneven Development*, 1990; Smith, 'Geography, difference and the politics of scale', 1992.
49. See, e.g., Carter et al., *Space and Place*, 1993.
50. See Bird et al., *Mapping the Futures*, 1993; Gregory and Urry, *Social Relations and Spatial Structures*, 1985; Keith and Pile, *Place and the Politics of Identity*, 1993.
51. On this point see, in particular, Keith and Pile, *Place and the Politics of Identity*, 1993.
52. Fisher, *Fighting Back in Appalachia*, 1993, p. 217.
53. Marx, *Grundrisse*, 1973, p. 101.
54. Marx, *Capital*, vol. 1, 1976, p. 102.

Chapter 9

1. Lefebvre, *The Survival of Capitalism*, 1976.

2. Harvey, 'The political economy of urbanisation', 1975.
3. Brenner, *The Boom and the Bubble*, 2002.
4. Gowan, *The Global Gamble*, 1999.
5. See, e.g., Wade and Veneroso, 'The Asian crisis', 1998.
6. Panitch, 'The new imperial state', 2000; Gowan et al., 'The state, globlisation and the new imperialism', 2001; Petras and Veltmayer, *Globalisation Unmasked*, 2001; Amin, 'Imperialism and globalisation', 2001; Cooper, 'The new liberal imperialism', 2002.
7. Carchedi, 'Imperialism, dollarisation and the euro', 2002.
8. Hegel, *The Philosophy of Right*, 1967.
9. Julien et al., 1949.
10. Arendt, *Imperialism*, 1968, p. 15.
11. Henderson, 'Uneven crises', 1999.
12. Gowan, *The Global Gamble*, 1999.
13. Ibid., pp. 23, 35.
14. Editorial, *Buenos Aires Herald*, 31 December 2002, p. 4.
15. Bhagwati, 1998.
16. Brenner, *The Boom and the Bubble*, 2002; Gowan, *The Global Gamble*, 1999.
17. Luxemburg, *The Accumulation of Capital*, 1968, pp. 452–3.
18. Such as Perelman, *The Invention of Capitalism*, 2000.
19. Marx, *Theories of Surplus Value*, Part 1, 1967.
20. Braudel, *Afterthoughts on Material Civilization and Capitalism*, 1967.
21. Wade and Veneroso, 'The Asian crisis', 1998.
22. Johnson, *MITI and the Japanese Miracle*, 1982; Webber and Rigby, *The Golden Age Illusion*, 1996.
23. Wade and Veneroso, 'The Asian crisis', 1998.
24. See, e.g., Brecher and Costello, *Global Village or Global Pillage?*, 1994; Gills, *Globalisation and the Politics of Resistance*, 2000; Bello, *Deglobalisation*, 2002; Falk, *Predatory Globalisation*, 2000.
25. Arendt, *Imperialism*, 1968, p. 28.
26. Armstrong et al., *Capitalism since World War II*, 1991.
27. Gowan, *The Global Gamble*, 1999, pp. 21–2.
28. Walton, *Reluctant Rebels*, 1984.
29. Petras, 'A rose by any other name?', 2002.
30. Anderson, 'Internationalism: a breviary', 2002; Soederberg, 'The new international financial architecture', 2002.
31. Burkett and Hart-Landsberg, 'Crisis and recovery in East Asia', 2001.
32. Brenner, *The Boom and the Bubble*, 2002.
33. Arrighi and Silver, *Chaos and Governance*, 1999, pp. 31–3.
34. Gowan, *The Global Gamble*, 1999, p. 123.
35. Arrighi and Silver, *Chaos and Governance*, 1999, pp. 288–9.
36. Cooper, 'The new liberal imperialism', 2002.

37. Mehta, *Liberalism and Empire*, 1999.
38. Arendt, *Imperialism*, 1968, pp. 6–9.
39. Williams, *Empire as a Way of Life*, 1980.

Chapter 10

1. Shiller, 'Housing bubbles are few and far between', 2011.
2. World Bank, *World Development Report 2009*, 2009.
3. Ibid., p. 206.
4. Harvey, 'Assessment: Reshaping economic geography', 2009.
5. Harvey, *The Condition of Postmodernity*, 1989, pp. 145–6, 169; Turner, *The Credit Crunch*, 2008.
6. Shiller, *Irrational Exuberance*, 2000.
7. Bardhan and Walker, 'California, pivot of the Great Recession', 2010; English and Gray, *The Coming Real Estate Crash*, 1979; Tabb, *The Long Default*, 1982; Harvey, *A Brief History of Neoliberalism*, 2005.
8. Goetzmann and Newman, 'Securitisation in the 1920's', 2010.
9. White, 'Lessons from the great American real estate boom and bust of the 1920s', 2010.
10. Marx, *Grundrisse*, 1973, pp. 88–100.
11. Marx, *Capital*, vol. 2, 1978, p. 357.
12. Marx, *Grundrisse*, 1973, p. 89.
13. Tronti, 'The strategy of refusal', 1966; Negri, 1989.
14. Goetzmann and Newman, 'Securitisation in the 1920's', 2010.
15. Marx, *Capital*, vol. 3, 1978, chs 24, 25.
16. Harvey, *The Limits to Capital*, 1982, ch. 8.
17. See Harcourt, *Some Cambridge Controversies*, 1972.
18. Marx, *Capital*, vol. 3, 1978, p. 573.
19. See Harvey, *The Urbanisation of Capital*, 1985; Harvey, *The Enigma of Capital*, 2010.
20. Thomas, *Migration and Economic Growth*, 1973.
21. Grebler et al., *Capital Formation in Residential Real Estate*, 1956; Long, *Building Cycles and the Theory of Investment*, 1940; Gottlieb, *Long Swings in Urban Development*, 1976.
22. Marx, *Capital*, vol. 3, 1978, ch. 25.
23. Marx, *Capital*. vol. 1, 1976, p. 793.
24. Logan and Molotch, *Urban Fortunes*, 1987.
25. See 'Cities in the Great Depression', www.wikipedia.org.
26. See Boddy, *The Building Societies*, 1980.
27. Kerner Commission, *Report of the National Advisory Commission on Civil Disorders*, 1968.
28. Weisman, 'Reagan policies gave green light to red ink', 2004; Greider, 'The education of David Stockman', 1981.

29. Stockman, 'The bipartisan march to fiscal madness', 2011; Buffett, 'In class warfare, guess which class is winning', 2006.
30. Marx and Engels, *The Communist Manifesto*, 2008, p. 4.
31. Ehrenreich and Muhammad, 'The recession's racial divide', 2009.
32. Morgenson and Rosner, *Reckless Endangerment*, 2011.
33. Sagalyn, 'Mortgage lending in older neighborhoods', 1983.
34. Bradsher, 'China announces new bailout', 2004.
35. Barboza, 'Building boom in China stirs fears of debt overload', 2011; Anderlini, 'Fate of real estate is global concern', 2011; Cookson, 'China bulls reined in', 2011.
36. Barboza, 'A city born of China's boom', 2010.
37. Anderlini, 'Fate of real estate is global concern', 2011.
38. International Monetary Fund and International Labour Organisation, *The Challenges of Growth*, 2010.
39. Hille and Anderlini, 'China: Mao and the next generation', 2011.
40. Ness and Azzellini, *Ours to Master and to Own*, 2011.
41. Castells, 1984; Gould, *Insurgent Identities*, 1995; Harvey, *Paris, Capital of Modernity*, 2003.
42. Tully, 'Green Bans and the BLF', 2004.
43. Wines, 2011; Leavitt and Blasi, 'The Los Angeles Taxi Workers Alliance', 2010.
44. Excluded Workers Congress, *Unity for Dignity*, 2010.
45. Kohn, *Radical Space*, 2003.
46. Fletcher and Gapasin, *Solidarity Divided*, 2008.
47. Ibid., p. 174.
48. Jaggi et al., *Red Bologna*, 1977.
49. Lefebvre, *Writings on Cities*, 1996; Marx, *Capital*, vol. 1, 1976.
50. Sugranyes and Mathivet, *Cities for All*, 2010.

Bibliography

Abadie, P. (1988), *Paul Abadie, Architecte, 1812–1884*, Paris: Ministère de la Culture, de la Communication, des Grands Travaux et du Bicentennaire, Editions de la Réunion de Musées Nationaux.

Agnew, J. and J. Duncan (eds) (1989), *The Power of Place: Bringing Together the Geographical and Sociological Imaginations*, Boston, MA: Unwin Hyman.

Alexander, D. (1990), 'Bioregionalism: science or sensibility', *Environmental Ethics*, 12: 161–73.

Allison, J. (1932), *Monsieur Thiers*, New York: Norton.

Alonso, W. (1964), *Location and Land Use*, Cambridge, MA: MIT Press.

Althusser, L. and E. Balibar (1970), *Reading Capital*, London: New Left Books.

Amin, S. (1973), *Accumulation on a World Scale*, New York: Monthly Review Press.

Amin, S. (2001), 'Imperialism and globalisation', *Monthly Review*, 53: 2.

Anderlini, J. (2011), 'Fate of real estate is global concern', *Financial Times*, 1 June.

Anderson, P. (2002), 'Internationalism: a breviary', *New Left Review*, 14a.

Arendt, H. (1968), *Imperialism*, New York: Harcourt Brace.

Armstrong, P., A. Glyn and J. Harrison (1991), *Capitalism since World War II: The Making and Break-up of the Great Boom*, Oxford: Basil Blackwell.

Arrighi, G. and B. Silver (eds) (1999), *Chaos and Governance in the Modern World System*, Minneapolis: University of Minnesota Press.

Attfield, R. (1991 edn), *The Ethics of Environmental Concern*, Athens: University of Georgia Press.

Ball, M. (1983), *Housing Policy and Economic Power: The Political Economy of Owner Occupation*, London: Routledge.

Baran, P. (1957), *The Political Economy of Growth*, New York: Monthly Review Press.

Barboza, D. (2010), 'A city born of China's boom, still unpeopled', *New York Times*, 20 October.

Barboza, D. (2011), 'Inflation in China poses big threat to global trade', *New York Times*, 17 April.

Barboza, D. (2011), 'Building boom in China stirs fears of debt overload', *New York Times*, 7 July.

Bardhan, A. and R. Walker (2010), 'California, pivot of the Great Recession',
Working Paper Series, Institute for Research on Labor and Employment,
University of California, Berkeley.

Barrett Brown, M. (1974), *The Economics of Imperialism*, Baltimore, MD: Penguin.

Bate, J. (1991), *Romantic Ecology: Wordsworth and the Environmental Tradition*,
New York: Routledge.

Baudrillard, J. (1981), *For a Critique of the Political Economy of the Sign*, St Louis,
MO: Telos Press.

Baudrillard, J. (1986), *L'Amérique*, Paris: Grasset.

Bell, D. (1978), *The Cultural Contradictions of Capitalism*, New York: Basic Books.

Bello, W. (2002), *Deglobalisation: Ideas for a New World Economy*, London: Zed
Books.

Bennett, J. (1976), *The Ecological Transition: Cultural Anthropology and Human
Adaptation*, New York: Pergamon Press.

Benton, T. (1989), 'Marxism and natural limits: an ecological critique and
reconstruction', *New Left Review*, 178: 51–86.

Benton, T. (1992), 'Ecology, socialism and the mastery of nature: a reply to Reiner
Grundmann', *New Left Review*, 194: 55–74.

Berkowitz, B. (1984), 'Economic development really works: Baltimore, MD', in R.
Bingham and J. Blair (eds), *Urban Economic Development*, Beverly Hills, CA:
Sage.

Bernal, J. (1971), *Science in History*, 4 vols, Cambridge, MA: MIT Press.

Berry, B. and F. Horton (1970), *Geographic Perspectives on Urban Systems*,
Englewood Cliffs, NJ: Prentice-Hall.

Bhagwati, J. (1998), 'The capital myth: the difference between trade in widgets and
dollars', *Foreign Affairs*, 77(3): 7–12.

Bianchini, F. (1991), 'The arts and the inner cities', in B. Pimlott and S. MacGregor
(eds), *Tackling the Inner Cities*, Oxford: Clarendon Press.

Birch, C. and J. Cobb (1981), *The Liberation of Life: From the Cell to the Community*,
Cambridge: Cambridge University Press.

Bird, J., B. Curtis, T. Putnam, G. Robertson and L. Tickner (eds) (1993), *Mapping
the Futures: Local Cultures Gobal Change*, London: Routledge.

Bluestone, B. and B. Harrison (1982), *The Deindustrialisation of America*, New
York: Basic Books.

Blunkett, D. and K. Jackson (1987), *Democracy in Crisis: The Town Halls Respond*,
London: Hogarth Press.

Boddy M. (1980), *The Building Societies*, London: Macmillan.

Boddy, M. (1984), 'Local economic and employment strategies', in M. Boddy and C.
Fudge, *Local Socialism*, London: Macmillan.

Bohm, D. and F. Peat (1987), *Science, Order and Creativity*, London: Routledge.

Bookchin, M. (1985), 'Ecology and revolutionary thought', *Antipode*, 17(2/3): 89–97.

Bookchin, M. (1990), *The Philosophy of Social Ecology: Essays on Dialectical Naturalism*, Montreal: Black Rose Books.

Bookchin, M. (1990), *Remaking Society: Pathways to a Green Future*, Boston, MA: South End Press.

Booth, A. and H. Jacobs (1990), 'Ties that bind: Native American beliefs as a foundation for environmental consciousness', *Environmental Ethics*, 12: 27–43.

Borneman, E. (ed.) (1976), *The Psychoanalysis of Money*, London: Urizen Books.

Bouinot, J. (ed.) (1987), *L'Action Economique des Grands Villes en France et à l'Etranger*, Paris: Centre de Formation des Personnels Communaux.

Boyer, C. (1988), 'The return of aesthetics to city planning', *Society*, 25(4): 49–56.

Bradsher, K. (2004), 'China announces new bailout of big banks', *New York Times*, 7 January.

Bramwell, A. (1989), *Ecology in the Twentieth Century: A History*, New Haven, CT: Yale University Press.

Braudel, F. (1967), *Afterthoughts on Material Civilisation and Capitalism*, Baltimore, MD: Johns Hopkins University Press.

Braudel, F. and E. Labrousse (eds) (1976), *Histoire Economique et Social de la France*, vol. 3, Paris: Presse Universitaires de France.

Brecher, J. and T. Costello (1994), *Global Village or Global Pillage? Economic Reconstruction from the Bottom Up*, Boston, MA: South End Press.

Brenner, R. (2002), *The Boom and the Bubble: The US in the World Economy*, London: Verso.

Bruhat, J., J. Dautry and E. Terson (1971), *La Commune de 1871*, Paris: Edns Sociales.

Brundtland Report (1987), *Our Common Future*, World Commission on Environment and Development, Oxford: Oxford University Press.

Buffett, W. (2006), 'In class warfare, guess which class is winning', interview with Ben Stein, *New York Times*, 26 November.

Burkett, P. and M. Hart-Landsberg (2001), 'Crisis and recovery in East Asia: the limits of capitalist development', *Historical Materialism*, 8.

Butzer, K. (1982), *Archaeology as Human Ecology*, Cambridge: Cambridge University Press.

Calvino, I. (1981), *If on a Winter's Night a Traveller*, New York: Harcourt Brace Jovanovich.

Capra, F. (1975), *The Tao of Physics*, Berkeley, CA: Shambhala.

Capra, F. (1982), *The Turning Point: Science, Society, and the Rising Culture*, New York: Simon and Schuster.

Carchedi, G. (2002), 'Imperialism, dollarisation and the euro', *Socialist Register*, London: Merlin Press.

Carter, E., J. Donald and J. Squires (eds) (1993), *Space and Place: Theories of Identity and Location*, London: Lawrence and Wishart.

Castells, M. (1983), *The City and the Grassroots*, Berkeley: University of California Press.

Chambers, I. (1987), 'Maps for the metropolis: a possible guide to the present', *Cultural Studies*, 1: 1–22.

Cheney, G. (1999), *Values at Work: Employee Participation Meets Market Pressures at Mondragon*, Ithaca, NY: ILR Press.

Clark, J. (1989), 'Marx's inorganic body', *Environmental Ethics*, 11: 243–58.

Cochrane, A. (ed.) (1987), *Developing Local Economic Strategies*, Milton Keynes: Open University Press.

Cockburn, C. (1977), *The Local State, Management of Cities and People*, London: Pluto Press.

Cohen, S. and L. Taylor (1978), *Escape Attempts: The Theory and Practice of Resistance to Everyday Life*, Harmondsworth: Penguin.

Collingwood, R. (1960), *The Idea of Nature*, Oxford: Oxford University Press.

Colquhoun, A. (1991), 'On modern and postmodern space', in A. Colquhoun, *Modernity and the Classical Tradition: Architectural Essays, 1980–87*, Cambridge, MA: MIT Press.

Commoner, B. (1990), *Making Peace with the Planet*, New York: Pantheon.

Cooke, P. (1989), *Localities: The Changing Face of Urban Britain*, London: Unwin Hyman.

Cookson, R. (2011), 'China bulls reined in by fears on economy', *Financial Times*, 1 June.

Cooper, R. (2002), 'The new liberal imperialism', *Observer*, 7 April.

Cox, K. and A. Mair (1989), 'Levels of abstraction in locality studies', *Antipode*, 21: 121–32.

Cronon, W. (1983), *Changes in the Land: Indians, Colonists, and the Ecology of New England*, New York: Hill and Wang.

Cronon, W. (1991), *Nature's Metropolis: Chicago and the Great West*, New York: Norton.

Crosby, A. (1986), *Ecological Imperialism: The Biological Expansion of Europe, 900–1900*, Cambridge: Cambridge University Press.

Dansette, A. (1965), *Histoire Religieuse de la France Contemporaine*, Paris: Presse Universitaires de la France.

Dauncey, G. (1988), *After the Crash: The Emergence of the Rainbow Economy*, Basingstoke: Green Print.

Davies, H. (1980), 'The relevance of development control', *Town Planning Review*, 51: 7–24.

Dicken, P. (1986), *Global Shift: Industrial Change in a Turbulent World*, London: Sage.

Dickens, P. (1992), *Society and Nature: Towards a Green Social Theory*, London: Harvester Wheatsheaf.

Dobson, A. (1990), *Green Political Thought*, London: Unwin Hyman.

Dreyfus, R. (1928), *Monsieur Thiers contre l'Empire: La Guerre et la Commune*, Paris: Grasset.

Duncan, S. and M. Savage (1989), 'Space, scale and locality', *Antipode*, 21: 179–206.

Dworkin, D. and L. Roman (eds) (1993), *Views beyond the Border Country: Raymond Williams and Cultural Politics*, London: Routledge.

Eagleton, T. (ed.) (1989), *Raymond Williams: Critical Perspectives*, Cambridge: Cambridge University Press.

Eckersley, R. (1992), *Environmentalism and Political Theory: Toward an Ecocentric Approach*, London: UCL Press.

Edwards, S. (1971), *The Paris Commune*, Chicago, IL: Quadrangle.

Ehrenreich, B. and D. Muhammad (2009), 'The recession's racial divide', *New York Times*, 12 September.

Elkin, S. (1987), *City and Regime in the American Republic*, Chicago, IL: University of Chicago Press.

Ellen, R. (1982), *Environment, Subsistence and System: The Ecology of Small-Scale Social Formations*, Cambridge: Cambridge University Press.

Emmanuel, A. (1972), *Unequal Exchange*, London: New Left Books.

Engels, F. (1935 edn), *The Housing Question*, New York: Lawrence and Wishart.

Engels, F. (1940 edn), *The Dialectics of Nature*, New York: International Publishers.

Engels, F. (1987 edn), *The Condition of the Working Class in England*, Harmondsworth: Penguin.

English, J. and E. Gray (1979), *The Coming Real Estate Crash*, New Rochelle, NY: Arlington House.

Enzensberger, H.-M. (1974), 'A critique of political ecology', *New Left Review*, 84: 3–31.

Excluded Workers Congress (2010), *Unity for Dignity: Excluded Workers Report*, c/o Inter-Alliance Dialogue, New York, December.

Falk, R. (2000), *Predatory Globalisation: A Critique*, Cambridge: Polity Press.

Fanon, F. (1967), *The Wretched of the Earth*, Harmondsworth: Penguin.

Firey, W. (1960), *Man, Mind and the Land*, Glencoe, IL: Free Press.

Fisher, F. (ed.) (1993), *Fighting Back in Appalachia*, Philadelphia, PA: Temple University Press.

Fletcher, B. and F. Gapasin (2008), *Solidarity Divided: The Crisis in Organised Labor and a New Path Toward Social Justice*, Berkeley: University of California Press.

Fortune Magazine (1970), *Special Issue on the Environment*, February.

Foucault, M. (1984), *The Foucault Reader*, ed. P Rabinow, Harmondsworth: Penguin.

Foulon, M. (1934), *Eugène Varlin: Relieure et Membre de la Commune*, Clermont Ferrand: Edns Mont-Louis.

Fox, W. (1990), *Toward a Transpersonal Ecology: Developing New Foundations for Environmentalism*, Boston, MA: SUNY Press.

Frank, A. (1969), *Capitalism and Underdevelopment in Latin America*, New York: Monthly Review Press.

Frug, G. (1980), 'The city as a legal concept', *Harvard Law Review*, 93(6): 1059–1153.

Fuss, D. (1984), *Essentially Speaking: Feminism, Nature and Difference*, London: Routledge.

Gaillard, J. (1977), *Paris, La Ville, 1852–1870: L'Urbanisme Parisien à l'Heure d'Haussmann: Des Provinciaux aux Parisiens: La Vocation ou Les Vocations Parisiennes*, Paris, H. Champion.

Gerratana, V. (1973), 'Marx and Darwin', *New Left Review*, 82: 60–82.

Gertler, M. (1988), 'The limits to flexibility: comments on the post-Fordist vision of production and its geography', *Transactions of the Institute of British Geographers, New Series*, 13: 419–32.

Gills, B. (ed.) (2000), *Globalisation and the Politics of Resistance*, New York: Palgrave.

Gilroy, R. (1987), *There Ain't No Black in the Union Jack*, Chicago, IL: University of Chicago Press.

Glacken, C. (1967), *Traces on the Rhodian Shore*, Berkeley: University of California Press.

Goetzmann, W. and F. Newman (2010), 'Securitisation in the 1920's', Working Papers, National Bureau of Economic Research.

Goldsmith, E. (1992), *The Way: An Ecological World View*, London: Rider.

Goncourt, E. (1969), *Paris under Siege, 1870–71*, From the Goncourt Journals, edited by G. Becker, Ithaca, NY: Cornell University Press.

Goodin, R. (1992), *Green Political Theory*, Cambridge: Polity Press.

Goodman, R. (1979), *The Last Entrepreneurs*, Boston, MA: South End Press.

Gosselink, J., E. Odum and R. Pope (1974), *The Value of the Tidal Marsh*, Baton Rouge: Center for Wetland Resources, Louisiana State University.

Gottlieb, M. (1976), *Long Swings in Urban Development*, New York: National Bureau of Economic Research.

Gottlieb, R. (1988), *A Life of Its Own: The Politics and Power of Water*, New York: Harcourt Brace Jovanovich.

Goudie, A. (1986), *The Human Impact on the Natural Environment*, Oxford: Basil Blackwell.

Gould, R. (1995), *Insurgent Identities: Class Community and Protest in Paris from 1848 to the Commune*, Chicago, IL: University of Chicago Press.

Gowan, P. (1999), *The Global Gamble: Washington's Bid for Global Dominance*, London: Verso.

Gowan, P., L. Panitch and M. Shaw (2001), 'The state, globlisation and the new imperialism: a roundtable discussion', *Historical Materialism*, 9.

Granovetter, M. (1985), 'Economic action and social structure: the problem of embeddedness', *American Journal of Sociology*, 91: 481–510.

343

Grebler, L., D. Blank and L. Winnick (1956), *Capital Formation in Residential Real Estate*, Princeton, NJ: Princeton University Press.

Green, H. (1988), 'Retailing in the new economic era', in Sternlieb, G. and J. Hughes (eds), *America's New Market Geography*, New Brunswick: Rutgers University Press.

Gregory, D. and J. Urry (eds) (1985), *Social Relations and Spatial Structures*, London: Palgrave Macmillan.

Greider, W. (1981), 'The education of David Stockman', *Atlantic Monthly*, December.

Grigsby, W., L. Rosenberg, M. Stegman and J. Taylor (1971), *Housing and Poverty*, Philadelphia: Institute for Environmental Studies, University of Pennsylvania.

Grundmann, R. (1991), 'The ecological challenge to Marxism', *New Left Review*, 187: 103–20.

Grundmann, R. (1991), *Marxism and Ecology*, Oxford: Oxford University Press.

Guha, R. (1989), *The Unquiet Woods: Ecological Change and Peasant Resistance in the Himalaya*, Berkeley: University of California Press.

Guillemin, H. (1956), *Cette Curieuse Guerre de 70: Thiers, Trochu, Bazaine*, Paris: Gallimard.

Gundle, S. (1986) 'Urban dreams and metropolitan nightmares: models and crises of communist local government in Italy', in *Marxist Local Governments in Western Europe and Japan*, 66–95.

Gurr, T. and D. King (1987), *The State and the City*, Chicago, IL: University of Chicago Press.

Haila, Y. and R. Levins (1992), *Humanity and Nature: Ecology, Science and Society*, London: Pluto Press.

Hajer, M. (1992), 'The politics of environmental performance review: choices in design', in E. Lykke (ed.), *Achieving Environmental Goals: The Concept and Practice of Environmental Performance Review*, London: Belhaven Press.

Hall, S. (1989), 'Politics and letters', in T. Eagleton, *Raymond Williams: Critical Perspectives*, Cambridge: Cambridge University Press.

Haraway, D. (1989), *Primate Visions: Gender, Race and Nature in the World of Modern New York*, New York: Routledge.

Harcourt, G. (1972), *Some Cambridge Controversies in the Theory of Capital*, Cambridge: Cambridge University Press.

Hardin, G. (1968), 'The tragedy of the commons', *Science*, 162: 1243–8.

Harrison, B. and B. Bluestone (1988), *The Great U-Turn: Capital Restructuring and the Polarisation of America*, New York: Basic Books.

Harvey, D. (1974), 'Population, resources, and the ideology of science', *Economic Geography*, 50: 256–77.

Harvey, D. (1975), 'The political economy of urbanisation in advanced capitalist countries', in G. Gappert and H. Rose (eds), *The Social Economy of Cities*, Beverly Hills, CA: Sage.

Harvey, D. (1982), *The Limits to Capital*, Oxford: Basil Blackwell.

Harvey, D. (1985), *The Urbanisation of Capital*, Oxford: Basil Blackwell.

Harvey, D. (1989), *The Condition of Postmodernity*, Oxford: Basil Blackwell.

Harvey, D. (1990), 'Between space and time: reflections on the geographical imagination', *Annals, Association of American Geographers*, 80: 418–34.

Harvey, D. (2003), *The New Imperialism*, Oxford: Oxford University Press.

Harvey, D. (2003), *Paris, Capital of Modernity*, New York: Routledge.

Harvey, D. (2005), *A Brief History of Neoliberalism*, Oxford: Oxford University Press.

Harvey, D. (2009), 'Assessment: reshaping economic geography: the World Development Report', *Development and Change*, 40(6): 1269–77.

Harvey, D. (2010), *The Enigma of Capital, and the Crises of Capitalism*, London: Profile Books.

Harvey, D. (2012), 'History versus theory: a commentary on Marx's method in *Capital*', *Historical Materialism*, 20(2): 3–38.

Hayter, T. and D. Harvey (eds) (1993), *The Factory and the City: The Story of the Cowley Auto Workers in Oxford*, Brighton: Mansell.

Heidegger, M. (1966), *Discourse on Thinking*, New York: Harper and Row.

Heidegger, M. (1971), *Poetry, Language, Thought*, New York: Harper and Row.

Heilbroner, R. (1974), *An Inquiry into the Human Prospect*, New York: Norton.

Henderson, J. (1999), 'Uneven crises: institutional foundations of East Asian economic turmoil', *Economy and Society*, 28(3).

Hille, K. and J. Anderlini (2011), 'China: Mao and the next generation', *Financial Times*, 2 June.

Hobson, J. (1938), *Imperialism*, London: Allen and Unwin.

Horvath, R. and K. Gibson (1984), 'Abstraction in Marx's method', *Antipode*, 16: 12–25.

Ingold, T. (1986), The *Appropriation of Nature: Essays on Human Ecology and Social Relations*, Manchester: Manchester University Press.

International Monetary Fund and International Labour Organisation (2010), *The Challenges of Growth, Employment and Social Cohesion*, Geneva: International Labour Organisation.

Jacks, G. and R. Whyte (1939), *Vanishing Lands*, New York: Doubleday.

Jacobs, J. (1984), *Cities and the Wealth of Nations*, New York: Random House.

Jaggi, M. et al. (1977), *Red Bologna*, London: Writers & Readers.

Jameson, F. (1988), 'Cognitive mapping', in C. Nelson and L. Grossberg (eds), *Marxism and the Interpretation of Culture*, Urbana: University of Illinois Press.

Jellinek, F. (1937), *The Paris Commune of 1871*, London: Victor Gollancz.

Jencks, C. (1984), *The Language of Post-Modern Architecture*, London: Academy Editions.

Jessop, B. (1983), 'Accumulation strategies, state forms and hegemonic projects', *Kapitalistate*, 10/11: 89–112.

Johnson, C. (1982), *MITI and the Japanese Miracle: The Growth of Industrial Policy, 1925–75*, Stanford, CA: Stanford University Press.

Johnson, C. (2000), *Blowback: The Costs and Consequences of American Empire*, New York: Henry Holt.

Johnson, H. (1971), 'The Keynesian revolution and the monetarist counter-revolution', *American Economic Review*, 16(2): 1–14.

Jonquet, R. (1892), *Montmartre Autrefois et Aujourd'hui*, Paris: Dumoulin.

Judd, D. and R. Ready (1986), 'Entrepreneurial cities and the new politics of economic development', in G. Peterson and C. Lewis (eds), *Reagan and the Cities*, Washington, DC: Rowman and Littlefield.

Julien, C-A., J. Bruhat, C. Bourgin, M. Crouzet and P. Renovin (1949), *Les Politiques d'Expansion Impérialiste*, Paris: Presses Universitaires de France.

Kapp, K. (1950), *The Social Costs of Private Enterprise*, New York: Schocken.

Keith, M. and S. Pile (eds) (1993), *Place and the Politics of Identity*, London: Routledge.

Kern, S. (1983), *The Culture of Time and Space, 1880–1918*, London: Harvard University Press.

Kerner Commission (1968), *Report of the National Advisory Commission on Civil Disorders*, Washington, DC: Government Printing Office.

Kohn, M. (2003), *Radical Space: Building the House of the People*, Ithaca, NY: Cornell University Press.

Kuhn, T. (1962), *The Structure of Scientific Revolutions*, Chicago, IL: University of Chicago Press.

Kuznets, S. (1961), *Capital in the American Economy: Its Formation and Financing*, Princeton, NJ: National Bureau of Economic Research.

Lave, L. (1970), 'Congestion and urban location', *Papers of the Regional Science Association*, 25: 133–52.

Lazare, L. (1872), *La France et Paris*, Paris: Bureau de la Bibliothèque Municipale.

Leavitt, J. and G. Blasi (2010), 'The Los Angeles Taxi Workers Alliance', in R. Milkman, J. Bloom and V. Narro (eds), *Working for Justice: The LA Model of Organising and Advocacy*, Ithaca, NY: ILR Press.

Lee, D. (1980), 'On the Marxian view of the relationship between man and nature', *Environmental Ethics*, 2: 1–21.

Lee, K. (1989), *Social Philosophy and Ecological Scarcity*, London: Routledge.

Lefebvre, H. (1976), *The Survival of Capitalism: Reproduction of the Relations of Production*, New York: St Martin's Press.

Lefebvre, H. (1991), *The Production of Space*, Oxford: Blackwell.

Lefebvre, H. (1996), *Writings on Cities*, trans. and ed. E. Kofman and E. Lebas, Oxford: Basil Blackwell.

Leiss, W. (1974), *The Domination of Nature*, Boston, MA: Beacon Press.

Leitner, H. (1989), 'Cities in pursuit of economic growth: the local state as entrepreneur', Ms, Department of Geography, University of Minnesota, Minneapolis.

Lenin, V. (1963 edn), *Imperialism: The Highest Stage of Capitalism*, Moscow: Progress Publishers.

Leopold, A. (1968), *A Sand County Almanac*, New York: Oxford University Press.

Lepidis, C. and E. Jacomin (1975), *Belleville*, Paris: H. Veyrier.

Lesourd, P. (1973), *Montmartre*, Paris: France-Empire.

Levine, M. (1987), 'Downtown redevelopment as an urban growth strategy: a critical appraisal of the Baltimore renaissance', *Journal of Urban Affairs*, 9(2): 103–23.

Levins, R. and R. Lewontin (1985), *The Dialectical Biologist*, Cambridge, MA: Harvard University Press.

Lewontin, R. (1982), 'Organism and environment', in Plotkin, H. (ed.), *Learning, Development and Culture*, Chichester: Wiley.

Lissagaray, P.-O. (1976 edn), *Histoire de la Commune*, Paris: Maspero.

Logan, J. and H. Molotch (1987), *Urban Fortunes: The Political Economy of Place*, Berkeley: University of California Press.

Lomnitz-Adler, C. (1991), 'Concepts for the study of regional culture', *American Ethnologist*, 18: 195–214.

Long, C. (1940), *Building Cycles and the Theory of Investment*, Princeton, NJ: Princeton University Press.

Lovejoy, A. (1964 edn), *The Great Chain of Being*, Cambridge, MA: Harvard University Press.

Luxemburg, R. (1968), *The Accumulation of Capital*, London: Routledge.

Lyall, K. (1982), 'A bicycle built for two; public–private partnership in Baltimore', in S. Fosler and R. Berger (eds), *Public–Private Partnership in American Cities*, Lexington, MA: Lexington Books.

Lyotard, J. (1984), *The Postmodern Condition*, Manchester: Manchester University Press.

McCay, B. and J. Acheson (1987), *The Question of the Commons: The Culture and Ecology of Human Resources*, Tucson: University of Arizona Press.

McEvoy, A. (1988), 'Towards an interactive theory of nature and culture: ecology, production and cognition in the California fishing industry', in D. Worster (ed.), *The Ends of the Earth*, Cambridge: Cambridge University Press.

McGann, J. (1983), *The Romantic Ideology: Critical Investigation*, Chicago, IL: University of Chicago Press.

McHale, B. (1987), *Postmodernist Fiction*, London: Routledge.

McLuhan, M. (1966), *Understanding Media: The Extensions of Man*, New York: Signet Books.

Mandel, E. (1975), *Late Capitalism*, London: New Left Books.

347

Markusen, A. (1986), 'Defense spending: a successful industrial policy', *International Journal of Urban and Regional Research*, 10: 105–22.

Marsh, G. (1965), *Man and Nature*, Cambridge, MA: Harvard University Press.

Martin, E. (1991), 'The egg and the sperm: how science has constructed a romance based on stereotypical male–female roles', *Signs*, 16: 485–501.

Martin, E. (1992), 'The end of the body?', *American Ethnologist*, 19: 121–40.

Martin, P. and D. Cohen (n.d.), 'Socialism 30 in China', the-diplomat.com.

Martin, R. and B. Rowthorn (eds) (1986), *The Geography of Deindustrialisation*, London: Palgrave Macmillan.

Marx, K. (1964), *The Economic and Philosophic Manuscripts of 1844*, New York: International Publishers.

Marx, K. (1967), *Theories of Surplus Value*, Part 1, New York: International Publishers.

Marx, K. (1968), *Theories of Surplus Value*, Part 2, New York: International Publishers.

Marx, K. (1970), *A Contribution to the Critique of Political Economy*, New York: International Publishers.

Marx, K. (1971), *Colonialism*, New York: International Publishers.

Marx, K. (1971), 'On the Jewish question', in D. McClellan (ed.), *Karl Marx: Early Texts*, Oxford: Basil Blackwell.

Marx, K. (1972), *Theories of Surplus Value*, Part 3, New York: International Publishers.

Marx, K. (1973), *Grundrisse*, Harmondsworth: Penguin.

Marx, K. (1976 edn), *Capital*, vol. 1, London: New Left Books (Penguin).

Marx, K. (1978 edn), *Capital*, vol. 2, London: New Left Books (Penguin).

Marx, K. (1978 edn), *Capital*, vol. 3, London: New Left Books (Penguin).

Marx, K. (1965), *Wages, Price and Profit*, Peking: Foreign Languages Press.

Marx, K. and F. Engels (1955), *Selected Correspondence*, Moscow: Progress Publishers.

Marx, K. and F. Engels (1970), *The German Ideology*, New York: International Publishers.

Marx, K. and F. Engels (1975), *Collected Works*, vol. 5, New York: International Publishers.

Marx, K. and F. Engels (2008 edn), *The Communist Manifesto*, London: Pluto Press.

Marx, K. and V. Lenin (1968 edn), *The Civil War in France: The Paris Commune*, New York.

Massey, D. (1991), 'The political place of locality studies', *Environment and Planning A*, 23: 267–81.

May, R. (1992), 'How many species inhabit the earth?', *Scientific American*, 267(4): 18–24.

Mehta, U. (1999), *Liberalism and Empire*, Chicago, IL: University of Chicago Press.

Merchant, C. (1980), *The Death of Nature: Women, Ecology and the Scientific Revolution*, New York: Harper and Row.

Merrifield, A. (1993), 'Place and space: a Lefebvrian reconciliation', *Transactions of the Institute of British Geographers, New Series*, 18: 516–31.

Meszaros, I. (1970), *Marx's Theory of Alienation*, London: Merlin Press.

Mitman, G. (1992), *The State of Nature: Ecology, Community, and American Social Thought, 1900–1950*, Chicago, IL: University of Chicago Press.

Mollenkopf, J. (1983), *The Contested City*, Princeton, NJ: Princeton University Press.

Molotch, H. (1976), 'The city as a growth machine: the political economy of place', *American Journal of Sociology*, 82: 309–32.

Morgenson, G. and J. Rosner (2011), *Reckless Endangerment: How Outsized Ambition, Greed and Corruption Led to Economic Armageddon*, New York: Times Books.

Murray, F, (1983), 'Pension funds and local authority investments', *Capital and Class*, 230: 89–103.

Muth, R. (1969), *Cities and Housing*, Chicago, IL: University of Chicago Press.

Naess, A. (1989), *Ecology, Community and Lifestyle*, Cambridge: Cambridge University Press.

Nagel, E. (1961), *The Structure of Science: Problems in the Logic of Scientific Explanation*, New York: Hackett Publishing.

Nash, R. (1989), *The Rights of Nature: A History of Environmental Ethics*, Madison: University of Wisconsin Press.

Negri, A. (1991), *Marx beyond Marx: Lessons on the Grundrisse*, London: Autonomedia.

Ness, I. and D. Azzellini (eds) (2011), *Ours to Master and to Own: Workers' Councils from the Commune to the Present*, Chicago, IL: Haymarket Books.

Norberg-Schulz, C. (1980), *Genius Loci: Towards a Phenomenology of Architecture*, New York: Rizzoli.

Norgaard, R. (1985), 'Environmental economics: an evolutionary critique and a plea for pluralism', *Journal of Environmental Economics and Management*, 12: 382–94.

Noyelle, T. and T. Stanback (1984), *The Economic Transformation of American Cities*, Totowa, N.J.: Rowman and Allanheld.

O'Connor, J. (1988), 'Capitalism, nature, socialism: a theoretical introduction', *Capitalism, Nature, Socialism*, 1: 11–38.

Ollman, B. (1971), *Alienation: Marx's Conception of Man in Capitalist Society*, Cambridge: Cambridge University Press.

Ollman, B. (1990), 'Putting dialectics to work: the process of abstraction in Marx's method', *Rethinking Marxism*, 3: 26–74.

Ollman, B. (1993), *Dialectical Investigations*, New York: Routledge.

Ophuls, W. (1977), *Ecology and the Politics of Scarcity: A Prologue to a Political Theory of the Steady State*, San Francisco, CA: Freeman.

O'Riordan, T. (1981), *Environmentalism*, London: Pion.

Paehlke, R. (1989), *Environmentalism and the Future of Progressive Politics*, New Haven, CT: Yale University Press.

Panitch, L. (2000), 'The new imperial state', *New Left Review*, 11: 1.

Park, R., E. Burgess and R. McKenzie (1925), *The City*, Chicago, IL: University of Chicago Press.

Parsons, H. (ed.) (1977), *Marx and Engels on Ecology*, Westport, CN: Greenwood Press.

Pearce, D., A. Markandya and E. Barbier (1989), *Blueprint for a Green Economy*, London: Earthscan.

Pearson, H. (1957), 'The economy has no surplus', in K. Polanyi, C. Arensberg and H. Pearson (eds), *Trade and Markets in Early Empires*, New York: Henry Regnery Co.

Perelman, M. (2000), *The Invention of Capitalism: Classical Political Economy and the Secret History of Primitive Accumulation*, Durham, NC: Duke University Press.

Peterson, P. (1981), *City Limits*, Chicago, IL: University of Chicago Press.

Petras, J. (2002), 'A rose by any other name? The fragrance of imperialism', *Journal of Peasant Studies*, 29(2).

Petras, J. and J. Veltmayer (2001), *Globalisation Unmasked: Imperialism in the 21st Century*, London: Zed Books.

Pinkney, D. (1958), *Napoleon III and the Rebuilding of Paris*, Princeton, NJ: Princeton University Press.

Pred, A. (1984), 'Place as historically contingent process: structuration and the time-geography of becoming places', *Annals of the Association of American Geographers*, 74: 279–97.

Price, R. (1975), *The Economic Modernisation of France*, London: Croom Helm.

Raban, J. (1974), *Soft City*, London: Picador.

Redclift, M. (1987), *Sustainable Development: Exploring the Contradictions*, London: Methuen.

Rees, G. and J. Lambert (1985), *Cities in Crisis: The Political Economy of Post-War Development in Britain*, London: Hodder Arnold.

Relph, E. (1989), 'Geographical experiences and being-in-the-world: the phenomenological origins of geography', in D. Seamon and R. Mugerauser (eds), *Dwelling, Place and Environment: Towards a Phenomenology of Person and World*, New York: Columbia University Press.

Rochberg-Halton, E. (1986), *Meaning and Modernity: Social Theory in the Pragmatic Attitude*, Chicago, IL: University of Chicago Press.

Rohault de Fleury, H. (1903–09), *Historique de la Basilique de Sacré Coeur*, 4 vols (limited edn), Paris: F Levé.

Roman, L. (1993), 'On the ground with antiracist pedagogy and Raymond Williams' unfinished project to articulate a socially transformative critical realism', in D. Dworkin and L. Roman (eds), *Views beyond the Border Country: Raymond Williams and Cultural Politics*, London: Routledge.

Rose, H. and S. Rose (1969), *Science and Society*, Harmondsworth: Penguin.

Rougerie, J. (1965), *Procès des Communards*, Paris: Julliard.

Rougerie, J. (1971), *Paris Libre, 1871*, Paris: Seuil.

Rousseau, J.-J. (1973), *The Social Contract and Discourses*, London: Everyman.

Sagalyn, L. (1983), 'Mortgage lending in older neighborhoods', *Annals of the American Academy of Political and Social Science*, 465 (January), pp. 98–108.

Sagoff, M. (1988), *The Economy of the Earth: Philosophy, Law, and the Environment*, Cambridge: Cambridge University Press.

Said, E. (1989), 'Appendix: Media, margins and modernity', in R. Williams (ed.), *The Politics of Modernism*, London: Verso.

Sale, K. (1985), *Dwellers in the Land: The Bioregional Vision*, San Francisco, CA: Sierra Club.

Sassen-Koob, S. (1988), *Global Cities*, Princeton, NJ: Princeton University Press.

Sauer, C. (1956), 'The agency of man on earth', in W. Thomas (ed.), *Man's Role in Changing the Face of the Earth*, Chicago, IL: University of Chicago Press (2 vols).

Sayer, A. (1989), 'Post-Fordism in question', *International Journal of Urban and Regional Research*, 13: 666–95.

Schoenberger, E. (1988), 'From Fordism to flexible accumulation: technology, competitive strategies and location', *Society and Space*, 6: 245–62.

Scott, A. (1988), *New Industrial Spaces: Flexible Production Organisation and Regional Development in North America and Western Europe*, London: Pion.

Shiller, R. (2000), *Irrational Exuberance*, Princeton, NJ: Princeton University Press.

Shiller, R. (2011), 'Housing bubbles are few and far between', *New York Times*, 5 February.

Simmel, G. (1971), 'The metropolis and mental life', in D. Levine (ed.), *On Individuality and Social Form*, Chicago, IL: University of Chicago Press.

Simmel, G. (1978), *The Philosophy of Money*, London: Routledge and Kegan Paul.

Smith, M. (1988), *City, State and Market*, Oxford: Basil Blackwell.

Smith, M. and M. Keller (1983), 'Managed growth and the politics of uneven geographical development in New Orleans', in S. Fainstein et al. (eds), *Regime Strategies, Communal Resistance, and Economic Forces*, New York: Longman.

Smith, N. (1987), 'Dangers of the empirical turn', *Antipode*, 19: 59–68.

Smith, N. (1990), *Uneven Development: Nature, Capital and the Production of Space*, Oxford: Basil Blackwell.

Smith, N. (1992), 'Geography, difference and the politics of scale', in J. Doherty, E. Graham and M. Malek (eds), *Postmodernism and the Social Sciences*, London: Macmillan.

Smith, N. and P. O'Keefe (1985), 'Geography, Marx and the concept of nature', *Antipode*, 12(2): 30–39.

Snedeker, G. (1993), 'Between humanism and social theory: the cultural criticism of Raymond Williams', *Rethinking Marxism*, 6: 104–13.

Soederberg, S. (2002), 'The new international financial architecture: imposed leadership and "emerging markets"', *Socialist Register 2002*, London: Merlin.

Soja, E. (1988), *Postmodern Geographies: The Reassertion of Space in Critical Social Theory*, London: Verso.

Spoehr, A. (1956), 'Cultural differences in the interpretation of natural resources', in W. Thomas (ed.), *Man's Role in Changing the Face of the Earth*, Chicago, IL: University of Chicago Press.

Spretnak, C. (1985), 'The spiritual dimension of Green politics', in C. Spretnak and F. Capra, *Green Politics: The Global Promise*, London: Paladin.

Spretnak, C. and F. Capra (1985), *Green Politics: The Global Promise*, London: Paladin.

Stanback, T. (1982), *Cities in Transition: Changing Job Structures in Atlanta, Denver, Buffalo, Phoenix, Columbus (Ohio), Nashville, Charlotte*, Totowa, NJ: Allanheld Osmun.

Steiner, G. (1992 edn), *Heidegger*, London: Fontana.

Sternlieb, G. (1966), *The Tenement Landlord*, New Brunswick, NJ: Rutgers University Press.

Stockman, D. (2011), 'The bipartisan march to fiscal madness', *New York Times*, 23 April.

Stoker, R. (1986), 'Baltimore: the self-evaluating city', in C. Stone and H. Sanders (eds), *The Politics of Urban Development*, Lawrence, KS: University Press of Kansas.

Sugranyes, A. and C. Mathivet (eds) (2010), *Cities for All: Proposals and Experiences towards the Right to the City*, Santiago: Habitat International Coalition.

Swyngedouw, E. (1986), 'The socio-spatial implications of innovations in industrial organisation', Working Paper no. 20, Johns Hopkins European Centre for Regional Planning and Research, Lille.

Swyngedouw, E. (1989), 'The heart of the place; the resurrection of locality in an age of hyperspace', *Geografiska Annaler*, 71.

Swyngedouw, E. (1992), 'The mammon quest; globalisation, international competition and the new monetary order, the search for a new spatial scale', in M. Dunford and G. Kafkalis (eds), *Cities and Regions in the New Europe*, London: John Wiley.

Swyngedouw, E. (1992), 'Territorial organisation and the space/technology nexus', *Transactions of the Institute of British Geographers, New Series*, 17: 417–33.

Szanton, P. (1986), *Baltimore 2000*, Baltimore, MD: Morris Goldsecker Foundation.

Tabb, W. (1982), *The Long Default: New York City and the Urban Fiscal Crisis*, New York: Monthly Review Press.

Taylor, B. (1987), *Modernism, Post-Modernism, Realism: A Critical Perspective for Art*, Winchester School of Art Press.

Thomas, B. (1973), *Migration and Economic Growth: A Study of Great Britain and the Atlantic Economy*, Cambridge: Cambridge University Press.

Thomas, E. (1966), *The Women Incendiaries*, New York: George Braziller.

Thomas, E. (1967), *Rossel 1844–71*, Paris: Gallimard.

Thomas, W. (ed.) (1956), *Man's Role in Changing the Face of the Earth*, Chicago, IL: University of Chicago Press (2 vols).

Todes, D. (1989), *Darwin without Malthus: The Struggle for Existence in Russian Evolutionary Thought*, Oxford: Oxford University Press.

Toffler, A. (1970), *Future Shock*, New York: Random House.

Tronti, M. (1966), 'The strategy of refusal', Turin: Einaudi, libcom.org.

Tully, J. (2004), 'Green Bans and the BLF: the labour movement and urban ecology', *International Viewpoint Online*, 357, internationalviewpoint.org.

Turner, G. (2008), *The Credit Crunch: Housing Bubbles, Globalisation and the Worldwide Economic Crisis*, London: Pluto Press.

Urry, J. (1990), *The Tourist Gaze*, London: Sage.

Valdès, N. (1971), 'Health and revolution in Cuba', *Science and Society*, 35: 311–35.

Virilio, P. (1980), *L'Esthétique de la Disparition*, Paris: Galilée.

Wade, R. and F. Veneroso (1998), 'The Asian crisis: the high debt model versus the Wall Street–Treasury–IMF complex', *New Left Review*, 228.

Walton, J. (1984), *Reluctant Rebels: Comparative Studies on Revolution and Underdevelopment*, New York: Columbia University Press.

Weale, A. (1992), *The New Politics of Pollution*, Manchester: Manchester University Press.

Webber, M. and D. Rigby (1996), *The Golden Age Illusion: Rethinking Post-War Capitalism*, New York: Guilford Press.

Weisman, J. (2004), 'Reagan policies gave green light to red ink', *Washington Post*, 9 June.

White, E. (2010), 'Lessons from the great American real estate boom and bust of the 1920s', Working Papers, National Bureau of Economic Research.

Williams, R. (1960), *Border Country*, London: Chatto and Windus.

Williams, R. (1961), 'The achievement of Brecht', *Critical Quarterly*, 3: 153–62.

Williams, R. (1964), *Second Generation*, London: Chatto and Windus.

Williams, R. (1973), *The Country and the City*, London: Chatto and Windus.

Williams, R. (1977), *Marxism and Literature*, Oxford: Oxford University Press.

Williams, R. (1979), *The Fight for Manod*, London: Chatto and Windus.

Williams, R. (1980), *Problems in Materialism and Culture*, London: Verso.

Williams, R. (1983), *Keywords*, London: Fontana.

Williams, R. (1985), *Loyalties*, London: Chatto and Windus.

Williams, R. (1989), *People of the Black Mountains: The Beginning*, London: Chatto and Windus.

Williams, R. (1989), *Resources of Hope*, London: Verso.

Williams, R. (1990), *People of the Black Mountains: The Eggs of the Eagle*, London: Chatto and Windus.

Williams, W. Appleman (1980), *Empire as a Way of Life*, New York: Oxford University Press.

Wilson, A. (1992), *The Culture of Nature: North American Landscape from Disney to the Exxon Valdez*, Oxford: Basil Blackwell.

World Bank (2009), *World Development Report 2009: Reshaping Economic Geography*, Washington, DC: World Bank.

Worster, D. (1985), *Nature's Economy: A History of Ecological Ideas*, Cambridge: Cambridge University Press.

Worster, D. (1985), *Rivers of Empire: Water, Aridity and the Growth of the American West*, New York: Pantheon Books.

Young, I. (1990), *Justice and the Politics of Difference*, Princeton, NJ: Princeton University Press.

Young, R. (1985), *Darwin's Metaphor: Nature's Place in Victorian Culture*, Cambridge: Cambridge University Press.

Zeldin, T. (1958), *The Political System of Napoleon III*, London: Macmillan.

Zeldin, T. (1963), *Emile Ollivier and the Liberal Empire of Napoleon III*, Oxford: Clarendon Press.

Zeldin, T. (1973), *France, 1848–1945*, vol. 1: *Ambition, Love and Politics*, Oxford: Oxford University Press.

Zimmerman, M. (1988), 'Quantum theory, intrinsic value, and panentheism', *Environmental Ethics*, 10: 3–30.

Zola, E. (1967), *L'Argent*, Paris: Pléiade.

Index